THE POETRY BOOK

THE POETRY BOOK

DK LONDON

SENIOR ART EDITOR
Nicola Rodway

SENIOR EDITOR
Victoria Heyworth-Dunne

SENIOR US EDITOR
Megan Douglass

EDITORS
John Andrews, Anna Cheifitz, Tim Harris,
Dorothy Stannard, Andy Szudek, Ed Wilson

PROJECT EDITOR
Rose Blackett-Ord

EDITORIAL ASSISTANT
Bonnie Macleod

PERMISSIONS CONSULTANT
Rachel Thorne

ILLUSTRATIONS
James Graham

JACKET DESIGNER
Stephanie Cheng Hui Tan

JACKET DESIGN
DEVELOPMENT MANAGER
Sophia MTT

SENIOR PRODUCTION EDITOR
Andy Hilliard

PRODUCER
Nancy-Jane Maun

SENIOR MANAGING ART EDITOR
Lee Griffiths

MANAGING EDITOR
Gareth Jones

ASSOCIATE PUBLISHING DIRECTOR
Liz Wheeler

ART DIRECTOR
Karen Self

DESIGN DIRECTOR
Philip Ormerod

PUBLISHING DIRECTOR
Jonathan Metcalf

DK DELHI

SENIOR ART EDITOR
Chhaya Sajwan

ART EDITOR
Aanchal Singal

SENIOR EDITOR
Janashree Singha

PROJECT EDITOR
Hina Jain

MANAGING EDITOR
Soma B. Chowdhury

SENIOR MANAGING ART EDITOR
Arunesh Talapatra

SENIOR JACKET DESIGNER
Suhita Dharamjit

SENIOR JACKETS COORDINATOR
Priyanka Sharma Saddi

DTP DESIGNERS
Mrinmoy Mazumdar, Nityanand Kumar,
Rakesh Kumar

PROJECT PICTURE RESEARCHERS
Mamta Panwar, Nunhoih Ching Guite

PRE-PRODUCTION MANAGER
Balwant Singh

PRODUCTION MANAGER
Pankaj Sharma

CREATIVE HEAD
Malavika Talukder

SANDS PUBLISHING SOLUTIONS

EDITORIAL PARTNERS
David and Silvia Tombesi-Walton

DESIGN PARTNER
Simon Murrell

original styling by
STUDIO 8

First American Edition, 2023
Published in the United States by DK Publishing
1745 Broadway, 20th Floor, New York, NY 10019

Copyright © 2023 Dorling Kindersley Limited
DK a Division of Penguin Random House LLC
23 24 25 26 27 10 9 8 7 6 5 4 3 2 1
001–329233–Nov/2023

A catalog record for this book
is available from the Library of Congress.
ISBN: 978-0-7440-8083-4

Printed and bound in China

For the curious
www.dk.com

This book was made with Forest Stewardship Council™
certified paper—one small step in DK's commitment
to a sustainable future.
For more information go to
www.dk.com/our-green-pledge

CONSULTANTS & CONTRIBUTORS

ELIZABETH BLAKEMORE

Elizabeth Blakemore is a writer, specializing in early modern Spanish literature.

HELEN DOUGLAS-COOPER

Helen Douglas-Cooper is a freelance writer, with a degree in English from the University of East Anglia.

SEAN FREDERICK FORBES

Sean Frederick Forbes is Assistant Professor-in-Residence and Director of the Creative Writing Program at the University of Connecticut.

BETHANY HICOK

Bethany Hicok is a lecturer in English at Williams College.

MARK COLLINS JENKINS

Mark Collins Jenkins is a freelance writer and has a Master's degree in English from the University of Virginia.

ANDREW KERR-JARRETT

Andrew Kerr-Jarrett has an MA in English Literature from Cambridge University and has special interests in Spanish, French, and English poetry.

SHIAMIN KWA

Shiamin Kwa received her PhD in Chinese Literature from the Department of East Asian Languages and Civilizations at Harvard University.

ROBIN LAXBY

Robin Laxby studied English Language and Literature at Magdalen College, Oxford. He is the author of eight published books of poetry.

SARAH LUSACK

Sarah Lusack is a writer and poet. She has an MA in Creative and Critical Writing from Birkbeck, University of London.

MAUD BURNETT MCINERNEY

Maud Burnett McInerney is the Laurie Ann Levin Professor of Comparative Literature at Haverford College.

ABIGAIL MITCHELL

Abigail Mitchell is a poet and a postgraduate researcher in English at the University of Southampton.

BRUNO VINCENT

Bruno Vincent has written or contributed to more than 30 books. He has a keen interest in ancient and epic poetry.

JULIANNE WERLIN

Julianne Werlin is an associate professor in the English Department at Duke University.

CONTENTS

REASON AND THE SUBLIME
1700–1900

THE MODERN AGE
1900–1940

POST-WAR AND CONTEMPORARY
1940–PRESENT

INTRODU

CTION

Dating back to prehistoric times in its oral forms, and at least 4,000 years as a written medium, poetry has been used to record events, inspire, inform, offer spiritual insight, and entertain. Whatever its intent, the genre in all its forms always reflects the careful choice and arrangement of words by a poet trying to connect with another—a specific individual, a live audience, or an anonymous reader. This drive for connection remains the life force of poetry, and underpins its historical development.

From song to verse

Poetry was originally an oral form, composed for recital. Its musicality or incantatory resonance was an important part of its appeal, drawing in listeners during live performances around a camp fire, or at a castle, court, or temple. This sonic quality made the information in poems easier to remember and pass on.

Music's historical connection with poetry also explains the origin of poetic building blocks—rhyme, refrains (repeated lines), rhythm, meter, and sound effects such as alliteration and assonance. Not just mnemonic devices, these elements have been used by poets of all eras to give structure to their works, to aid understanding, and to fashion

diction. Alliteration (the use of the same letter or sound to begin consecutive or nearby words) is found in some of the earliest written verse in Old English (Anglo-Saxon), Old Norse, Old Irish, and Sanskrit. The echoing "music" of repeated vowel sounds—assonance—is also used in the first written verses of the medieval period, probably taken from the traditional sung ballad.

While it is clear that some oral poems circulated for many hundreds of years before being transcribed, there is often little evidence for this process of transformation from performance piece to written text. We know, for example, that the two ancient Greek epics ascribed to Homer, *The Odyssey* and *The Iliad*, date from the late 8th or early 7th

Genuine poetry can communicate before it is understood.
T. S. Eliot

century BCE, but they do not appear to have been written down until the 6th century BCE.

At the other end of the poetry timeline, the rise of performance poetry in the 21st century shows that despite the availability of poetry in printed form since the 1500s, there has been an enduring desire to listen to spoken verse. A line can be traced from the troubadour poets of medieval Europe to 20th-century Modernist poems such as T. S. Eliot's *The Waste Land*, which has been performed as a theater piece, and the cryptic soundscapes of Welsh poet Dylan Thomas (influenced by the Celtic bards). Rap poetry, usually recited from memory, and slam poetry events, where participants perform their poems competitively before a live audience or judging panel, are just some of the more recent manifestations of oral verse.

Evolving formats

In the 4th century BCE, ancient Greek philosopher and writer Aristotle classified poetry into three types—lyric, dramatic, and epic—and these have continued to influence poetic forms. Lyric poems were originally short pieces intended to be sung, but the modern definition is broader, encompassing poetry

that expresses emotions (directly or obliquely) or feelings. This form is exemplified by love poetry, which can be personal and self-revealing, but at certain cultural junctures (such as the European Renaissance) also drew on, and promoted the use of, a great variety of established forms, ideas, and images. The sonnets of William Shakespeare demonstrate how some of the most imaginative poets used traditions to their advantage, playing or overturning literary conventions to produce works of great originality.

Dramatic and epic forms

Aristotle's second type of poetry—verse in the context of drama—was much used by Shakespeare, who wrote five of his plays in poetic verse. This form of poetry would give rise to the dramatic monologue, a form popularized by English poets of the Victorian era such as Alfred Tennyson and Robert Browning.

The epic form—a long, poetic narrative—dates back to at least the early 3rd millennium BCE, when the ancient Akkadian *The Epic of Gilgamesh* is thought to have been composed. In Western literature, the ancient epics of Homer and Virgil have come to define the epic tradition, but poets have continued to bring their own interpretations to the form. In the 19th century, Lord Byron wrote a comedic "mock" epic, *Don Juan*; while in the 1990s, Derek Walcott set his modern epic *Omeros* in the Caribbean but still referenced Homer's Classical works.

Content and ideas

The power of poetry lies in the ability of poets to handle language with skill, originality, and insight, avoiding linguistic and conceptual clichés. The choice of language—or poetic diction—may be influenced by the style of a poem, its subject, or audience. However, it also reflects cultural forces—often signifying whether a poet is reflecting their times or protesting against them.

Choice of content and subject matter can also be reactive, often echoing wider social, political, or cultural moods. In the 18th century, Romanticism valued the imagination and the expression of deep emotions (especially those prompted by love or nature), and this remained a strong influence into the 20th century, despite the calls of some poets for demystification. Among these, the anti-Romantic poets of the early 20th-century Modernist movement pitched intellect and innovation against emotion and nostalgia—sometimes producing poetry that has challenged readers.

Whether intentionally aiming to challenge, or indirectly initiating change, the history of poetry has been shaped by a multitude of "big ideas"—evolutions and innovations in format, language, content, and delivery. This book focuses on 100 poems, arranged in chronological order, that are landmarks in the emergence, implementation, and development of these ideas.

Each poem is an attempt at perfect communication, an effort by the poet to connect with readers or listeners and to elicit a response through the use of imagination. Key to the enjoyment of poetry, is the poet's ability to apprehend something the reader may have experienced or felt, perhaps only fleetingly or even subconsciously, and bring it vividly to life. In this regard, poetry is, in the words of the Greek philosopher Plato "nearer to vital truth than history." ∎

Poem quote style

For the purposes of this book, a single slash (/) is used in poem quotes to indicate a line break, and double slashes (//) are used to indicate a stanza break.

MYTHS
HEROES
c. 2100 BCE—700 CE

AND

The earliest surviving heroic saga, the ancient Sumerian **Epic of Gilgamesh**, is recorded on clay tablets in Mesopotamia.

c. 2100 BCE

The Sanskrit epic **Mahabharata**, describing a power struggle between two cousins, is composed in India.

9TH—4TH CENTURIES BCE

Sappho produces **lyric poems in Greek** on the island of Lesbos.

c. 630—570 BCE

11TH—7TH CENTURIES BCE

In **China**, lyrical poems based on ancient folk songs, prayers, and hymns are compiled into the **Classic of Poetry or Book of Odes**.

c. LATE 8TH CENTURY BCE

Homer's **Iliad and Odyssey** are **set down in writing** for the first time.

The works that survive from this earliest era of poetic composition demonstrate the great importance of storytelling and song. Before the invention of writing, oral recitation was the only way poets could pass on their ideas, thoughts, and knowledge. With the birth of writing and the refinement of scripts, ancient tales and songs were gradually written down and structured into the forms that we now recognize as "poetry."

Epic stories

The poetic tradition of storytelling began with tales of heroic deeds or epic narratives. Performed by a bard (in Greek a *rhapsode*), these stories usually related the deeds of a hero—a warrior who defended his people and slayed monsters, or a traveler who journeyed around the world, or sometimes beyond it. In some epics, these heroes were gods or demigods with superhuman powers, such as the Sumerian Gilgamesh, who slayed the giant Humbaba and the Bull of Heaven, and roamed the world in search of immortality, or Arjun, a central figure of the Indian *Mahabharata* (9th–4th centuries BCE). In others, the heroes were simply human, like Homer's Odysseus, the son of Laertes, who undertook an epic journey home after the Trojan War.

Whether mortal or supernatural, epic heroes embodied the traits most admired by their culture, such as courage, generosity, or cleverness. Very few, however, were perfect: prone to rage, pride, grief, even fear, just like the rest of us. The epic hero may be more than we are, but he is also like us. What attracted people to these stories thousands—even millions—of years ago still draws us to them today.

Performing early poetry

Circulating orally, epic poems were continually altered in the telling, often adapted to a particular time of audience. A bard might, for example, have flattered a local dignitary by including his great grandfather in the list of heroes at an important battle; he might have added an episode upon request, or left out an exploit praising ancestral enemies.

Rhythmic schemes such as the Homeric dactylic hexameter (six feet per line, each foot consisting of one long syllable followed by two short syllables) or the Sanskrit *shloka* (couplet)—the first forms of meter—evolved to help performers memorize these stories, but also

Horace publishes
books 1 to 3 of his
Odes; their format
and style will be
much emulated by
medieval poets.

The **Song of Songs** is
devised by an unknown
poet **in Hebrew**.

C. 3RD CENTURY BCE

23 BCE

498 BCE

29–19 BCE

8 CE

**Pindar writes
Pythian 10**, the first in
his series of **victory
odes** celebrating the
winners of the Pythian,
Olympian, Isthmian,
and Nemean games.

Virgil's **Aeneid**
establishes a
**foundation myth
for Rome**.

Ovid writes
Metamorphoses,
stories in verse derived
from **Greek and
Roman mythology**.

provided a base framework when adjusting their content. Many ancient poems were performed with musical accompaniment, which enhanced their rhythmic and melodic qualities, and some may have been sung.

Songs of praise or sorrow

Many early poetic works took the form of songs linked to rituals or traditions, such as hymns, prayers, eulogies, or folk tunes. Some praised a divinity, an ancestor, a ruler, or a beloved: the Old Testament *Song of Songs* (c. 3rd century BCE), for example, is a passionate, erotic declaration of love shared between a male voice and a female one. Writing in ancient Greece around the 6th century BCE, Sappho's lyrical poems also expressed intense emotion and desire, but between women.

The works of the Chinese *Classic of Poetry*, compiled between the 11th and the 7th centuries BCE, were more wide-ranging in their veneration. They included poems that glorified the founders of the Zhou dynasty, as well as others praising the beauty of young women and fruit trees.

Sorrow also found expression in verse—in dirges, elegies, and laments for the dead. Some of these songs of grief were built into longer epic works. Poetry, with its close connection to music and power to move the hearer, was establishing itself as an appropriate vehicle for the deepest human feelings from these earliest of times.

Recitation to transcription

Early oral poetry eventually took on fixed forms in writing. Once transcribed, these works began

a new life, translated and widely shared as tablets and manuscripts. Later writers drew on these ancient compositions to craft poems in new contexts. The *Epic of Gilgamesh* (c. 2100 BCE) likely influenced Homer's poems *The Iliad* (c. 700 BCE) and *The Odyssey* (c. 725–675 BCE), which in turn inspired, directly or indirectly, many later poems of Western European literature.

The ongoing influence of early poems is demonstrated by the works of Ovid, who was writing poetry at the start of the 1st century CE. A linchpin between the Classical world and that of early Medieval Europe, his poem *Metamorphoses* (8 CE) reconfigured ancient myths but also inspired some of the writers in the next chapter of this book, such as Dante Alighieri and Geoffrey Chaucer. ■

THE GODS BOWED THEMSELVES, AND SAT DOWN, AND WEPT
THE EPIC OF GILGAMESH (c. 2100–1200 BCE)

The world's oldest surviving work of literature, *The Epic of Gilgamesh* lay undiscovered for more than 4,000 years before being found by archaeologists in the 19th century.

Written in cuneiform (ancient cone-shaped script) on clay tablets, *Gilgamesh* was translated in the 1870s by British Assyriologist George Smith.

At the start of the poem, the warrior-king Gilgamesh rules as a tyrant over his people in Uruk (a city-state on the Euphrates River in present-day Iraq). The gods create Enkidu to stop Gilgamesh from oppressing his subjects, but after Gilgamesh wins a test of strength between the two men, they become friends and travel together to the Cedar Forest, home of the gods.

When Enkidu is killed by the gods, Gilgamesh experiences loss for the first time. Torn apart by grief, he searches for meaning in the world and locates the only man on Earth who has escaped death: Utnapishtim, survivor of the Great Flood. Meeting him, Gilgamesh perceives eternal life not as paradise but as a desert. He returns home a wiser man and a kinder monarch.

Epic traits

Composed during the Bronze Age, *Gilgamesh* is typical of epic poetry and includes tales of characters who are forced into interactions with gods or superhuman forces. It was a performance piece, probably recited at festivals, as indicated by internal rhymes and puns that become apparent when the text is spoken in Akkadian, its original language. ∎

> I looked over the sea and a calm had come,
> And all mankind were turned into mud [...]
> **The Epic of Gilgamesh (Tablet 11, lines 133–134)**

(NOW SING WE) HOW THIS ORIGIN OCCURRED
CLASSIC OF POETRY (11TH–7TH CENTURIES BCE)

IN CONTEXT

FOCUS
Ancient Chinese poetry

OTHER KEY POET
Li Bai

AFTER
c. 450–221 BCE *Songs of the South*, another major anthology of classical Chinese verse, is compiled. It is also known as *Verses of Chu* or *Elegies of Chu*.

c. 200 BCE Along with the *I Ching* (a mystical method for predicting fortunes) and three other texts, the *Classic of Poetry* forms the Five Classics of Confucianism, the foundation of all Chinese culture under the Western Han dynasty.

2nd century CE Written by an unknown author or authors, the anthology *Nineteen Old Poems* presents works that contain five Chinese characters per line.

P roviding a glimpse into the lives and concerns of ordinary people in rural China three millennia ago, the *Classic of Poetry* (or *Shijing*) is the earliest example of ancient Chinese literature. The 305 poems in this anthology were probably composed during the Western Zhou period (1046–771 BCE). Many are crafted in simple language about everyday situations—for example, spouses yearning for absent partners or a girl worried about her family's disapproval of her lover. They also conjure rustic images of activities such as farming and housework.

Confucius is the named editor, although it is more likely that this is in recognition of the fact that the poems promote virtue in all forms of public and private life, in line with Confucian philosophy. The collection has been studied for its metaphorical meaning and instructive moral qualities.

The book consists of "Odes of the Domains" (the tales of ordinary life mentioned above), but also "Elegances" and "Hymns," which

The wisdom of Confucius is clearly present in the *Classic of Poetry*. The great philosopher was a keen advocate of the values of earlier eras.

were used by the upper echelons of Chinese society at rituals and state occasions. At court in ancient China, it is probable that most educated people would have known the whole book by heart. Even today, the "Odes" in particular are easy to enjoy: the imagery is simple and the human emotions clear and resonant. ∎

See also: The Song of Solomon 20–21 ▪ *Mahabharata* 22–23 ▪ Fragment 31 32–33 ▪ "Fighting" 52 ▪ "The Old Pond" 110–111

LET HIM KISS ME WITH THE KISSES OF HIS MOUTH
THE SONG OF SOLOMON (10TH–2ND CENTURIES BCE)

IN CONTEXT

FOCUS
Ancient Hebrew poetry

OTHER KEY POETS
Enheduanna, Pindar

BEFORE
c. 500 BCE The Chinese *Classic of Poetry* is written down. It contains powerful poems about love and longing, often using images from nature.

AFTER
c. 300 BCE The Song of Solomon influences works in ancient Egypt and Mesopotamia, as well as the Greek poems of Theocritus.

1947 Three shepherds discover the first of the Dead Sea Scrolls in a cave in Qumran. Dating back to the 1st century CE, nearly 1,000 years earlier than the oldest manuscripts known, the scrolls contain extracts from The Song of Solomon.

The **Song of Solomon** conveys erotic desire in several ways:

Explicit references to the **lovers' bodies**

Allusions to **vineyards and wine**, suggesting **intoxication**

Accounts of **dreams** in which love is initially **thwarted**, heightening the **sense of longing**

Images drawn from **nature** to convey **fecundity and procreation**.

The inclusion of The Song of Solomon in the Bible is an engaging mystery that has perplexed religious academics through the ages. This collection of love poems is not only devoid of any overt mention of God but is also the most erotic passage in the entire Bible. Although the Song is credited to 10th-century BCE King Solomon, it is purely as a gesture of respect.

The language of infatuation
Even to modern readers, the Song is delightfully surprising and perhaps shocking, with its references to naked breasts and nighttime embraces, as well as its tone of enthralled, erotic infatuation. The poem, which reads like a dialogue between a man and a woman who long to be together, is lush with visual metaphors as the two narrators describe each other adoringly. The man compares his beloved's lips to "a thread of scarlet" (4:3), and she responds by saying that his lips are "*like* lilies, dropping sweet smelling myrrh" (5:13).

The couple are intoxicated by love, and they project their passion onto the world around them, seeing it with vivid intensity in plants, animals, and fruit, as well as in

King Solomon and the Queen of Sheba, the latter with an animal head in the top left of this 14th-century illustration, are often identified as the Song's narrators.

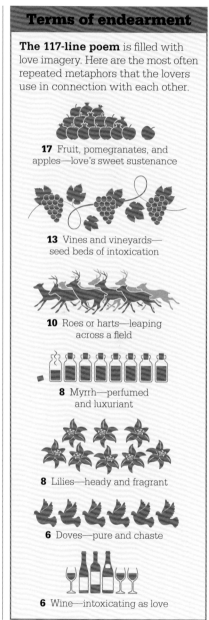

Terms of endearment

The 117-line poem is filled with love imagery. Here are the most often repeated metaphors that the lovers use in connection with each other.

17 Fruit, pomegranates, and apples—love's sweet sustenance

13 Vines and vineyards— seed beds of intoxication

10 Roes or harts—leaping across a field

8 Myrrh—perfumed and luxuriant

8 Lilies—heady and fragrant

6 Doves—pure and chaste

6 Wine—intoxicating as love

various foods, wine, and precious jewels. The consummation of their love is relayed in similar terms: "Let my beloved come into his garden, and eat his pleasant fruits" (4:16).

Interpreting the Song

Reading the poem as an allegory makes it possible to attach deeper and more spiritual meanings to the lush descriptions of physical attributes and carnal pleasures. Hebrew clerics, for example, interpreted the Song as a metaphor for the love between God and the people of Israel.

The 3rd-century biblical scholar Origen of Alexandria extended the allegorical Hebrew reading to a Christian audience, arguing that the Song was about the love of Christ for the Church. However, Origen also advised the spiritually immature to abstain from reading the Song, lest its erotic content lead them into temptation.

The Song in Passover rites

Despite the theological readings of the Song, it is possible that it was included in the Bible simply to preserve an exquisite example of Israelite literary culture.

All Hebrew poetry, as far as we know, was written to be sung or chanted, probably accompanied by instruments. The Song itself came to be recited at Passover, the feast commemorating the Israelites' escape from Egypt. Whether raising eyebrows or spiritual fervor, this series of love poems seems wholly worthy of one of its alternative names, Song of Songs. ∎

Set me as a seal upon thine heart, as a seal upon thine arm: for love *is* strong as death [...]
The Song of Solomon 8:6 (King James Version)

NO WRITER OF THIS WORK IS TO BE FOUND ON EARTH
MAHABHARATA (9TH–4TH CENTURIES BCE)

IN CONTEXT

FOCUS
Sanskrit epic

OTHER KEY POET
Homer

BEFORE
c. 1000–500 BCE The brief verse epic the *Suparnakhyana* includes the story of the divine bird Garuda, which is later expanded in the first book of the *Mahabharata*.

AFTER
c. 100 BCE The Sanskrit texts *Upanishads* detail Hindu rituals and philosophy.

1940 Previously passed down in dance form, the epic *Khamba Thoibi*, in the Northeast Indian Meitei language, is committed to paper in full for the first time.

With the English-language translation running to nearly 4,000 pages and 1.8 million words across its 18 *parvas*, or books, the *Mahabharata* is probably the longest poem ever written. To put that within the context of other epics, it is 10 times the length of Homer's *Iliad* and *Odyssey* put together. A story of dynastic power struggles, battle, honor, kingdoms, wisdom gained, love, loss, sacrifice, family, and duty, the *Mahabharata* is a world in itself. Its advocates claim that it encompasses every aspect of life in ancient India and that one can study it for a lifetime and never exhaust its wonders.

As with other Hindu Sanskrit epics—for example, the *Ramayana* (c. 700–300 BCE)—the *Mahabharata* is composed almost entirely in the ancient Indian verse called *shloka*, comprising a couplet in which each line typically contains 16 syllables.

The plot of the *Mahabharata* is compelling and exciting, and it concerns itself with two warring sides of the same family, the Pandavas and the Kauravas. A detailed family tree would be useful in keeping track of the large cast of characters in the two warring factions.

Historical background

Itihasa (literally meaning "that which happened") refers to an ancient narrative tale that potentially includes some vestiges of historical events and people. (*The Iliad* would also fall into this category.) It is very different from the older Indian *Vedas*, scriptures that delineate religious customs, rituals, laws, and gathered wisdom. Although the *Mahabharata* is an *itihasa* text, it is not intended to be taken as history.

The *Mahabharata* is far too long to be performed at a single sitting, but over the years it has become

> As the full-moon [...] expandeth the buds of the water-lily, so [the *Mahabharata*] hath expanded the human intellect.
> **Mahabharata (Book I, Section I)**

See also: *The Epic of Gilgamesh* 18 ▪ *The Odyssey* 24–31 ▪ *Metamorphoses* 40–43 ▪ "Fighting" 52 ▪ "The Guest House" 56 ▪ *Gitanjali* 15 178–179

This illustrated extract comes from a palm-leaf manuscript of the *Mahabharata*. The edges of the page are decorated with floral details.

If there is one central message in such a vast text, *dharma* is it. The term means different things in the main Indian religions (Hinduism, Sikhism, Buddhism, and Jainism), but in the *Mahabharata* it means that each person has their place in the world and in society, and it is their sacred duty to fulfill this position with honor. Arjun's family has suffered grievous wrongs, and it is his *dharma* to bring justice and achieve victory for his side.

The resulting number of casualties is of epic proportions; however, after an 18-day battle, balance is restored to the world. ▪

widely accessed as reference material. Parts of it were (and are) used for the purposes of ethical learning, spiritual guidance, codes of conduct, the study of human nature, and sheer entertainment.

Fulfilling one's *dharma*

As the final conflict approaches, in Book VI, the hero Arjun (of the Pandavas) races to battle in his chariot drawn by white steeds. He has a crisis of conscience and asks the Lord Krishna (his friend and charioteer) whether violence can ever be truly justified. What follows (often printed separately in book form) is one of the great world texts of religious philosophy: the *Bhagavad Gita*, also written in poetic *shloka* verses. In it, Lord Krishna explains to Arjun that he must follow and fulfill his *dharma*.

The wisdom of this work [...] hath opened the eyes of the inquisitive world blinded by the darkness of ignorance.
***Mahabharata* (Book I, Section I)**

Authorship

As might be expected of such a massive and ancient book, there are multiple layers of authorship to the *Mahabharata*. The original authors are likely to remain forever unknown, but the scribe is traditionally identified as Krishna Dvaipayana, also known as Ved Vyasa (literally "compiler"). This legendary Indian sage dictates the events to Ganesha, the elephant-headed Hindu deity. Since authorship of many of the important Hindu texts is ascribed to this person, some believe that Vyasa was a subsequent title given to a lineage of scribes.

The first full English translation was undertaken in the 1880s by Kisari Mohan Ganguli at the behest of Kolkata bookseller and publisher Pratap Chandra Roy; it took 13 years. Ganguli chose to leave his name off the books, in case he died before the enormous project could be completed. Consequently, however, after the publication of the first four volumes, publisher Roy was accused of posing as the translator. With the release of the complete edition, Ganguli finally allowed himself to be credited.

HOW PRONE ARE HUMAN-KIND TO BLAME / THE POW'RS OF HEAV'N!

THE ODYSSEY (c. 700 BCE), HOMER

IN CONTEXT

FOCUS
Ancient Greek epic

OTHER KEY POETS
Hesiod, Virgil, Ovid

BEFORE
c. 1800 BCE The Bronze Age work *The Epic of Gilgamesh* follows a great hero on a journey of discovery.

AFTER
c. 30 BCE Virgil's *Aeneid* tells the story of the Trojan warrior Aeneas, who fled to Italy after the Siege of Troy.

c. 1320 Dante writes his *Divine Comedy*, an epic work in which Virgil features as a character, guiding Dante through the Underworld.

1990 *Omeros*, a modern epic poem by Saint Lucian writer Derek Walcott, takes its inspiration from Homer and characters in *The Iliad*.

Homer, the supreme and influential poet of ancient Greece, is veiled in mystery: there is no definitive evidence for his name, the details of his life, or even his existence. However, we do know that the epics ascribed to him—*The Iliad* and *The Odyssey*—were composed in the late 8th or early 7th centuries BCE.

The word "epic" comes from the ancient Greek *epos*, meaning not only "story" but also "poem." Epics are long, complex narrative poems, featuring a large cast of characters facing battles, conflicts, and other physical and mental challenges. Initially told orally, these tales were later embellished, formalized, and finally written down.

The Iliad and *The Odyssey* are composed in dactylic hexameter, the usual choice for epic poetry in both Greek and (later) Latin. *Dactyl* is Greek for "finger." Just as there are three phalanges in a finger, so there are three components to a dactyl: each is one long syllable followed by two short ones, creating a hypnotic, rhythmic effect.

A homecoming tale

Both of the Homeric epics take their inspiration from the Trojan War, a mythical battle between the Achaeans (an alliance of Greek states) and the city of Troy. In each, various gods interfere in human affairs, for and against different combatants.

Whereas *The Iliad*, which tells the tale of the Trojan War itself, is an ensemble piece following many key characters, *The Odyssey* focuses mainly on the adventures of one protagonist—Ulysses (the Roman variant of his original Greek name Odysseus)—as he tries to find his

> I am Ulysses, fear'd in all the earth
> For subtlest wisdom, and renown'd to heaven,
> The offspring of Laertes; my abode
> Is sun-burnt Ithaca [...]
> **The Odyssey (Book IX, lines 22–25)**

Homer

Little is known about Homer's life. He was born sometime around the 8th century BCE and was possibly a blind traveling bard. The text of his two great epics, *The Iliad* and *The Odyssey*, has changed little since around the 6th century BCE. One theory is that the Athenian ruler Pisistratus legislated against changes to the text, in order to preserve the version of Homer that he had loved as a child.

Many modern scholars agree that there is enough consistency of tone and sensibility in Homer's two texts to indicate a single editorial personality, if not necessarily a single author. Perhaps Homer merely brought the text together from multiple sources, unifying it as an authored work. Other scholars maintain that the single authorial voice is little more than evidence of hundreds of talented storytellers.

Additional works, including several of the lesser Trojan epics, were once credited to Homer, but these attributions were never universally accepted.

Other key work

c. 700 BCE *The Iliad*

Dactylic hexameter

Ancient Greek (and, later, Latin) poetry has a basic rhythmic structure called dactylic hexameter. Each line is divided into sections known as feet. A foot contains two or more syllables, which are arranged in patterns based on the length of their vowels, creating a rhythm when they are spoken aloud. The most common patterns are long-short-short and long-long.

> In dactylic hexameter, each line has six feet. Foot 6 must be a spondee, and Foot 5 a dactyl. The other four may be either dactyls or spondees.

Foot 1	Foot 2	Foot 3	Foot 4	Foot 5	Foot 6
daah-da-da	**daah**-**daah**	**daah**-da-da	**daah**-da-da	**daah**-da-da	**daah**-**daah**
long-short-short	long-long	long-short-short	long-short-short	long-short-short	long-long

> A syllable is long or short depending on the pronunciation of the word.

> Long-long syllable patterns are known as spondees.

> Long-short-short syllable patterns are known as dactyls.

way home after the Siege of Troy. This is therefore a tale of peacetime but also of homecoming—what the Greeks called *nostos*.

The poem opens on the troubled island of Ithaca, where Ulysses is the king. At this point absent for almost 20 years (the Trojan War accounting for 10 of those), Ulysses is presumed dead. A vast number of male suitors have gathered around his wife Penelope, each trying to persuade her to marry him—thus gaining kingship of the isle.

Nonlinear structure

Ulysses does not appear at all in the first four books of *The Odyssey*. Then, once Penelope's suitors start plotting the murder of his son Telemachus, the action switches to a homesick and weary Ulysses.

Penelope is no less cunning than her husband Ulysses. The shroud she says she must make before considering her suitors' offers will never be finished because by night she unpicks her work.

He has been trying to get back to Ithaca for nine years, seven of which he has spent as a prisoner of the goddess Calypso on the island of Ogygia. After the gods order Calypso to release him ("For fate ordains him not to perish here"), Ulysses suffers a shipwreck but manages to swim to the land of the good-natured Phaeacians. Renowned for their seafaring skills, the Phaeacians offer him

hospitality and agree to help Ulysses on his way by granting him "A vessel of prime speed."

In Book IX, Ulysses starts to tell his hosts about the adventures that have led him to their shores. Prior to his captivity in Ogygia, he had escaped the giant one-eyed Cyclopes and temptresses such as the goddess Circe, and avoided the whirlpools and multiheaded beasts that killed his shipmates. **»**

At the end of his narrative—during which "the whole assembly silent sat, / Charm'd into ecstacy with his discourse"—Ulysses leaves for Ithaca. The rest of the poem—his homecoming and the resolution of Penelope's story line—plays out in chronological order.

Through adopting a nonlinear structure and focusing on Penelope and Telemachus in Books I–IV, Homer sets up what is at stake, so whetting the audience's appetite for Ulysses' appearance and a resolution to the troubles in Ithaca.

A master of deceit

The first line of *The Odyssey* tells us that the poem is about a man who is "for shrewdness famed."

This Greek vase (c. 470–80 BCE) depicts Ulysses—who is shown tied to the ship's mast—and his crew sailing past the Sirens, which are portrayed as winged creatures.

Indeed Ulysses himself, when revealing his identity to the Phaeacians, defines himself as "fear'd in all the earth / For subtlest wisdom." Besides being a valiant warrior, Ulysses is a thinker and a problem-solver. During the Siege of Troy, he had come up with the idea of the Trojan Horse. As told in Book VIII of *The Odyssey*, this huge, wooden, horse-shaped gift was used to sneak soldiers into the city of Troy, ending the war and securing victory for the Greeks.

There is a very fine line between Ulysses' "subtlest wisdom" and his reliance on subterfuge to progress his cause. Deception and wiliness are key themes in *The Odyssey*, with the hero living and surviving by guile. In his glorious adventures, battling against fate and the gods to find his way home, tricks have been Ulysses' stock in trade—from the episode of the Trojan Horse, to blinding and tricking the Cyclops Polyphemus.

Survival through ingenuity

Ulysses' deceit goes hand in hand with his cunning and ingenuity. Wishing to hear the voice of the Sirens, whose "mellifluous song" no living soul has heard without being dragged to destruction, Ulysses orders his crew to tie him to the ship's mast. The sailors, in turn, stuff their own ears with wax.

Ulysses' patron deity is Athena, the goddess of warfare and crafts, such as weaving. Athena adores wit and craftiness, and she encourages Ulysses to use them. She guides Penelope, too, in her games to elude the suitors. Penelope maintains she cannot marry until she has woven her father-in-law Laertes a shroud. All day she weaves—and by night she unpicks the threads so the task will never be finished.

Ulysses' adventure timeline

The chronology of *The Odyssey* is impressively jumbled. This diagram shows how books I–IV and V–VIII play out simultaneously. They deal respectively with Penelope and the suitors on Ithaca; and Ulysses' journey to the land of the Phaeacians. Books IX–XII are a flashback to action that precedes Book V.

Sequence of poem	Chronology of events
Book I	Book IX
Book II	Book X
Book III	Book XI
Book IV	Book XII
Book V	Books I & V
Book VI	Books II & VI
Book VII	Books III & VII
Book VIII	Books IV & VIII
Book IX	
Book X	
Book XI	
Book XII	
Books XIII–XXIV	Books XIII–XXIV

Time and again, Athena appears in disguise to help Ulysses: as a shepherd boy (Book XIII); as a little girl (Book VI); and as an elderly man named Mentor (Book II and others), the origin of the word for a knowledgeable tutor. Ulysses also uses a disguise, pretending to be a beggar in his own home. He sees Penelope playing tricks on the suitors, requesting gifts from them in order to guarantee her hand in marriage, and is delighted, knowing that the gifts will be useless.

When tricks backfire

One of the problems with so much use of deception is that it makes it difficult for those closest to Ulysses to believe the truth—and even for Ulysses himself. When Calypso tells him he has been granted his freedom (Book V), Ulysses urges her to promise there is no trick.

In Book XXIV, when Ulysses reveals his identity to his father Laertes, he is told in response, "If thou hast come again, and art indeed / My son Ulysses, give me then the proof." Although he is able to assuage his father's suspicions by showing him a childhood scar, it is a cruel irony that when Ulysses speaks the truth, people initially refuse to believe what he says.

Recurring themes

Homer's twin epics of *The Iliad* and *The Odyssey* are each based on a fundamental notion to which

they return again and again. In *The Iliad*, this is *kleos*, which means lasting fame or renown. The warriors at the Siege of Troy are all hoping to be remembered throughout history.

In *The Odyssey*, the crucial concept is that of *xenia*, which loosely translates as "hospitality." Nearly every character in *The Odyssey* is at one time a *xenos*, simultaneously a friend, stranger, foreigner, host, and guest. Simply put, people who are strangers to one another are bound by the sacred duty of *xenia*, the reciprocal extension of hospitality. Only after a stranger has received

Ovid's story of Baucis and Philemon, a poor couple scraping together a meal for Jupiter and Hermes in disguise (depicted here by Rubens), shows the proper application of *xenia*.

hospitality can the host ask their name. To do otherwise meant to offend the gods, in particular Zeus, who was the sponsor of this ritual and sometimes known as Zeus Xenios.

The rules of *xenia* are repeatedly alluded to in *The Odyssey*. When Ulysses and his crew land on the island home of the Cyclopes (Book IX), the monstrous Polyphemus attacks and eats several of the sailors whole—two for dinner, two for breakfast. Conversely, when Ulysses later finds himself shipwrecked on the island of the Phaeacians (Book VI), he is welcomed at the court of King Alcinous and nurtured back to health. This allows him to surprise and thrill his hosts by revealing at a feast that he is the famous hero **»**

> [...] by the fiction only of a name,
> Slight stratagem! I had deceived them all.
> Then groan'd the Cyclops wrung with pain and grief,
> And, fumbling with stretch'd hands, remov'd the rock
> From his cave's mouth [...]
> **The Odyssey (Book IX, lines 486–490)**

> At length, with conjugal endearment both
> Satiate, Ulysses tasted and his spouse
> The sweets of mutual converse. She rehearsed,
> Noblest of women, all her num'rous woes
> Beneath that roof sustain'd […]
> **The Odyssey (Book XXIII, lines 355–359)**

of Troy. As was customary, the Phaeacians have previously been too well mannered to ask their guest's name.

The gravest offenders against *xenia* (at least among the poem's human characters) are Penelope's 108 suitors on Ithaca, all but 12 of whom are outsiders. *Xenia* must be reciprocal, and there is a duty not to abuse hospitality. However, these suitors stay on, year after year, eating away at the wealth of the kingdom and offering nothing in return—even evicting Ulysses' beloved dog Argus from his own home. Worst of all, they conspire to murder Telemachus.

When Ulysses finally returns home, it is his duty to restore *xenia* by massacring the suitors. Only in this way can his *nostos*, his homecoming, be fully achieved.

Pain and loss

The original Greek name of the character Ulysses is Odysseus. Folk etymology suggests this name derives from a word associated with grievance and pain. There are few who come into contact with Ulysses who do not later experience pain and loss. When, at the court of the Phaeacians, he hears the bard Demodocus singing the tale of the Trojan Horse, Ulysses is overcome by emotion about the slaughter that occurred during the Sack of Troy: "Ulysses melted, and tear after tear / Fell on his cheeks."

From its very first line, *The Odyssey* is about the nature of this one man—to cause and receive pain, to trick and endure tricks, but, finally, to fight his way home and to correct the sins against *xenia*.

Composed for recital

The modern reader of Homer is often surprised by the number of repetitions, with specific phrases quoted verbatim several times. This was a key part of long texts that were designed to be read aloud. Like a repeated guitar riff or vocal refrain in a pop song, this repetition gives the listener something familiar to latch on to during the performance.

One of these repetitions is used to underline the theme of *xenia*. On the three occasions when Ulysses wakes to find himself on a foreign shore, he asks one of the essential

The Missing Epics of the Troy saga

The so-called Missing Epics once connected and completed the story of the events surrounding the Trojan War. *The Iliad* would have been the opening chapter of the whole saga, while *The Odyssey* served as the finale.

These lost works have passed through the ages only in the form of fragments and references in other writings. Homer's poems are the only surviving epics relating to the siege and its aftermath.

The Aethiopis is named after Memnon the Ethiopian, who comes to fight alongside the Trojans after the death of Hector.

In **The Little Iliad**, Achilles' armor is awarded to Ulysses rather than Ajax. Overcome with shame, Ajax dies by suicide. Paris is killed by Philoctetes.

The stories of the Trojan Horse and the death of King Priam are relayed in **The Iliupersis**. Some of this text can possibly be gleaned from Virgil's *Aeneid*.

The Nostoi details the homeward journeys of various characters, many of whom—such as Helen and Menelaus—are beset by obstacles and delays caused by unhappy gods.

The wooden horse being led into Troy is a key plot point (and another story of disguise) in the war for the city, yet it is mentioned only briefly in *The Odyssey* and not at all in *The Iliad*.

questions of the human condition. He wonders what greeting he can expect and whether he will be recognized as a *xenos*: "what mortal race inhabit here? / Rude are they [...] / Or hospitable [...] ?" The first time Ulysses asks this question, he is very fortunate (he is shortly to be rescued by princess Nausicaa in Book VI); the second time, he is unlucky (in the land of the Cyclopes). The third time, Ulysses has finally but unknowingly returned home. The land and people are his own, and the matter of *xenia* is in his hands to set straight.

Oral performances

The first printed edition of *The Odyssey* (in Greek) was published in Italy in 1488. In antiquity, the format of the poem would have been a set of papyrus rolls; there may have been 24 rolls, one for each of the 24 books of the epic (although this division is usually believed to postdate Homer's involvement).

It was expected that each roll would take about an hour to perform. At the beginning of both books V and IX is a narrative recap, which

was probably intended as a way to bring new audience members up to date and to refresh the memory of those returning for the next installment—effectively signaling a return to the story after a break in the performance. Although no such recaps occur in the subsequent books, it can be deduced that the four-hour performance pattern would have been followed throughout the poem, meaning that the entire *Odyssey* would have been performed over the course of six days (four rolls recited on each).

There is further support for this four-hour interval theory toward the end of Book VIII, where the blind bard Demodocus is paid a tip of a fine cut of meat: "Herald! bear it to the bard / For his regale, whom

I will soon embrace / In spite of sorrow; for respect is due / And veneration to the sacred bard." This may have been a hint for audiences to dip into their pockets as the entertainment drew to a close.

Our impressions of Homer, derived from later writers in Greek, include the supposition that he himself, like Demodocus, was blind. Some scholars, however, believe that physical blindness is a metaphor for oral composition and performance in a pre-literate age.

An epic legacy

It is not possible to trace how much of this story of gods, monsters, and warriors comes from the author's imagination and how much from popular stories of the day. Classic Greek mythology is clearly a major source, though, at least for the tale's assorted gods and goddesses.

The importance of Homer's epic works cannot be overestimated. His use of nonlinear structure in *The Odyssey* continues to inspire writers to this day. More importantly, though, his name lives on, just as the names of his heroes live on, through two masterpieces of poetic art that have informed not only storytelling through the centuries but also the very definition of epic. ∎

Ulysses! matchless valor thou hast shewn
Recov'ring thus thy wife; nor less appears
The virtue of Icarius' daughter wise,
The chaste Penelope, so faithful found
To her Ulysses, husband of her youth.
The Odyssey (Book XXIV, lines 231–235)

A THIN FLAME RUNS UNDER / MY SKIN

FRAGMENT 31 (600 BCE), SAPPHO

IN CONTEXT

FOCUS
Love poetry

OTHER KEY POETS
Ovid, John Donne, Lord Byron, Elizabeth Barrett Browning, Kamala Das

BEFORE
c. 650 BCE On the island of Paros, Greek poet Archilochus writes the earliest-known lyric poetry on personal themes.

AFTER
c. 65 BCE The Roman poet Catullus writes 25 love poems addressed to a woman he calls "Lesbia." They are most likely a homage to Sappho, who came from Lesbos.

1650s–60s Anglo-Welsh poet Katherine Philips celebrates female love and friendship in her work, earning the moniker "the English Sappho".

1666 English poet Ben Jonson pens the lyrical love poem "Song: to Celia."

An exquisite, gently ironic rendering of the pains of erotic desire, Fragment 31 is one of the few snippets of poetry by ancient Greek poet Sappho to survive to the present day. The poem depicts a fortunate man, able—because he is male—to sit in the attitude of a lover with the female poet's beloved: "He is a god in my eyes—/ the man who is allowed / to sit beside you." This "godlike" man is permitted to enjoy the "sweet murmur" of the beloved's voice and her "enticing // laughter."

Obliged to keep her distance, the poet is denied such intimacies, but even setting eyes on the focus of her adoration is enough to set her heart racing and deprive her of the power of speech. She, the hopeless lover, now becomes the poem's focus, with a list of the symptoms of her infatuation: "a thin flame" running under her skin, blindness, noises in her ears, a cold sweat, and trembling, until it seems that death cannot be far off. At this point, tantalizingly, the fragment breaks off. Though truncated, the poem's bittersweet, tragicomic depiction of sexual longing keeps its force.

The lyric emerges

In contrast to epic verse and drama, which drew on myths and historical narrative, lyrical poems were short and intimate, speaking of personal emotions, hopes, fears, aspirations, and events—including the feelings aroused by love and passion. Sappho was among the earliest poets to write lyric works, and she helped to refine and perpetuate the tradition with her deft, often ironic flair. She is now best remembered for her depictions of same-sex desire, with poems praising the beauty of other women living on Lesbos at the time. Aside

[...] If I meet you suddenly, I can't

speak—my tongue is broken; [...]
Fragment 31 (lines 9–11)

See also: "To My Dear and Loving Husband" 100 ■ *In Memoriam A.H.H.* 148–149 ■ "How Do I Love Thee?" 150–151 ■ "The Looking Glass" 270–271

from personal works such as Fragment 31, many of her poems are wedding songs or songs for religious rites, such as those honoring the goddess Aphrodite.

The Sapphic legacy

Sappho was highly regarded by her contemporaries and successors in the Greek and Hellenistic worlds and into the Roman era. By the early Middle Ages, however, most of her work had been lost. Surviving fragments were often quotations within other writings, to which scholars during the past 150 years have added further rediscoveries, some preserved on papyri.

Despite this loss, the appeal of Sappho's personality endured through the centuries, as did the legacy of her formal mastery. This includes the "Sapphic stanza," consisting of three lines of eleven syllables, followed by a shorter fourth line of five syllables, which is a wonderfully fluid instrument of poetic expression, as evidenced in Fragment 31. It has often been imitated, famously by the Victorian poet Algernon Swinburne in a poem simply entitled "Sapphics," as well as by others including 20th-century poets Ezra Pound and W. H. Auden.

The survival of the Sapphic stanza makes it one of the oldest Western poetic measures. The deeply personal focus of Sappho's work and her dissection of the nature of love were influential upon many later poets: a thread that runs from the Classical era through to the poetry of our own times. ■

Sappho is pictured on a Greek vase (c. 470 BCE) with the poet Alcaeus. Their lyres show how they accompanied the performance of their emotion-filled, songlike—"lyrical"—poems.

Sappho

Sappho was born between 630 BCE and 610 BCE on Lesbos, an island in the northeast Aegean, near modern Türkiye. Little is known for certain about her life but she seems to have come from an aristocratic family. She possibly had a daughter named Cleis, which may also have been her mother's name.

Sappho spent most of her life in Lesbos's chief city, Mytilene, a major trading and cultural hub with links to the mainland kingdom of Lydia and across the Mediterranean. She seems to have established herself as an acclaimed poet and performer during her lifetime; her works were probably first published as books in the 5th century BCE. Sometime around 600 BCE, an unknown political upheaval forced Sappho and her family into exile in the Greek city of Syracuse on Sicily. Sappho eventually returned to Lesbos, where she died around 570 BCE.

Other key works

c. 600 BCE Fragment 44
c. 600 BCE "The Brothers' Song"
c. 600 BCE "Hymn to Aphrodite"

HE WON / THE LATIAN REALM, AND BUILT THE DESTIN'D TOWN

THE AENEID (29–19 BCE), VIRGIL

IN CONTEXT

FOCUS
The foundation myth

OTHER KEY POETS
Homer, Hesiod, Ovid, Apollonius of Rhodes

BEFORE
c. 200 BCE Ennius writes *Annales*, the first influential Roman epic poem, in the ancient Greek verse format of dactylic hexameter.

AFTER
c. 1136 *History of the Kings of Britain*, by Geoffrey of Monmouth, recounts the tale of the legendary King Arthur.

c. 1200 In the Danube region of Austria, an anonymous poet writes *Nibelungenlied* (*Song of the Nibelungs*). Said to be based on events of the 5th and 6th centuries, this national poetic epic of the Germanic peoples later inspires Wagner's operatic *Ring* cycle.

To have a clear view of one's origins is a deep-seated human need. It is seen at a communal level when a creation myth is devised to explain how the world began. The equivalent at the political level is the foundation myth—an origin story enabling people to understand and take pride in the roots of their culture.

In Virgil's *Aeneid*—the most admired of Western foundation-myth poems, written 29–19 BCE to honor the city of Rome—the hero Aeneas is aware of his destiny. He embodies *pietas*, the combined Roman virtues of loyalty to state and family and reverence for the gods.

Aeneas in pre-Virgilian writings was admirable enough for Emperor Julius Caesar (r. 46–44 BCE), the adoptive father of Augustus, to have placed himself proudly within the same bloodline. The semidivine parentage attributed to Aeneas (his father was Anchises, a Trojan prince; his mother, Venus, goddess of love) made him ideal as an imperial ancestor. As well as possessing prized character traits, Aeneas helped justify Roman imperialism through his military exploits.

Troubled memories

Virgil had witnessed traumatic times for the Roman Republic. Octavian had vanquished his rivals Antony and Cleopatra at the Battle of Actium in 31 BCE—a victory prophetically depicted in *The Aeneid* on the hero's divinely forged shield. By this time, Virgil had just started his great work. Octavian, renamed Augustus, appeared more secure in his rule. However, instability remained a painful memory—one that an inspiring national epic might help put to rest.

> [Neptune] saw the Trojan fleet dispers'd, distress'd,
> By stormy winds and wintry heav'n oppress'd.
> Full well the god his sister's envy knew,
> And what her aims and what her arts pursue.
> **The Aeneid (Book I)**

Virgil

Born Publius Vergilius Maro in 70 BCE, Virgil was the son of a farmer from a village near Mantua, in Cisalpine Gaul (now northern Italy). His education in Cremona and Milan familiarized him with Greek and Roman literature. Later, he abandoned a course in rhetoric in Rome to study Epicurean philosophy in Naples. He met the poet Horace, as well as Gaius Maecenas, a patron of the arts and adviser to Emperor Augustus (Octavian).

Around 39–38 BCE, Virgil published a collection of pastoral poems, the *Eclogues*, that won esteem, as well as support from Augustus. He was given a house in Rome, near Maecenas's.

The Aeneid took 11 years to write. Although Augustus admired it, Virgil remained dissatisfied. He died in 19 BCE, aged 50, on a trip to Greece.

Reflecting Virgil's lasting influence, Dante imagined him as a guide to hell in his own masterpiece, *Inferno*.

Other key works

c. 39–38 BCE *Eclogues*
c. 37–29 BCE *Georgics*

Anticipated in the poem is the foundation of Rome, 333 years after *The Aeneid*'s narrative ends. The reader is told that Romulus and other early rulers of the city are descendants of Aeneas's marriage to Lavinia, an Italian princess. Augustus (r. 27 BCE–14 CE), who is said to be able to trace his lineage back to Romulus, could therefore claim to descend from Aeneas himself. Aeneas linked him with the prestige of an ancient culture, and Lavinia with his native land of Italy.

The epic's morale-boosting intention was also conveyed in several prophetic passages that look forward to Virgil's own era. In these glimpses of the future, Augustus is praised, and hope is expressed for a period of peace under his strong leadership.

The Homeric background

Virgil, narrating the foundation story of his homeland, was consciously following in the footsteps of his Greek predecessor Homer, author of two great epics, *The Iliad* and *The Odyssey*, about the Trojan War. Written down around 700 BCE, these Greek poems describe a war that, in Virgil's time, was believed to have occurred around 1100 BCE. When Virgil began his epic, Homer's tales were already well embedded in the public mind, so he chose to build on them for the purpose of glorifying Rome.

Homer's epics describe the Trojan War itself (*The Iliad*) and Odysseus's obstacle-filled journey »

Venus gives Aeneas a shield that she commissioned from her husband Vulcan. It is adorned with images that foretell the founding of Rome, including Romulus and Remus being suckled by a she-wolf.

> These figures, on the shield divinely wrought,
> By Vulcan labor'd, and by Venus brought,
> With joy and wonder fill the hero's thought.
> Unknown the names, he yet admires the grace,
> And bears aloft the fame and fortune of his race.
> **The Aeneid (Book VIII)**

back home after the war (*The Odyssey*). By setting *The Aeneid* in the aftermath of the Trojan War, Virgil makes it clear that he wishes his epic poetry to be measured against Homer's. Treating war and a homecoming in a single work, rather than two separate poems, Virgil tries to outshine his Greek predecessor.

Aeneas plays a minor role in *The Iliad*, showing bravery in battle under the protection of his mother Aphrodite (known as Venus to the Romans) and the sea god Poseidon (Neptune), who prevents him from being killed by the Greek warrior Achilles. Virgil, however, places this warrior-prince center stage.

Grand style

In a break from Homeric precedent, Virgil presents *The Aeneid* in 12 books rather than 24. However, like other classical epics, he adopts dactylic hexameter as its meter.

Each line comprises six metrical feet—generally five dactyls (each with one long then two short syllables), followed by a spondee (two long syllables). This pattern was considered appropriate to the grandest poetry in both Greek and Latin traditions. There are no rhymes; however, in English, some translators adopted rhyming to popularize or enliven the poetry. A notable example is John Dryden, whose version from 1697 is used in the quotations offered here.

There are also thematic parallels with *The Iliad* and *The Odyssey*. Just as Odysseus is aided by Athena, goddess of wisdom, Aeneas is aided by Venus, his mother. Divine intervention in human affairs is a major strand of all three epics. Another common theme is prophecy. Early on, *The Iliad* reveals that the Greeks are fated to vanquish the Trojans,

Aeneas and Dido are doomed from the start in Virgil's poem. Dido kills herself after Aeneas deserts her. On her deathbed, she warns of eternal conflict between her city of Carthage and Rome.

while in *The Odyssey*, the blind seer Tiresias tells Odysseus that he will make it home alive. Similarly, in Book II of *The Aeneid*, Aeneas is told by the ghost of Hector (a Trojan warrior-prince featured in *The Iliad*) that he will leave the ruins of Troy to found a new city. Both Homer's Achilles and Virgil's Aeneas carry shields with elaborate decoration that is described in great detail.

Lengthy wanderings

The first six books of *The Aeneid* focus on Aeneas's seven-year sea journey after escaping burning Troy and setting out to found a glorious new city in the West—not Rome, as it turns out, but Lavinium, a port city 4 miles (6 km) to the south from which Rome would later emerge. This first half of the work includes a number of passages that echo *The Odyssey*. In both epics, the hero journeys around the Mediterranean, facing similar challenges, and descends to the Underworld to glean information from the dead.

Forced by a storm to land on the Libyan coast, Aeneas becomes a guest of the widowed Queen Dido of Carthage, to whom he tells his

Roman and Greek deities

The gods and goddesses mentioned in Virgil's *Aeneid* are given their Roman names, whereas the same characters in Homer's *Iliad* and *Odyssey* are referred to by their Greek names, reflecting the authors' origins.

Specific god or goddess	Roman	Greek
King of the gods	Jupiter	Zeus
Queen of the gods	Juno	Hera
Messenger god	Mercury	Hermes
Goddess of wisdom	Minerva	Athena
God of truth, healing, and sunlight	Phoebus	Apollo
Goddess of sexual love	Venus	Aphrodite
God of desire	Cupid	Eros
God of the sea	Neptune	Poseidon
Goddess of hunting	Diana	Artemis
God of war	Mars	Ares
God of metalwork	Vulcan	Hephaestus

tale; stories within stories are also common in *The Odyssey*. They fall in love; but Jupiter, king of the gods, sends Aeneas a message to remind him of his destiny. He deserts Dido, who then kills herself. This episode emphasizes the supremacy of duty but also shows Aeneas as capable of emotional cruelty. Virgil is too great a poet to deal only in one-dimensional heroism.

Aeneas's descent into the Underworld (Book VI), where he encounters the ghosts of Dido and his father Anchises, is another key event in the epic's first six books. This episode gives Virgil the opportunity, via the prophetic understanding of Anchises, to foreshadow the golden age of Rome. For the modern reader, there is fascination, too, in the inhabitants of Virgil's afterlife being treated according to the lives they led on Earth. This concept was later explored in Dante's *Divine Comedy*.

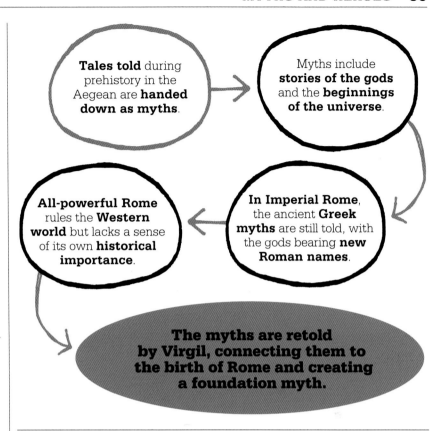

Tales told during prehistory in the Aegean are **handed down as myths**.

Myths include **stories of the gods** and the **beginnings of the universe**.

In Imperial Rome, the ancient **Greek myths** are still told, with the gods bearing **new Roman names**.

All-powerful Rome rules the **Western world** but lacks a sense of its own **historical importance**.

The myths are retold by Virgil, connecting them to the birth of Rome and creating a foundation myth.

War ending

The second half of *The Aeneid*, books VII to XII, concentrates on military conflict in Latium (where the wandering Trojans have finally settled), prompted by a quarrel over a woman, the princess Lavinia. It depicts suffering and grief, as well as action; and ultimately, the fate of thousands comes down to a conflict between two great warriors, just as it does in *The Iliad*.

The epic ends with Aeneas fighting Turnus, leader of the Rutuli tribe, the enemies of the Trojan settlers. Aeneas is prepared to spare his foe's life until he notices that Turnus is wearing the belt of Aeneas's friend Pallas over his shoulder. Enraged, the hero despatches Turnus with a thrust of his sword. Aeneas's dutiful commitment to his destiny has been swamped by a surge of emotion. Again, Virgil portrays the hero of his tale as a complex, very human character.

Some critics have argued that the epic's abrupt ending suggests incompleteness, and perhaps this is why Virgil, when he realized he was close to death, asked for the manuscript to be destroyed. However, Augustus ordered it to be published, not least for use as a tool of propaganda for his golden age of empire.

Looking forward

The Aeneid has long been seen as a masterpiece of Latin literature, comparable in achievement to *The Iliad*. Its influence on later poetic works extended to Dante's *Divine Comedy*, Spenser's *The Faerie Queene*, and Milton's *Paradise Lost*.

Irish poet Seamus Heaney translated Book VI, attracted by its elegiac tone, its otherworldly strangeness, and its meeting between a son and his deceased father in the afterlife. ∎

> Deep in his bosom drove the shining sword.
> The streaming blood distain'd his arms around,
> And the disdainful soul came rushing thro' the wound.
> **The Aeneid (Book XII)**

IMMORTAL GODS / INSPIRE MY HEART

METAMORPHOSES (8 CE), OVID

IN CONTEXT

FOCUS
Mythological poetry

OTHER KEY POETS
Homer, Hesiod, Horace

BEFORE
c. 2000 BCE The ancient
Mesopotamian poem *The Epic
of Gilgamesh* contains elements
common to other great works
of mythological literature, such
as a voyage to the Underworld.

c. 700 BCE Hesiod's *Theogony*
explains in 1,000 lines the
origins of all the Greek gods.

AFTER
c. 1320 In *The Divine Comedy*,
Dante frequently discusses the
debt he owes to Ovid.

1820 *Hyperion*, an unfinished
poem by John Keats, deals with
the mythical beginnings of the
universe, when the Titans, led
by Saturn, gave way to the
Olympians, led by Jupiter.

Like Homer and Virgil before
him, the Roman poet Ovid
drew inspiration from the
much-loved stories of Greek
mythology. However, while Homer
dealt with heroic battles (*The Iliad*)
and a homecoming fraught with
difficulties (*The Odyssey*), and
Virgil's national epic *The Aeneid*
celebrates the importance of Rome,
Ovid used the stories to explore his
true interest: matters of the heart.

Ovid had pursued this subject
from his earliest writings. His
first poetry collection, *Amores*,
consisted of love poems written in
elegiac couplets; and he wrote his
Heroides poems as though they
were letters from mythical women

to their male lovers—Penelope to Ulysses, and Helen to Paris, for example—giving voice to their side of the story, which had been ignored by earlier writers.

When Ovid came to write *Metamorphoses*, he turned to myth to explain emotional experiences. In an act of breathtaking ambition, he decided to tell the entire story of the world—from the creation, to the murder of Julius Caesar in 44 BCE, the year before his own birth. Only with such an epic undertaking could he fully map the human heart.

An epic with a difference

Metamorphoses is an epic in every technical sense. It is written in the sonorous rhythm of dactylic hexameter, just like the works of Homer and Virgil (and other less famous epics, such as the *Annales* by the early Roman poet Ennius). It is 12,000 lines long, split into 15 books. (*The Iliad* is 15,000 lines over 24 books, and *The Aeneid* is just under 10,000 lines across 12 books.)

> Before the ocean and the earth appeared—
> Before the skies had overspread them all—
> The face of Nature in a vast expanse
> Was naught but Chaos uniformly waste.
> ***Metamorphoses* (Book I)**

Vast in scope, the sprawling tale has gods interacting with humans and connects ancient events with Ovid's contemporary Rome. Like *The Aeneid*, and according to the custom of the time, *Metamorphoses* is politely dedicated to Emperor Augustus, whose godlike status is lionized. Indeed, the poem ends with Augustus's adopted father Julius Caesar being turned into a star in the sky. In an unusual move, *Metamorphoses* has no main character and no story line; instead, it is an anthology of classical stories about change.

Mixing and matching

The central belief that emerges from Ovid's *Metamorphoses* is that chaos is the natural order of things and that everything (Earth, nature, the human mind) is always changing. To attempt to make one grand story—one with an ending, happy or otherwise—out of this worldview would have undermined the whole enterprise.

Such was the closeness between the Greek and Roman worlds that it can be hard to extricate them from each other. Many Greek statues and works of art and literature are known only through Roman copies of lost Greek originals. *Metamorphoses* is a perfect example of this act of reproduction. Ovid's stories give a Roman patina to the original Greek tales, and he was so successful in making the Greek stories his own that his versions are often better known than the originals. »

Ovid

Publius Ovidius Naso was born in 43 BCE into an ancient equestrian family, the highest elite of Roman society other than the patrician class. Although a career in government had been planned for him, he instead devoted himself to writing, claiming that whenever he wrote, only poetry came out.

As well as writing about myths, Ovid penned works about erotic love, at odds with the morals of his time. Emperor Augustus promoted traditional values, and infidelity was illegal; however, Ovid was creating guides to seduction and detailing locations for illicit trysts.

He was exiled to Tomis (now Constanța, Romania), right at the edge of the Roman Empire.

Even in exile, Ovid remained a prolific writer, but this was a harsh sentence for a man of words. The locals did not speak Latin, so he had to communicate with them in gestures.

In Rome, where Ovid's wife remained, it was illegal to speak his name. He died in 17/18 CE, still petitioning for a reprieve.

Other key work

2 CE *Ars amatoria*

> ["...] Much more remains to me
> In all my utmost sorrow, than to you,
> You gloater upon vengeance—Undismayed,
> I stand victorious in my Field of Woe!"
> **Metamorphoses (Book VI)**

Narcissus was so enthralled by the sight of his own reflection—as shown in this painting of 1597–1599 by Italian master Caravaggio—that he was incapable of loving anyone else.

The myth of ill-fated lovers Pyramus and Thisbe, who "lived in adjoining houses," is of little significance in Greek literature, but Ovid's timeless tale of the couple inspired the plot of *Romeo and Juliet*. Their union was prohibited by their fathers, "yet the passion that with equal strength / Inflamed their minds no parents could forbid" (Book IV).

Twists and transformations

The great majority of the changes inflicted upon the various characters throughout *Metamorphoses* are forms of punishment meted out by capricious deities for real or perceived slights against them.

The agony and shock of physical metamorphosis are presented in graphic detail. In one tale, as Dryope suckles her infant Amphissos, she takes a flower from a tree that was previously the nymph Lotis (another victim of transformation). As a punishment for the pain this causes to the sentient Lotis, Dryope begins to turn into a tree, the bark growing up her body. Terror hits the reader as Amphissos feels "his mother's bosom harden to his touch" (Book IX).

Ovid's genius lay in his ability to recognize how love and passion twist and transform us in terrible ways. His work is so timeless that many characters have given rise to words we still use to this day. In the myth of Narcissus, for example, the beautiful male nymph becomes besotted with his own reflection and cannot love anyone else; this retelling of the Greek story gives us the word narcissism, to mean morbid self-obsession.

Another familiar story is that of Pygmalion, who disparages women and can only adore the statue of a woman that he himself has carved. Ovid's work inspired George Bernard Shaw to write the play *Pygmalion*, which later became the musical *My Fair Lady*. In the original myth, the object of Pygmalion's love is not even granted a name.

Ruthless deities

The modern reader can find a lot of misogyny and sexual violence in these ancient stories. Male gods frequently prey on human women, seemingly without consequences for themselves.

The female gods can be just as unforgiving as the male ones. When Jupiter (sometimes called Jove) sees the maiden Callisto, a follower of the virgin goddess Diana, he takes on Diana's form

This painting by Flemish artist Peter Paul Rubens shows the moment when the goddess Diana discovers that her maid Callisto is pregnant by Jupiter, Diana's father.

in a bid to lure her to him, then rapes her. When the real Diana learns that Callisto is pregnant, she is disgusted and casts her out from the sacred springs.

Jupiter's consort Juno is equally venomous: learning Callisto has borne Jupiter's son, she turns Callisto into a bear to be hunted by her human son. Only at the last moment before Callisto in bear form is killed does Jupiter take pity. He spirits them both into the sky to become the constellations Ursa Major and Ursa Minor.

Inspiring later artists

Metamorphoses is a deep treasure trove of fantastical stories and human truths. It includes more than 250 myths.

The collection continued to be much read in the Middle Ages, when its various stories were read allegorically as revealing truths about the human condition. In addition, Ovid's depiction of the Flood seemed to confirm the version in the Bible's Book of Genesis.

The influence of *Metamorphoses* is immense across multiple art forms. It has inspired many great painters from the Renaissance onward, including Italians Sandro Botticelli and Titian, Flemish Peter Paul Rubens, and Spaniards Diego Velázquez and Pablo Picasso. The story of Orpheus is the subject of Italian composer Claudio Monteverdi's 1607 opera *L'Orfeo*.

Other writers through the ages have also borrowed from Ovid. In Chaucer's *Canterbury Tales*, the

Ovid's transformations

Throughout the text of *Metamorphoses*, many characters are turned into creatures and objects. Here is a selection.

Character	Transformed into
Actaeon (herdsman)	Stag
Alcithoe (princess)	Bat
Alcyone and Ceyx (king and queen)	Birds
Arachne (weaver)	Spider
Cadmus (slayer of monsters)	Serpent
Cyparissus (huntsman)	Cypress tree
Daphne (nymph)	Laurel tree
Hippomenes (hunter)	Lion
Lycaon (king)	Wolf
Myrrha (princess)	Myrrh tree
Narcissus (nymph)	Flower
Niobe (bereaved mother)	Weeping rock
Picus (king)	Woodpecker
Pierides (singers)	Magpies
Scylla (princess)	Monster
Talus (inventor)	Partridge
Tiresias (shepherd)	Woman (and back into a man)

Wife of Bath begins to tell the story of Midas but leaves it unfinished, instructing her fellow pilgrims to read Ovid for the conclusion. *Metamorphoses* had a great impact on Shakespeare, too, appearing as a prop in both *Titus Andronicus* and *Cymbeline*, as well as providing the theme of transformation for

A Midsummer Night's Dream. The blind seer Tiresias of Thebes in Book III later features as a key figure in T. S. Eliot's *The Waste Land* (1922). Franz Kafka's most famous story, *Metamorphosis* (1915), unapologetically displays its inspiration in its own title, as does *Tales from Ovid* (1997), by British poet Ted Hughes.

The influence is ongoing. The last lines of *Metamorphoses* show Ovid already knew this to be the case. The final transformation is his own, from human to legend: "If Poets' prophecies / Have any truth, [...] / I shall live in fame." ∎

> And now, I have completed a great work,
> Which not Jove's anger, and not fire nor steel,
> Nor fast-consuming time can sweep away.
> ***Metamorphoses* (Book XV)**

THE ME
WORLD
c. 700 CE–1450

DIEVAL

The **epic poem** *Beowulf* is composed in Old English by an anonymous poet in England.

Japanese poet Ono no Komachi writes "How Sad," one of her many famous **tanka poems**.

Hildegard of Bingen composes "O virga mediatrix," a poem to music that **celebrates the Virgin Mary's role** in the Salvation.

700–1000 CE   **c. 880 CE**   **c. 1150**

8 CE   **c. 1100–1350**   **MID-14TH CENTURY**

Li Bai produces **over 1,000 poems** on various subjects, including many based on his own life, in **Tang dynasty** China.

Troubadour poetry flourishes in the feudal courts of southern France.

Persian poet Rumi's **ghazal** "The Guest House" provides a philosophy for living.

The poetry of the medieval era was rooted in ancient and Classical traditions, but it was also shaped by the defining characteristics of its times. These included the increasing power of the Christian Church, as well as the growing patronage of poets by secular rulers and nobles. By the end of the period, aristocratic courts were responsible for a flowering of poetry in vernacular dialects, new themes (such as courtly love), and new forms, which include the tanka pioneered in Imperial Japan, the ghazal from the Umayyad court in Arabia, and the European sonnet.

New quests and warriors

In Western poetry, the narrative epic continued to be a popular genre, but evolved to accommodate new heroes and quests. Beowulf, slayer of monsters, has much in common with the Sumerian Enkidu from the *Epic of Gilgamesh* (c. 2100 BCE), but the Anglo-Saxon poem that tells his story was written down by scribes living in a world governed by Christian rather than Pagan values.

In his *Divine Comedy* (1308–1321), Dante drew on the work of Classical authors such as Virgil and Ovid, while also presenting the ultimate Christian hero—an everyman whose quest is to save his own soul by coming to a greater understanding of God's universal plan. Chaucer's *Canterbury Tales*, written in the late 14th century after reading the *Divine Comedy*, references Dante as well as Classical and Christian traditions. Chaucer remade the epic quest as a pilgrimage, melding religious and worldly matters: his journey is shared by knights, monks, and ordinary people who recount tales ranging from the devout to the highly scurrilous.

Secular and sacred love

The genre of chivalric romance, a further evolution of the epic form, brought heroic traits into a new Christian context. In poems such as *Sir Gawain and the Green Knight* (late 14th century), knights seek to balance a dedication to honor with their devotion to God.

From the 12th century, these poems also began to feature the rituals of courtly love or *fin amour*. An idealized form of courtship based on heroic qualities, courtly love was a stylized expression of an ennobling passion that was both spiritual and erotic. This code of love was popularized and spread from the courts of Occitania (now

Dante, in exile from his home town of Florence, writes the **Divine Comedy**, an **allegorical journey** through the afterlife.

1308–1321

An anonymous poet writes the **chivalric romance** **Sir Gawain and the Green Knight**; one of the most important texts in **Middle English**.

LATE **14TH CENTURY**

Christine de Pizan is a **prolific author of both prose and verse**, writing many poems **in defense of women**.

1393–1430

1327–1368

Petrarch composes more than 300 sonnets to his idealized beloved, Laura, perfecting the **sonnet form** that bears his name.

1387–1400

Chaucer creates the **Canterbury Tales**, a collection of **24 stories in verse** told by fictional pilgrims, influenced by Italian writers Dante, Boccaccio, and Petrarch.

---

southern France) in the works of the troubadours—poet-performers who composed a new form of lyrical verse in vernacular languages. The most renowned composers, such as Bernart de Ventadorn, would inspire the love sonnets of later poets such as Dante and Petrarch; their influence can still be detected in love songs and poetry today.

The writings of Benedictine abbess Hildegard of Bingen show that medieval religious poetry could be as passionate as secular verse. Her songs to the Virgin, collected in *Symphonia* (c. 1150), use intense, beautiful, and often erotic metaphors in praise of the Mother of God.

The ghazal, a poetic form that originated in Arabia then spread across the Muslim world from Spain to India, also meshes the sacred and spiritual. The emotion expressed in

these works can be directed to a male or a female beloved, who may or may not represent a divine being. The Persian poet Rumi wrote thousands of ghazals that celebrate the mystical union of the poet with his God. In a different mode, many of the most famous poems of the Chinese poet Li Bai celebrate the passions that fueled his life—not least the joys of wine, which he exalted in quasi-religious terms.

Poems by women

A remarkable number of medieval poems were authored by women. In their subject matter, style, and the religious or secular careers of their authors, they characterize wider poetic developments during the medieval era, which laid the foundations for the works of the Renaissance period that followed.

The rapid growth of Church institutions in the medieval age resulted in improved literacy and more opportunities for education; for religious women such as Hildegard of Bingen, the Church also provided financial support and an audience for their compositions.

In the secular realm, Christine de Pizan became a celebrated and professional poet at the French royal court. She wrote in French (not Latin) and her works were widely circulated. Catering to the ongoing appetite for love poems, she wrote hundreds of lyrical ballads, but her poems also addressed more serious matters. Her *Letter to the God of Love* (1399) is a spirited attack on the misogynist rhetoric of centuries of male writers, and its reasoned and philosophical approach heralds the works of Renaissance poets. ∎

SONGS OF OLD, / BOUND WORD TO WORD IN WELL-KNIT RIME

BEOWULF (c. 700–1000 CE)

IN CONTEXT

FOCUS
Old English oral poetry

OTHER KEY POETS
Homer, Ovid, Geoffrey Chaucer

BEFORE
After 450 CE "The Seafarer" is an anonymous philosophical work about a man trapped at sea on a raft.

c. 680 CE Caedmon, a monk at Whitby Abbey in northern England, writes a hymn that is the earliest known example of Old English poetry.

AFTER
c. 1000 CE *The Song of Roland*, an epic poem from France, espouses many of the same virtues as *Beowulf*.

c. 1470 Sir Thomas Malory composes *Le Morte d'Arthur*, which relates the tales of the legendary British king Arthur.

The epic tale of a valiant warrior-prince, *Beowulf* is the most important example of poetry composed in Old English, or Anglo-Saxon, originally to be read to an audience. Almost impenetrable to modern ears, this language developed from those spoken by Germanic peoples such as the Angles, Saxons, and Jutes, who invaded Britain in the 5th century CE. Old English remained in common usage until the Norman Conquest of 1066–1071.

Beowulf's date of composition is unknown. However, it is unlikely that any poet in England would have chosen to rhapsodize about the adventures of a Scandinavian

See also: *The Epic of Gilgamesh* 18 ▪ *The Odyssey* 24–31 ▪ *The Aeneid* 34–39 ▪ *Sir Gawain and the Green Knight* 57 ▪ *The Canterbury Tales* 64–71

Kennings

A brilliant piece of wordplay predominantly found in Norse and Icelandic poetry, a kenning describes something by using an unusual combination of words that makes one look at the original concept with fresh eyes. Examples in *Beowulf* include:

Kenning	Meaning
Battle-sweat	Blood
Rapture-of-heaven	Sun
Shaft-of-slaughter	Spear
Weeds of battle	Armor
Whale-path	Sea

Heaney's *Beowulf*

In 1999, the Irish poet and playwright Seamus Heaney published a translation of *Beowulf* that became a huge success, winning the UK's Whitbread Book of the Year award and having the unusual distinction of being a poetry book in the bestseller list.

When Heaney began the translation, he was teaching in the US and was looking for an "anchor" that would keep his poetry rooted "to the Anglo-Saxon sea-bed." He said that translating such a great work from a language in which he was not an expert was "like trying to knock down a megalith with a toy hammer." Eventually, he found the poem's voice in the sonorous diction of the stern male relatives he had heard while growing up in Northern Ireland.

Rather than sticking unswervingly to the regularity of the poem's meter, Heaney allowed himself occasional transgressions so that the piece would sound natural when spoken. This is most evident in the audiobook of the translation, performed by Heaney himself.

hero after the ferocious Viking invasions that began in 793 CE, so the story (at least in its original telling) probably precedes that date.

Epic storytelling

Set in what is now Denmark and southern Sweden, *Beowulf* is historical in nature, dealing with the adventures of its eponymous hero. In this respect, it sits alongside classic epics such as Homer's *Iliad* and *Odyssey* and Virgil's *Aeneid*.

Just like Odysseus and Aeneas in their respective sagas, Beowulf is a storyteller: more than once in the poem, he regales enthralled audiences with his heroic deeds. For example, when a servant of Hrothgar, the Danish king, claims that Beowulf lost in a swimming contest against his childhood friend Breca, Beowulf turns the story on its head. He concedes that Breca might have been the first to reach the shore, but he continues by saying "that I had more of might in the sea / than any man else." This is because he also had to contend with a number of sea monsters: "Of night-fought battles / ne'er heard I a harder 'neath heaven's dome," he says.

Ending the tale of his perilous adventures with a faux humble "I boast not of it!" Beowulf establishes his prowess and proves that he is more than qualified to deal with Grendel, the monster that has been terrorizing Hrothgar's kingdom.

A tale of three monsters

In lines 815–36, Beowulf mortally wounds Grendel and hammers the monster's arm into the wall of »

[…] the fiend trod on,
ireful he strode; there streamed from his eyes
fearful flashes, like flame to see.
***Beowulf* (lines 725–727)**

King Hrothgar's hall, where it hangs as an emblem of his victory. Later (lines 1276–82), Grendel's mother appears, even more formidable than her offspring. After a brutal battle in her underwater lair, Beowulf murders her, too.

Crowned in heroic glory, Beowulf lives 50 years as king of a prosperous clan before he confronts an even fiercer monster than either Grendel or his mother—a rampaging dragon protecting a hoard of gold. This time, however, Beowulf has finally met his match: although he slays the dragon, he dies from the injuries sustained in the fight.

The world of *Beowulf*—much like the spirit of the age—is one of bleak survival, underscored by a sense of inescapable catastrophe. The poem pours adulation on Beowulf and his epic achievements, but it does not shy away from the fact that his death leaves his people bereft and in danger. A mourner

Beowulf kills Grendel by cutting off the monster's arm after a gruesome battle, as illustrated in this early 20th-century print by British artist John Henry Frederick Bacon.

Beowulf's verse structure

Each line of *Beowulf* consists of two pairs of beats (stressed syllables) separated by a pause. Generally, the first three beats alliterate (have the same sound), but the fourth does not.

> These lines from *Beowulf* show how the consonants alliterate.

while **wield**ed **words**   the **win**some **Scyld**,

the **lead**er be**loved**   who **long** had **ruled** …

> The first and/or second beats usually alliterate with the third, which "controls" the alliteration.

> A pause in a line of poetry is known as a caesura.

at his funeral bemoans "the doleful days to come, / deaths enow, and doom of battle, / and shame."

A sense of impending doom

Although *Beowulf* celebrates its hero's exploits, the author repeatedly reminds the audience of the transitory nature of heroism. When Beowulf is awarded a golden neck ring, the reader is immediately told it will be lost later in a failed raid; Beowulf saves King Hrothgar's mighty mead hall, but the reader is told it will later be devoured by fire; when Beowulf is in his full pomp, celebrating after his victory in the first half of the poem, Hrothgar himself warns him not to forget that he will lose everything—that no matter how great his feats, every warrior is fated to meet the same end.

The lesson of transience is also true for the greatest treasure of all: the hoard of gold beneath the dragon's belly. This, the poem says, belonged to some forgotten chieftain, and the reader might infer that it could sustain Beowulf's clan for a great while, if not in perpetuity. However, tragedy strikes when all of Beowulf's hand-picked warriors desert him in the heat of battle. Wiglaf, the only one who remains by his side (and the one who returns with his tale), makes the moral clear to the others: they are not worthy of the gold that Beowulf has won for them.

The poem ends the way it began: with a magnificent mournful ritual. Just as King Scyld's funeral boat at the start of the poem carried untold treasures, so is Beowulf's pyre decorated with riches—the very gold that cost him his life.

> [S]he offered, to honor him, arm-jewels twain,
> corselet and rings […]
> on the last of his raids this ring bore with him […]
> […] and that gorgeous ring;
> weaker warriors won the spoil […]
> **Beowulf (lines 1194–1195, 1203, 1211–1212)**

Beowulf's death spells doom for his people. A bleak age of darkness begins to encroach again, after a brief respite.

Rhythmic verses

There are no rhymes in *Beowulf*. Instead, the verses are rich with assonance and alliteration. Thus, Beowulf's final opponent is described as a "naked foe-dragon flying by night / folded in fire" and "folk-destroyer, fire-dread dragon," creating a mesmerizingly rhythmic pattern.

In addition, the text is filled with descriptive phrases and word usages that are unique to this poem—for example, the synonyms and compounds used for the word "sword." These include "keenest blade," "warriors' heirloom," and "edge of iron." The *Beowulf* author manipulates the language in which he composes, transforming it and enriching it with variety and complexity of expression.

Christianity and history

Enthralled by *Beowulf*'s heroic journeys, fearsome dragons, and troll-like monsters, J.R.R. Tolkien devoted himself to becoming an expert on the subject. The British author of the fantasy saga *The Lord of the Rings* delivered a lecture on *Beowulf* in 1936, by which time he had also completed his own translation of the epic poem. This was published posthumously, in 2014.

Tolkien thought that *Beowulf* was a pagan poem to which some unconvincing elements of Christianity had been added by later scribes, perhaps in an attempt to make it respectable. However, recent critics disagree, pointing out that there are so many Christian references in the poem that Christianity must have been part of its original fabric. For example,

> [...] Cain cut down
> with edge of the sword his only brother,
> his father's offspring: outlawed he fled [...]
> [...] There woke from him
> such fate-sent ghosts as Grendel [...]
> **Beowulf (lines 1261–1263, 1265–1266)**

God is invoked 39 times; monsters such as Grendel are said to be children of Cain, the murderous first-born son of Adam and Eve; the sword that Beowulf takes to kill Grendel's mother has a carving of Noah's ark on its hilt; and a bard sings a creation myth similar to the one in the Book of Genesis.

There are also real characters from history in *Beowulf*. Ancient poets were often inspired by true (or presumed-true) events and heroes—from Homer using the Trojan War in *The Iliad*, to Turold writing about the 778 CE Battle of Roncevaux Pass in *The Song of Roland* (c. 1100). By including real people and events, authors could give their fantastic tales of dragons and monsters a sense that it might be true history.

In his *Ten Books of Histories*, Gregory of Tours (538–594 CE) recorded a raid in which the Danish warrior Hygelac was killed. In the poem *Beowulf*, Hygelac is the uncle of the title character, meaning that the tale unfolds on the fringes of recorded history, giving it a grounding in truth.

Beowulf's perilous journey

The poem only narrowly escaped oblivion. From about the year 1000, it survived in a single manuscript

copy that passed through various private owners and was nearly destroyed by fire at the ominously named Ashburnham House in central London, in 1731.

Most surviving Old English writing consists of lives of the saints, biblical translations, sermons, and legal acts. Writing was a specialist pursuit—and an expensive activity. For an original composition to be copied frequently enough to survive, it had to stand out—and *Beowulf*, bristling as it does with action and poetic brilliance, certainly did. Finally published in 1815, it is now rightly appreciated as a masterpiece of Old English oral poetry. ∎

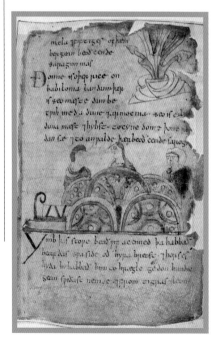

The only extant manuscript of *Beowulf* is one of several works in the illustrated 11th-century Nowell Codex, which is held by the British Library in London.

THE BEACONS ARE ALWAYS ALIGHT

"FIGHTING" (c. 750), LI BAI

IN CONTEXT

FOCUS
Tang Era poetry

OTHER KEY POETS
George Herbert, Ezra Pound, Dylan Thomas

BEFORE
c. 1100–600 BCE Two foundational collections of Chinese poetry, the *Shijing* and the *Shujing*, are assembled. They later provide inspiration for Li Bai.

AFTER
1522 *Romance of the Three Kingdoms* by Chinese writer Luo Guanzhong is published. Like Li Bai's "Fighting" this is partly based on real historical conflicts.

1925 The first edition of *The Cantos*, by American poet Ezra Pound, is published. Pound is greatly influenced by Li Bai's poetry.

The Tang era (618–907) was a golden age for Chinese art and literature, and Li Bai and his friend Du Fu were its finest poets. They wrote about friendships, travel, and personal experiences.

Poet and legend

Although Li Bai was a man of action—a rider, hunter, skilled swordsman, and fighter of chivalrous duels—his poem "Fighting" is about the stupidity of war. It starts out mournful, turns gorily grotesque— "Crows and hawks peck for human guts / Carry them in their beaks"— and ends simply numb at the pointlessness of it all. There is no heroism here.

Li Bai the poet hated war, adored friendship, and worshipped nature. Judging by his output he was more at home writing couplets on the joys of wine, looking out over the countryside, and living rapturously in the moment. Li Bai the man was born in what is now Kyrgyzstan and raised in Sichuan, China. He traveled the Yangzi River, gave away a fortune, married four times, was elevated to the imperial court, and later exiled. It was said he drowned trying to scoop the reflection of the moon from a river.

"Fighting" bemoans the conflicts breaking out near the end of Li Bai's life; he did not live to see the return of peace and prosperity. His style is marked by strict formal mastery and respect for poetic traditions: in some poems, every single line and phrase is a reference or quote from a classic work. His talent was to work them with apparent effortlessness into poems that seem utterly personal. ∎

> Captains and soldiers are smeared on the bushes and grass;
> The General schemed in vain.
> **"Fighting" (lines 17–18)**

See also: *Classic of Poetry* 19 ▪ "The Skylark" 54–55 ▪ "The Old Pond" 110–111 ▪ "Dulce et Decorum Est" 192–193 ▪ Canto LXXXI 232–235

LIGHT / BURST FROM YOUR UNTOUCHED / WOMB LIKE A FLOWER

"ALLELUIA-VERSE FOR THE VIRGIN" (12TH CENTURY), HILDEGARD OF BINGEN

IN CONTEXT

FOCUS
Visionary poetry

OTHER KEY POETS
Teresa of Avila, John Milton, William Blake

BEFORE
c. 90 CE An unknown author writes the Book of Revelation, an apocalyptic prophecy and the final book of the Bible's New Testament.

AFTER
c. 1420 Julian of Norwich's *Revelations of Divine Love* is the first visionary text by an English female mystic.

c. 1438 *The Book of Margery Kempe* describes an English Christian mystic's visions and conversations with God; it is probably the first English-language autobiography.

1793 English poet William Blake turns his visions into radical verse in *The Marriage of Heaven and Hell*.

An author, teacher, composer, philosopher, visionary, mystic, indomitable spirit, and scourge of her enemies, Saint Hildegard of Bingen's achievements were many. Born to an aristocratic family and educated by Benedictine nuns, she joined the order at the age of 15, became abbess in time, and in middle age published a book describing the astonishing religious visions she had experienced since childhood. It made her famous across Europe. The visions were euphoric and apocalyptic, wondrous and ambiguous, qualities that are vividly captured in Hildegard's musical compositions and poetry.

Hymn cycle

Hildegard's "*O virga mediatrix*" ("Alleluia-verse for the Virgin"), to be sung during the gospel at Catholic mass, is part of a cycle of hymns she composed praising the magical power of the Virgin Mary. The Virgin is also a "*virga*" (of the verse title)—a growing limb of the life-giving "world-tree" that is Christianity. Through Mary's flesh,

Hildegard of Bingen's talents went far beyond worship. She wrote learned works on mathematics, botany, and sexuality—and even invented her own language.

the poem claims, life is transformed, death is denied, a whole new world is given birth to, and salvation is achieved—"a flower / on the farther side / of death." Her blessed femininity is a blossoming and transfiguration (Mary is the transforming medium, the "*mediatrix*") of the life spirit into something utterly new, pure, and eternal that saves all humanity. ∎

See also: The Song of Solomon 20–21 ▪ "Let Mine Eyes See" 80 ▪ Paradise Lost 102–109 ▪ "London" 122–125

A FOOL UPON LOVE'S BRIDGE AM I
"THE SKYLARK" (1145–1175), BERNART DE VENTADORN

IN CONTEXT

FOCUS
Occitan troubadours

OTHER KEY POETS
Turold, Marie de France, Dante, Petrarch, Ezra Pound

BEFORE
c. 1102 English chronicler Orderic Vitalis describes the poems of William IX Duke of Aquitaine, considered to be the first troubadour.

AFTER
c. 1255 Compilation of the *King's Songbook*, containing more than 600 troubadour verses; such collections provided the template for later anthologies of poetry.

c. 1296 Dante writes his sestina "On the Short Day," using a stanza form innovated by celebrated 12th-century troubadour Arnaut Daniel.

1925 Ezra Pound's first *Cantos* are influenced by the forms and themes of troubadour verse.

During the 11th century, the first vernacular poetry in Europe began to be produced by poets in the feudal courts of southern France. Composing works in their local language of Old Occitan, these poets became known as "troubadours," from the Occitan *trobar*—"to find" or "to compose." Their new style of lyrical poetry was sung to music and explored secular topics purely for entertainment, in contrast to the religious, and more instructional or edifying, subjects of contemporary Latin works. By the 12th century, the *"cançon"* or "love song" had become the genre's most popular form, and Bernart de Ventadorn one of their most celebrated composers.

Bernart's poem "The Skylark" exemplifies the style and themes of troubadour poetry, including its preoccupations with the trials of love. The poem begins with a description of a lark soaring carefree, allowing itself to drift, unfettered because "all his heart is glad and gay." In contrast, the speaker—the troubadour—is a captive; trapped by an unrequited love, he is unable to "control this heart that flies / To her who pays love no return." Shown no "mercy" by his beloved, the poem concludes with the speaker decrying love—he will give up on women and "leave, exiled to pain."

Promoting courtly love

The pain, joys, and passions described in "The Skylark" are those of courtly love or *"fin'amor."* This idealized and ritualized form of courtship, promoted by the poems of the troubadours, was based on codes of conduct associated with knighthood, such as bravery, devotion, and honor. Just as a knight might display these characteristics in service to his lord,

> Ay! such great envies seize my thought
> To see the rapture others find,
> I marvel that desire does not
> Consume away this heart of mine.
> **"The Skylark" (lines 5–8)**

See also: *Sir Gawain and the Green Knight* 57 ▪ "Death, Be Not Proud" 94–95 ▪ "How Do I Love Thee?" 150–151 ▪ Canto LXXXI 232–235

in courtly love they were directed toward a noble lady, usually unobtainable because she was married. In a feudal society where women were married off for financial, social, or political gain, courtly love verse was revolutionary in evoking a world with a new balance of power, where women held sway.

Redefining poetic form

Courtly ideology, fashioned by the troubadours, had a far-reaching influence on European society and literature, finding its way into romance narratives, such as the *lais* of Marie de France, and shaping enduring ideas about romantic love. The innovative poetic models and language of troubadour verse were equally influential: admired by writers such as Petrarch and Dante in the 14th century, they would have a lasting impact on European writing traditions.

In "The Skylark", Bernart's mastery of poetic expression and lyrical form showcase these most admired aspects of the troubadours' art. His description of love in physical terms employs idioms that have found their way from the 12th century into contemporary songs and verse: the speaker is "drowned in sighs," his heart has been stolen, and the rejection of his love feels like a "death." Bernart enhances these images through the musicality of his words—his control of meter, rhythm, and rhyme. The result is a master class in the troubadour literary techniques that established many of the basic ground rules of later European poetry. ▪

Troubadour poetry was designed to be sung before an audience, not read; some performances would have involved musical accompaniment with a fiddle, lute, harp, or wind instrument.

Bernart de Ventadorn

Born in Corrèze, France, in about 1130–1140, Bernart de Ventadorn may have been the son of a baker at the castle of Ventadour. Here he appears to have learned to sing and write verse and, encouraged by the lady of the castle, Marguerite de Turenne, was elevated to the post of court composer. However, his love songs for Marguerite eventually led to his exile from the castle, and he was forced to seek employment elsewhere. After joining the court of Eleanor of Aquitaine, he followed her to England when, in 1152, she married the Duke of Normandy (later King Henry II).

Bernart later returned to France, spending his last years in a monastery in the Dordogne region. He died around 1190–1200. Celebrated during his lifetime and after death, more of his works survive than any other 12th-century troubadour—an unprecedented 45 poems, of which 18 have musical scores.

Other key works

1145–1175 "When Fresh Breezes Gather"
1145–1175 "Time Comes, and Goes, and Runs Away"

GOOD AND ILL FORTUNE BECOME GUESTS IN THY HEART
"THE GUEST HOUSE" (c. 1265), RUMI

IN CONTEXT

FOCUS
Spiritual poetry

OTHER KEY POETS
Dante, St. Teresa of Avila, George Herbert, John Milton

BEFORE
1010 Ferdowsi writes the epic poem *Shahnameh* (*The Book of Kings*), one of the seminal works of Persian literature.

1177 *The Conference of the Birds* is the most famous work of Persian Sufi poet Attar of Nishapur.

AFTER
1485 Sufi poet Jami, author of the Persian classic *Haft Awrang* ("seven thrones"), is credited with calling Rumi's *Masnavi* "the Qur'an in Persian."

1818 Austrian diplomat Joseph von Hammer-Purgstall introduces Western readers to Rumi's poetry with his German translations.

I n a passage from his six-book poem of spiritual reflection *Masnavi-ye Ma'navi* (meaning "the spiritual couplets"), Persian-speaking mystic Jalal al-Din Rumi writes, "O (dear) soul, regard thought as a person." In this section—widely known as "The Guest House"—Rumi says that each thought that comes and goes in the body should be treated as "an honored guest."

With teachings akin to those of modern mindfulness, Rumi invites his reader to entertain all thoughts,

Followers of the Mevlevi Order
practice a meditative turning dance that has led to them being best known in the West as whirling dervishes.

whether happy or not. Even a sorrowful thought is also "making preparations for joy": it "violently sweeps thy house clear of (all) else, in order that new joy from the source of good may enter in."

Born in 1207 on the borders of modern Afghanistan, Rumi spent most of his life in the city of Konya in modern Türkiye. He was already a teacher of Islam in 1244, when he fell under the spell of a Sufi mystic called Shams Tabrizi. For Rumi, it was a kind of spiritual love affair, releasing in him the flood of his lyric poems. He wrote more than 3,000 *ghazals*, or love poems, which form part of a collection known as *Divan-i Shams* ("the collected poems of Shams"), after his mentor. In the last 10 years or so of his life, Rumi composed the *Masnavi*.

Following his death, Rumi's disciples perpetuated his teachings and spiritual practices in the Sufi Mevlevi Order, which exists to this day. His poetry was hugely influential in the Islamic world and has become increasingly popular in the West. ∎

See also: "Alleluia-verse for the Virgin" 53 ▪ *The Divine Comedy* 58–61 ▪ "Let Mine Eyes See" 80 ▪ "Prayer" 96–99 ▪ *Paradise Lost* 102–109

WHAT MAY A MAN DO BUT PROVE HIS FATE?

SIR GAWAIN AND THE GREEN KNIGHT
(LATE 14TH CENTURY)

Although not published until the 19th century (the one manuscript copy having lain undiscovered for centuries), *Sir Gawain and the Green Knight* was quickly recognized as one of the finest romances in Middle English, the language spoken by commoners rather than the elite.

Tests of virtue

Unfolding over 101 stanzas, the story takes place in an area close to the Welsh border, probably where the unknown author lived. It features plot points common to many tales of medieval romance—such as a solitary quest and an unquestioning loyalty to the chivalric code—but revolves around legendary King Arthur's nearly perfect knight Sir Gawain. His virtue is tested by a series of challenges, most notably a terrifying contest with the grim, supernatural Green Knight, a battle that ends with one of them losing his head. Such tests are folklore motifs, but the poet has reworked them so that Gawain's qualified victory—he acknowledges a moral shortcoming, having "lack[ed] a little" judgment—has made him sympathetic to readers.

This complex but beautifully rendered tale is an outstanding example of the "alliterative revival" in poetry that swept northern and western England in the late 14th century. However, if those bards had hoped to steer English verse back to its Anglo-Saxon metrical roots, they would be disappointed. English poets left alliterative verse behind, instead adopting Chaucer's most famous accentual-syllabic line, the iambic pentameter. ∎

> Sometimes he fought with dragons and wolves; sometimes with wild men that dwelt in the rocks […]
> ***Sir Gawain and the Green Knight* (Part II)** (Jessie L. Weston prose translation)

See also: *The Odyssey* 24–31 ▪ *The Aeneid* 34–39 ▪ *Beowulf* 48–51 ▪ *The Canterbury Tales* 64–71 ▪ *The Faerie Queene* 82–85 ▪ *The Waste Land* 198–205

ALL HOPE ABANDON, YE WHO ENTER IN!

THE DIVINE COMEDY (1308–1320), DANTE ALIGHIERI

IN CONTEXT

FOCUS
Quest narrative

OTHER KEY POETS
Homer, Virgil, Chaucer, John Milton, W. B. Yeats, T. S. Eliot

BEFORE
c. 2100–1200 BCE The ancient *Epic of Gilgamesh* relates a hero's quest for eternal life.

c. 700 BCE Homer's *Odyssey* takes the hero to the edge of Hades in his quest for home.

29–19 BCE Virgil's *Aeneid* recounts the legendary journey of Aeneas, which will lead to the foundation of Rome.

AFTER
1667 John Milton's biblical epic *Paradise Lost* describes the Fall of Adam and Eve.

1943 T. S. Eliot publishes *Four Quartets*, a spiritual odyssey indebted to Dante's vision.

I talian poet Dante Alighieri hoped that his poem *The Divine Comedy* might remove "those living in this life from the state of misery" by leading them into "the state of felicity." But the work is more than a spiritual manual. Using a quest narrative that follows the hero from the Underworld (or realm of the dead) to Paradise, Dante gives physical form to the spiritual journey of the soul toward God. This allegory of intellectual and spiritual growth would become the literary touchstone of medieval Europe.

The concept of a descent to the Underworld (*katabasis* in Greek), and the return ascent (*anabasis*), if there was one, was an established

See also: *The Epic of Gilgamesh* 18 ▪ *The Odyssey* 24–31 ▪ *The Aeneid* 34–39 ▪ *Sonnet 1* 62–63 ▪ *The Canterbury Tales* 64–71 ▪ *Paradise Lost* 102–109

Terza rima

Terza rima is a poetic form that uses three-line groupings of interlocking rhymes. At the end of the poem or canto, a single line completes the rhyme scheme (as in Dante's work), or a couplet can be used (as by Percy Bysshe Shelley).

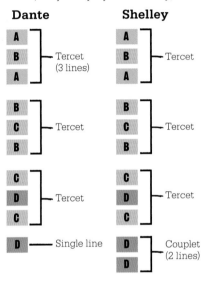

literary trope even in ancient times. Such journeys feature, for example, in Homer's *Odyssey* and in Virgil's *Aeneid*. Drawing on this tradition in *The Divine Comedy*, Dante melds Classical myth and epic narrative with medieval theological doctrine.

Church teaching

A letter from Dante to his patron, Cangrande delia Scala, in which he states that the subject of his poem will be "the state of souls after death" provides a clue to *The Divine Comedy*'s physical and spiritual landscape. While Christian concepts of Heaven and Hell were well established by the time Dante was writing, beliefs about Purgatory—an interim state, where souls could be purified in order to enter Heaven—had only just been formalized.

In 1274, The Second Council of Lyon set out Church doctrine on Purgatory for the first time, stating that after death, repentant souls would enter Purgatory where they could be cleansed by "purifying punishments." The notion that Purgatory was a physical place (not than just a spiritual state) was also gaining traction. In *The Divine Comedy*, Dante fills out the details of this new landscape with vivid and unprecedented imagery.

Significant structure

Dante divides his poem into three parts, or canticles: "Inferno" (Hell), "Purgatorio" (Purgatory), and "Paradiso" (Heaven). This reflects the three landscapes of the afterlife through which his hero must travel, while also referencing the structure of the Christian Trinity—God the father, God the son, and God the holy spirit. Each of the poem's canticles consists of 33 or 34 cantos (large sections of poetry), so that the work has 100 cantos overall.

The significance of "threes" continues with the poem's rhyme scheme, terza rima (see above). »

Dante Alighieri

Born around 1265, Dante Alighieri grew up in a family with noble associations. He claimed to have fallen in love with eight-year-old Beatrice Portinari while visiting her house at age nine, but at 12 he was promised in marriage to Gemma di Manetto. His love for Beatrice endured, and after her premature death in 1290, Dante elevated her into a literary symbol of divine grace and beauty. His poems to her are contained in his courtly love collection *La Vita Nuova* (*The New Life*).

Dante's involvement in the bitter politics of Florence, resulted in his exile on pain of death in 1302. Although he saw neither his native city nor his wife again, he spent his years of exile writing *The Divine Comedy*. Dante's use of a Tuscan vernacular for this work, for his essay *Convivio* (*The Banquet*), and for *La Vita Nuova*, was key in establishing the vernacular as a respected literary language, replacing Latin. He died in 1321.

Other key works

1294 *La Vita Nuova*
1304–1307 *Convivio*

> Midway upon the journey of our life
> I found myself within a forest dark,
> For the straightforward pathway had been lost.
> **The Divine Comedy ("Inferno", Canto I, lines 1–3)**

Thought to derive from lyrical forms used by the Provençal troubadours, Dante is the first to employ terza rima in a written poem. In its units of three lines (a "tercet"), the end-word of the second line supplies the rhyme for the first and third lines of the next unit. At the end of each canto, Dante closes his tercet sequence with a single line which rhymes with the second line of the final tercet; later poets, such as the Romantics, would experiment with a two-line rhymed ending.

Entering the wood

It is no coincidence that Dante's quest takes place over Easter, the period linked to Christ's atonement for human sin and the Resurrection, which provide a wider context for the protagonist's personal salvation story. The narrative begins on the night of Maundy Thursday, not with a traditional epic or chivalric hero, but with a poet—Dante (widely

Beatrice explains the hierarchy of the universe to Dante (creatures without reason at the bottom; Heaven above) in an illustration from a mid-15th-century manuscript of *The Divine Comedy*.

> But I, why thither come, or who concedes it?
> I not Aeneas am, I am not Paul,
> Nor I, nor others, think me worthy of it.
> **The Divine Comedy ("Inferno", Canto II, lines 31–33)**

regarded as the poet himself)—lost in sin, symbolically represented as a dark wood. His passage to safety up a mountain (salvation) is blocked by a lion, a female wolf, and a leopard, each representing a different type of sin. In this state of exile, Dante is already setting out his multiple narrative threads—a personal spiritual crisis, the exile of humankind from God's grace by Original Sin, and a representation of his own forced exile due to the political situation in Italy, in which he is composing his poem.

A journey to salvation

On Good Friday, Dante is eventually rescued from the wood by the spirit of Virgil, who has been sent to help him by Beatrice, a symbol of Divine Love. The poet's choice of a Classical guide, who is also a historical figure and a fellow author of epic poems, is significant in giving Dante's quest narrative a degree of structural, moral, and intellectual integrity.

Virgil offers to lead Dante through Hell (a *katabasis*), and they enter through gates marked with an ominous inscription: "Abandon all hope, ye who enter here…." Crossing the river Acheron, the poets enter a colossal cavern, ringed with ledges that spiral downward—the nine circles of Hell. The first circle, Limbo, houses virtuous pagans, including the great thinkers and writers of Classical antiquity. They must dwell in this twilight world because they lived before the light of Christianity dawned, but their location at the top of the hierarchy of Hell reflects their celebrated achievements.

Moving downward through the circles of Hell, the seriousness of the sinners' crimes, and severity of their punishments increase. Dante

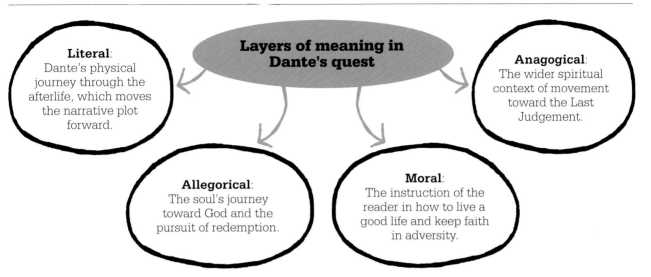

Layers of meaning in Dante's quest

Literal: Dante's physical journey through the afterlife, which moves the narrative plot forward.

Anagogical: The wider spiritual context of movement toward the Last Judgement.

Allegorical: The soul's journey toward God and the pursuit of redemption.

Moral: The instruction of the reader in how to live a good life and keep faith in adversity.

passes those accused of a spectrum of vices, including lust, greed, anger, and treachery, culminating in Satan in the deepest pit.

Having survived Hell, Dante and Virgil arrive at the island-mountain of Purgatory on Easter Sunday, ready to begin the second stage of the quest. In a Classical epic narrative, this part of the story might mark the *anabasis*—the hero's return from the Underworld. However, in Dante's tale, the hero needs further guidance on how to live a good life.

Climbing the mountain of Purgatory, Dante traverses seven terraces, corresponding to the seven deadly sins. Here, penitent sinners accept punishment; but unlike Hell, the focus is on spiritual growth guided by concepts of pure love. Symbolizing his return to Divine Grace, Dante finally reaches Earthly Paradise—the Garden of Eden— at the top of the mountain, where absolved souls regain the state of innocence that existed before the Fall of Adam and Eve.

As a pagan and a representation of earthly reason, Virgil cannot accompany Dante on the last part of his quest—the journey through Heaven. Beatrice, Dante's idealized

symbol of Divine Love, takes his place as guide. Densely theological, with more visionary imagery than other sections of the poem, the third canticle records Dante's passage through nine celestial spheres to the Empyrean, a wholly spiritual realm. This is where he fulfills his quest, experiencing the real *anabasis* or return, when he finally sees God in a moment of spiritual union.

An influential narrative

The immediate popularity of Dante's poem led to the wide dissemination of manuscript, and later printed editions, throughout Renaissance Italy. His graphic depiction of the afterlife in words was also quickly translated into pictures: inspired by his imagery, Sandro Botticelli was the first of many artists to illustrate Dante's work, when he produced 92 drawings for the first Florentine edition of the poem in 1481.

While an English translation of *The Divine Comedy* was not published in full until 1802, it is clear that English writers were already familiar with the poem by the late 14th century. Chaucer's *Canterbury Tales*, begun in 1387, while a different type of pilgrimage quest, quotes and references Dante directly.

In the 17th century, English writer John Bunyan's allegory *The Pilgrim's Progress* was heavily indebted to Dante's masterpiece, and diverted the stream of quest epics away from poetry and into prose fiction. W. B. Yeats's work in general and T. S. Eliot's *Four Quartets* in particular, carried the influence of the Dantean spiritual universe into the 20th century. Eliot summed up the legacy of *The Divine Comedy* when he famously claimed that "Dante and Shakespeare divide the modern world between them: there is no third." ∎

> [...] There is no greater sorrow
> Than to be mindful of the happy time
> In misery [...]
> *The Divine Comedy* ("Inferno", Canto V, lines 121–123)

WORLDLY JOY IS STILL A SHORT, SHORT DREAM

SONNET 1 (14TH CENTURY), PETRARCH

IN CONTEXT

FOCUS
The Petrarchan sonnet

OTHER KEY POETS
Dante, Sir Thomas Wyatt, Edmund Spenser, William Shakespeare

BEFORE
1230–1240 Giacomo da Lentini, a lawyer in the court of King Frederick II of Sicily, writes the first sonnets by modifying a Provençal verse form.

1294 Dante's *La Vita Nuova* (The New Life), a mixture of prose and verse, includes 25 sonnets in Italian to his beloved Beatrice.

AFTER
1631 John Milton's "On His Being Arrived at the Age of Twenty-Three," on the subject of aging, follows the Petrarchan rhyme scheme but without a clear break between the octave and sestet.

The sonnet is one of the West's oldest and most versatile verse forms. Although comprising only 14 lines, its scope is often extended into a sonnet series or sequence.

From the start, the appeal of the sonnet was its compactness and its harmonious division into two unequal parts of eight lines (octave) and six lines (sestet) with a "turn" (volta) between them. The volta is a hinge on which an argument may revolve, such as an observation followed by a conclusion. At the turn, the rhyme scheme alters, too.

The term "Petrarchan" comes from Petrarch, the prime exponent of the form in the 14th century. Petrarch adapted the sonnet and

brought it to maturity in the Italian Renaissance. The octave in his version rhymes abbaabba, while the sestet is either cdcdcd or cdecde.

The so-called Italian sonnet is in fact an English development of the Petrarchan one, with the sestet rhyming cddcee. This pattern was incorporated by Sir Thomas Wyatt and others into the English sonnet, which included a different approach to the rhyming scheme (see p.91).

Patient love

Petrarch's sonnets have a grace that is reminiscent of Dante, but the musicality of the rhymes can only be fully appreciated in Italian. The poet expresses a lover's feelings of excitement and despair, longing and loss, with a subjective immediacy that hugely contributed to the evolution of later love poetry.

Il Canzoniere (*The Songbook*) is dominated by 317 sonnets about the object of Petrarch's unrequited love, Laura, whom he portrays as an ideal of beauty. Sonnet 1 says

Petrarch's muse Laura is depicted here alongside the poet. She holds a laurel branch that indicates the origin of her name, while he wears one as the poet laureate.

See also: *The Divine Comedy* 58–61 ▪ Sonnet 130 88–93 ▪ *Paradise Lost* 102–109 ▪ "My Last Duchess" 144–145
▪ "How Do I Love Thee?" 150–151

Petrarch

Petrarch is the anglicized name of Francesco Petrarca, a learned Italian poet born in 1304 in Arezzo, Tuscany. His father, a lawyer, was a friend of Dante's.

Petrarch spent much of his early life in southern France, after his father moved there to be close to Pope Clement V at Avignon. He studied law at Montpellier and Bologna and later worked as a minor church official in Avignon.

In 1341, Petrarch was made poet laureate of Rome after writing an epic poem in Latin about Scipio Africanus, the Roman military leader, as well as many sonnets in Italian. Rediscovering lost texts in Latin, Petrarch was renowned as a scholar, but he knew no Greek.

Although his role within the Church meant he was not permitted to marry, Petrarch had two children. He was also one of the earliest humanists.

Petrarch died in Arquà (now known as Arquà Petrarca), near Padua, in 1374. His *Canzoniere* was published posthumously, almost 100 years after his death, and contains 366 poems, most of them love sonnets.

nothing about Laura, though elsewhere Petrarch talks of her golden hair, slim white hands, and milky neck; in another poem, her beauty is said to have the power to reshape mountains and rivers. Instead, Sonnet 1 is a record of infatuation, seen retrospectively from a viewpoint of maturity. It speaks of "the mixed strain which here I do compound."

In other sonnets, the poet admits to having carnal feelings, though he knows he will never satisfy them. After many years, Laura finally looks at him. In Sonnet 201, Petrarch returns her lost glove.

In *The Canzoniere*'s final 103 poems, written after Laura's death, Petrarch places her in heaven. She reveals that she resisted his love for the sake of their mutual salvation.

Petrarch's legacy
The Petrarchan sonnet offered an attractively compact and logically organized form for many later poets. Even after the Italian and English sonnet versions had become available, many poets preferred

(at least on occasion) to avoid the final rhyming couplet and instead built their rhymes more organically, in the Petrarchan style, leaving the closing sestet with no epigrammatic flourishes. Examples of this can be seen in John Milton's "On His Blindness" (published in 1673) and Elizabeth Barrett Browning's "How Do I Love Thee?" (1850). John Donne, William Wordsworth, and Robert Browning also made notable use of the Petrarchan sonnet form. ▪

Troubadour **courtly love poetry** has a form known as the ***canso or canzone***, with stanzas divided into two parts, separated by a turn.

The first sonnets, by Giacomo da Lentini, have **14 lines of 11 syllables**, with the octave rhyming abababab.

Petrarch, in his **sonnets about Laura**, favors abbaabba for the **octave** and either cdcdcd or cdecde for the **sestet**.

Abbaabba (closed rhyme) followed by cdecde (interlaced rhyme) becomes established as a classic sonnet form, used often in later centuries.

LAT EVERY FELAWE TELLE HIS TALE

THE CANTERBURY TALES (c. 1387–1400), GEOFFREY CHAUCER

IN CONTEXT

FOCUS
The frame narrative

OTHER KEY POETS
Virgil, Ovid, Dante, Edmund Spenser

BEFORE
9th–4th centuries BCE The *Mahabharata* contains the philosophical text *Bhagavad Gita*, a tale within the tale.

9th century CE In the Middle Eastern collection *One Thousand and One Nights*, Princess Scheherazade tells a story every day to distract the king and delay her execution.

AFTER
1798 In Samuel Taylor Coleridge's *The Rime of the Ancient Mariner*, the sailor tells his story to a wedding guest.

1856 Elizabeth Barrett Browning's epic *Aurora Leigh* incorporates a framing device within its nine-book structure.

> " Whan that Aprill with his shoures soote
> The droghte of March hath perced to the roote,
> And bathed every veyne in swich licour,
> Of which vertu engendred is the flour [...]
> *The Canterbury Tales* (General Prologue; Fragment 1, lines 1–4)

Geoffrey Chaucer is widely acknowledged as the first great poet in the English language. His poetry has earned him this accolade for its wit, humanity, and narrative brilliance. However, luck was involved, too, especially in the early days, when the patronage of John of Gaunt (Duke of Lancaster and father of future king Henry IV) gave Chaucer a close connection to the ruling dynasty. The links with the royal family grew even stronger when John of Gaunt married his third wife Katherine Swynford, Chaucer's sister-in-law.

There is little doubt that it was Chaucer's deliberate intention to be acknowledged as the father of English literature. This is revealed not just by his choice of language—instead of writing in French (the courtly language of his time),

Chaucer used the vernacular, or Middle English—but also by the vast scope of his greatest work, *The Canterbury Tales*, which includes verse and prose, borrowed and original elements, silly and serious themes, and observations both profound and profane. Indeed, Chaucer's narrative tapestry is so rich and his characters so diverse that 17th-century poet and literary critic John Dryden suggested, "Here is God's plenty."

The frame narrative
In the poem, Chaucer places himself among a group of pilgrims traveling from the Tabard Inn in London's Southwark to the shrine of Thomas Becket in Canterbury Cathedral. The party also includes the owner of the tavern, Harry Bailly, who is referred to as the Host. It is his idea to have a

Geoffrey Chaucer

Born into a middle-class family in London around 1342, Geoffrey Chaucer grew up to become a well-known public figure with close links to royalty. After serving in the Hundred Years' War, he traveled widely around Europe, meeting authors such as French poet Jean Froissart and possibly an elderly Petrarch. Later, he held a senior position as a customs officer, while writing poetry at night.

Chaucer is credited with introducing the rhyme royal (also known as the Chaucerian stanza) to English poetry. This format, which he used in his poems *Troilus*

and Criseyde and *The Parliament of Fowls* (1380–1382), consists of seven lines rhyming ababbcc.

Although he gained much acclaim for his verses in his lifetime, it was for his public works that Chaucer was buried inside Westminster Abbey when he died in 1400, in the area that later became known as Poets' Corner.

Other key works

1368–1372 *The Book of the Duchess*
Mid-1380s *Troilus and Criseyde*

Canterbury Cathedral was a popular destination among medieval pilgrims. Every year, thousands made the journey to pay their respects at the shrine to Thomas Becket.

storytelling contest as a way of keeping the company entertained during the long journey.

The pilgrimage becomes a framing device—the overarching story that contains the travelers' various tales. The traveling party includes a knight and his squire, a miller, a merchant, and several members of the clergy, ranging from prioress to parson.

Exploring genres
By having "a compaignye / Of sondry folk" narrate their tales, Chaucer gives himself the freedom to explore disparate literary genres and themes. Some tales, such as "The Miller's Tale", are fabliaux—a sort of bedroom farce featuring sex, misunderstandings, and coarse humor. Others ("The Friar's Tale" and "The Summoner's Tale") are comic tales of bad behavior by men of the Church—a genre known as antifraternal satire. At the opposite end of the spectrum are devotional stories such as "The Prioress's Tale," about the power of the Holy Virgin, and "The Second Nun's Tale," a retelling of the story of the Roman virgin martyr St. Cecilia.

There are also courtly romances, such as "The Knight's Tale," with two valiant heroes competing for the affection of the same lady, and animal tales in the vein of Aesop's fables—such as "The Nun's Priest's Tale," which tells of a rooster who outwits a fox to save his life.

The Decameron's influence
A superlatively well-read man, Chaucer had also translated other writers' works, both ancient and modern. He was certainly familiar with the work of the Italian poet Giovanni Boccaccio, whose poem »

Boccaccio's *Decameron* and the "anxiety of influence"

Chaucer was keen to hide from his English audience how much *The Canterbury Tales* was influenced by *The Decameron*, a collection of stories by Italian writer Giovanni Boccaccio (1313–1375). There is reason to believe that Boccaccio himself adopted a similar strategy.

Boccaccio completed *The Decameron* before 1353. In the work, 10 young Florentines flee their plague-ridden city for the country, where they while away the time by narrating tales of love, lust, and fortune.

In his book *The Anxiety of Influence: A Theory of Poetry* (1973), American critic Harold Bloom maintained that many authors feel the need to be markedly different from the great writers who preceded them, particularly those who are closest to them in time. Thus, Boccaccio demonstrated the influence of ancient authors in his work: he learned to write prose from the letters of Roman statesman Cicero and was influenced by the Roman philosopher Boethius, whose great themes are fortune and chance, on which Boccaccio's stories often dwell. The influence of Ovid is also evident in the theme of erotic love, which he writes about in a witty style.

The huge influence of Dante's *Divine Comedy* is shown in what Boccaccio does not do. While Dante writes in the complex terza rima verse form, Boccaccio writes in prose. Dante was spiritual and allegorical, whereas Boccaccio's work was gritty, realistic, and bawdy.

[…] Emelye, that fairer was to sene
Than is the lylie upon his stalke grene,
And fressher than the May with floures newe—
For with the rose colour stroof hire hewe,
I noot which was the fyner of hem two […]
The Canterbury Tales (The Knight's Tale; Fragment 1, lines 1035–1039)

Il Filostrato (meaning "the love-struck") was the source for Chaucer's Troilus and Criseyde.

Boccaccio's The Decameron, which also develops within a frame narrative, is the obvious influence on The Canterbury Tales. However, Chaucer's work differs in important ways. While Boccaccio's storytellers are affluent young Florentines, Chaucer's pilgrims come from all over the country ("from every shires ende / Of Engelond") and from all walks of life. The group does not feature anybody extremely wealthy (they would not travel in a group with others) or anybody who was without financial income (since they could not afford such a journey).

While Boccaccio's characters talk (in the tradition of Ovid) mainly about matters of love, Chaucer's narrate all manner of tales. They have only the loosest brief (set by the Host), which is to tell stories that combine "best sentence and moost solaas"—that is, highest merit and greatest amusement.

The art of "quiting"

There is a degree of uncertainty about the order in which the tales were gathered, and the sequence differs across several of the published versions and extant manuscript fragments. It is possible that Chaucer never made a final decision on the arrangement. Nevertheless, a clear order can be established in certain sections by the way different characters interrupt each other or respond to stories they do not like by starting to tell their own. This connecting process is called "quiting," which means requiting, responding to, or matching; it threads through much of the poem, making its first appearance at the end of "The Knight's Tale," the opening story of the contest.

William Blake's engraving of 1810 depicts the pilgrims making their way to Canterbury. Chaucer himself is portrayed as the second traveler from the left, on the black horse.

Loosely based on Boccaccio's epic poem Teseida, "The Knight's Tale" is a chivalric romance worthy of its narrator, who holds the highest status of all the characters. It explores a love triangle in ancient Greece, ending with a wedding that is "alle blisse and melodye."

The Host suggests that the Monk might like to follow up with another story, but the drunken Miller has other ideas. He announces, "I kan a noble tale for the nones, / With which I wol now quite the Knyghtes tale." A considerably less worthy take on a love triangle, "The Miller's Tale," the story of a carpenter's wife being unfaithful, is a comic and ribald fabliau. It features sex and a case of mistaken identity, plus a red-hot plow blade thrust into a man's backside and various jokes about breaking wind.

Spiteful counterattacks

The Reeve (who, it transpires, is a carpenter) takes exception to a member of his trade being mocked as a cuckold. He quites (responds to) the Miller by telling another love

> And which of yow that bereth hym best of alle—
> That is to seyn, that telleth in this caas
> Tales of best sentence and moost solaas—
> Shal have a soper at oure aller cost
> Heere in this place, sittynge by this post [...]
> **The Canterbury Tales** (General Prologue; Fragment 1, lines 796–800)

triangle story—but this time, it is a miller who is made to look like a fool, with his daughter and wife being sexually ill-used by two university students. Although "The Reeve's Tale" is less scurrilous than "The Miller's Tale" it is more offensive, with a mean-spirited streak running through it. The lack of consent to the various sexual dalliances deprives it of the jolly lustfulness seen in the previous tale.

A similarly vengeful tit-for-tat occurs later, when the Friar narrates the story of a corrupt ecclesiastical officer, or summoner; in return, "The Summoner's Tale" focuses on an evil friar.

Incomplete narratives

Not every tale in the collection is neatly concluded and followed by a "quiting." For example, "The Cook's Tale," which seems set to deal with

> Whoso shal telle a tale after a man,
> He moot reherce as ny as evere he kan
> Everich a word, if it be in his charge,
> Al speke he never so rudeliche and large,
> Or ellis he moot telle his tale untrewe,
> Or feyne thyng, or fynde wordes newe.
> **The Canterbury Tales (General Prologue; Fragment 1, lines 731–736)**

sex work and debauchery, comes to a sudden halt after only a few dozen lines. Some scholars suggest that Chaucer lost enthusiasm for the downward trajectory established after "The Knight's Tale" and that he decided to spare his readers another vulgar story.

"The Squire's Tale" also comes to an abrupt ending, but for different reasons: this time it's a fellow pilgrim who loses interest and intervenes. Upon hearing that

the Squire's long-winded tale of magic is about to enter a third act, the Franklin cuts him off: "thow hast thee wel yquit" (you have acquitted yourself well), he says. Then it is his (the Franklin's) turn, and he launches into another, more succinct tale of magic.

A similar fate to that of the Squire also befalls the character of Chaucer himself. When his turn to entertain his fellow travelers comes around, he narrates "Sir Thopas," »

Occupations in *The Canterbury Tales*

With a handful of exceptions (the Wife of Bath among them), the pilgrims traveling to Canterbury are referred to by their jobs—the Miller, the Cook, and the Merchant, for example.

However, among the occupations that appear in the poem, several no longer exist. Below is a brief explanation of these lost medieval professions.

Pardoner: One who sold "official" pardons to people who repented of their sins, reducing their time in Purgatory.

Summoner: A kind of bailiff who delivered judgments made by ecclesiastical courts.

Manciple: A provisioner, or person in charge of supplies, for a monastery, college, or Inn of Court.

Franklin: A wealthy landowner, perhaps of upper middle-class status but not of noble birth.

Reeve: An overseer or local official. The term "shire reeve" later evolved to become the word "sheriff."

Canon: A member of the clergy who is also connected to a cathedral.

Yeoman: A freeholder with his own allotment of land to work. In Chaucer, it refers to a middle-ranking servant.

Nun's priest: A priest dedicated to a convent, taking care of the spiritual needs of the nuns.

Shipman: A common sailor.

Haberdasher: A seller of items used in sewing.

a parody of a minstrel romance told in amusingly (and deliberately) substandard verse. The Host stops the clunky narrative: "Namoore of this, for Goddes dignitee," he cries, before giving his well-considered critique: "Thy drasty rymyng is nat worth a toord!"

In spite of this harsh rebuke, Chaucer is given another chance to narrate a story, though the Host encourages him to steer clear of rhymes and "telle in prose." For his second attempt, he shares "The Tale of Melibee," a lengthy moral allegory on the subject of patience and correct behavior, complete with scholarly quotations, erudite opinions, and traditional proverbs to support the various points he makes. At this point, Chaucer might well have fallen foul of the rules laid down by the Host at the start of the pilgrimage,

> ["…] And whan that I hadde geten unto me,
> By maistrie, al the soveraynetee,
> And that he seyde, 'Myn owene trewe wyf,
> Do as thee lust the terme of al thy lyf;
> Keep thyn honour, and keep eek myn estaat' […"]
>
> **The Canterbury Tales** (The Wife of Bath's Prologue; Fragment 3, lines 817–821)

by initially telling a tale of too much "solaas" (entertainment) and then following it with one of too much "sentence" (moral).

A colorful portrayal

For many modern readers, one of the stand-out characters in *The Canterbury Tales* is the Wife of Bath. This is not so much for her tale but for her remarkable prologue, which—at 800 lines— is longer than the tale itself.

One of the funniest and most outspoken characters in English literature, the Wife of Bath has had five husbands. She claims to have worn out the first four with her voracious sexual appetite, with which they were unable to keep up. However, it is her fifth husband, Jankyn, whom she really misses. He was in the habit of reading aloud from a book of tales that focused on the flaws of women throughout all of history—from Eve in the Bible ("That womman was the los of al mankynde"), to Clytemnestra of Greek legend, who plotted with her lover to kill her husband Agamemnon.

One night, the Wife of Bath says, she ripped a few pages out of the book, which led to a terrible physical fight. Worried that one of his blows might have killed her, Jankyn repented and yielded all authority to her: "He yaf me al the bridel in myn hond." Thus matrimonial harmony was restored.

The message of "The Wife of Bath's Prologue" is unequivocal: women must be given absolute control in a marriage, in order for both husband and wife to be happy.

Women's sovereignty

In her actual tale, set in the times of legendary King Arthur, the Wife of Bath reiterates a woman's desire for sovereignty. A knight guilty of raping a young maiden is sentenced by the queen to go forth

Rhyming schemes

There are six key ways in which the lines of a poem can rhyme, but which lines rhyme depends on the poem's rhyming scheme. For example, an abba rhyming scheme is one in which the first and fourth lines rhyme in one way, and the second and third lines rhyme in another.

Type	Definition
Masculine rhyme	A rhyme between the final stressed syllables of two lines, such as **fox** and **socks**.
Feminine rhyme	A rhyme in which both stressed and unstressed syllables rhyme with their counterparts, such as **breezy** and **sleazy**.
Slant rhyme	A rhyme in which either the vowels or the consonants of stressed syllables are identical, such as **height** and **size**, or **fears** and **fires**.
Eye rhyme	Words that look similar on the page, but do not rhyme when spoken aloud, such as **move** and **love**.
Rich rhyme	Words that are pronounced the same, but have different spellings and meanings, such as **slay** and **sleigh**.
Internal rhyme	Words that rhyme in the middle of a line rather than at the end, such as "he **fights** the demons and **rights** the wrongs."

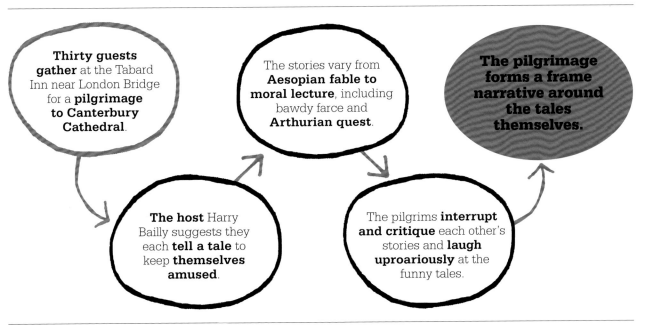

Thirty guests **gather** at the Tabard Inn near London Bridge for a **pilgrimage to Canterbury Cathedral**.

The stories vary from **Aesopian fable to moral lecture**, including bawdy farce and **Arthurian quest**.

The pilgrimage forms a frame narrative around the tales themselves.

The host Harry Bailly suggests they each **tell a tale** to keep **themselves amused**.

The pilgrims **interrupt and critique** each other's stories and **laugh uproariously** at the funny tales.

for a year and a day to discover what women want—or be killed. At the end of his long quest, having come no closer to finding a definitive answer, the knight puts his trust in an old crone, who tells him that she will share her wisdom if he gives her what she wants.

On his return to the court, the knight delivers the result of his findings: "Wommen desiren to

have sovereynetee." That appears to be the right answer. Not only is his life spared, but the old woman (whose desire was to marry him) transforms into a beautiful maiden.

Critics continue to debate the Wife of Bath and whether she is a grotesque caricature or a brilliant proto-feminist creation. After all, she is depicted as ugly, opinionated, and violent. However, she is also powerful, and her radical view of matrimonial harmony based on female sovereignty (at a time when women were regarded as little more than chattel) makes her stand out. Traditionally, women in medieval texts were graceful and mannered. There is, however, a blueprint for the Wife of Bath in La Vieille, a character in Jean de Meun's section of *The Romance of the Rose*, a 13th-century French poem about courtly love left unfinished by Guillaume de Lorris.

The Wife of Bath is described as well dressed and red-faced. She is also an experienced pilgrim, having previously traveled to Rome and Spain's Santiago de Compostela.

Unfinished business

Chaucer's ambitious plans for *The Canterbury Tales* were not fully realized. The poem was supposed to feature four stories by each of the 30 pilgrims—two on the way to Canterbury, and two on the way back—making 120 tales altogether, which would have exceeded the 100 tales in Boccaccio's *Decameron*. Instead, only 24 pilgrims narrate a story. The poem comes to an end just outside Canterbury, and the winner of the storytelling contest is never announced. As a consequence, Chaucer's framing device is also incomplete.

After "The Parson's Tale," a lengthy prose sermon about the Seven Deadly Sins, the reader is presented with Chaucer's Retraction, a passage in which Chaucer the writer (not the pilgrim) apologizes for the coarser aspects of his entire life's work. Although this may not have been intended as part of *The Canterbury Tales*, it has traditionally been used as the closing section of the work since at least the 18th century. ∎

OF DAMAGE DONE, OF BLAME AND BLEMISHED NAME

"LETTER OF THE GOD OF LOVE" (1399), CHRISTINE DE PIZAN

IN CONTEXT

FOCUS
Literary argument

OTHER KEY POETS
Hildegard of Bingen, Bernart de Ventadorn, Alexander Pope

BEFORE
8th century *Conflictus Veris et Hiemis* (*Contention of Spring and Winter*) is probably written by English scholar Alcuin.

13th century An anonymous Middle English poem, *The Owl and the Nightingale*, recounts a debate between the two birds.

AFTER
1674 John Wilmot's "A Satyr Against Reason and Mankind" provokes fellow English poet Edward Pococke to compose a poetic response.

1714 English poet Anne Finch composes "The Answer" in response to Alexander Pope's *Rape of the Lock*, which she considers misogynistic.

ourtly love and chivalric themes were favorite topics in the literature of late medieval Europe. In the 13th century, French poet Guillaume de Lorris's *Le Roman de la Rose* (*The Romance of the Rose*), about a knight's attempt to reach the woman he loved, swept through Europe, winning universal approval.

An illustration from Christine de Pizan's *Book of the City of Ladies*—in which she creates an allegorical community of famous women—shows her giving a lecture to a group of men.

Some 50 years later, another French poet, Jean de Meun, made substantial additions to the poem. In around 1275, he added more than 17,000 lines, changing the tone and substance of the work. His additions promoted the guile of the male lover and advocated tricks and deceit in the pursuit of his sexual goal—and they also depicted women as vile seducers and the cause of all evil.

Christine de Pizan, court writer for French king Charles V, had achieved success with her book *Cent Ballads* (*One Hundred*

See also: "Alleluia-verse for the Virgin" 53 ▪ "The Skylark" 54–55 ▪ *An Essay on Criticism* 116–117 ▪ "Because I Could Not Stop for Death" 168–169

Ballads), which included love poetry, albeit overshadowed by her mourning for her beloved husband.

When a French courtier praised Jean de Meun's version of *The Romance of the Rose*, Christine felt a response was needed. First, though, she wrote "Letter of the God of Love," a poem written from the viewpoint of Cupid, the Roman god of love. It admonishes men and male writers for taking a negative view of women, urging them to see reason and describing the virtues and blessings of women—which those same men had deliberately ignored for their own advantage. Referring to Jean de Meun's poem directly, she writes: "So many efforts made and ruses found / To trick a virgin—that, and nothing more! / And that's the aim of it, through fraud and schemes."

A feminist voice

Surprisingly, perhaps, when viewed from our own argumentative times, this lone feminine voice caused no furore or rebuke. Christine undertook other volumes on the same theme. In 1402, she wrote a specific, targeted response to *The Romance of the Rose* entitled *The Tale of the Rose*, which dismantled the misogynistic suppositions in the work.

Christine's technique was always gently persuasive, taking in learned arguments from her exceptionally wide reading (in Charles V's large library) and her knowledge of history and literature. She examined the lives of women from the Bible, from ancient Greece, and throughout history, emphasizing their goodness, kindness, and wisdom as examples for male readers to appreciate and female ones to replicate.

Allegory and persuasion

In 1405, Christine wrote *The Book of the City of Ladies*, an allegory in which three women, named Reason, Justice, and Rectitude, build a city with the help of the author. Some scholars have described it as proto-feminist literature. She also wrote *The Book of the Three Virtues*, a guide to a virtuous and happy life for women.

Christine's authorial voice is strong, her tone is never strident, and she uses the rhetorical device of sardonic antiphrasis—saying the opposite of what is actually meant—feigning ignorance and pleading with readers to follow her examples and make up their own minds. She was influenced by Dante's style and use of allegory, and her pen was quickened by the misogyny she discovered in the love poems of Roman poet Ovid. In turn, Christine influenced many generations of women after her, not only writers but royalty, playwrights, tapestry weavers, campaigners, and philosophers. ▪

Christine de Pizan

Born in Venice in 1364, but raised in France, Christine de Pizan was suddenly widowed at age 25, with three children, her mother, and an aunt to support. Refusing to remarry, she became possibly the first professional female author in medieval Europe. She had the advantages of being well born and well connected and pursued her profession with determination.

Many of Christine's 42 completed works survive; the constant in all of them is their exposure of misogyny posing as chivalry. She exhibited deep professionalism, close attention to detail, mastery of every stage of book production, and dedication to the memory of her husband, as seen in the melancholy tone of her love poems. It was as a writer of romantic ballads that she first gained prominence, but she also wrote a guide to modern warfare. Christine died around 1430.

Other key works

c. 1390 *Rondeaux* (*Roundels*)
c. 1390 *Les Cent Ballades* (*The Hundred Ballads*)
c. 1400 "*Seulete sui*" ("Alone Am I")

> [...] complaints have come
> To us, and plaints so very piteous,
> From women, both the young and older ones [...]
> **"Letter of the God of Love" (lines 9–11)**

REVIVAL REBIRT
1450–1700

AND

Ludovico Ariosto draws on elements of the **Classical epic and chivalric romance** in *Orlando Furioso*; his work will influence poets across Europe.

Thomas Wyatt uses a **sonnet form** originated by Italian poet **Petrarch** for his poem "Whoso List to Hunt."

Carmelite nun Teresa of Ávila experiences the first of the spiritual visions that will inspire her **mystical poetry**.

Two editions of Christopher Marlowe's **narrative verse epyllion** *Hero and Leander* are issued posthumously.

1516   **c. 1520–1540**   **1559**   **1598**

1517   **1558**   **1596**

German theologian Martin Luther's *Ninety-Five Theses* questions Catholic practices and beliefs, igniting the **Protestant Reformation**.

Queen Elizabeth I ascends to the throne of England.

Edmund Spenser publishes the second half of his **allegorical epic**, *The Faerie Queene*.

The two centuries covered in this chapter involved great growth and experimentation in poetry, promoted by increased literacy across Europe. More people learned to read and write in their native languages, resulting in the formalization and standardization of vernaculars such as Modern English.

Poets writing in the English language were vital contributors to the era's linguistic creativity, coining new words and pushing syntax to its limits. They imported poetic forms from both Classical works and contemporary European poetry, including epics, odes, sonnets, and sestinas (forms developed further afield, such as the haiku in Japan, would be imported much later), and shaped the system of meter still in use today. Literary innovation also led to the first theories of poetics in English, as readers attempted to understand what the courtier, soldier, and poet Philip Sidney called "the sweet mysteries of poetry."

Courtly makers

In 1557, an anthology titled *Songes and Sonnettes* included poems by two courtiers of Henry VIII—Henry Howard, the Earl of Surrey, and Sir Thomas Wyatt. Both electrifying writers, they drew freely on Italian, French, and Latin verse. Wyatt's intense but ambivalent love poems adapted Italian writer Petrarch's (1304–1374) sonnet form to the dangerous intrigues of the Tudor court. Howard's partial translation of Virgil's *Aeneid* pioneered the use of blank verse, or unrhymed iambic pentameter, helping to codify English meter. Later Renaissance poets would revere Howard and Wyatt as the "courtly makers," who brought medieval English literature into the modern, cosmopolitan era.

In the Elizabethan age, the court continued to exercise a strong grip on poetic imagination: the Queen even featured in allegorical form as Gloriana in Edmund Spenser's epic *The Faerie Queene* (1596). Love poetry was a particular feature of these years, with the monarch and courtiers providing much of the inspiration. William Shakespeare and John Donne gave a new twist to this courtly tradition, writing love poems that were by turns deeply moving and disconcertingly ironic. Christopher Marlowe, another court favorite, produced a different type of love poetry with *Hero and Leander* (1598), an epyllion or short epic about young lovers that drew on Greek mythology.

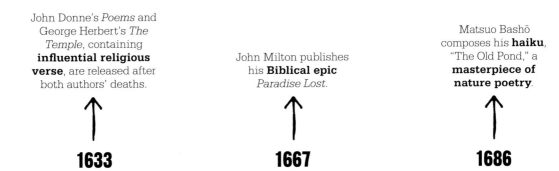

John Donne's *Poems* and George Herbert's *The Temple*, containing **influential religious verse**, are released after both authors' deaths.

John Milton publishes his **Biblical epic** *Paradise Lost*.

Matsuo Bashō composes his **haiku**, "The Old Pond," a **masterpiece of nature poetry**.

1633

1667

1686

1609

1641–1643

1681

The first edition of Shakespeare's *Sonnets* is printed; these compositions will become the **most famous love poems** in the English language.

In North America, Puritan Anne Bradstreet writes "To My Dear and Loving Husband," **a poetic expression of earthly and heavenly love**.

Andrew Marvell's **metaphysical love poem** "To His Coy Mistress" is published posthumously.

The popularity of sonnets, lyrics, and narrative verse celebrating love in all its forms continued into the 17th century, when it was also explored in more philosophical or metaphysical terms by poets such as Andrew Marvell.

Sacred songs

Far removed from earthly loving, the poems of Spanish religious reformer and nun Teresa of Ávila expressed her deeply spiritual love for God. Her verses, and those of Donne who wrote devotional works alongside his love poetry in England, reveal another aspect of Renaissance poetics—its immersion in the period's complex religious culture.

As Protestant reformers began to question Catholic practices and doctrine, initiating the Reformation during the 16th century, European society became embroiled in violent religious conflict, and many poets responded. In England, some drew inspiration from the first liturgical texts issued in English, such as *The Book of Common Prayer* (1549). Other poets, including Philip Sydney and Mary Sidney Herbert, translated the psalms into verse, experimenting with new meters and stanza forms to bring the rhythms of Hebrew into English diction.

A widening world

John Milton's *Paradise Lost* (1667), a Biblical epic in blank verse that set out to do "things unattempted yet in prose or rhyme," was one of the greatest religious poems of this age, but also groundbreaking in more than form and content. Issued as a printed book from the start, rather than a written manuscript, it epitomized the boom in printing that was bringing poetry to a much wider audience. Milton's epic quickly traveled beyond England, becoming one of the first works of English poetry to be translated into other languages, and the first to become a classic of European literature.

Anne Bradstreet's *The Tenth Muse Lately Sprung Up in America* (1650), the first English poetry book written in the Americas, reveals the possibilities of this moment. With Bradstreet, English poetry left the British Isles and became part of a global literature that would spread in tandem with colonialism in the centuries that followed. Her work also reveals a widening of literary culture by the end of the 17th century, with poems written, published, and read by new groups of people, including women. ∎

IN A NET I SEEK TO HOLD THE WIND

"WHOSO LIST TO HUNT, I KNOW WHERE IS AN HIND" (c. 1520–1540), SIR THOMAS WYATT

IN CONTEXT

FOCUS
Accentual-syllabic meter

OTHER KEY POETS
Geoffrey Chaucer, Edmund Spenser, Mary Sidney Herbert, William Shakespeare, John Dryden, Alexander Pope

BEFORE
1380s Geoffrey Chaucer's *Troilus and Criseyde* is one of the first poems in English to use iambic pentameter.

AFTER
c. 1540 The first blank verse in English is written by Henry Howard, Earl of Surrey, for his translation of books II and IV of Virgil's *Aeneid*.

1582 Sir Philip Sidney writes his *Astrophel and Stella* sonnet sequence in iambic pentameter.

1590s Christopher Marlowe's pastoral poem "The Passionate Shepherd to His Love" adopts the iambic tetrameter.

Accentual-syllabic meter is a cumbersome phrase for the metrical mode most widely used in English, European, and American poetry from the Renaissance to at least the 1960s. It refers to the calibration of a line by stresses and syllables to create a satisfying rhythm.

The stresses are those syllables that receive emphasis when spoken. For example, the word "behind" has the stress on the second syllable; the first syllable is weakly pronounced. This word makes an iamb—a unit ("foot") of unstressed and stressed syllables. A poem using this pattern systematically is said to be in iambic meter.

The patterns of feet and of syllables are independent of each other. An iamb can be two monosyllables; or alternatively, one four-syllable word could account for two iambs. It is possible for a two-syllable word to have one syllable in one iamb and one in another. In some verse forms, a particular line within each stanza is shorter than others. Rather than following a chosen meter consistently, poets often

Sir Thomas Wyatt

Born in 1503 at Allington Castle, Kent, England, Thomas Wyatt probably studied at St. John's College, Cambridge.

After marrying in 1520, Wyatt became esquire of the king's body and clerk of the royal jewels. He translated many of Petrarch's sonnets, prompted originally by Catherine of Aragon, Henry VIII's first wife.

Wyatt separated from his wife around 1524, and from 1536 he had a relationship with courtier Elizabeth Darrell.

He may also have had a liaison with Anne Boleyn, for which he was imprisoned for a month in the Tower of London. That same year, Wyatt was made sheriff of Kent and served as ambassador to King Charles V of Spain.

After the fall of his patron Thomas Cromwell, in 1541 Wyatt was arrested again, for disloyalty, but appears to have been pardoned. Wyatt died in Dorset in 1542.

Other key work

1557 "They Flee from Me"

See also: Sonnet 1 62–63 ▪ *The Canterbury Tales* 64–71 ▪ Sonnet 130 88–93 ▪ *Paradise Lost* 102–109 ▪ "Song of Myself" 152–159 ▪ "The Windhover" 166–167

Rhythm

Most poetry written in meter is composed of primary beats called feet, which are defined by the way in which their syllables are stressed. There are seven key feet in all, and the number of times they are used in a line defines a poem's meter. For example, using an iamb five times per line is known as iambic pentameter. An alternative kind of meter is quantitative meter, in which the poet prolongs (rather than stresses) certain vowel sounds.

Foot	Stress	Example
Iamb	da-**dah**	in-**deed**
Trochee	**dah**-da	**wel**-come
Spondee	**dah-dah**	**TV**
Anapest	da-da-**dah**	un-a-**ware**
Dactyl	**dah**-da-da	**cer**-tain-ly
Amphibrach	da-**dah**-da	al-**read**-y
Pyrrhic	da-da	in the

Meter	Number of feet
Monometer	1 per line
Dimeter	2 per line
Trimeter	3 per line
Tetrameter	4 per line
Pentameter	5 per line
Hexameter	6 per line
Heptameter	7 per line
Octameter	8 per line

Meter generated by stressing (or not stressing) syllables is known as qualitative meter.

Eight is generally accepted as the maximum number of feet per line.

tend to introduce some slight variations in lines, as a way to prevent rhythmic monotony.

The English sonnet

Written in the 1520s or '30s but not published until 1557, Sir Thomas Wyatt's "Whoso List to Hunt, I Know Where Is an Hind" is one of the first English sonnets. It is typical of Wyatt's work, in both theme and form. Owing a debt to Petrarch's Sonnet 190, it is part translation and part imitation. It offers a description of courtly love metaphorically, in terms of hunting. Wearily, the poet decides that wooing a particular lady is like trying to catch the wind. She wears a diamond necklace, a gift that indicates "ownership" by another man. The poem ends with a couplet: "*Noli me tangere*, for Caesar's I am, / And wild for to hold, though I seem tame." Her diamonds seem to be saying, "Do not touch me, for I belong to someone powerful": Caesar may represent King Henry VIII, and the woman may be Anne Boleyn, Henry's second wife.

Wyatt, writing for an elite circle in King Henry's court, was the most important English poet of the first half of the 16th century. A pioneer of poetics, he forged approaches to form and meter that were inspired by both continental and classical models, while also showing Chaucer's influence.

In Wyatt's sonnets, artificial conceits (elaborate metaphors) and antitheses (war/peace; fire/ice) abound, following Petrarchan practice. However, there is also a tendency at times to subvert Petrarchan values—not least in Wyatt's refusal to play by the conventions of courtship.

A more regular meter

Typically for Wyatt, "Whoso List to Hunt" uses the iambic pentameter (five iambs per line)—but inexactly: the very first line has a weak extra syllable before the stress on "list," and there are other irregularities, too, prioritizing natural speech over metrical regularity. Later, Sir Philip Sidney and, at the turn of the century, William Shakespeare perfected Wyatt's metrical experiments in sonnets that were technically more polished and syntactically more sophisticated, while retaining the feel of speech. ▪

LET MINE EYES SEE THEE, / AND THEN SEE DEATH

"LET MINE EYES SEE" (MID- TO LATE 16TH CENTURY), TERESA OF ÁVILA

IN CONTEXT

FOCUS
Mysticism

OTHER KEY POETS
Hildegard of Bingen, Rumi, Dante, William Blake, Rainer Maria Rilke

BEFORE
12th century In his poetry book *Masnavi*, the Persian mystic Rumi treats love as a flame that consumes everything except God.

1472 In Canto 31 of *Paradiso*, printed posthumously, Dante focuses on the image of the Mystic Rose, a symbol linked to the Virgin and used in Catholic meditation.

AFTER
1923 Lebanese poet Kahlil Gibran's collection *The Prophet*, written in English, offers a hopeful message about the essential goodness of humankind, inspired by a mixture of Christian and Buddhist thinking.

ysticism is the direct understanding of the divine. Believers maintain that while poetry is capable of approximating the mystical experience, it can never capture it exactly, because the most profound truths about life and spirit lie beyond the power of words.

Although they may at times use literal descriptions, mystic poets are valued more for their attempts at the near-impossible: using imagery and other linguistic effects to convey how their insights have felt to them. In her poem "Let Mine Eyes See," addressed to Jesus, Spanish Carmelite nun Teresa of Ávila writes of his face, "All blossoms are therein." The metaphor is simple yet layered, expressing

> Nothing I require
> Where my Jesus is;
> Anguish all desire,
> Saving only this [...]
> **"Let Mine Eyes See"**

a physical impossibility that takes the reader outside the laws of nature. The implied reference to gardens offers an echo of the two most important gardens in the Bible: Eden and Gethsemane. Within the work of a Middle Eastern mystic such as Rumi—who was writing in a desert setting—gardens, growth, and water gain even deeper metaphorical significance.

Use of contradictions

The image repertoire of mystic poets also includes the sun, stars, and the moon. The ecstasy of the mystic may also be presented as sensual or even sexual. Paradox plays a large part, too, since there are fundamental contradictions in mysticism—for example, that one can gain inner wealth by caring nothing for possessions.

In his collection *The Book of Hours*, Austrian poet Rainer Maria Rilke explores his relationship with God by overturning preconceptions: he finds God on Earth rather than in the heavens, and sees Him as son rather than father. ■

See also: "Alleluia-verse for the Virgin" 53 ▪ "The Guest House" 56 ▪ *The Divine Comedy* 58–61 ▪ "The First Elegy" 206

TO SPREAD THY PRAISE / WITH TUNED LAYS
"PSALM 57" (1595), MARY SIDNEY HERBERT

IN CONTEXT

FOCUS
Translating the psalms

OTHER KEY POETS
Sir Thomas Wyatt, John Milton, John Dryden

BEFORE
c. 730 CE Bede, the early English saint, translates a version of the Gospel of John.

1382–1395 John Wycliffe translates the Bible from Latin into English so ordinary people can read or hear biblical texts for themselves.

AFTER
1652 Welsh metaphysical poet Henry Vaughan's collection *The Mount of Olives* shows the powerful influence of the Sidney Psalter.

1991 Through his translations in *A Poet's Bible*, American poet David Rosenberg seeks to foster a renewed appreciation of the art inherent in Old Testament verses.

I t is unfortunate that Mary Sidney Herbert (the Countess of Pembroke) is often mentioned only in relation to her older brother, Sir Philip Sidney. Herbert was a brilliant poet and intellectual in her own right, as well as a champion of her brother's legacy.

At the time of his death, Sir Philip left behind an unfinished poetry translation of the biblical Book of Psalms, having completed only 43 of the 150 poems. Fluent in Latin, French, and Italian, Herbert translated the remaining 107 psalms, including Psalm 119's 22 poems, one for each letter of the Hebrew alphabet. She utilized 127 different verse forms, showing a great mastery of English poetry. The completed work became known as the Sidney Psalter.

"Psalm 57" is considered the poet's most personal. It cries out to God for protection from the barbs of enemies, but by repetition and assertion of faith, the narrator realizes that the enemies will only be harmed by their own weapons: "Holes they dig but their own holes."

Mary Sidney Herbert established a literary circle at Wilton House, her mansion near Salisbury. Members of the group included Edmund Spenser.

The line lengths give a sense of anguish, each stanza beginning with a long line followed by two shorter ones; then two slightly longer ones, and finally a peaceful resolution. It is like the fluttery breath of panic of someone under extreme duress, gradually talking themselves back to calmness through the act of contemplation. ∎

See also: The Song of Solomon 20–21 ▪ "Alleluia-verse for the Virgin" 53 ▪ "Letter of the God of Love" 72–73 ▪ "Prayer" 96–99 ▪ *Paradise Lost* 102–109

MIRROUR OF GRACE AND MAJESTY DIVINE

THE FAERIE QUEENE (1590), EDMUND SPENSER

IN CONTEXT

FOCUS
Allegory

OTHER KEY POETS
Dante, William Langland, Geoffrey Chaucer, Christine de Pizan, John Milton

BEFORE
1321 Dante's *Divine Comedy* is an allegory for the spiritual journey of a troubled soul through Hell and Purgatory to Paradise.

1374–1385 Geoffrey Chaucer writes *The House of Fame*, an allegorical dream vision in which he reflects on the nature of worldly renown.

AFTER
2016 British poet Simon Armitage publishes his translation of the 14th-century allegorical work *Pearl*, possibly by the same author as *Sir Gawain and the Green Knight*.

he first canto of Edmund Spenser's *The Faerie Queene* opens *in media res*—right in the middle of heroic action, with a knight "pricking on the Plain." He is riding at full pelt, his steed foaming at the bit. Beside him rides Una, a lady who has been dispossessed of her kingdom and is in need of a hero. They are headed toward the lair of a monster, the "infernal Fiend" that has been terrorizing Una's parents, in order to kill it and restore order in the land.

Widely regarded as the first epic in the modern English language, *The Faerie Queene* draws heavily on the medieval tradition, appearing as a sequence of Arthurian

See also: *The Odyssey* 24–31 ▪ *The Aeneid* 34–39 ▪ *Metamorphoses* 40–43 ▪ "Alleluia-verse for the Virgin" 53 ▪ *The Divine Comedy* 58–61 ▪ *Paradise Lost* 102–109 ▪ "Ozymandias" 132–135 ▪ *The Waste Land* 198–205

Dragons through the ages

The Redcrosse Knight in the First Book defeats "a Dragon horrible and stearne." These mythical beasts have featured in global storytelling for thousands of years.

2. Quetzalcoatl
c. 100 BCE: Mesoamerican cultures worshipped the Feathered Serpent, also known as Quetzalcoatl, god of sun and wind.

3. *Beowulf*
c. 700 CE: In this Anglo-Saxon epic, a dragon guarding a hoard of gold is killed by a hero with a magic sword.

5. *The Hobbit*
1937: J.R.R. Tolkien's novel is published. Its famous dragon Smaug loses out to a humble halfling with a magic ring.

1. Chinese dragon
c. 5000 BCE: Ancient Chinese peoples considered themselves "the gods of the dragon," and images of dragons date back several millennia.

4. The *Völsunga Saga*
c. 1270: The dragon Fáfnir is killed by the hero Sigurd in this Icelandic/Norse myth that also contains a doomed magic ring.

romances—tales narrating the heroic exploits of the knights of legendary King Arthur, with a focus on courtly love and Christian chivalry. The poem is also a clever allegory—a story that presents difficult or controversial themes in a simplified form or cloaked under a layer of symbolism.

Allegorical readings

As an allegory, Spenser's poem works on multiple levels. The valiant knights fighting dragons and vicious foes represent the human soul battling the monsters of temptation and doubt, the age-old battle between good and evil.

More specifically, *The Faerie Queene* is also an allegory for the religious turmoil of mid- and late 16th-century England. Spenser was writing only a few decades after the short reign of Mary I, the Catholic sister of Elizabeth I, a Protestant. At this time, the battle between Protestantism and Roman Catholicism was still smoldering. In his poem, Spenser champions both Elizabeth and Protestantism. Thus

in Book I, the chaste and steadfast lady Una represents the One True Church (the Church of England). This makes the knight (who wears a red cross on his shield and is later identified as St. George) a defender of the faith against enemies such as falsehood and the Roman Catholic Church (both embodied in the duplicitous temptress Duessa).

Lastly, the poem is an allegory for the Tudor court of Elizabeth I, who is obsequiously addressed in the prologue as "Mirrour of Grace and Majesty Divine." Several characters in the poem embody the monarch—first and foremost, Gloriana, "That greatest glorious Queen of *Fairy* Lond," who looms large over the proceedings, though she never makes an appearance. There are also traits of Elizabeth I in the characters of Belphoebe, »

Walter Crane, a leading British Arts and Crafts illustrator, produced 88 woodblock engravings for an 1897 edition of *The Faerie Queene.*

> Oftimes it haps, that sorrowes of the mynd
> Find remedie vnsought, which seeking cannot fynd.
> ***The Faerie Queene* (Book VI, Canto IV, Stanza XXVIII)**

whose celibacy echoes that of the Virgin Queen, and of Britomart, the female knight at the heart of Book III and the very embodiment of Chastity. During an encounter with the wizard Merlin, Britomart learns that she is to be the founder of a great line of English monarchs. He then goes on to prophesize the ascension of Elizabeth I, saying, "Then shall a Royall Virgin raine."

Mixed royal reactions

Spenser used allegory as a device to distance himself from the royal court while still commenting on contemporary political and religious matters. However, some of the characterizations in the poem are thinly veiled. Duessa, for example, is easily identified as Mary, Queen of Scots—right down to her being tried for treason, found guilty, and

Queen Elizabeth I is celebrated in the poem as a paragon of virtue. Spenser also establishes a connection between the Virgin Queen and the golden age of King Arthur.

sentenced to death (Book V). Mary's son, James VI of Scotland, was so incensed by this unflattering portrayal that he banned the poem in his kingdom.

James VI's negative assessment had the unfortunate effect of diminishing Spenser's poem in the eyes of Elizabeth I, turning it from glorious tribute to political liability and straining her relationship with the Scottish Crown.

Private moral virtues

In a letter written in 1589 to English statesman and explorer Sir Walter Raleigh, who may have given him

financial assistance to write *The Faerie Queene*, Spenser detailed his proposed structure for the poem. He planned to include 12 books, each focusing on one of the "private Moral Vertues, as *Aristotle* hath devis'd."

Ultimately, Spenser completed only six books, each centered on a different knight going about his own adventurous quest, although many feature in each other's stories. The brave knights embody the virtues of Holiness, Temperance, Chastity, Friendship, Justice, and Courtesy. According to Spenser's letter to Raleigh,

> It falls me here to write of Chastity,
> That fayrest vertue, far above the rest:
> For which what needes me fetch from Faëry
> Forreine ensamples it to have exprest?
> Sith it is shrined in my Soveraines brest [...]
> **The Faerie Queene (Book III, Prologue, Stanza I)**

Ludovico Ariosto's *Orlando Furioso*

The Italian epic poem *Orlando Furioso* (*Orlando's Frenzy*, 1516) is a continuation by Ludovico Ariosto of the 1495 poem *Orlando Innamorato* (*Orlando in Love*) by Matteo Maria Boiardo. The poem (one of the longest in European literature, at 38,736 lines) has a similar setting to the 11th-century work *The Song of Roland* by Turold: the conflict between the Christian armies of Charlemagne and the invading Arab Muslims ("Saracens"). However, Ariosto introduces

fantastical elements, including a trip to the moon and a winged horse called a hippogriff.

The story has two main arcs. The first tells of a knight named Orlando, who falls in love with a pagan princess, Angelica. She lures him from the fighting and drives him mad with despair when she leaves him. The second concerns a female Christian soldier, Bradamante, who falls in love with Ruggiero, a Saracen warrior. According to legend, Bradamante and Ruggiero were

the ancestors of the Este family in Italy, who became Boiardo's and Ariosto's patrons.

Allegories feature heavily in Ariosto's poem—for example, the bloated, monstrous servants of the sorceress Alcina (who is believed, by some scholars, to be a blueprint for Spenser's Duessa in *The Faerie Queene*) are seen as embodiments of human vices.

Elizabeth I commissioned an English translation of *Orlando Furioso* in 1591, the year after hearing *The Faerie Queene*.

these moral attributes were to be brought together in the person of Prince Arthur ("before he was King"), who would represent the highest virtue: Magnificence.

In the letter, Spenser also hinted at the possibility of further books: "I may be, perhaps, encourag'd to frame the other part of Politick Vertues in his Person, after that he came to be King." This ambition was to remain unfulfilled: Spenser died while writing Book VII. Even in its unfinished state, though, *The Faerie Queene* is one of the longest poems in the English language.

Spenser also broke new ground in his grand project, creating his own verse form. The Spenserian stanza builds on the Chaucerian rhyme royal (ababbcc) and the Italian ottava rima (abababcc) from Ariosto's epic poem *Orlando Furioso*. Its ababbcbcc rhyme structure includes eight lines in iambic pentameter and a final line (an alexandrine) in iambic hexameter.

The real magic is in the rhythm and the way Spenser often ends a line just as he is reaching the quickening moment in a phrase, sending the reader racing to the next line in the story and making for a joyous momentum.

An allegory of the self

The first three books of *The Faerie Queene* were written between 1581 and 1590 at Spenser's castle in County Cork. He presented the poem to court in 1590 and read part of it to Queen Elizabeth I. Confident in the brilliance of his poem celebrating the glory of England and its monarch, he may have expected it to be received as a majestic triumph. However, he was disappointed. In recognition of the work, Spenser received an annuity of £50, which he thought unequal to his efforts. Disillusioned, Spenser returned to Ireland, where he composed three more books for *The Faerie Queene*; these appeared in the 1596 edition.

There may be one final layer of allegory attached to *The Faerie Queene*, particularly in the last three books. It is possible that Spenser ended up describing his own journey, portraying himself as a lonely, determined, brilliant hero performing wonderful deeds for no immediate accolade other than the inner reward of having accomplished them and knowing the motivations to be pure.

After Spenser

The use of allegory remained popular with English poets after Spenser's death in 1599. John Milton employed it in *Paradise Lost* (1667), as did Alexander Pope in the mock-epic *The Rape of the Lock* (1712); Percy Bysshe Shelley's *Masque of Anarchy* (1819) puts allegorical figures to powerful political use, introducing the concept of nonviolent resistance. From the 20th century, however, the use of allegory in poetry has become much less commonplace. ∎

Edmund Spenser

Born around 1552 in London, probably to a middle-class family, Edmund Spenser was educated at Cambridge. In 1580, he moved to Ireland to work for Lord Deputy Arthur Grey (the English governor of Ireland), and he served alongside Sir Walter Raleigh who likely sponsored his writing. Later that same year, following the massacre of surrendering Catholic rebels at the Siege of Smerwick, a disgraced Lord Grey was recalled to England, but Spenser stayed on.

Spenser owned several properties in Ireland, including a castle at Kilcolman that was burned during a rebellion in 1598. According to English poet Ben Jonson, Spenser's infant child was killed in the fire.

After his first wife's death in 1594, Spenser married the much younger Elizabeth Boyle. He died in 1599.

Other key works

1595 *Amoretti*
1596 *Prothalamion*

"Renowmed kings, and sacred emperours,
Thy fruitfull ofspring, shall from thee descend;
Brave captaines, and most mighty warriours,
That shall their conquests through all lands extend,
And their decayed kingdomes shall amend [...]"
The Faerie Queene (Book III, Canto III, Stanza XXIII)

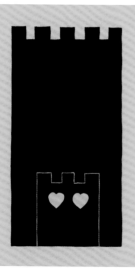

SUCH FORCE AND VIRTUE HATH AN AMOROUS LOOK

HERO AND LEANDER (1598), CHRISTOPHER MARLOWE (AND GEORGE CHAPMAN)

IN CONTEXT

FOCUS
The epyllion

OTHER KEY POETS
Homer, Ovid, Edmund Spenser, William Shakespeare, Alexander Pope, Lord Byron

BEFORE
3rd century BCE In ancient Greece, Callimachus writes *Hecale*, a 1,000-line epyllion about a noblewoman who gives shelter to Theseus.

c. 8 CE Ovid's *Metamorphoses* shows the influence of the epyllion, especially in the story of Baucis and Philemon.

AFTER
1773 Phillis Wheatley writes the epyllion "Niobe in Distress," based on a story from Ovid's *Metamorphoses*.

1853 British poet Matthew Arnold mimics Homeric grandeur in his epyllion *Sohrab and Rustum*.

An epyllion is a miniature epic, generally on a mythological or romantic theme—or both. Its key features tend to be a mock-heroic tone; a dynamic presentation of action; erudite allusions; and an uneven narrative scale, with some episodes elaborated on and some treated briefly. The term epyllion did not come into use until the 19th century, when it was applied retrospectively to the poetry of antiquity.

Style and form
Poems that fit the description of epyllion were most popular during the Greek Alexandrine era (3rd–2nd centuries BCE), notably in the works of Theocritus and Callimachus. In

---

Christopher Marlowe takes inspiration from a **mythical tale**, previously the subject of a **6th-century** work.

⬇

Despite the story's **tragic ending**, Marlowe presents his two sections in a **playful, mock-heroic style**.

⬇

Marlowe **flatters and entertains** the educated reader with **allusions** to the heroes and deities of **Roman myth**.

⬇

The author presents an epic, hedonistic view of life, based mainly on sensory pleasure.

addition to Christopher Marlowe's *Hero and Leander*, outstanding examples of epyllions written in English include Shakespeare's *Venus and Adonis* (1593) and *The Rape of Lucrece* (1594).

The usual verse form employed is the dactylic hexameter, the meter favored in the epics of Homer and Virgil. However, the characteristics of the meter differ according to the language. In Latin and Greek verse, a dactyl consists of one long syllable followed by two short ones, but in English, the key feature of a dactyl is stress: one stressed syllable followed by two unstressed, with six feet per line. As a result, lines in dactylic hexameter are awkward in English verse; Henry Wadsworth Longfellow's *Evangeline* (1847) is one of the few attempts to adapt it to the language.

Crossing the Hellespont

Marlowe was murdered before he could finish *Hero and Leander*, of which only two sestiads (sections) survive. The poem takes the form of rhyming couplets in iambic pentameter, and it tells the story of two lovers who live on opposite sides of the Hellespont, the strait separating Europe from Asia.

Hero is a priestess of the cult of Venus, living a life of chastity at Sestos. When the pair fall in love, Leander arranges to swim across each night, guided by the lamp Hero leaves for him in her tower. The poem breaks off after Hero has submitted to his amorous advances on their second night.

Playful but knowing

One characteristic of the epyllion is its inclusion of a digression, and Marlowe follows convention. Cleverly, he includes an account of how scholars came to be impoverished from 6th-century Greek poet Musaeus Grammaticus (on whose work *Hero and Leander* is based).

Hero and Leander is playful, sensual (with a lascivious focus on the body), elaborately decorative, and animated. It is also full of lively invention, such as Hero's veil woven with flowers so realistic that "honey bees [...], / [...] beat from thence,

Neptune sees Leander swimming across the Hellespont. Mistaking him for the beautiful youth Ganymede, the sea god flirts with him.

have lighted there again." There is a good smattering of light-hearted hyperbole, too—for example, in the idea that Leander's hair, if shorn, would prompt a quest akin to that for the Golden Fleece.

Allusions to myth are plentiful throughout, but sometimes names are withheld: it is assumed that the reader will know who leapt into water to embrace his own reflection (Narcissus). This is poetry for those schooled in the classics. ▪

As with many classical tales, the story of Hero and Leander ends with poignant sorrow, the doomed lovers united in death.

Pleasure and morality

After Marlowe's untimely death, *Hero and Leander* was completed by George Chapman, who added four extra sestiads. The first edition to fuse the work of the two authors appeared in 1598. Chapman's style is convoluted and his tone moralistic: he begins with a long passage (49 lines) in which the goddess Ceremony criticizes Leander for his unbridled lust. By contrast, Marlowe's treatment delights in the pleasures of the flesh and embraces classical, Ovidian allusions to eroticism.

The story of Hero and Leander ends tragically. One night, a storm extinguishes the beacon, and Leander drowns. In response, Hero throws herself down from her tower. On the shore, the corpses of the lovers embrace in death.

It is difficult to see how Marlowe's playful style could have accommodated the tragic ending. Because of this, some critics believe that, having got as far as the dawn of the lovers' first morning together, Marlowe simply could not face finishing the poem.

A FAR MORE PLEASING SOUND

SONNET 130 (1609), WILLIAM SHAKESPEARE

IN CONTEXT

FOCUS
The Shakespearean sonnet

OTHER KEY POETS
**John Donne, George
Herbert, John Keats,
W. B. Yeats, Claude McKay,
Edna St. Vincent Millay**

BEFORE
14th century The sonnets
in Petrarch's *Canzoniere* extol
the virtues of Laura, whom the
poet can only love from afar.

1595 Edmund Spenser's
Amoretti, a cycle of 89 sonnets,
details the poet's courtship
of the woman who would
become his wife.

AFTER
1609–1610 John Donne writes
his *Holy Sonnets*, marking a
new thematic development in
the English sonnet tradition.

1850 Elizabeth Barrett
Browning publishes *Sonnets
from the Portuguese*, reviving
the English sonnet cycle.

In the 16th century, English poet and playwright William Shakespeare popularized a new sonnet form—the English, or Shakespearean, sonnet—which departed from the traditional format of Italian Renaissance poets.

The original Italian sonnet form appears to have reached England in the 1530s through translations of the works of Francesco Petrarca (Petrarch) by poets Sir Thomas Wyatt and Henry Howard, Earl of Surrey. Also called the Petrarchan sonnet, this poetic form contains 14 lines set within a standardized scheme: two four-line stanzas, or quatrains (combined to make an octave), in iambic pentameter and rhyming abba abba, followed by six lines, or a sestet, rhyming cdecde.

The octave usually establishes a viewpoint, with a "turn," or volta, occurring at the sestet that provides a conclusion or counterargument. This makes for two almost equal divisions in which to express a poetic thought, theme, or metaphor.

Sonnet form

The English sonnet form, which was primarily expounded by Henry Howard, varies from the Petrarchan

This illustration from the Codex Manesse anthology of medieval German poetry shows a display of courtly love as a knight takes leave of his lady.

sonnet in rhyme and division. Instead of an octave and a sestet, the sonnet tends to be divided into three quatrains, followed by a final couplet. This makes room for a more staged development of a poetic idea. The first stanza can announce it, and the second and third ones follow it more logically, each supported

Sonnet 130 is written by Shakespeare as a **parody**.

The first quatrain **sets up the reversal** of tropes, or literary devices, traditionally **used to glorify** the lady in **courtly love romances**.

The pattern continues in the second and third quatrains, resulting in the **revelation** of an **ordinary, everyday woman**.

The concluding couplet "turns" the thought: despite her ordinariness, her qualities outrank any list of false comparisons.

See also: Sonnet 1 62–63 ▪ "Whoso List to Hunt, I Know Where Is an Hind" 78–79 ▪ "Death, Be Not Proud" 94–95 ▪ "How Do I Love Thee?" 150–151

by its own rhyming scheme (abab, cdcd, and efef). The turn is usually reserved for the couplet (rhyming gg), which can wrap everything up with a satisfying flourish.

Howard never saw his name attached to his newly devised sonnet—he was beheaded by King Henry VIII at the age of 29. Although works such as Sir Philip Sidney's sonnet cycle *Astrophel and Stella* popularized the form, it was Shakespeare who became known as its chief proponent because he used it so adroitly in all but three of his sonnets.

Departing from convention

Shakespeare's Sonnet 130 is one of 154 poems in a sequence, or cycle, of sonnets published in 1609 that differ from Petrarchan convention in more than just form. Petrarch had been a key exponent of both the sonnet sequence—a series of sonnets linked by a common theme and the nature of its subject matter, which was usually the trials of courtly love. With its roots in medieval romance, the archetypal story line involved a knight's service to a highborn lady, forever unattainable because she is already married. Idolized, the lady's perfection is praised using elaborate metaphors, often relating to nature; the tormented knight's suffering is usually—though not always—played out in a series of attempts to win the lady's heart.

Sonnet styles

A sonnet is a 14-line poem that traditionally presents a single idea and then comments on it (after a volta, or turn of thought). Petrarch (see pp.62–63), Spenser (see pp.82–85), and Shakespeare each developed their own style of sonnet. Although they differed in their rhyming schemes and in the length and number of their stanzas, they all shared the use of the volta, at which the sonnet's subject is questioned.

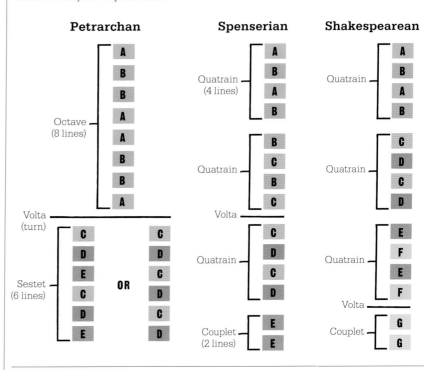

Although they were embraced by Elizabethan poets such as Edmund Spenser (*Amoretti*), these tropes were considered clichés by the time Shakespeare began writing his sonnets in the 1590s. Consequently, in Sonnet 130, Shakespeare chose to turn Petrarchan convention on its head, thereby parodying and satirizing not only the poets who were still using this style but also their overblown language.

Unflattering parallels

Traditionally, a sonnet opens with a panegyric (words of praise) to the beauty of the courtly heroine. In Shakespeare's Sonnet 130, however, the panegyric is hardly conventional. Describing a woman who has become known as the "Dark Lady," Shakespeare makes a series of ironic comparisons. His lady is not fair, as expected »

> Coral is far more red than her lips' red;
> If snow be white, why then her breasts are dun;
> If hairs be wires, black wires grow on her head.
> **Sonnet 130 (lines 2–4)**

of an ideal courtly heroine, but dark-haired, dull-eyed, and olive-skinned. The first quatrain uses one-line comparisons to establish the picture quickly. The next two quatrains—as prescribed in the English sonnet form—elaborate on this set of rather unfavorable comparisons, using two-line descriptions to fill out the scene. The lady's cheeks are not rosy, or "damasked," and her breath "reeks." While he loves to "hear

> Therefore my mistress' eyes are raven black,
> Her eyes so suited, and they mourners seem
> At such who, not born fair, no beauty lack,
> Sland'ring creation with a false esteem […]
> **Sonnet 127 (lines 9–12), 1609**

her speak," her voice could never be called musical. Nor does the lady glide across palace floors; instead, she "treads on the ground." Here, Shakespeare overturns all the usual compliments that would have been familiar to his audience.

In the sonnet's final couplet, however, Shakespeare delivers a masterstroke by reversing the reversal and returning the reader to something like the conventions of courtly love: "And yet, by heaven, I think my love as rare / As any she belied with false compare." He does appreciate her beauty, but he is not going to praise it using the overwrought metaphors of courtly

love. This introduces an anti-Petrarchan concept: praise and love for an ordinary woman. The heroines of other sonnets cannot possibly live up to their exaggerated qualities; Shakespeare's lady, however, is not only authentic but superior.

The realities of love

Like Sonnet 130, the other poems in Shakespeare's 1609 collection share a degree of truth and real experience not found in sonnets based on the Petrarchan model. Instead of depicting idealized love, the poet makes little attempt to hide the anguish, self-loathing, lust, lies, and betrayal that get snarled up in human love.

In total, there are 26 sonnets (127–152) featuring the Dark Lady, but not all of them reinforce the heartwarming picture of an ordinary man's love for an ordinary

The aristocratic Mary Fitton, a maid of honor to Queen Elizabeth I, is often thought to be the Dark Lady of Shakespeare's sonnets. In this portrait of 1595, she would have been about 17.

William Shakespeare

Born in Stratford-upon-Avon in the English Midlands in 1564, William Shakespeare probably attended the local grammar school. At age 18, he married 26-year-old Anne Hathaway, who was already pregnant with their first child. After disappearing from historical records for much of the 1580s, by the early 1590s Shakespeare reemerged in London as a young playwright and founder member of a theater company called The Lord Chamberlain's Men.

Over the next 25 years, a tremendous outpouring of poetry and plays made Shakespeare the most revered writer in English literature. This occasioned some disbelief, with some scholars attributing his works to other worthies, such as Sir Francis Bacon or Edward de Vere, Earl of Oxford. In 1611, Shakespeare retired to Stratford-upon-Avon, where he died in 1616.

Other key works

1593 *Venus and Adonis*
1601 *The Phoenix and the Turtle*

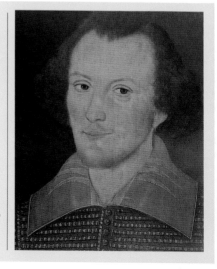

"Mr. W. H."

The first published quarto of Shakespeare's sonnets includes the printer's dedication to a Mr. W. H., the "onlie begetter" of the poems. There has been much speculation on the identity of W. H. Might he be the Fair Youth of the sonnets? Among the individuals who have been suggested is William Herbert, third Earl of Pembroke, who is known to have had an affair with Mary Fitton, often said to be the Dark Lady. Shakespeare's *First Folio*, or complete works, published in 1623, after his death, was dedicated to Herbert. Another possible candidate, if the initials were reversed to protect his identity, is Henry Wriothesley, third Earl of Southampton and Shakespeare's patron in the early 1590s.

Both Herbert and Wriothesley had been urged to wed and produce heirs, which they both delayed (Herbert to the point of never having any offspring). Shakespeare may have been enlisted in that cause—his first 17 sonnets all urge the Fair Youth to marry and have children.

TO.THE.ONLIE.BEGETTER.OF.
THESE.INSVING.SONNETS.
Mr.W.H. ALL.HAPPINESSE.
AND.THAT.ETERNITIE.
PROMISED.

BY.

OVR.EVER-LIVING.POET.

WISHETH.

THE.WELL-WISHING.
ADVENTVRER.IN.
SETTING.
FORTH.

This page of the first edition of Shakespeare's sonnets has a dedication from the printer rather than the usual one from the author.

woman. In other sonnets, the Dark Lady is seen as alluring—a sexually promiscuous "bad angel" (Sonnet 144), a temptress who incites jealousy and frustration.

The Fair Youth sonnets

The other major character in the unfolding drama of the sonnet cycle is a "Fair Youth," who dominates the first 126 sonnets. Subversion may again be at play here, with a handsome young man described as an object of desire in place of a courtly heroine. This idea was not original to Shakespeare: Richard Barnfield's 1594 poem *The Affectionate Shepherd* and its sequel *Cynthia* (1595) had been widely condemned for their homoerotic subtext. Shakespeare's poems to the Fair Youth are not dramatically different—indeed, the Victorians considered them so overtly homoerotic that they tried to rewrite them.

The Fair Youth sonnets include those with such famous opening lines as "Shall I compare thee to a summer's day?" (Sonnet 18) and "When to the sessions of sweet silent thought / I summon up remembrance of things past" (Sonnet 30). Many of them deal with conventional themes such as the passage of time versus the immortality of art, and most of them are written from the vantage point of a patronage-based relationship. However, sonnets 78–86, in which the Fair Youth has an affair with a "Rival Poet," are filled with such fury, self-abnegation, and pain that they are regarded as springing from a genuinely traumatic heartbreak in Shakespeare's life.

He is even forced to admit to his own small infidelities and betrayals while continuing to force honesty to the surface. A good example is Sonnet 112, generally overlooked, which begins with Shakespeare acknowledging the eruption of a "vulgar scandal" before turning to the Fair Youth: "You are my all the world, and I must strive / To know my shames and praises from your tongue; / None else to me, nor I to none alive." Eventually, the poet braces up and carries on. Sonnet 126 is his farewell to the Fair Youth, and the following poem introduces the Dark Lady, beginning a new chapter of turmoil.

A revived form

Shakespeare's sonnet sequence was published for the first time in the spring of 1609 by the printer Thomas Thorpe. Never reprinted during Shakespeare's lifetime, the publication appears to have coincided with a decline in the popularity of sonnets with love as a central theme. Shakespeare's sonnets were largely ignored in the 17th century, though sonnet-writing continued, with John Donne and John Milton both introducing new themes and variations. In the early 19th century, the Romantic movement revived the sonnet, with Shakespeare's poems widely read and newly valued for their skill and emotional insights. ∎

> So long as men can breathe or eyes can see,
> So long lives this, and this gives life to thee.
> **Sonnet 18 (lines 13–14), 1609**

DEATH, THOU SHALT DIE

"DEATH, BE NOT PROUD" (1633), JOHN DONNE

IN CONTEXT

FOCUS
Address

OTHER KEY POETS
**Homer, Virgil, William
Shakespeare, Percy Bysshe
Shelley, John Keats,
Walt Whitman, Charles
Baudelaire, Lucille Clifton**

BEFORE
8th century BCE The call to
the muse that begins *The Iliad*
and *The Odyssey* is a form of
apostrophe, Greek for "turning
away" from the reader or
listener toward another.

1609 William Shakespeare's
Sonnet 146 takes the form of
an address to his mortal soul.

AFTER
1820 Percy Bysshe Shelley
uses apostrophe in his poem
"To a Skylark."

1952 Wallace Stevens writes
"To an Old Philosopher in
Rome," an address to Spanish
poet George Santayana.

In the early 20th century, British critic Edmund Gosse declared John Donne to be "one of the greatest Churchmen of the seventeenth century, and one of the greatest, if the most eccentric, of its lyrical poets." Of all the vast output of Donne's poetry and sermons, that combination of spiritual and lyrical is most clearly seen in his *Holy Sonnets*. Published posthumously, most of these 19 poems were composed in 1609–1610, but some were written nearly a decade later.

Throughout the *Holy Sonnets*, Donne bares his soul in sometimes terrifying detail, fearing the mighty wrath of God and the fate of his immortal soul. The certainty of the approaching Day of Judgment is

Death has no reason to be **"proud,"** and we have no reason to **fear it**.

At best, **death** is really **akin to rest** and **sleep**.

Mostly, **Death** should be seen as a **slave or servant** whose job is **"soul's delivery."**

Death is merely a short sleep until the Resurrection, when Death itself must die.

See also: *The Odyssey* 24–31 ▪ *The Aeneid* 34–39 ▪ *The Divine Comedy* 58–61 ▪ "Let Mine Eyes See" 80
▪ "To My Dear and Loving Husband" 100 ▪ "To Autumn" 138–141 ▪ "The Windhover" 166–167

John Donne

Born in London in 1572, John Donne was apparently full of contradictions. As a young man, he was an adventurer in both love and war; later in life, he was the deeply religious dean of St. Paul's Cathedral. His poetry championed both sex and God.

Donne wrote poems in astonishingly innovative rhythms and meters that anticipated the metrical experiments of Victorian poets such as Gerard Manley Hopkins more than two centuries later. In addition to poems, Donne also wrote sermons, letters, and essays, but most of his considerable output remained unpublished until after his death in 1631. Four centuries later, many of his lines—including "Death, be not proud," "No man is an island," and "for whom the bell tolls"—have become English-language catchphrases.

Other key works

1611 "The First Anniversary: An Anatomy of the World"
1612 "The Second Anniversary: Of the Progress of the Soul"

---

never questioned, which is key to understanding Holy Sonnet X, better known by its opening words, "Death, be not proud."

Direct address

By writing to a personification of death, Donne uses a device known as apostrophe, or direct address to someone or something not actually present. The sonnet puts forward a scenario in which the poet confronts Death, which also places it within another literary tradition: *ars moriendi*, or "art of dying."

The tone is certain and assured, because the poet is confident that God will destroy Death, in line with St. Paul's prophecy: "The last enemy *that* shall be destroyed *is* death." Hence, Death must not be "proud" and is certainly not as "mighty and dreadful" as most human beings assume—a declaration made in five strongly stressed syllables: "for thou art not so." You might think you overthrow us, the poet tells Death, but that is not the case: "nor yet canst thou kill me."

Death diminished

In the second quatrain, Death is humbled further, being compared to "rest and sleep," something healthy and restorative. In the third quatrain, Death is described as a "slave to fate, chance, kings, and desperate men"—an assembly of disparate categories that stress the universality of its servitude. The companions it keeps—"poison, war, and sickness"—merely use its instruments; even the narcotic "poppy" promises a more satisfying sleep.

So far, the poem has been a series of declarations verging on warnings, the threat of punishments if a now thoroughly cowed Death even thinks about resuming its former terrifying aspect. Then comes the turn, in the final couplet: "One short sleep past, we wake eternally / And death shall be no more; Death, thou shalt die."

The poet suggests that death is merely the sleep preceding the Resurrection, after which it "shall be no more" (four single-syllable words). Death, the universal servant, will have discharged its function—"soul's delivery"—and can now leave the stage. The poetic thought concludes with four more strongly stressed syllables having the force of an injunction: "Death, thou shalt die."

Among the *Holy Sonnets* are several that could be considered prayers as much as address poems to God. However, in Holy Sonnet IV, "Oh My Black Soul!", Donne apostrophizes his own immortal spirit, urging it to repent in advance of his imminent death. ▪

> Death, be not proud, though some have called thee
> Mighty and dreadful, for thou art not so [...]
> **"Death, Be Not Proud" (lines 1–2)**

THE SOUL IN PARAPHRASE, HEART IN PILGRIMAGE

"PRAYER" (1633), GEORGE HERBERT

IN CONTEXT

FOCUS
Metaphysical poetry

OTHER KEY POETS
William Shakespeare, John Donne, Andrew Marvell

BEFORE
1601 William Shakespeare's "The Phoenix and the Turtle," the first great Metaphysical poem, weaves a Neoplatonic myth about the union between an immortal phoenix and a mortal turtle dove.

AFTER
1650–1655 Henry Vaughan's *Silex Scintillans* shows the influence of George Herbert.

1681 Andrew Marvell's *Miscellaneous Poems* is published posthumously. It includes "The Coronet," whose garland conceit explores the poet's attitude to Christ.

S amuel Johnson coined the phrase "Metaphysical poets" in his book *Lives of the Most Eminent English Poets* (1779–1781). He used the term (unfavorably) to refer to a loose group of 17th-century British poets, whose work employs startling comparisons and contrasts drawn from science and philosophy.

Common traits

Metaphysical poetry concerns itself with reality, identity, space, time, and other questions about our human existence and the world. John Donne's "To His Mistress Going to Bed," for example, describes his lover as "my America! my new-found-land"—a playful and

See also: Sonnet 130 88–93 ▪ "Death, Be Not Proud" 94–95 ▪ "To His Coy Mistress" 101 ▪ "Because I Could Not Stop for Death" 168–169 ▪ "Machines" 296–297

Metaphysical elements

Not all Metaphysical poets used scientific imagery in reference to everyday situations—for example, to express a romantic relationship. These are the main ingredients of their poetic approach:

Type of element	Definition
Antithesis	This brings disparate ideas together, often with wit.
Argument	The poem contains a complex line of thought through a persuasive line of reasoning.
Concentration	The argument is often densely woven.
Drama	In an age of great theater, drama surfaced in poetry, too, especially in arresting openings.

inventive reference to Christopher Columbus's 1492 arrival in the Americas that simultaneously suggests life-changing discovery and hands exploring skin.

In another poem, "The Sun Rising," Donne turns old and new astronomy on their heads by declaring himself and his beloved the center of the universe. This is an allusion to Nicolaus Copernicus proving in 1543 that Earth orbited the sun and not vice versa.

Elaborate "conceits" (extended metaphors) are a key characteristic of Metaphysical poetry, as is the use of antithesis—the juxtaposition of incongruous ideas.

Another Metaphysical tendency is the use of argument. In some poems, Donne writes on behalf of his own libido; and in others (in a manner more consistent with his later role as Dean of St. Paul's Cathedral), he argues to ennoble love as a value of the soul.

George Herbert expertly used Metaphysical devices to explore spiritual subjects. A self-sacrificing parish priest, he crafted well-constructed arguments in verse about "the many spiritual conflicts that have passed betwixt God and my soul," until he was able to find peace by trusting in Jesus.

Spiritual eloquence

Herbert's sonnet "Prayer" is a fine example of the Metaphysical method of bringing disparate ideas together, whether in a conceit or a simple phrase, to startling effect. Like Donne, Herbert shows a boundless imagination that goes to the limits of the known world to conjure an image.

Unusually, "Prayer" has no main verbs, only a series of noun phrases, painting a composite picture of what prayer means. In choosing the sonnet form, Herbert gives a degree of conciseness to his pondering of the question.

Herbert uses antithesis from the start, stating in the first line that prayer (a soulful experience) is "the church's banquet" (a bodily one). Even more surprising is the notion »

George Herbert

Born in 1593 in Montgomery Castle, Wales, George Herbert was brought up by his mother, having lost his aristocratic father at a young age. He attended Westminster School in London and was elected fellow at Trinity College, Cambridge. A Latin and Greek scholar, he was fluent in Italian, Spanish, and French. He also played the lute and wrote songs.

Disappointed (due to the death of his patrons) in his ambition to become a secretary of state, Herbert resolved to commit himself to a pure and simple life and so took holy orders—unusual for someone of noble birth. Unlike John Donne, he wrote no secular poetry. In 1630, Herbert became priest of Bemerton (now a suburb of the city of Salisbury), where he died three years later. His poetry collection *The Temple: Sacred Poems and Private Ejaculations* was published shortly after his death.

Other key works

1633 "The Altar"
1633 "The Collar"

of prayer as a siege engine, an "Engine against th' Almighty," which contradicts the presumption that God should be worshipped rather than assailed. However, there is nothing arbitrary about such an image, since prayer can be seen as a benevolent bombardment.

Metaphysical imagery

God (like Zeus or the Norse god Thor in pre-Christian times) is often portrayed wielding a thunderbolt. In "Prayer," the image is turned around, with the act of prayer sending that surge of power back where it came from ("Reversed thunder").

In using the compound phrase "Christ-side-piercing spear," Herbert anticipates Gerard Manley Hopkins, the priest-poet of the late 19th century; the term marks another startling shift, as the prayer morphs into the centurion's weapon used to wound Christ on the cross. The 11th line, "Heaven in ordinary, man well drest," continues the strand of antithesis, since heaven is normally far from ordinary, and leads into the poem's last three lines, a triumph of contrasting scales, starting with the "milky way" and "the bird of Paradise," representing cosmic,

> " The Christian plummet sounding heav'n and earth
> Engine against th' Almighty, sinner's tow'r [...]
> **"Prayer" (lines 4–5)**

terrestrial (the bird), and heavenly (Paradise) extremes. (The bird of Paradise was thought to hover perpetually in the air.)

The penultimate line, "Church-bells beyond the stars heard," is one of the most beautiful of all Metaphysical concoctions, juxtaposing the local and the universal. However, that brilliance is then taken even further: "the soul's blood" provides another startling two-word antithesis (spiritual and corporeal), while "The land of spices" suggests a trip to a far-flung exotic region of earthly pleasures.

The last phrase of the poem—"something understood"—succeeds on multiple levels. The eye rhyme (similarity in spelling) and half-rhyme with "soul's blood" closes the sonnet with an appropriately imperfect clinch, since a true rhyme would have sounded artificially conclusive. The switch to plain, understated speech also

Herbert compares prayer to a siege engine. Although seemingly unusual, this concept is also expressed in one of John Donne's sermons.

puts all preceding inventiveness into a mature perspective—as if to say imagery can suggest truth, but it can never be truth. The reticence of the phrase "something understood" emphasizes the moral dimension: Herbert is now showing humility before God. Implicit, too, is the idea that spiritual wisdom lies beyond the reach of words.

Drama in moderate tones

In his works, Herbert combines the conversational rhythms of Donne with the musicality of Renaissance lyric, creating subtle rhythms and using assonance and alliteration with unparalleled skill. His one poetry collection, *The Temple*, is consistent throughout in its modulated tone of voice. Herbert avoids Donne's flamboyance, but there is no shortage of drama within his work. In "The Collar," a succession of agonized complaints about his life in the Church is

Metaphysical conceits

A conceit (derived from the Latin term *conceptum*) is a poetic comparison that appeals to the mind rather than the senses. It is more elaborate than simple exaggeration and is often intended as a display of wit or as a stage in a line of argument. Essentially, a conceit is an extended metaphor, sometimes sustained over an entire poem.

In George Herbert's poem "The Pulley" (published in 1633), God is seen, at the creation of mankind, to be pouring his

blessings from a glass. But God withholds rest, or peace, since someone "rich [in nature's bounty] and weary" is more likely to turn to God for comfort: "If goodness lead him not," God says, "yet weariness / May toss him to my breast."

In Andrew Marvell's "The Definition of Love," the poet and his loved one, who are apart, are likened to two parallel lines, which, "Though infinite, can never meet." This turns absence, attributed to Fate being envious, into a sign of superiority—the "opposition of the stars."

suddenly soothed by God calling "*Child!*" and the poet responding quietly, "*My Lord.*" In the poem "Redemption," the metaphorical search for a new deal with his landlord—representing God—ends with the poet finding Christ on the cross, "Who straight, *Your suit is granted*, said, and died."

Other Metaphysical poets

Herbert's sense of moderation is matched in the work of fellow Metaphysical poet Andrew Marvell by what T. S. Eliot called a "tough reasonableness beneath the slight lyric grace." In "The Garden" (published in 1681's *Miscellaneous Poems*), Marvell plays wittily with biblical notions, referencing a "fall," "Ripe apples," and "paradise."

More than any of the other Metaphysical poets, Marvell was the master of the rhyming couplet, hiding serious depth beneath the superficially simple form. This trick is used to great effect in the likes of "The Mower to the Glow-Worms" (also in *Miscellaneous Poems*). One of the best-known *carpe diem* ("seize the day") poems, Marvell's "To His Coy Mistress" begins with amorous persuasion but turns macabre. The poet pictures the lovers devouring time like "amorous birds of prey."

Among other exponents of the movement is Welshman Henry Vaughan. His poem "The World" begins, "I saw Eternity the other night," with a Metaphysical antithesis between the sublime vista of the infinite and the offhand idiom of "the other night."

Simile
Saying that one thing is like another thing, such as that one's love is "like a red, red rose."

Metaphor
Suggesting that one thing is another thing, as in the moon is a "galleon in the sky."

Metonymy
Replacing a word with a related word, such as calling the monarchy "the Crown."

Figurative language
Many poets use nonliteral language to enhance their work. In "The Agony," George Herbert uses the expression "liquor sweet and most divine" to describe love, going on to add, "Which my God feels as blood; but I, as wine."

Personification
Describing a nonhuman thing or idea in human terms—for example, saying, "Death draws near, carrying his scythe."

Synecdoche
Referring to something by one (or some) of its parts—for example, describing an army as "boots on the ground."

Symbol
Using something mundane, such as a butterfly, to suggest something abstract, such as transformation.

The mystic leanings in the work of Catholic poet Richard Crashaw differed from Vaughan's, showing the influence of the divine feminine and offering a tenderness that was rare in the English tradition.

Renewed appreciation

Few of the Metaphysical poets were highly thought of until the 20th century, when T. S. Eliot helped revive their reputation. Eliot's Anglicanism was one of the reasons he was drawn to Herbert and Donne in particular.

Two major poetry anthologies edited by Herbert Grierson (1921) and Helen Gardner (1957) were instrumental in popularizing the Metaphysicals. Gardner found precursors of their approach in Shakespeare and Sir Walter Raleigh, and she extended the term "Metaphysical" to cover Restoration pieces by English poets Edmund Waller and Lord Rochester.

W. H. Auden admired Herbert, impressed by his modest persona and elegantly plain language. ∎

I struck the board, and cried, "No more;
I will abroad! [...]"
"The Collar" (lines 1–2), 1633

IF EVER TWO WERE ONE, THEN SURELY WE

"TO MY DEAR AND LOVING HUSBAND" (1641–1643), ANNE BRADSTREET

IN CONTEXT

FOCUS
Marital eroticism

OTHER KEY POETS
**Edmund Spenser,
William Shakespeare,
John Milton, Elizabeth
Barrett Browning**

BEFORE
1611 English poet Aemilia
Lanyer publishes *Salve Deus
Rex Judaeorum*, the first
volume of original, secular
English-language verse
written by a woman.

1650 Bradstreet's brother-in-
law publishes *The Tenth Muse
Lately Sprung Up in America*,
her first collection of poems to
be written in colonial America.

AFTER
1956 American poet John
Berryman publishes *Homage
to Mistress Bradstreet*, in
which he considers the
balance between her family
life and her poetry.

I n "To My Dear and Loving Husband" by American poet Anne Bradstreet, the speaker describes her marriage as a union between two people who have become one. In a reference to the Song of Solomon, in the Old Testament, she says her love for him is unquenchable, linking her feelings to the Bible and her faith.

Such intense expressions of love between wife and husband were in keeping with the doctrines of the Puritan community in which Bradstreet lived after moving to America from England in 1630. The Puritans believed a passionate, loving relationship would produce a strong marriage, and one that reflected Christ's love for his church.

Amorous writings

Bradstreet's varied output included intimate and affectionate poems written to her husband, for his eyes only, and published posthumously. In this amorous work, Bradstreet uses the structure of a traditional Elizabethan love poem, which was more commonly employed by male poets to address their mistresses. She builds the intensity through a series of statements in rhyming couplets, while weaving together private passion and religious faith.

After expressing her feelings of inadequacy—"Thy love is such I can no way repay"—the poet reveals her wish that her husband be appropriately rewarded in heaven. The poem ends with the hope that their reciprocal love will earn them both everlasting life. ∎

Anne Bradstreet now stands [...] as one of the two true poets of seventeenth-century New England.
Jeannine Hensley
The Works of Anne Bradstreet (1967)

See also: "Whoso List to Hunt, I Know Where Is an Hind" 78–79 ∎ Sonnet 130 88–93 ∎ "How Do I Love Thee?" 150–151

HAD WE BUT WORLD ENOUGH AND TIME
"TO HIS COY MISTRESS" (c. 1650s), ANDREW MARVELL

IN CONTEXT

FOCUS
The carpe diem poem

OTHER KEY POETS
Catullus, Horace, Ovid, Li Bai, John Donne, Charles Baudelaire

BEFORE
23 BCE In *Odes* 1.11, Horace writes, *carpe diem, quam minimum credula postero* ("seize the day, put little faith in tomorrow").

1648 English poet Robert Herrick writes "To the Virgins, to Make Much of Time" (also known as "Gather Ye Rose-Buds While Ye May").

AFTER
1938 American poet Robert Frost publishes the aptly titled "Carpe Diem," in which he considers the concept.

1944 In "A Song on the End of the World," Polish-American poet Czesław Miłosz ponders the unpredictability of calamity.

The carpe diem poem is a lyric that attempts sexual seduction by appealing to the brevity of life and the inevitability of death. In "To His Coy Mistress," Andrew Marvell embraces this classical tradition started by the Roman poet Catullus.

A member of Oliver Cromwell's English government and an admirer of John Milton, Marvell escaped punishment after the restoration of King Charles II.

Seize the day
In "To His Coy Mistress," the poet (or a persona he has created) is trying to persuade his mistress to make love to him. At his disposal is a delightfully cheeky and risqué arsenal of words. He suggests they should seize the day. If we had forever, he says, that would be the perfect amount of time to worship her with his love. He goes on to say that he would spend "two hundred [years] to adore each breast, / But thirty thousand to the rest" of her body. However, time is fleeting: if they don't make love now, they risk wasting away in marble tombs, where "worms shall try / That long-preserved virginity."

In a typically metaphysical twist, Marvell turns the lovers from hunted to hunters: they should become "like amorous birds of prey" and "tear our pleasures with rough strife."

The poem is playfully absurd in its grandiosity—but deliberately so. It is also charming, persuasive, and seductive, reimagining well-known literary conventions through the hyperbolic, self-conscious wit typical of the metaphysical poets. ∎

The grave's a fine and private place, But none, I think, do there embrace.
"To His Coy Mistress" (lines 31–32)

THINGS UNATTEMPTED YET IN PROSE OR RHIME

PARADISE LOST (1667), JOHN MILTON

IN CONTEXT

FOCUS
Miltonic blank verse

OTHER KEY POETS
**Christopher Marlowe,
William Shakespeare,
William Wordsworth,
Alfred Tennyson,
Robert Browning**

BEFORE
c. 1540 Henry Howard, Earl
of Surrey, translates Book II
and Book IV of Virgil's *Aeneid*
in blank verse. It is thought to
be the first time blank verse
is used in English poetry.

AFTER
1798 "Tintern Abbey" by
William Wordsworth uses
blank verse in an informal,
conversational style.

1833 Alfred Tennyson writes
"Ulysses" in the form of a
dramatic monologue.

1920 W. B. Yeats's "The Second
Coming", a 22-line poem in
blank verse, is published.

From his days as a student at Cambridge University, English poet John Milton had always harbored ambitions of writing an epic poem. When the time finally came, he discounted his early idea of writing about the legendary King Arthur and decided instead to tell a "true" story: that of man's salvation.

Paradise Lost was first published in 1667 as a 10-book poem. Seven years later, Milton revised his work and rearranged it into 12 books, in reference to Virgil's *The Aeneid*.

An epic in blank verse

Until then, the closest thing to an English poetic epic had been Edmund Spenser's *The Faerie Queene*. That poem was composed in Spenserian stanzas—eight lines of rhymed iambic pentameter closed by a ninth line in iambic hexameter. Most contemporary English poets attempting an epic would likely have followed that standard.

For his poem, Milton chose blank verse, a poetic format in which the lines do not rhyme, though they are written in a regular meter, or rhythm—in English, this is always iambic pentameter.

Oliver Cromwell (right) dictates a letter to a blind John Milton (left) in this 1877 painting by Ford Madox Brown. Milton translates it into Latin, penned by his secretary Andrew Marvell.

Although blank verse was well established long before its use by Milton, it had rarely been employed in English other than for translations or by playwrights, notably Christopher Marlowe and William Shakespeare.

Milton may have opted for this poetic form because of the latter's influence—"Thy easy numbers flow," he once wrote of Shakespeare's art. His daring choice of meter elevated blank verse to the highest ranks of

John Milton

Born in 1608 to a prosperous family in London, John Milton was a prodigy in learning and mastered several languages, including Latin and Greek. He earned two degrees from Cambridge University and, at the age of 30, traveled to Italy. There he met polymath Galileo Galilei, who was being held under house arrest by the Catholic Church. The meeting helped form Milton's hatred of censorship and distrust of Roman Catholicism.

An outspoken supporter of the English Revolution, Milton was made secretary for foreign tongues for the Commonwealth of England.

Imprisoned at the start of the Restoration (1660) for republican views, Milton was released after the intervention of influential friends, perhaps including English poet Andrew Marvell.

Milton was in late middle age and blind by the time he wrote *Paradise Lost*. He composed at night and dictated the verses to his daughters and other helpers in the morning. He died in 1674.

Other key works

1638 "Lycidas"
1671 *Paradise Regained*

See also: *The Odyssey* 24–31 ▪ *The Aeneid* 34–39 ▪ *Beowulf* 48–51 ▪ *The Faerie Queene* 82–85 ▪ *Hero and Leander* 86–87 ▪ "I Wandered Lonely as a Cloud" 126–129 ▪ "Ozymandias" 132–135 ▪ *In Memoriam A.H.H.* 148–149 ▪ *The Waste Land* 198–205

English poetry. Running to almost 11,000 lines, Milton's mighty flow of blank verse in *Paradise Lost*—whether vivid and pounding, or supple and stately—is unrivaled by any other single poem in the English language.

Mixing Bible and classics

Inspired by Homer's *Odyssey* and Virgil's *Aeneid*, Milton cast his story as these classical poets had theirs: as a tale of heroic action. However, his hero was Christ, and his principal characters the fallible Adam and Eve and a reprobate former angel named Satan. The poem is therefore an authentically Christian tale encased within the framework of a classical epic.

Milton's intention to marry a biblical subject with a classical form is hinted at in the prologue to Book I. Here, like Homer and Virgil before him, he invokes his "Heav'nly Muse," later identified as Urania, Greek muse of astronomy. A few lines later, though, he also replicates the opening words of the Old Testament: "In the Beginning."

In the first line of the prologue, Milton announces his theme: "Of Mans First Disobedience," meaning the eating of the forbidden fruit in the Garden of Eden, and Adam and Eve's consequent banishment from Paradise. Twenty-six lines later, the prologue ends with the promise that the book-length poem will "justify the wayes of God to men," suggesting that what follows is

---

Iambic pentameter

The most common meter in English poetry is iambic pentameter—that is, the repetition of the iambic foot five times per line (see p.79). It was first used in English by Chaucer (see pp.64–71), and was embraced by both William Shakespeare (see pp.88–93) and John Milton, who used it in *Paradise Lost*.

Foot 1	Foot 2	Foot 3	Foot 4	Foot 5
Of **Mans**	First **Dis**	o-be-	dience, **and**	the **Fruit**
Of **that**	For-**bid**-	den **Tree**,	whose **mor**-	tal **tast**
Brought **Death**	in-**to**	the **World**,	and **all**	our **woe**

English iambic pentameter that does not rhyme is known as "blank verse."

---

a drama of human destiny. That drama is the Christian cycle of redemption, circling down from the Creation to the Fall of Man, and upward via Judgment and Redemption to a New Creation.

Satan's origin story

Classical epics always begin *in medias res*—that is, in the middle of the story. So it is in *Paradise Lost*, where readers find themselves dropped into the deepest recesses of Hell, along with the terrible figure of Satan and his troop of rebel angels, who have just been hurled out of Heaven.

Paradise Lost's first two books are set in the "darkness visible" of this infernal place, where stands the capital of Hell, Pandemonium, a word meaning "all demons" that

was coined by Milton and has since come to signify a situation of utter chaos and disarray.

In Pandemonium, Satan holds an assembly of devils, concocting a plan to wreck God's newly minted Creation. A parody of heavenly courts, this demonic council also bears a certain resemblance to the human governments of the day. After all, Milton was writing in the wake of a particularly turbulent time in British history: 14 years of civil war (1639–1653) had led to Oliver Cromwell's short-lived republican Commonwealth of England (1653–1659) and the 1660 restoration of the monarchy. Contemporary readers who had firsthand knowledge of these momentous events would have been able to link Satan's chaotic court with their recent history.

It is not until Book III that the reader glimpses Heaven, with its dazzling light; and not until Book V, almost halfway through the poem, that the Archangel Raphael reveals Satan's story to Adam in Eden. »

[…] long is the way
And hard, that out of Hell leads up to Light […]
Paradise Lost (Book II, lines 432–433)

In a time before time, when God chose his Son as his "effectual might", the Archangel Lucifer, "fraught / With envie," rebelled, persuading a third of the angels to follow him and instigating a war in Heaven. On the third day of battle, the Son of God emerges triumphant, and Satan and the rebel angels are cast into Hell. Only then does the Son of God go about the act of Creation, which culminates in Adam (and eventually Eve) in the Garden of Eden. That divine work is what Satan, after a lonely and epic quest through the wastes of Chaos, seeks to destroy.

Embroidering the Bible

Paradise Lost details the Fall of Man and the events leading to it with both psychological acuity

> [...] Him the Almighty Power
> Hurld headlong flaming from th' Ethereal Skie
> With hideous ruine and combustion down
> To bottomless perdition, there to dwell
> In Adamantine Chains and penal Fire [...]
>
> **Paradise Lost (Book I, lines 44–48)**

and poetic grandeur. The narrative of the Creation in Book VII of *Paradise Lost* closely follows the accounts in the Book of Genesis. However, as each of the seven days passes, Milton expands on and embroiders the original story. Thus, different species are established, grow, proliferate, give rise to more life on the land, in the sea, in the air—a burst of creation that is reflected in an equal expansion of poetic skill and richness of imagery. A hymn or a dance, or both, it celebrates the glories of the created order.

At this point, Satan finally appears in the Garden of Eden, "Sat like a Cormorant" in the Tree of Life, eyeing Adam and Eve, who have been set in the Garden to tend to its exuberant life.

Satan's complex portrayal

No proper epic is complete without a huge cast of players. *Paradise Lost* abounds with named characters, whether dwelling in the highest heaven or the lowest hell. Yet Milton offers only conventional portrayals of God and his Son. Even Raphael, the most approachable of the angels, is haloed with holiness.

Satan, however, is an extremely complex and layered character. He questions authority, is willing to argue, and is clearly courageous, traversing the realms alone to strike at divine tyranny. He is subtle and dangerous, but also despairing: "Which way I flie is Hell; my self am Hell." He mirrors many of the facets of human nature.

The archetypal rebel, Satan has been seen by some readers as the epic's true hero. English poet and painter William Blake wrote that, in *Paradise Lost*, Milton was "of the Devil's party without knowing it."

Above all, Satan is fiendishly clever. He is never more insidious than in the masterful temptation scene in the Garden of Eden (Book

Milton decides to write a **Christian epic** poem on the **Fall of Man** from a state of innocence to one of sin.

↓

He chooses to cast it in a **classical mold**, taking **Virgil's *Aeneid*** as his **primary influence**.

↓

However, the traditional Latin **dactylic hexameter**, or "heroic line," **does not scan well** in English.

↓

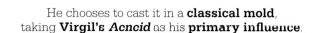

An admirer of English drama and classical translations, Milton adopts blank verse for its flexibility.

Satan and his rebel angels are cast from Heaven in this 1866 illustration by French artist Gustave Doré. Many artists through the ages have striven to capture the richness of *Paradise Lost*.

VIII). While strolling among the flowers, Eve encounters that most charming of rogues, the Arch-Flatterer. Disguised as a serpent, Satan approaches Eve, appealing to her vanity and praising her resplendent beauty. She is familiar with snakes, "but not with human voice endu'd." The Serpent explains that he was "at first as other Beasts that graze," but since eating the fruit of the Tree of Knowledge, he can turn his thoughts to "Speculations high or deep."

God has expressly forbidden Adam and Eve to eat the fruit of the Tree of Knowledge; nevertheless, after being regaled with luscious descriptions of the fruit that appeal to her five senses, "she pluck'd, she eat." Adam inevitably follows, passion overwhelming reason. Afterward, "in Lust they burne," and Creation heaves a deep, mournful sigh.

Satan's tragic flaw

Milton presents a very different Satan when he returns him to Hell in Book IX. Once a figure of Titanic proportions—"in bulk as huge / As whom the Fables name of monstrous size"—he is now considerably diminished. Although victorious in ruining Creation, he is greeted not by triumphant applause but by a "dismal universal hiss, the sound / Of public scorn." Satan and his demons have turned into hideous serpents—"punisht in the shape he sin'd."

Satan embodies the tragic flaw of pride, which according to St. Augustine is the root of all sin.

He "hath offended the majesty of God by aspiring to Godhead"—as Milton put it in his revised second edition of *Paradise Lost*—but then dug his pit even deeper. "Evil be thou my Good" was his choice. Satan fell due to his own malice; man fell as a result of Satan's malice, not his own.

Better things to come

Paradise Lost concludes with a motif borrowed from Virgil's *Aeneid*: the revelation of future greatness for the protagonists. Whereas Aeneas learns that his wanderings will eventually lead »

> [...] abasht the Devil stood,
> And felt how awful goodness is, and saw
> Vertue in her shape how lovly, saw, and pin'd
> His loss [...]
> **Paradise Lost (Book IV, lines 846–849)**

The image of the Devil as a likable rascal is used often in marketing material, as in this 1899 ad for the City Cork Hat Company in London.

The names of Satan

In *Paradise Lost*, Milton calls him the Prince of Darkness, but Satan goes by many names elsewhere. As an angel in Heaven, he was Lucifer, and the Old Testament word "Satan" comes from the Hebrew word *ha-satan*, meaning "adversary." In the Old Testament, Satan went by the name of Beelzebub, also known as "the lord of the flies" (an epithet made infamous by William Golding's 1954 novel of the same name). In the first book of the New Testament, "the Devil" tempts Jesus in the desert; but in the last (the Book of Revelation), Satan is also a red dragon with seven heads, ten horns, and a tail that drags a third of the stars of heaven with it.

In Christopher Marlowe's play *Doctor Faustus* (1592), the Devil is called Mephistopheles. Satanic monsters include Leviathan, which features in William Blake's book *Jerusalem*, while Italian writer Dante's epic *Divine Comedy* described the center of Hell as featuring a Devil called Dis, another name for Pluto, the Roman god of the Underworld.

to the establishment of the mighty Roman Empire, in Book X of Milton's poem, Adam is presented with a detailed pageant of biblical history culminating in the life, death, and resurrection of Christ, and the promise of "Joy and eternal Bliss."

The 20th-century American philosopher Arthur O. Lovejoy wrote about this revelation by the Archangel Michael in the poem as the "paradox of the fortunate Fall." Eating the forbidden apple set in motion a sequence of sacred history resulting in the redemption of man and nature—"And evil turn to good." Thus are the ways of God justified to man. Although it means exile from Eden—a paradise lost—the Archangel Michael assures Adam and Eve that in return, they will have "A Paradise within thee, happier farr."

Breadth of knowledge
An enormous and complex work of art, *Paradise Lost* allowed Milton to display his prodigious range of learning. All classical epics sought to be encyclopedic in scope; they were to be the mirrors of their age. However, Milton went beyond the encyclopedic: he cast such a wide range of learning across his pages that even early editions of the poem, printed at a time when readers were more familiar with classical and Biblical references, were filled with explanatory aids.

Milton's imagery is strikingly modern, influenced by the 17th-century discoveries of Italian astronomer and physicist Galileo Galilei, whose telescope had just revealed a universe much vaster than any previous estimate. When Raphael, "prone in flight," takes wing from Heaven to Earth, he "Sailes between worlds & worlds"—just as, earlier, the Son of God had set out on his chariot "to create new Worlds." He uses a pair of golden compasses to chart the boundaries between ordered cosmos and formless chaos, to "circumscribe / This Universe, and all created things," before following the Milky Way home to Heaven. When Satan leaves Hell to subvert this new world, he reverses that pattern, traversing chaos to arrive at the cosmos, an epic journey if ever there was one.

Poetic virtuosity
Milton's narrative of Creation is sprinkled with images that underline the vastness of the universe that surrounds us. He talks about "the vast immeasurable Abyss," the "dark unbottom'd infinite Abyss," the "vast abrupt," and "Starrs, that seem to rowle / Spaces incomprehensible"—expressions that frame that first vision of Earth.

The rich imagery, description, and characterization are all carried on Milton's torrent of unrhymed iambic pentameter. The alternating

> Which way I flie is Hell; my self am Hell;
> And in the lowest deep a lower deep
> Still threatning to devour me opens wide,
> To which the Hell I suffer seems a Heav'n.
> *Paradise Lost* (Book IV, lines 75–78)

> So hand in hand they passd, the lovliest pair
> That ever since in loves imbraces met,
> *Adam* the goodliest man of men since borne
> His Sons, the fairest of her Daughters *Eve*.
> **Paradise Lost (Book IV, lines 321–324)**

stressed and unstressed syllables are always effectively harnessed. Additionally, lines are often syncopated—stress patterns playing off each other—with spondees, or metrical feet of two stressed syllables: "Rocks, Caves, Lakes, Fens, Bogs, Dens, and shades of death."

As Satan makes his solitary way through Chaos, the reader must clamber over an avalanche of spondees: "Ore bog or steep, through strait, rough, dense, or rare, / With head, hands, wings, or feet pursues his way, / And swims or sinks, or wades, or creeps, or flyes."

The sibilants employed in the universal "hissing through the Hall" of Pandemonium are highly evocative: "Scorpion and Asp, and *Amphisbaena* dire, / *Cerastes* hornd, *Hydrus*, and *Ellops* drear, / And *Dipsas*."

Critical judgment

Milton's barrage of blank verse with its freight of learning and theology was overwhelming for some later critics. The adjective "Miltonic" came to be associated with Latinate, baroque, affected, grandiloquent, and even pompous writing. In 1781, wading through *Paradise Lost*, the English writer and literary critic Samuel Johnson commented with exasperation, "None ever wished it longer than it is." T. S. Eliot in 1936 conceded that Milton was "a very great poet indeed," but he also argued that his lines were often outrunning the real human emotion they were meant to carry, leading to a "dissociation of sensibility," a dogged artificiality.

This criticism is like chipping away at a mountain: *Paradise Lost* is immovable, a massive feature that looms over the landscape of English poetry. It is a towering achievement of poetic verse that honors poetic traditions but also alters them. Perhaps its most compelling quality, however, lies in the conflict at its heart. It is a story of disobedience written by a devout and puritanical man. ■

The Archangel Raphael admonishes Adam and Eve, telling them of Satan's fall from Heaven. This illustration of the scene from Book V of *Paradise Lost* is by Gustave Doré (1866).

PLOP!— WATER

"THE OLD POND" (1686), MATSUO BASHŌ

The poetry of 17th-century Japan prized immediacy of perception, following the Zen Buddhist ethos of simplicity and awareness. This idea was mastered in the short poem form called haiku. Its subject was usually a detail or process of nature, perceived mindfully in the moment.

A haiku written in Japanese usually consists of three phrases containing a *kireji* ("cutting word," or break) and a *kigo* (seasonal reference). The standard form has phonetic units arranged as 5-7-5. Some translators follow this as a syllable count in their three-line renderings, although a less restrictive approach allows for the translation to be more faithful to the original meaning.

Initially called *hokku*, the haiku originated in the 13th century as the opening scene-setter for a *renga*, an oral verse form, usually of 100 linked stanzas. Later, it acquired independent life as a popular literary entertainment. From 1679, Matsuo Bashō used the form as a vehicle for philosophical contemplation on the transience of the living world. Having studied Zen Buddhism, Bashō believed in stilling and opening the mind to receive sense impressions untainted by egotism or materialism.

Haiku structure

A Japanese haiku traditionally captures a single moment in time—typically a natural event, such as a sunrise or a bird taking flight—usually by bringing together two ideas. Its focus on small observed details links it to meditative practice.

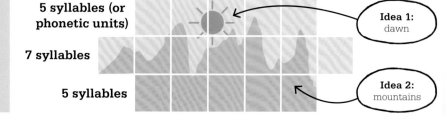

See also: "The Sparrow" 216–217 ▪ Canto LXXXI 232–235

Three great poets of old Japan

Matsuo Bashō (1644–1694) transformed the haiku into a serious expression of insight. His work gets straight to the point through expert use of vivid description.

Blades of summer grass—
all that is left
of warriors' dreams.

Yosa Buson (1716–1784) was a master of *haiga* (a combination of painting and poem). His writing is highly visual, showing an affinity for colors and shapes.

Only Mount Fuji
escapes being buried
by young leaves.

Kobayashi Issa (1763–1828) wrote more than 21,000 haiku. They often offer wry glimpses into human activity in everyday language, or have a focus on small creatures.

Don't squash it!
The fly rubbing its hands,
rubbing its legs.

> The old pond.
> A frog jumps in.
> Plop!—water.
> **"The Old Pond"**

Evolving style

Bashō's most famous haiku, "The Old Pond," is typical in its focus on a specific moment in nature, minimalistically described, without metaphor or rhyme. There is no allusion to the time of year, though frogs may have been more active at certain times than others. The original Japanese is sparser than the translated version quoted above, with a reference to just the "sound of water" in the final line. In English-language renditions of the poem, the word "Plop!" or "Splash!" is commonly inserted for animation. However, a Japanese audience would have been satisfied without this enlivening touch: loyalty to the haiku's rules gave pleasure in itself, combined with *kensho*—a flash of enlightenment, facilitated through the observation of an everyday natural wonder.

Bashō's style encompassed two ideals of Zen thinking. One was *sabi*, an acceptance that beauty is fleeting; the other was *wabi*, linked with monastic austerity and detachment, as well as an appreciation of the commonplace (notably in the tea ceremony).

A poet's focus on transient nature particularly came to the fore in the brief cherry-blossom season, when viewing parties (*hanami*) were held. Haiku could alternatively have a human subject, and some practitioners favored comedy over evocation. When Masaoka Shiki revived the haiku's waning fortunes in the late 19th century, he brought to it a new freshness of natural observation.

The modern age

In the early 20th century, the haiku was popular in Britain and the US. Ezra Pound's two-line haiku-like "In a Station of the Metro" (1913) became a key text of the Imagist movement, which sought to crystallize meaning in sparse, vivid images. In the second half of the 20th century, the genre enjoyed a new vogue among Western poets. It has been practiced by, among others, Americans Jack Kerouac and Robert Hass. Irish poet Paul Muldoon's "Hopewell Haiku," a 90-poem sequence in his 1998 collection *Hay*, rhymes aba and shows an enjoyably subtle irony. ▪

> Your poetry issues of its own accord when you and the object have become one.
> **Matsuo Bashō**
> *The Narrow Road to the Deep North*

Bashō is portrayed as a wanderer stopping to converse with two tea-drinking farmers in this late 19th-century woodblock print by Tsukioka Yoshitoshi.

REASON
THE SUB
1700–1900

AND
LIME

Alexander Pope issues ***An Essay on Criticism***, his discussion on how to be a literary critic composed in rhyming couplets.

1711

1773

Phillis Wheatley publishes *Poems on Various Subjects, Religious and Moral*, the **first volume of poetry by a Black American poet**.

The **French Revolution** begins. Marking the start of Romanticism, it will inspire a new **focus on freedom, equality**, and the **individual**.

1789

1786

Robert Burns publishes ***Poems, Chiefly in the Scottish Dialect***.

1794

William Blake prints ***Songs of Experience***; it includes poems such as "London" exposing social injustice.

Lyrical Ballads, a collaboration between William Wordsworth and Samuel Taylor Coleridge, signifies the start of the **English Romantic movement**.

1798

1819

John Keats publishes his *Odes*. His **intensely lyrical style** has a profound **impact on poetry**.

The 18th and 19th centuries were an era of huge social change in which the old kingdoms of Europe transformed into modern, capitalist societies. European empires brought much of the world under colonial rule even as radical political movements argued for new rights for the individual.

In poetry, as in politics, a mass culture developed alongside an unprecedented emphasis on writers as individuals. National canons were formed through the selection of notable authors, including many of the poets featured in this volume. Literary biographies, essays, and reviews, published in the newly popular periodical press, allowed readers to follow the careers of their favorite writers. The most famous poets became celebrities, such as Lord Byron, who inspired writers around the world, from Alexander Pushkin in Russia to Edgar Allan Poe in the US. In this environment, a new understanding of poetry developed, focusing on originality, self-expression, and authenticity.

The Neoclassical style

During the early 18th century, Neoclassicism became the leading poetic style. As the movement's name indicates, Neoclassical poets were deeply influenced by Classical Greek and Roman literature. Unlike their Renaissance predecessors, however, they sought to imitate the ambitions of the classics, rather than importing their idioms directly into modern languages. They used neatly balanced verse forms such as the rhyming couplet, and often favored longer genres, such as the verse essay or satire, over the lyric poem. Writing at a time later known as the Enlightenment, when the power of reason and science were celebrated, Neoclassical poets also explored the nature and limitations of the human mind in a breezily philosophical style. "Two principles in human nature reign," Alexander Pope wrote in *An Essay on Man* (1733–1734), "Self-love, to urge, and reason, to restrain."

Neoclassicism influenced writers far beyond England. Pope's admirers included enslaved poet Phillis Wheatley, the first Black American to publish a volume of verse, whose elegant, moving poems made a powerful case for abolitionism.

Romantics and revolution

Toward the end of the 18th century, a new literary movement took hold in Europe: Romanticism. Inspired

In Russia, Alexander Pushkin produces the first complete edition of **Eugene Onegin**, a **novel in verse** featuring a Byronic antihero.

French writer Charles Baudelaire publishes the first edition of **Les Fleurs du Mal**. In subject matter and style, the collection marks the decline of Romanticism.

In his sonnet "The Windhover," English poet Gerard Manley Hopkins pioneers a new meter— **"sprung" rhythm**—which **imitates natural speech**.

Paul Laurence Dunbar publishes his first volume of poetry, **Oak and Ivy**, which contains his **earliest dialect poems**.

1833   **1857**   **1877**   **1893**

1855   **1861–1865**   **1890**

American poet Walt Whitman completes the first edition of **Leaves of Grass**. His use of **unmetered lines** helps to inspire the **free verse movement**.

The **American Civil War** results in the **abolition of slavery**.

In the US, the first volume of **Emily Dickinson's Poems** is released four years after her death.

---

by philosophers such as German thinker Immanuel Kant and Swiss-born Jean-Jacques Rousseau, Romantic writers believed that art originated in emotion and the imagination, in self-reflection, and communion with nature. The poets who embraced this aesthetic often favored lyric forms, such as odes, sonnets, and ballads, combining musicality with mysticism and highly evocative imagery.

Galvanized by revolutions in America (1775–1783), France (1789–1799), and Haiti (1791–1804), the Romantic writers were not just inward-looking. Poets, Percy Bysshe Shelley claimed in 1821, were "the unacknowledged legislators of the world," and many Romantics, including William Blake and William Wordsworth, wrote poetry that spoke fiercely against social inequalities

and injustice. Echoing their reformist sentiments, Shelley urged the common people of England to "Shake your chains to earth like dew."

Freedom and free verse

In the newly independent US, poets sought to create forms that reflected the values of a democratic society— values violently contradicted by the institution of slavery. For Walt Whitman, democratic poetry meant literary freedom, realized through the use of free verse (verse without meter) and exuberant depictions of humanity in his collection *Leaves of Grass* (1855). "Each of us limitless," Whitman proclaimed, "each of us with his or her right upon the earth." Other American writers also introduced new forms. In *Oak and Ivy* (1893), for example, Paul Laurence Dunbar sought to represent the lives

of Black Americans by using dialect, bringing a new linguistic strain into English poetry.

European poets were becoming equally experimental. In England, Alfred Tennyson, Robert Browning, and Gerard Manley Hopkins tested poetic styles that used the rhythms or structures of everyday speech, while Christina Rossetti used shifting rhythms and meter in her narrative poem "Goblin Market" (1862). At the end of the 19th century—perhaps partly inspired by Whitman's work—successors of Baudelaire in France began calling for the use of *vers libre* (free verse), which sparked a wider movement of experimentation and poetic freedom. The conventions that had governed all aspects of European poetry since the Renaissance were beginning to loosen. ∎

BE HOMER'S WORKS YOUR STUDY AND DELIGHT
AN ESSAY ON CRITICISM (1711), ALEXANDER POPE

IN CONTEXT

FOCUS
Neoclassicism

OTHER KEY POETS
Homer, Virgil, Horace, Ovid, John Dryden, Anne Finch

BEFORE
c. 800 BCE Homer composes *The Odyssey*, the first great work to be composed in heroic or epic style.

c. 18 CE Horace writes *Ars Poetica* (*The Art of Poetry*).

1674 *L'Art Poétique* (*The Poetic Art*), by French poet Nicolas Boileau, deals with the basic rules of classical verse writing.

1681 Dryden's poem *Absalom and Achitophel*, a political satire, is published.

AFTER
1728 Pope's satire *The Dunciad* is published; it is a parody of Virgil's *Aeneid*, and an epic of idiocy in all its forms.

Eighteenth-century English poet Alexander Pope wrote as an outsider, someone who was a fierce critic of society even as he gained influence within it. He saw stupidity in all its forms all around him—selfishness, shallowness, shortsightedness, and meanness—and spent his whole life writing and railing against it.

Pope's *An Essay on Criticism* is a verse epistle, like Augustan Age Roman poet Horace's *Ars Poetica* (*The Art of Poetry*), laying down rules for authors and critics alike. He encourages poets to pursue the muse and never give up, even though every challenge surmounted leads to an even greater one. Over the course of 744 lines in three parts, he warns critics against considering poems in part, rather than in their entirety, as well as judging different poems by unequal criteria. He also says that the poet and critic must not collaborate to produce poems so strictly obedient in form that they

put readers to sleep: "Still humming on, their drowsy course they keep, / And lash'd so long, like tops, are lash'd asleep." Most of all, poets must use their skill to express what they truly mean and not make empty flourishes.

Challenging fashion

Pope was writing at a time when a brand-new industry of critics, authors, booksellers, publishers, and pamphleteers had sprung into being relatively quickly. Sensationalism and backbiting were rampant, with authors and critics publishing pamphlets attacking each other and gaining notoriety, one writer even writing the attacks upon himself and his defenses to improve his fame.

Pope's contention was that to escape from the merely fashionable and rediscover true value, one should judge things that are unchangeable: nature and the ancient classics. The works that

> A little learning is a dang'rous thing;
> Drink deep, or taste not the Pierian spring [...]
> **An Essay on Criticism (Part 2, lines 15–16)**

Pope and fellow Neoclassicist John Dryden particularly admired were those of Homer. In *An Essay on Criticism*, Pope writes, "Be Homer's works your study and delight, / Read them by day, and meditate by night."

The beauty of decorum

Pope and Dryden emulated Virgil and Homer very consciously. Most importantly, they translated them. Dryden published Virgil's *Aeneid* in English in 1697, and Pope made himself wealthy with his *Iliad* and *Odyssey* translations in the 1720s.

What Pope prized most in poetry was "decorum" (a poem's style should be appropriate to its subject), which the ancient authors had achieved, and in which one could perceive the beauty of nature. Here were standards beyond the reach of fashion. By reading these authors and basking in their brilliance, poets could not but be edified by their influence. Pope claimed Homer and Virgil had not invented poetic decorum but *discovered* it, and that it was as natural as the beauty of streams and mountains. ▪

The evolution of Neoclassicism
A cultural movement later described as Neoclassicism became popular in Europe from the late 17th century. Drawing inspiration from the art of classical antiquity, it impacted literature—including poetry—architecture, theater, and music.

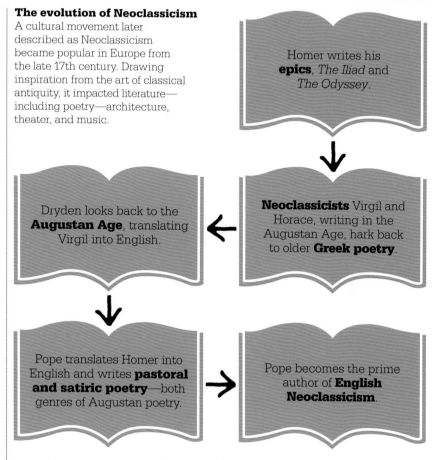

Homer writes his **epics**, *The Iliad* and *The Odyssey*.

Neoclassicists Virgil and Horace, writing in the Augustan Age, hark back to older **Greek poetry**.

Dryden looks back to the **Augustan Age**, translating Virgil into English.

Pope translates Homer into English and writes **pastoral and satiric poetry**—both genres of Augustan poetry.

Pope becomes the prime author of **English Neoclassicism**.

Alexander Pope

Born into a Catholic family in London in 1688, Pope suffered a childhood illness that left him permanently disabled and of small stature. Anti-Catholic sentiment forced his family to move out of London in 1700. It later led to him being barred from holding public office or attending university. However, Pope showed a talent for writing from an early age, his first book of poems (*Pastorals*) being published in 1709.

Pope's witheringly scornful satires against the ills of society were terrifically popular, and his poetry is perhaps the most quoted in the English language with the exception of William Shakespeare. He edited the latter's works, publishing a six-volume edition in 1725, and was a skilled translator of the classics. His poems and other work made him both very rich and a great celebrity. Pope died in 1744.

Other key works

1714 *The Rape of the Lock*
1728 *The Dunciad*
1734 *An Essay on Man*

ONCE I REDEMPTION NEITHER SOUGHT NOR KNEW

"ON BEING BROUGHT FROM AFRICA TO AMERICA" (1773), PHILLIS WHEATLEY

IN CONTEXT

FOCUS
Antislavery poetry

OTHER KEY POETS
Alexander Pope, Paul Laurence Dunbar, Robert Hayden, Derek Walcott

BEFORE
1688 The Quaker Germantown Petition Against Slavery is the first written document to argue for equality of rights for enslaved Africans in England's American colonies.

AFTER
1776 The US Declaration of Independence states all men are created equal, but this does not extend to enslaved citizens.

1778 African American poet Jupiter Hammon publishes his celebratory verse "An Address to Miss Phillis Wheatley."

1788 English poet William Cowper writes "The Negro's Complaint," quoted by civil rights activist Martin Luther King, Jr., in the 1950s and '60s.

U nlike much of her work, Phillis Wheatley's poem "On Being Brought from Africa to America" directly addresses the racial issues of her day. On one level, it underlines the Christian view that all suffering—including slavery—is part of God's purpose. But Wheatley also uses her faith to build a case for the equality of Black and white people. This duality reflects her own experience as both an African and an American. She uses this double identity to speak as an enslaved African, while addressing white Christian Americans.

[…] if the authoress *was designed for slavery* […] the greater part of the inhabitants of Britain must lose their claim to freedom.
Thomas Clarkson
Antislavery campaigner
(1760–1846)

The poem begins, "'Twas mercy brought me from my *Pagan* land, / Taught my benighted soul to understand / That there's a God, that there's a *Savior* too: / Once I redemption neither sought nor knew." Wheatley says "mercy" saved her from Africa, which she sees as a heathen land. Her good fortune in being taken to America lies in her subsequent Christian religious awakening—she now knows the light of God. This is the paradox of the poem: in the process of being physically enslaved, Wheatley considered herself to be spiritually set free.

Linguistic dualities
Paradoxes are also apparent in the language of the poem, which can be interpreted literally or figuratively. In describing her soul as "benighted," Wheatley references the darkness of her skin, but also the prevailing notion of the superiority of the Western Christian world.

Wheatley was greatly influenced by early 18th-century English poet Alexander Pope and turned his stylistic forms to her purpose. The poem uses "heroic" couplets (rhyming pairs of lines in iambic pentameter—aabbccdd), a form

See also: *Metamorphoses* 40–43 ▪ *An Essay on Criticism* 116–117 ▪ "We Wear the Mask" 170–171 ▪ "I, Too" 208–213 ▪ "Middle Passage" 230–231 ▪ *Omeros* 300–303

championed by Pope and usually associated with translations of, or tributes to, the classical epic verse of writers such as Virgil and Ovid. By using the respected forms of the day, Wheatley added weight to her message and presented it in familiar terms to a contemporary audience.

Overturning assumptions

The first half of Wheatley's poem has sometimes been interpreted as condoning enslavement, but the remainder suggests a more subtle intention. In the poem's last four lines, Wheatley shifts the focus from her view of herself to the opinions of others, encouraging her—white Christian—readers to reconsider their assumptions about Black people. With the words, "Some view our sable race with scornful eye," she speaks as a member of this collective—"our" race—now setting herself apart from her readers.

In the final lines of the poem, Wheatley turns the tables. She again addresses her fellow Christians as a member of their community, while exposing and indicting their prejudice and "un-Christian" views: "Remember, *Christians*, *Negros*, black as *Cain*, / May be refin'd, and join th' angelic train." She subverts the racial myth that Black people are descended from Cain—the first murderer in the Bible—by using God's protection of Cain to prove her point that Black people are capable of salvation. Having identified herself as a former pagan at the start of the poem, she is the ultimate proof.

Inspiring change

Phillis Wheatley's work was a catalyst for the fledgling anti-slavery movement, inspiring other writers as well as encouraging abolitionist debate in both England and the US. Perhaps more importantly, Wheatley's literary talents—built on traditional Western language and style—communicated the message that African Americans were as capable, creative, and intelligent as any other humans. ▪

Phillis Wheatley

Born in Senegal or The Gambia, West Africa, in about 1753, Phillis Wheatley Peters was kidnapped at the age of seven or eight and transported to North America. Arriving in Boston, she was bought as a domestic servant by the Wheatley family. They taught her to read and write and, on seeing her talent, encouraged her to compose poetry. With the aid of the family, Wheatley traveled to London to find a publisher for her work. Her first collection, *Poems on Various Subjects, Religious and Moral*, issued in 1773, was the first volume of poetry by an African American to be published in modern times.

Freed from enslavement in 1774, Wheatley continued to write, but failed to secure a publisher for her next poetry collection. Impoverished, she was forced to take work as a maid when her husband was imprisoned for debt. She died in 1784 at the age of 31.

Other key works

1773 *Poems on Various Subjects, Religious and Moral*
1775 "To His Excellency, George Washington"

A poetic case against slavery

Christian faith	✝	Argues that **all Christians** (Black and white) **are deserving of**, and capable of, **salvation**.
Reason	💡	Uses the **"heroic"** rhyming couplets of 18th-century **Neoclassical verse** to **give the poem** literary and, by association, **moral and political authority**.
Equality and freedom	=	Implies that **social and political equality is implicit in religious equality**: if all are **equal in the eyes of God**, all must be equal in society.
Loyalty to America	🇺🇸	Asserts that **America** can provide the conditions in which **spiritual equality** (and therefore **democracy and social equality**) can prevail.

WEE, SLEEKET, COWRAN, TIM'ROUS BEASTIE
"TO A MOUSE" (1786), ROBERT BURNS

IN CONTEXT

FOCUS
Dialect poetry

OTHER KEY POETS
John Clare, W. B. Yeats, Paul Laurence Dunbar, Langston Hughes, Seamus Heaney

BEFORE
1375 Scottish poet John Barbour writes the epic *Brus* (*The Bruce*) in early Scots; it becomes the most influential vernacular poem in Scottish literature.

AFTER
1844 English poet William Barnes publishes *Poems of Rural Life in the Dorset Dialect*.

1893 The Gaelic League (*Conradh na Gaeilge*) is formed to promote the use of Irish language and dialect in poetry and prose.

1913 Paul Laurence Dunbar's verse collection *Humour and Dialect* is published posthumously.

While plowing his field, just south of Kilmarnock in Scotland, in 1785, the young farmer-turned-poet, Robert Burns, struck something beneath the soil. The blade on his plow had ripped through the nest of a mouse, sending its inhabitant scurrying. Burns carried on plowing, composing a poem as he trudged along. Its eight stanzas, each with the rhyme scheme aabcbc, are cast as an apostrophe (address) to the little mouse. Much of the poem is written in Scots dialect, which lends its story a unique flavor and places an emphasis on the short last three lines of each stanza.

Natural comrades
The use of dialect creates a sense of fellowship, emphasizing the plowman-poet's care for the tiny mouse, and his commiseration with its plight—mouse trials and labors are likened to human ones. Burns sadly acknowledges that "Man's dominion," symbolized by the "cruel coulter," will always upset the harmony of "Nature's social union." The mouse is his "earth-born companion / An' fellow-mortal"— a surprising admission from an 18th-century farmer, as mice were regarded as destructive pests.

Burns decides he can easily spare a few ears of corn from the sheaves in the barn (the meaning of the Scots words in stanza three); they would never be missed. He even feels bad about the destroyed nest—a flimsy thing made of leaves and stubble, but to the mouse it was hearth and home ("house or hald").

In the last two stanzas, Burns's use of dialect broadens the comradeship of this mouse and man into an existential reflection on their parallel lives. Mouse, the poet says, you are not alone in providing for the future only to see your plans wrecked by unforeseen

But house or hald,
To thole the Winter's sleety dribble,
An' cranreuch cauld!
"To a Mouse" (lines 34–36)

See also: "I Wandered Lonely as a Cloud" 126–129 ▪ "Song of Myself" 152–159
▪ *for colored girls who have considered suicide / when the rainbow is enuf* 284–285

events. Bringing the poem close to ordinary speech, with its metaphors drawn from working life, dialect also extends this comradeship to Burns's Scottish readers.

Politics and subversion

Speaking to more than fellowship, Burns's Scots dialect shows the politicizing of language and the forging of identity. Dialect literature developed as a result of the spread of Standard English, promoted by a publishing industry and government centralized in London. In the poem's language, as well as its subject, Burns makes a political statement.

The mouse understands Burns in the poem; and Burns the mouse. So do Burns's drinking friends in Ayrshire. However, their English or Anglicized overlords do not understand Scots. Dialect can be conspiratorial on a number of levels. In Scotland in 1785, both mice and men are sharing the same fates.

They are both being turned out of their houses—one by the plow, the other (the tenant farmer) by landlords clearing their land of people in order to replace them with more profitable sheep. The implicit political and egalitarian functions of dialect were soon taken up by other poets.

By the end of the 18th century, the English Romantic poets were championing the value of everyday language that could be understood by all. In late 19th-century Ireland, the writers of the Irish literary renaissance employed dialect as an expression of regional consciousness and cultural inheritance, and as an instrument of activism—faculties that have been used by poets of many other nationalities since. ▪

A 19th-century print of Alloway, Robert Burns's birthplace in Ayrshire, reflects the idealized view of local identity promoted by the Gaelic revival and Romantic movements.

Robert Burns

Born in Ayrshire, southern Scotland, in 1759, Robert Burns was the son of a tenant farmer and continued to farm while practicing as a poet. The hard labor of farming left him bent and stooped at an early age. Fluent in both Scots and English, Burns's first book (which included "To a Mouse") entitled *Poems, Chiefly in the Scottish Dialect*, established him as a champion of Scottish culture, but he would also greatly influence the English Romantic poets.

Burns was a collector and celebrated composer of Scottish folk songs. He wrote the words to "Auld Lang Syne," and his "Scots Wha Hae" has been termed an unofficial national anthem. A committed social reformer, he penned fierce political tracts and commentaries, and his verse captures the spirit of Scotland better than that of any poet before or after him. He died in 1796, aged just 37.

Other key works

1786 *Poems, Chiefly in the Scottish Dialect*
1788 "Auld Lang Syne"
1791 "Tam O'Shanter"
1794 "A Red, Red Rose"

AND MARK IN EVERY FACE I MEET / MARKS OF WEAKNESS, MARKS OF WOE
"LONDON" (1794), WILLIAM BLAKE

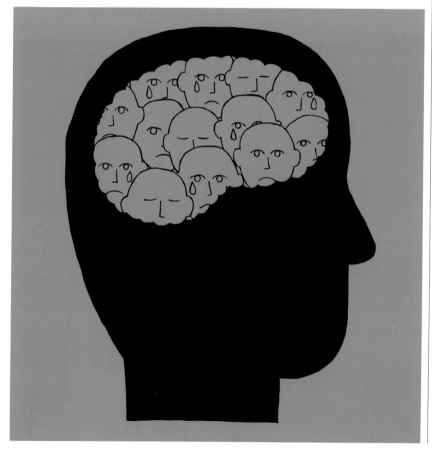

IN CONTEXT

FOCUS
Poetry of social conscience

OTHER KEY POETS
William Langland, Percy Bysshe Shelley, Langston Hughes, Adrienne Rich, Rita Dove

BEFORE
14th century William Langland's *Piers Plowman* depicts peasants and criticizes corruption within the church.

AFTER
1839 Percy Bysshe Shelley's "A Song: 'Men of England'" calls for armed struggle.

1903 "The Haunted Oak" by Paul Laurence Dunbar, whose parents were enslaved, describes a lynching in the American South.

1971 American poet Denise Levertov protests against the Vietnam War in *To Stay Alive*.

P oetry has often given voice to the oppressed, and has sometimes gone further by campaigning for social change. In the late 18th and early 19th centuries, a group of poets later known as the Romantics were inspired by the revolutionary spirit of the period to challenge the status quo. William Wordsworth and William Blake, for example, welcomed the 1789 French Revolution as a new dawn, before eventually rejecting its excesses. Blake also supported the American Revolution (1775–1783)—he was a friend of English-born activist and philosopher Thomas Paine, whose pamphlet *Common Sense* gave the

See also: "On Being Brought from Africa to America" 118–119 ▪ "I, Too" 208–213 ▪ *Poem Without a Hero* 265 ▪ "Diving into the Wreck" 278–283 ▪ "Still I Rise" 288–289 ▪ *Sonata Mulattica* 305

Blake's illustration for "London" shows a child, perhaps symbolizing the fresh approach and energy needed for reform and redemption, leading an old man ("London") toward an open door.

American patriots moral authority. Outraged by the 1819 Peterloo Massacre in Manchester, England, when peaceful protesters were killed by cavalry, Percy Bysshe Shelley wrote an impassioned poem about the event, "The Masque of Anarchy."

City of sorrows

Blake, who lived on the margins of poverty himself, wrote about the exploitation and oppression of the urban poor. "London," a poem in his 1794 collection *Songs of Experience*, shows concern for "every cry of every Man," building an impression of the city as a place of sorrow, before narrowing the gaze to a chimney sweep, soldier, and sex worker. The poem is framed as a walk, with an enclosing reference to the streets in the first and last of four stanzas.

Blake weaves an analysis of the causes of suffering through the poem. He begins with institutional inequities and restraints. Already disenfranchised by discriminatory legal and societal strictures (even

the Thames is "charter'd"), the disempowered are also subject to "mind-forg'd manacles." These internal chains are as debilitating as the systemic inequalities. Blake viewed "energy" and "reason" as forces in opposition; he implies that reason can shackle the imagination, depriving people of the vision or energy to emancipate themselves. A victim mindset is also inferred: the poor have been indoctrinated to feel shame at their own suffering in a society structured by the privileged.

Immoral institutions

In stanza three, Blake's attention turns to abuses of power and the institutions that are failing society's most vulnerable. The Church is reneging on its moral duty to help the poor; the State has blood on its hands, using soldiers—who have no agency themselves—to violently enforce its will.

The miseries associated with the institution of marriage are covered in stanza four. Instead of the expected coach, we have the oxymoron of a "marriage hearse." Far from a joyful new beginning, Blake implies that marriage causes both spiritual and physical death. On a spiritual level, the wedding is a kind of funeral for lost innocence and hope; the

restrictions of marriage are also hypocritical as entrapment in loveless unions fosters sex work. Physical death occurs when men pass the sex workers' "curse" (venereal disease) on to their innocent wives and children.

Although the poem is set in London, Blake's criticism of institutional structures—and his repeat of the word "every"—has a universalizing effect. Blake is writing of soldiers, chimney sweeps, and sex workers everywhere. To some degree this is a poem about being trapped inside inexorable social straightjackets.

The chimney sweep

Comparable to "London" in its social radicalism is Blake's "The Chimney Sweeper," also in *Songs of Experience* (it echoes a companion poem with the same title in *Songs of Innocence*). This poem is an extended take on just two lines in "London": "How the Chimney-sweepers cry / Every blackning Church appalls." Owing to their conveniently small size, boys as young as four or five were employed to sweep chimneys in the late 18th and early 19th centuries. They were often badly treated, and some died from falling or from lung damage.

"The Chimney Sweeper," a dialogue between the speaker and a chimney sweep boy he finds weeping in the snow, attacks the Church's assertion that labor »

> The tigers of wrath are wiser than the horses of instruction.
> *The Marriage of Heaven and Hell*, 1790

William Blake

Born in London in 1757, William Blake experienced religious visions from early childhood, which later influenced his art and poetry. At the age of 10, he was enrolled in drawing classes, and at 14 was apprenticed to an engraver. In 1779, he entered the Royal Academy of Art's School of Design to study painting.

Blake married Catherine Boucher in 1782 and taught her to read, write, and draw; she helped him print his illustrated poems. In 1783, he published his first poetry collection. Blake knew radical thinkers, including Thomas Paine, William Godwin, and the feminist Mary Wollstonecraft. He was arrested for treason in 1803. Unappreciated (and thought mad) in his lifetime, Blake died in 1827.

Other key works

1790 *The Marriage of Heaven and Hell*
1794 *Songs of Innocence and of Experience*
1804 *Milton*
1804 *Jerusalem*

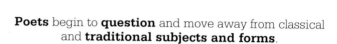

From the mid-18th century, **the Industrial Revolution changes the established social and political order**.

⬇

Poets begin to **question** and move away from classical and **traditional subjects and forms**.

⬇

Revolutions across Europe **inspire emotionally charged poetry** with a focus on social inequalities and political themes.

⬇

William Blake writes "London," among other poems in his *Songs of Experience* series, which highlights the exploitation of workers, including children.

and hardship should be endured for the sake of heavenly rewards to follow. The jaunty meter is appropriate to the good times the boy recalls, when he "was happy upon the heath," but the poem also offers a devastating counterpoint of pain. First, there is the vivid image of "a little black thing among the snow," weeping. Then we learn the boy's parents have provided a travesty of loving care: "They clothed me in the clothes of death, / And taught me to sing the notes of woe." Their pious ignorance of the harm they have caused runs through the poem.

The angry conclusion of "The Chimney Sweeper," like the marriage hearse at the end of "London," brings clashing opposites together. The parents "are gone to praise God and his Priest and King, / Who make up a heaven of our misery." The sentiment—typically for Blake— is fervently anti-Church and anti-monarchy.

The dark side

Blake's rich use of paradox in *The Songs of Experience* is a means for questioning established orthodoxy and exposing the issues of his times. The Industrial Revolution may have been bringing advances, but Blake also calls out the growing societal injustices, the child labor, poverty, pollution, and poor working conditions. Institutions are seen as both complicit and ineffective in the face of change. In his poem

The child chimney sweep, pictured here in a Victorian cartoon, epitomized the suffering and exploitation Blake sought to expose in his work.

"The Tyger," Blake encapsulates these contradictions in a stubborn theological question: what kind of God can make both tiger and lamb?

Blake's influence

Engagement with the dark side of urban living was a theme later picked up by other poets. In the 19th century, Charles Baudelaire documented urban distress in Paris. Forward from that, a line can be traced to T. S. Eliot's "Unreal City" in the first part of *The Waste Land* (1922), where the poet "had not thought death had undone so many."

Blake's expressions of social conscience, antiestablishment mood, and reformist ideology also foreshadowed the genre of protest poetry that voiced the calls of the US Civil Rights movement (1954–1968) to end racial segregation and discrimination, that expressed pacifist outrage at the Vietnam War (1955–1975), and that bolstered the women's rights movement of the 1960s and 1970s. In recent times, nature poetry has acquired a more political tone, as concerns about our planet have intensified.

Protest poems have often followed Blake's lead in their use of rhetoric to give urgency to their calls to action, and in avoiding ambivalence when questioning the status quo. Ella Wheeler Wilcox's anti-racist poem "Protest" (1914) exemplifies the debt to speech-writing: "Call no land free, that holds one fettered slave."

Some poets have focused on disturbing examples of individual suffering or injustice, including well-documented episodes. American activist poet Muriel Rukeyser (1913–1980) examined a grave miscarriage of justice in Alabama in "The Trial" (1935) and industrial tragedy in "The Book of the Dead" (1938), which commemorated silicosis deaths in West Virginia. Much as Blake addresses both the personal and universal in "London" and his chimney sweeper poems, these works have wider implications, giving validation to individuals subject to marginalization and discrimination, while attempting to reform society. ∎

Poetry with art

The artwork Blake used to illustrate his poems is now as lauded as his writing. To create them, he invented new engraving techniques, which involved painting his designs in reverse using varnish on a metal plate. The plate was then etched to produce a relief surface for printing (in contrast to the more usual intaglio method where designs are engraved). The text was printed in brown ink, then each page was colored by hand. The circulation of these crafted works was limited to friends and collectors—only 30 books were sold in Blake's own lifetime.

Blake's paintings do not appear on separate pages but create an enclosing frame for his words. For example, in his illustrated version of "The Tyger," tree branches sprout between the quatrains.

A color relief etching for "The Tyger" from one of Blake's last editions of *Songs of Innocence and of Experience*, printed around 1825.

[…] thousands of sweepers, Dick, Joe, Ned, & Jack,
Were all of them locked up in coffins of black […]
"The Chimney Sweeper" (lines 11–12), *Songs of Innocence*, 1789

THEY FLASH UPON THAT INWARD EYE / WHICH IS THE BLISS OF SOLITUDE

"I WANDERED LONELY AS A CLOUD" (1815), WILLIAM WORDSWORTH

IN CONTEXT

FOCUS
English Romantic poets: the first generation

OTHER KEY POETS
William Blake, Samuel Taylor Coleridge

BEFORE
1789 William Blake prints the first copies of his *Songs of Innocence and of Experience*.

1798 William Wordsworth and Samuel Taylor Coleridge publish the first edition of *Lyrical Ballads*, considered a manifesto of Romanticism.

AFTER
1818 Second-generation Romantic Lord Byron includes criticism of Wordsworth and Coleridge in his *Don Juan*.

1850 Posthumous publication of Wordsworth's *The Prelude* marks the end of the first generation of Romantic poets.

A walk in the countryside usually generated a spiritual communion between English poet William Wordsworth and the natural world around him. On many occasions, so intensely did he "see into the life of things," as he put it, that he returned to his desk with the germ of a poem in mind. Poetry was, he elaborated, "the spontaneous overflow of powerful feelings: it takes its origin from emotion recollected in tranquillity." This is how he wrote the poem "I Wandered Lonely as a Cloud."

The poem describes nature's ability to evoke strong emotions—a defining theme in the work of the

See also: "To a Mouse" 120–121 ▪ "London" 122–125 ▪ "Kubla Khan" 130–131 ▪ "Ozymandias" 132–135 ▪ *Don Juan* 136–137 ▪ "To Autumn" 138–141

A Lake District vista (c. 1755–1781) by Joseph Farington demonstrates the influence of nature on the Romantic movement, which encompassed art and music as well as poetry and literature.

"first generation" of English Romantic poets, William Blake, Samuel Taylor Coleridge, and William Wordsworth. Disenchanted with what they regarded as the elitist content and stilted style of Enlightenment era poetry, these poets felt that nature held democratic appeal, and could also act as a muse, a solace, and a source of personal inspiration.

Recollections in tranquillity
On April 15, 1802, Wordsworth and his younger sister Dorothy were taking a walk in England's Lake District. Sheltering from rough weather in some woods, they spied a long belt of daffodils carpeting the shore of the lake. Dorothy noted in her journal: "I never saw daffodils so beautiful […] some rested their heads upon these stones as on a pillow for weariness and the rest tossed and reeled and danced […] with the wind." Two years later, reclining in his study at Dove Cottage in nearby Grasmere, Wordsworth revisited this scene in his imagination. The resulting four-stanza lyric, "I Wandered Lonely as a Cloud," captures the vivid imagery of the daffodils using a simple rhyme scheme (ababcc) which has a waltz-like rhythm.

Wordsworth begins by imagining himself "lonely as a cloud," drifting across hills and vales, setting »

William Wordsworth

Born in 1770, in Cockermouth, near the English Lake District, Wordsworth looked to this area as a source of inspiration. Aside from his studies at Cambridge University; a spell in revolutionary France, where he fathered a daughter; and a few years spent in southern England, he lived in the Lake District all his life. It was there, from 1799 until 1815, that he had his most fruitful years, composing odes, sonnets, and long narrative poems imbued with a love of the land and the local people. In 1802, he married his childhood sweetheart.

Wordsworth's career was summed up by contemporary critic Thomas De Quincey: "Up to 1820 the name of Wordsworth was trampled underfoot […] from 1820 to 1830 it was militant; from 1830 to 1835 it has been triumphant." In 1843, Wordsworth became Poet Laureate, holding the post until his death in 1850.

Other key works

1798 *Lyrical Ballads*
1807 *Poems, in Two Volumes*
1850 *The Prelude*

> A host, of golden daffodils […]
> Ten thousand saw I at a glance,
> Tossing their heads in sprightly dance.
> **"I Wandered Lonely as a Cloud" (lines 4, 11–12)**

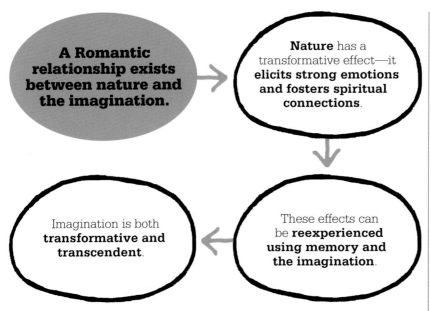

A Romantic relationship exists between nature and the imagination.

→

Nature has a transformative effect—it **elicits strong emotions and fosters spiritual connections**.

↓

These effects can be **reexperienced using memory and the imagination**.

←

Imagination is both **transformative and transcendent**.

out the characteristic Romantic relationship with nature. He suggests that we are an integral part of the scene and the natural world, not just outside observers. The details of this relationship are developed when Wordsworth encounters the vista of "golden daffodils," which are "[f]luttering and dancing in the breeze."

The word "danced" (probably taken from Dorothy Wordsworth's 1802 journal entry) becomes the poem's controlling metaphor. The daffodils are consistently portrayed as "dancing"; even "the waves beside [the flowers] danced." This universal dance is modified by words of a similar tone: "glee," "sprightly," "gay," and "jocund." It is a happy scene, notwithstanding the traditional symbolic association of flowers with transient beauty—a hint at Romantic concerns with transience and eternity, and what nature can teach us of these themes.

The use of personification strengthens the link between nature and humankind and allows an easy transference of emotion to both

poet and reader. The terms are also relatable and accessible. Fueled by the egalitarian fervor of revolutions in Europe, the first Romantics sought to write in direct, everyday language that could be understood by all, rather than the elitist diction of Classical literature. This striving for authenticity in language was matched by a new emphasis on the value of the personal, including the imagination.

The inward eye
A Romantic manifesto on the power of the imagination is introduced toward the end of the third stanza of the poem with the words, "but little thought / What wealth the show to me had brought." The word "wealth" suggests a treasure chest, overflowing with riches to be savored in the future. The

association with "golden daffodils" is unmistakable, but this is a treasure of a different kind—one that has everything to do with "emotion recollected in tranquillity." The daffodils—and the pleasure they invoke—are being experienced through imagination.

The Romantics aimed to topple "reason" from the throne of the mind and to crown "imagination" in its place. "The Imagination is not a State," declared William Blake, "it is the Human Existence itself." He also called it "Jesus, the Imagination," meaning salvation itself. Samuel Taylor Coleridge, Wordsworth's colleague on the seminal collection *Lyrical Ballads*, echoed Blake in his assessment: "The primary Imagination I hold to be the living power and prime agent of all human perception," he wrote in his *Biographia Literaria,* a meditation on Romantic literature and the imagination. "It acts by creating a oneness, even as nature, the greatest of poets, acts upon us when we open our eyes upon an extended prospect." This encapsulates the experience in the last stanza of Wordsworth's poem—he beholds an "extended prospect" of dancing daffodils while nature, greatest of poets, creates a oneness or fusion between him and what he sees.

Reliving experience
Wordsworth's heart "dances with the daffodils" in the poem's final lines. Enacting Coleridge's description of "Primary imagination" as a "living power," Wordsworth

> I gazed—and gazed—but little thought
> What wealth the show to me had brought [...]
> **"I Wandered Lonely as a Cloud"** (lines 17–18)

> [...] Poetry is passion:
> it is the history or
> science of feelings [...]
> **William Wordsworth**
> *Lyrical Ballads,*
> **1800 edition**

shows that this kind of experience is not mere reverie but actual recreation. As he explains in his Preface to *Lyrical Ballads*, when contemplating "in tranquillity" the intensity of the original emotion, a "kindred" emotion is produced, "and does itself actually exist in the mind." Imagination is therefore both transformative and transcendent— able to transport the poet from his present time and place, it also allows him to reexperience an earlier emotional state.

The poem is not a tribute to the day in 1802 when Wordsworth strolled along the lake shore with Dorothy, but a celebration of the power of imagination to recreate the occasion, with all its sensuous detail intact, so that the poet can truly dance with the daffodils in a scene, as Wordsworth put it in "Ode: Intimations of Immortality," imbued with all "the glory and the freshness of a dream."

Classic Romanticism

"I Wandered Lonely as a Cloud" was written in 1804, but it was not published until 1807, when it appeared in *Poems in Two Volumes*. In 1815, Wordsworth made some revisions to the poem, and this is the version widely familiar today. On publication, the poem garnered lukewarm reviews; Coleridge, in *Biographia Literaria*, dismissed its final stanza as another example of the "mental bombast" he thought he

Wordsworth's Lake District home inspired his most famous poems and helped him formulate a new kind of poetry in which nature was both a subject and a guide to enlightenment.

spied in some of Wordsworth's work (the two men were estranged by this point). Over time, the poem won a wider circle of admirers: it was short, pithy, upbeat, and easily memorized. Its accessibility, however, does not diminish its status as a classic expression, in miniature, of Romantic poetry's deep spiritual communion with nature and how exquisitely, as Wordsworth put it, "[t]he external World is fitted to the Mind." ∎

Lyrical Ballads

A slender volume first published in 1798, *Lyrical Ballads* would change the course of English poetry. Its authors, Samuel Taylor Coleridge and William Wordsworth, sought to cast aside the witty epigram, the hallmark of 18th-century verse, and replace it with the rhythms of everyday life. In so doing, they hoped to return English poetry to a lost tradition of simplicity, directness, and emotional immediacy. The advertisement for the volume read: "It is the honorable characteristic of poetry that its materials are found in every subject which can interest the human mind."

Wordsworth's "Preface," first issued with the 1800 edition, asserted that since poetry could be found in common life, everyday language should suffice to enshrine it in a new kind of blank verse. In trusting to the senses and to the alchemy of imagination to discover the innate poetry at the heart of ordinary things—and never to the "meddling intellect"—the collection initiated a new era of Romanticism.

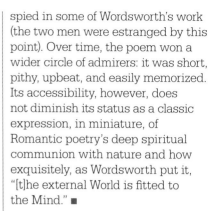

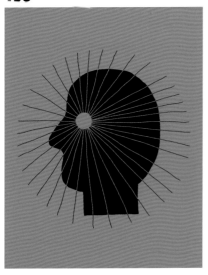

IN A VISION ONCE I SAW
"KUBLA KHAN" (1816), SAMUEL TAYLOR COLERIDGE

IN CONTEXT

FOCUS
Visionary Romanticism

OTHER KEY POETS
William Blake, William Wordsworth, Percy Bysshe Shelley, W. B. Yeats

BEFORE
14th century Chaucer's *Parliament of Fowls* is an early dream vision poem.

1797 Coleridge has the dream that inspires "Kubla Khan."

1805 Wordsworth, in *The Prelude* (Book 5), describes "visionary power" as dark and mysterious.

AFTER
1816 British critic William Hazlitt writes of "Kubla Khan" that Coleridge "can write better *nonsense* verse than any man in English."

1819 Keats's ballad "La Belle Dame sans Merci" spins a tale about a sorceress seducing a knight.

The Romantic poets valued emotion, imagination, and nature over reason. Drawn to wild places, they found excitement in the sublime, which trivialized human self-importance. The complexity of the inner self, however, was a rich source of inspiration: it had its own kind of sublimity.

Samuel Taylor Coleridge was the prime exponent of another Romantic mode: the visionary, employing the fantastic imagery of private visions in his poetry. Dreams fascinated the Romantic mind. Opium was a medicinal, not a recreational, drug at the time; it took its users to a hallucinatory state. Coleridge's "Kubla Khan," originating in an opium-induced reverie, expressed intuitive insights of the unconscious.

Xanadu

"Kubla Khan" is compromised for being implicitly imperialist in its view of Eastern culture, but it remains one of the most brilliant poems ever written about the poetic imagination. It begins with two Eastern names: Xanadu and Kubla Khan. Kublai Khan (the modern spelling) was the first Yuan dynasty emperor in China after the Mongol conquest, and Xanadu (Shangdu) was his summer capital. From Khan's "pleasure-dome," the Alph River—the name suggesting alpha, the first letter of the Greek alphabet—runs through caverns to a "sunless sea," conjuring a link between the unconscious and instincts both "sacred"—the description of the river—and primitive.

Kublai Khan (1215–1294), the fifth emperor of the Yuan (Mongol) dynasty, completed the conquest of China, an invasion that had been started by his grandfather Genghis Khan.

See also: "I Wandered Lonely as a Cloud" 126–129 ▪ "Ozymandias" 132–135 ▪ "To Autumn" 138–141
▪ "The Second Coming" 194–197

Samuel Taylor Coleridge

Born in Devon, England, in 1772, Coleridge was the son of the local vicar and headmaster. He studied at Jesus College, Cambridge but did not complete his degree. While there, he won an award for an ode attacking the slave trade and met radical poet Robert Southey, with whom he planned an unrealized utopian community (Pantisocracy) in Pennsylvania.

In the three years after meeting Wordsworth in 1795, Coleridge wrote prolifically, composing "The Rime of the Ancient Mariner" and "Kubla Khan," and publishing the groundbreaking collection *Lyrical Ballads* (with Wordsworth). In 1799, he settled in England's Lake District to be near Wordsworth. By this time, Coleridge's opium addiction was having a serious effect on his health and relationships. He moved to London in 1816, where he completed his major prose work, *Biographia Literaria*. He died in London in 1834.

Other key works

1796 *Poems on Various Subjects*
1798 *Lyrical Ballads*
1817 *Biographia Literaria*

The rhythm slows to a stately description of Khan's paradise before sharper notes emerge: a "romantic chasm"; a "savage place"; a woman "wailing for her demon-lover"; a fountain throwing up rocks; and Khan hearing "ancestral voices prophesying war!" The "sunny pleasure-dome" has caves of ice: the unconscious, where imagination mines its treasures, is unsettling.

The balance of opposites

At the beginning of the poem's third stanza, we hear of Coleridge's vision of the Abyssinian maid playing her dulcimer. If he could replicate her song, he says, he could create his own pleasure dome—which he has in fact done through poetry. But it would have caves of ice; and he, the magician, would generate fear. Onlookers would need to protect themselves ritually from his visionary fire. Paradise is both sustaining ("honey-dew" and "milk") and dangerous—like imagination and also, perhaps, like opium. The balance of opposites is exquisitely handled throughout the poem.

A mariner's tale

Coleridge's "The Rime of the Ancient Mariner," a narrative in ballad form, also features ice and honey-dew. The visions—"death-fires," seawater burning like "a witch's oils"—start with the hallucinations of sick crew members and continue with a death-ship, prompted by the killing of an albatross. But all this is framed within a pious morality tale about the ecological unity of nature, the nightmare—a temporary descent into hell—being a prelude to redemption. The longest poem by Coleridge, "The Rime of the Ancient Mariner" appeared in the first edition of *Lyrical Ballads* (1798), the collection Coleridge shared with Wordsworth. Its Gothic brand of visionary horror sits uncomfortably with its companion poems in the book, and Wordsworth considered dropping it from the second edition. On the other hand, its conversational tone conforms with Wordsworth's mission for a new kind of poetry, prioritizing "the real language of men in a state of vivid sensation."

Keats's "Lamia" and "The Eve of St. Agnes" (both 1820) are also narrative poems with dreamlike elements. They look forward to Robert Browning's "Childe Roland to the Dark Tower Came" and W. B. Yeats's "The Song of Wandering Aengus," while "Kubla Khan" foreshadows Yeats's "Sailing to Byzantium" in the self-referential way it spins magic from visionary imagination. ∎

> It was a miracle of rare device,
> A sunny pleasure-dome with caves of ice!
> **"Kubla Khan" (lines 35–36)**

LOOK ON MY WORKS, YE MIGHTY, AND DESPAIR!

"OZYMANDIAS" (1818), PERCY BYSSHE SHELLEY

IN CONTEXT

FOCUS
English Romantic poets: the second generation

OTHER KEY POETS
Lord Byron, John Keats, Felicia Hemans, John Clare

BEFORE
1798 William Wordsworth's preface to *Lyrical Ballads* sets out the principles of the first generation of Romantic poets.

1813 Shelley privately prints and distributes 250 copies of his radical, antiestablishment poem *Queen Mab*.

AFTER
1819 John Keats writes five of his classically inspired odes.

1820 Shelley publishes *Prometheus Unbound*, a lyrical drama, reflecting ongoing interest in mythology and the themes of tyranny, nature, and the imagination.

The "second generation" of English Romantic poets—the successors to William Blake, Samuel Taylor Coleridge, and William Wordsworth—were establishing their influence by 1817. Lord Byron, already popular, had just written the fourth canto of his lauded *Childe Harold's Pilgrimage*, introducing the classic Romantic character of the "Byronic hero." John Keats had published his first volume of verse. And Percy Bysshe Shelley's young wife, Mary Shelley, was awaiting the imminent publication of her gothic fantasy novel *Frankenstein*, which questioned the progress of science. Toward the end of 1817, Shelley

The head of the real "Ozymandias," now known to be Pharaoh Ramses II, was pulled on wooden rollers to the banks of the Nile before being taken to England by boat, arriving in 1818.

himself would create another and equally titanic figure in a 14-line sonnet that is now one of his best-known poems: "Ozymandias."

A contest

In late December 1817, when Shelley was living in Marlow, on the Thames River, northwest of London, he engaged in a sonnet-writing contest with his friend Horace Smith, a financier and part-time poet. The subject was to be "Ozymandias," a character known from the 1st-century BCE historian Diodorus Siculus, whose *Bibliotheca historica* Shelley had acquired in 1812.

Diodorus describes visiting a ruined temple in Egypt that housed a colossal statue of an enthroned king. An inscription on the statue stated: "I am Ozymandias, king of kings; if any would know how great I am, and where I lie, let him exceed me in any of my works." The literature, art, and philosophy of ancient Greece were already a source of inspiration for the second-

generation Romantics. However, the arrival of archaeologists, artists, and travel writers in Egypt in 1815, in the wake of the Napoleonic wars, had ignited a new passion for ancient, exotic, and oriental subjects in England. French engineers had identified the probable "Tomb of Ozymandias" at Thebes in Upper Egypt, and by 1816 a giant stone head and torso from this complex were en route to the British Museum, inspiring great excitement—and Shelley's sonnet-writing contest.

The sonnets were written at speed: in a later sonnet-writing contest between Shelley and Keats, each was allotted only 15 minutes. Shelley appears to have completed "Ozymandias" in three days, submitting it to Leigh Hunt, poet, essayist, and editor of London's *The Examiner*, who had promised to print both Shelley's and Smith's poems.

Romantic revolt

Shelley's sonnet was a triumph of tight language and narrative momentum; it also encapsulated the spirit, approach, and ideals of the second generation Romantic poets. In pursuing a more democratic style, the first generation Romantics had rejected the Classical language, »

Percy Bysshe Shelley

Born in 1792 in Sussex, England, the grandson of a baronet, Percy Bysshe Shelley attended Eton College and Oxford University before being expelled from the latter for his 1811 essay, "The Necessity for Atheism," his first attack on authority. It would not be his last. He made a reputation during his lifetime as a radical revolutionary and an apostle of free love who eloped twice: his first wife died by suicide; his second, Mary Shelley, wrote the novel *Frankenstein*.

Among the most gifted poets of his time, Shelley used an astounding variety of forms and measures, and achieved heights of lyric intensity rarely equaled. His lyrical drama *Prometheus Unbound* is generally regarded as his masterpiece. Shelley died at 29, drowning in a storm at sea off the coast of Italy in 1822. His body, when recovered, was cremated on the beach, like those of ancient Greek heroes.

Other key works

1813 *Queen Mab*
1819 "Ode to the West Wind"
1821 "Adonais: An Elegy on the Death of John Keats"

Half sunk a shattered visage lies, whose frown,
And wrinkled lip, and sneer of cold command,
Tell that its sculptor well those passions read
"Ozymandias" (lines 4–6)

the subject matter, and settings of traditional poetry. The second generation Romantics, with their revived interest in Classicism, preferred revolution through the poetic disruption—rather than the rejection—of archaic forms.

Search for truth

Like much second generation Romantic writing, "Ozymandias" makes use of an alternative reality (in this case, a legendary setting) to comment on contemporary concerns. The poem establishes this contrast between the legendary past and the present through a story-within-a-story told by two narrators. The first of these, the poet, is situated in the present and reflects the Romantic perception of the poet as prophet, signposting a better path through personal insight. The second narrator, "a traveler from an antique land," plunges the reader into an exotic world of romance and fable, where these insights are revealed. His initial declamation, "Two vast and trunkless legs of stone / Stand in the desert. ...," sets up some of the poem's themes: the fragility of power and the endurance of art.

The traveler's statement marks Shelley's first departure from his source (one also made by Smith) and hints at his radical intent. Shelley's statue is not the enthroned king of Diodorus, but a symbol of tyranny and autocratic authority overthrown. The statue's head is "half sunk" and "shattered"; the king's expressions "yet survive, stamped on these lifeless things" only through the skill of the sculptor—reinforcing the role of the artist as truth-teller.

The synecdoche (part standing for the whole) that ends the traveler's description of the head—"The hand that mocked them and the heart that fed"—has been variously interpreted. Most commentators believe that the "hand" is the sculptor's, which both "mocked up" the tyrant's features and, because his art survives, is now mocking the tyrant's demise. The "heart that fed" is widely assumed to have belonged to the tyrant, who had been sustained by feeding on vainglory, but the reference remains, perhaps deliberately, unclear.

Life's ironies

At the climax of his tale, the traveler relates the words on the king's pedestal: "My name is Ozymandias, King of Kings:/ Look on my Works, ye Mighty, and despair!" Shelley has again departed from his source to make the words more challenging. The contrast with what follows could not be more clear: "Nothing beside remains." To

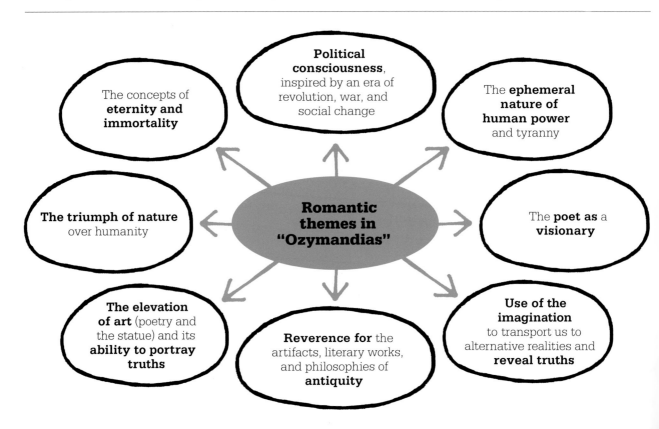

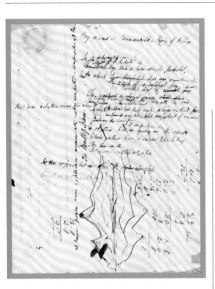

Shelley's draft of "Ozymandias" shows a phrase from Diodorus Siculus at the top—"My name is Ozymandias, King of Kings"—suggesting this was the key inspiration for his sonnet.

Poets are the unacknowledged legislators of the world.
Percy Bysshe Shelley
"A Defense of Poetry"
(1821)

emphasize the scale of obliteration, Shelley has also changed Diodorus's original setting, which described the statue amid ruined temple gates, courts, and galleries, to create a starker scene. The use of alliteration, which creates a punchy ending and reinforces the sense of lost power—the wreck is "boundless and bare," the "lone and level sands stretch far away"—confirms the poem as a masterpiece of irony.

Subversive form

Shelley's choice of the sonnet form for "Ozymandias" illustrates a preference for more complex and conventional language than the first generation of Romantic poets, but also a continued desire to disrupt tradition. His poem innovates by subverting a standard sonnet rhyme pattern (abab cdcd efef gg), instead using an abab acdc ede fef rhyme scheme that upends the traditional practice of never connecting the octave and sestet by rhyme. Shelley also uses slant, or slightly off, rhymes to give the poem a fragmented rhythm that echoes the king's crumbling statue. This bending of established rules serves to reinforce the nonconformist,

revolutionary, and idealistic undercurrents in Shelley's work. Poetic rules—as well as societal ones—are open to question.

Transient life

"Ozymandias" was published in *The Examiner* on January 11, 1818. Smith's sonnet, identically named, was published in the paper's February edition, but soon sank into oblivion. The most sweeping meaning of Shelley's poem is that time will annihilate everything, erasing even the most mighty works of human achievement. A reading that reflects Shelley's radical republicanism and Romantic revolutionary aspirations might be that tyrannies must inevitably topple and that social equality must ultimately prevail—hence "the lone and level sands" at the end of the poem. But "Ozymandias" also seems to suggest that destruction is not necessarily absolute. Might art endure? After all, the sculptor's

hand had fashioned the "sneer of cold command" on Ozymandias's features, which outlasted all of his mighty works.

A few years after the publication of "Ozymandias," all three of the major figures in the second generation of English Romantic poets would die young, and none would die in England. Their verse, however, survived and flourished, giving even greater resonance to their thematic preoccupations with the transience of life, the significance of art, the power of nature and the imagination, and our place in the world. ∎

The caesura

A caesura is the literary term for a halt in the middle of a line of poetry. Often (but not always) indicated by punctuation, such as a period or comma, it is a pause that interrupts the poem's cadence or metrical flow. The pause corresponds to taking a deep breath before continuing to read. A caesura can be a very effective tool of emphasis—in "Ozymandias," Shelley employs a number of caesurae over the poem's 14 lines for heightened dramatic effect.

Caesurae are categorized into two groups. A "masculine" caesura occurs after a stressed syllable and creates a hard, staccato effect: "My name is Ozymandias, || King of Kings || Look on my Works" (the double uprights mark the scansion—stress patterns—for the caesurae). A "feminine" caesura occurs after an unstressed syllable and creates a softer pause, as, for example, in "Near them, || on the sand" or "ye Mighty, || and despair!."

'TIS BUT / THE TRUTH IN MASQUERADE
DON JUAN (1819–1824), LORD BYRON

IN CONTEXT

FOCUS
Comic verse

OTHER KEY POETS
Alexander Pope, Edward Lear, Lewis Carroll, T. S. Eliot, W. H. Auden

BEFORE
1712 Alexander Pope's mock-heroic *The Rape of the Lock* satirizes the triviality of contemporary society.

1809 Byron publishes his first major satirical poem, *English Bards and Scotch Reviewers*, in response to criticism of his work in *The Edinburgh Review*.

1818 *Beppo*, a long poetic romp, is Byron's first use of the ottava rima rhyme scheme.

AFTER
1846 Edward Lear's *Book of Nonsense* popularizes the light humor of nonsense verse.

1937 W. H. Auden publishes *Letter to Lord Byron,* his humorous tribute to *Don Juan.*

C omedy—the cultivation of humor in the face of life's vicissitudes and human weaknesses—has featured in poetry since antiquity. It can fulfill a social or psychological function, may defy the limits of taste to provoke a response, and frequently attempts to challenge the status quo.

In ancient Rome, during the 1st century BCE, Horace composed gently satirical poems to mock vices and follies, while Juvenal launched more abrasive comic attacks. These methods of ridicule were revived in England in the early 18th century by writers such as Alexander Pope,

who looked to Classical models for his own satirical verse. Pope wittily held a mirror to upper-class vanities, criticizing a society that feigned high ideals and sensibilities but was riddled with hypocrisy. In the early 1800s, Pope's approach was followed by the English Romantic poet Lord Byron, an ardent fan of his work.

Byronic transgression

In *Don Juan*, a comic epic poem based on a Spanish folk legend, Byron takes aim at a variety of targets through the adventures of his antihero. Transgressive acts provide the basis for much of the poem's

The comic style of *Don Juan*

Mocks pretensions in poetry and life.

Satirizes human appetite, hypocrisy, and vanity **in a conversational style**.

Uses ottava rima rhyming style, with its clinching final couplet **for witty effect**.

See also: *The Canterbury Tales* 64–71 ▪ *Hero and Leander* 86–87 ▪ *An Essay on Criticism* 116–117 ▪ *Eugene Onegin* 142–143 ▪ "Not Waving but Drowning" 258–259

humor and include seductions, cannibalism, cross-dressing, and adultery. Juan is a highly sexed teenager from Seville, Spain, who flees by ship after being caught with the wife of a family friend. Afloat on an open boat after a shipwreck, the crew draw lots to decide who to eat, devouring Juan's tutor to survive. Juan is captured by pirates, sold into slavery, and kept in a harem dressed as a girl. Escaping, he joins the Russian army, witnesses war, and is desired by Catherine the Great. Sent to England as an envoy, he finds himself in an aristocratic country house when the poem ends abruptly (owing to Byron's death).

Mock-heroic verse

Don Juan's structure and form are key to its comedic success. The poem takes the characteristics of epic legend (including length—the poem extends over 16,000 lines in 17 cantos) then subverts them with a hapless protagonist and satiric style for mock-heroic effect. An ingenious rhyme scheme adds to the humor. Byron uses ottava rima, an eight-line stanza with the rhyme scheme abababcc. Following three rhymes, the concluding couplet provides Byron with the opportunity for a witty, often bathetic, ending which can be entertainingly disyllabic ("shaken / Bacon"; "gullet / pull it"). Byron often resorts to inverted word order and circumlocution, implying he does not take himself too seriously and wants readers to relish his linguistic acrobatics. The tone of voice is that of a tongue-in-cheek, worldly-wise anecdotalist—who in one sense is the hero of the poem.

Unlike the philosophical musings typical of much Romantic poetry, Byron used comedy in *Don Juan* for social commentary with full-blooded panache. Immediately popular, his work reinvigorated comic poetry as a serious genre, paving the way for later 19th-century poets such as Lewis Carroll, Edward Lear, and Oscar Wilde to popularize their own versions of light verse. ▪

The Shipwreck of Don Juan, painted by Eugène Delacroix in 1840, depicts the episode in Byron's poem when lots are drawn to decide who should be sacrificed to feed the others.

Lord Byron

Born in London in 1788, George Gordon Byron inherited his title and the ancestral home of Newstead Abbey, Nottinghamshire, when he was 10. Studying at Trinity College, Cambridge, he became friendly with Shelley and gained a reputation for financial profligacy. In 1809, Byron embarked on a tour of Europe and began writing *Childe Harold's Pilgrimage*, a Romantic verse travelogue that would make him famous.

Byron had numerous sexual adventures, including an affair with Anglo-Irish novelist Lady Caroline Lamb. In 1815, he married Anne Isabella (Annabella) Milbanke but they separated after a year. Moving to Switzerland, Byron settled near Shelley; his later amorous adventures were the subject of brilliant letters. While supporting the Greek War of Independence in 1824, Byron died from a fever in Missolonghi, Greece.

Other key works

1812–1818 *Childe Harold's Pilgrimage*
1814 "She Walks in Beauty"
1818 *Beppo: A Venetian Story*

SEASON OF MISTS AND MELLOW FRUITFULNESS

"TO AUTUMN" (1820), JOHN KEATS

IN CONTEXT

FOCUS
Romantic ode

OTHER KEY POETS
**William Wordsworth,
Samuel Taylor Coleridge,
Percy Bysshe Shelley,
John Clare**

BEFORE
1595 Edmund Spenser publishes "Epithalamion," among the first odes in English.

1802 In "Dejection: An Ode," Samuel Taylor Coleridge explores the interrelationship between nature and emotion.

1807 William Wordsworth's "Immortality Ode" ponders human insignificance.

AFTER
1830 Alfred Tennyson's introspective *Poems, Chiefly Lyrical* show Keatsian influence in their observations and melodic variety.

A type of lyric poetry with no fixed stanza form or rhyme scheme, the ode was devised in ancient Greece. It was embraced by all the Romantic poets, but the prime exponent of the form was John Keats. The six examples he wrote in 1819—on autumn, melancholy, indolence, psyche, a nightingale, and a Grecian urn—show a level of craftsmanship unsurpassed in the Romantic period.

The ode form

An ode celebrates a person, place, phenomenon, or idea. In the early 5th century BCE, the ancient Greek poet Pindar wrote a particular style of ode that was set to music and

See also: "I Wandered Lonely as a Cloud" 126–129 ▪ "Kubla Khan" 130–131 ▪ "Ozymandias" 132–135 ▪ "The Windhover" 166–167

> Where are the songs of spring? Ay, Where are they?
> Think not of them, thou hast thy music too […]
> **"To Autumn" (lines 23–24)**

accompanied by dance, mostly to celebrate athletic achievement. Each piece had three parts—the strophe (presenting the poem's main idea), antistrophe (extending or counterbalancing the idea), and epode (concluding the poem).

The main practitioner of the "Pindaric ode" in English was Abraham Cowley, writing during the 17th century CE. Like Pindar, Cowley emphasized mastery of technique—the triumph of language over a difficult form—but he devised his own irregular patterns of meter and rhyme. His style led to a new classification: the "irregular" or "Cowleyan" ode.

The Roman lyric poet Horace created a contrasting style of ode during the 1st century BCE. The "Horatian ode" used a structure of simple four- or two-line stanzas, all with the same meter. The best-known example in English is Andrew Marvell's "An Horatian Ode upon Cromwell's Return from Ireland," written in 1650.

Romantic reflections

In the Romantic period, the Pindaric ode proved a suitable medium for reflective poetry that either teases apart the strands of personal crisis or explores the thoughts and feelings conjured by an object, state, or phenomenon, as in the odes of Keats. Typically, there is a carefully wrought progression from the opening premise to the conclusion.

Keats's odes show unmistakable traits of the Romantic temperament: an interest in intoxication and trance, in solitary emotional states, in beauty (especially of nature), in life's brevity and the transitoriness of all things, in myth and the distant past, and in the personal experience of opening the senses to the world. Imagination is prized above reason—whether speculating on what the dancing figures on a Greek urn are doing or conjuring up a scriptural scene or spirit realm.

The abstract personified

Composed after a walk near Winchester, in southern England, Keats's "To Autumn" is the most serene of Keats's odes. More than a simple word-picture, it begins with a description of fruitfulness that could be interpreted as either personified description or apostrophe (speech to a person who is not present). Keats's second stanza clearly addresses the season as a woman, but there is nothing stilted in this. Keats creates immediacy in vignettes presented as multisensory gifts to the reader, while the use of exact rhymes and carefully placed enjambment (overrunning sentences beyond »

Keats's personification of autumn to convey sensual pleasure and abundance, as well as transience and mortality, is captured in the 1898 painting *Autumn* by Victorian artist William Stott.

John Keats

Born in 1795, John Keats was the son of an east London stable manager, who died when Keats was eight. For five years, he was apprenticed to an apothecary, before studying surgery at Guy's Hospital, London. He read widely in 17th- and 18th-century literature and published his first poetry collection in 1817.

In letters, Keats expressed influential ideas about poetry, including the concept of "negative capability." After the death of his brother Tom in 1818, he moved to a house near London's Hampstead Heath and fell in love with his neighbor, 18-year-old Fanny Brawne. He wrote poetry prolifically from 1818, including his great odes.

By 1820, Keats had developed consumption. He sailed for Italy later that year, hoping the climate would ease his symptoms. But in February 1821, he died in an apartment by the Spanish Steps, in Rome. He was 25.

Key works

1817 *Poems*
1818 *Endymion*
1820 *Lamia, Isabella, The Eve of St. Agnes and Other Poems*

the line endings) give a musical flow. Autumn comes to life "sitting careless on a granary floor," with "hair soft-lifted by the winnowing wind," which is an active agent in the harvest.

This type of anthropomorphism—the attribution of human qualities and characteristics—is also found in Keats's "Ode on a Grecian Urn" (the urn is an "unravish'd bride," a "foster-child," and a "Sylvan historian"). Quickly drawing the reader into the world of the poem, the device allows meditations on subjects linked to the human condition—the passage of time, mortality, and beauty.

Essential paradox

The poem goes on to visualize Autumn asleep, "Drows'd with the fume of poppies." The theme of intoxication, important to Keats, is developed at greater length in his "Ode to a Nightingale" and "Ode on Melancholy." The paradox of intoxication is that while it suspends reality and allows the imagination to flow, it also numbs the senses. Ultimately, it cannot halt the passage of time or nature's transformations. Although Autumn's nap has left some of the corn unharvested and entwined by flowers, as if it has protected the crop and blooms from the march of time, Keats makes it clear as the poem progresses that the cycle of seasons must continue, and transience is part of the beauty of autumn.

In "Ode to a Nightingale," intoxication offers a means of escape from the harsh realities

O for a
Life of Sensations
rather than of Thoughts!
John Keats
Letter to Benjamin Bailey (1817)

of a world where "youth grows pale, and spectre-thin, and dies." Here, intoxication is ultimately rejected in favor of poetry and the imagination, which (like Autumn's slumber) provides a brief freedom from conscious realities and temporarily makes immortality seem possible.

The passage of time

Musings on immortality sit alongside a progressive treatment of time in "To Autumn." The reader is reminded of summer in stanza one, of spring in stanza three. Keats concludes with a gentle foreboding of the one season the poem does not mention—winter. The swallows that "twitter" in the last line are gathering to fly south.

Although the ode is more subtle than to end with anxiety about the shortening days—its last nine lines are pure description and have no rhetorical questions—there are hints of something darker in the

"Beauty is truth, truth beauty,"—that is all Ye know on earth, and all ye need to know.
"Ode on a Grecian Urn" (lines 49–50), 1819

The structure of an ode invites a progression of thought

The object
A natural scene, emotional state, phenomenon, or object (autumn, a nightingale, melancholy, an urn) is described, using personification, sensual language, and imagery.

Meditation and argument
The object inspires a meditation on personal and universal themes, such as the passage of time, beauty, truth, mutability, and death.

Conclusion
A final insight (such as change is inevitable, without pain there is no joy, nature is immortal, or its beauty reflects inherent truths) draws the poem to an end.

season's beauty. The "mourn" of the "wailful choir" of gnats begs a question about what they are mourning (transience? brevity of life?). Even the wind "lives or dies." Four lines from the end, these melancholy overtones are qualified by the prospect of new life: "And full-grown lambs loud bleat from hilly bourn."

Before the final line, Keats includes a couplet (this is the only Keatsian ode with two consecutive rhyming lines), referring to crickets singing and a robin whistling. A couplet often has a clinching effect, as if winning an argument, and here the effect is to override any intimations of concern with the satisfying low-key music of the robin before the ode ends with the twittering swallows.

Negative capability
Minutely recorded observations of nature are woven throughout "To Autumn." From the "vines that round the thatch-eves run" to the

A painting by British artist Joseph Severn (c. 1845) imagines Keats hearing the song of a nightingale, the vehicle for reflection in one of his other famous odes published in 1819.

"barred clouds" that "bloom the soft-dying day," Keats celebrates the beauty of nature and its ability to communicate ultimate truths. This formed part of Keats's unique concept of "negative capability"—the idea that beauty, wonder, and sensation can stir the imagination and be as informative and important as fact.

Nature is also used as a catalyst for introspection—a route into ruminations on life's hardships, pleasures, and uncertainties. In "To Autumn" it is the sights and sounds of the season that kindle contemplation. In "Ode to a Nightingale," birdsong has the same effect.

Keats's influence
After Keats, innumerable poets took up his themes of introspection inspired by nature and attempted to express them with Keatsian atmosphere and euphony. Alfred Tennyson's "Ode to Memory" (1830) is one of several early poems by him that show the influence clearly. However, the seasonal personifications and nature imagery of Victorian poets were not always as accurately observational, and often tended to be purely decorative rather than vehicles for self-examination.

From 1848, the Pre-Raphaelite poets, notably Dante Gabriel Rossetti and Christina Rossetti, brought a more authentic note to their treatments of nature. This carried through to the work of Thomas Hardy, Gerard Manley Hopkins, and W. B. Yeats, who all drew upon Keats's influence while creating an imaginative vision that was uniquely their own. ■

ENJOY, FRIENDS, TILL IT'S ENDED, / THIS LIGHT EXISTENCE, EVERY DRAM!

EUGENE ONEGIN (1833), ALEXANDER PUSHKIN

IN CONTEXT

FOCUS
Verse novel

OTHER KEY POETS
William Wordsworth, Lord Byron, Robert Browning, Elizabeth Barrett Browning, Vikram Seth

BEFORE
c. 1350s The Petrarchan sonnet rhyme scheme is popularized by Italian poet Francesco Petrarch.

1818 Lord Byron completes his long narrative poem *Childe Harold's Pilgrimage*.

AFTER
1834 Polish writer Adam Mickiewicz publishes his epic poem *Pan Tadeusz*, which describes a feud between two noble families.

1856 Elizabeth Barrett Browning completes *Aurora Leigh*, a nine-book novel in blank verse based on her own experiences as a writer.

A novel in verse, completed in 1833 by Russian writer Alexander Pushkin, *Eugene Onegin* proved ground-breaking in both its form and content. Epic poems have a long history in Western literature—one of the earliest, the *Epic of Gilgamesh*, dates from the 2nd millennium BCE. Pushkin's *Onegin* was a poem of epic length written specifically to be read, not listened to; and, unlike John Milton's *Paradise Lost*, it was recognizably a novel.

Onegin contained another Pushkin innovation—the "Onegin stanza" or "Pushkin sonnet." This verse form (a step on from the sonnet forms used by Shakespeare and Petrarch) featured a rhyme scheme of AbAbCCddEffEgg, where lower case letters denote stressed final syllables. This scheme varied the stresses and rhyme structure to suit the rhythms of Pushkin's own succinct yet flowing style as well as the Russian tongue.

A superfluous man

Pushkin's hero, Onegin, was so truthfully observed and recognizable that he became a recurring character type in 19th-century Russian fiction. He is earnest, noble, educated, and caring; but like Shakespeare's Hamlet, he is also caught in the pinch of indecision, uncertain when and how to act. In the agony of hesitation, life passes him by. Onegin is presented with love but turns it down; later, when he realizes its value, it is too late.

Other Russian writers, such as Ivan Turgenev (in *Diary of a Superfluous Man*, 1850), Leo Tolstoy (with the character Bezukhov in *War and Peace* 1865–1869), and Fyodor Dostoevsky (with Prince Myshkin in *The Idiot*, 1868–1869),

[…] With you I've known
The things that every poet covets:
Oblivion, when the tempest buffets,
Sweet talk of friends. […]
Eugene Onegin (Chapter VIII, stanza 50, lines 4–7)

See also: *The Odyssey* 24–31 ▪ Sonnet 1 62–63 ▪ Sonnet 130 88–93
▪ *Don Juan* 136–137 ▪ "How Do I Love Thee?" 150–151 ▪ *Omeros* 300–303

created similar versions of this character, who came to be known as the "superfluous man."

The object of Onegin's love, Tatyana, is an equally significant creation. Despite speaking French, she was taken by generations of readers to represent the true soul of Russia: in love with its countryside, idealistic, heartfelt, and self-sacrificing. Initially spurned by Onegin, she rejects him in turn when he at last falls for her, as she is already (albeit unhappily) married by then.

Innovative form

Pushkin's verse novel is not just a story of self-thwarted love: it is also playful, witty, and structurally daring. As much as a third of the narrative consists of digressions by the narrator (a sort of fictionalized Pushkin), as he discusses topics as varied as Russian folk tales, Greek myths, the state of the roads, and the impossibility of land reform. Just as the story seems to be coming to its melancholy conclusion, the novel suddenly stops. The romantic implication is that the story's narrator cannot bear to finish the tale.

Eugene Onegin cemented the importance of the verse novel as a genre, with examples written by William Wordsworth and both Elizabeth Barrett Browning and Robert Browning, among many others, during the 19th century. The form was not taken up by modernist poets, but its use steadily increased in the second half of the 20th century, with authors such as Vikram Seth popularizing it in his 1986 verse novel *The Golden Gate*. ▪

The duel scene in chapter VI of *Eugene Onegin* fascinated celebrated Russian artist Ilya Repin, who produced a number of versions, including this watercolor in 1899.

Alexander Pushkin

Born in Moscow, Russia, in 1799, Pushkin was the great-grandson of an enslaved African who found favor in the imperial court of Czar Peter the Great and rose to become a military general. Growing up among nobility, Pushkin had an excellent education at the new Imperial Lyceum near St. Petersburg. He was a prodigy, well known as a poet by his early twenties, but also exiled from the city owing to his poems' satirical and sacrilegious content, and his liberal views. Pushkin struggled with debt and a gambling addiction and was considered a troublemaker by Czar Alexander I. Although Pushkin had many literary successes, including plays and novels, his primary masterpiece was *Eugene Onegin*. However, by the time of its publication he was in dire financial straits and a victim of his own fiery temper. He reputedly fought 29 duels—and was killed in the last of them in 1837.

Other key works

1820 *Ruslan and Ludmila*
1831 *Boris Godunov*
1833 *Eugene Onegin*

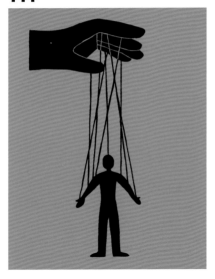

I GAVE COMMANDS; / THEN ALL SMILES STOPPED TOGETHER
"MY LAST DUCHESS" (1842), ROBERT BROWNING

IN CONTEXT

FOCUS
Dramatic monologue

OTHER KEY POETS
Elizabeth Barrett Browning, Alfred Tennyson, Christina Rossetti, T. S. Eliot, Elizabeth Bishop

BEFORE
1833 Tennyson composes "Ulysses," portraying the hero dealing with restlessness and aging after the Trojan War.

AFTER
1848 Elizabeth Barrett Browning publishes "The Runaway Slave at Pilgrim's Point," the monologue of an enslaved Black woman.

1915 "The Love Song of J. Alfred Prufrock," by T. S. Eliot, conveys the inner thoughts of a neurotic, repressed urban man.

1978 American poet Ai's "The Kid" is published, written in the voice of a 14-year-old boy who has killed his family.

From the 1840s, the dramatic monologue was a way of capturing in poetry the liveliness and essence of personality, as realistic novels by Charles Dickens and others were doing. Instead of the lyric "I" (usually the poet), the viewpoint is that of a character—real-life or fictional, contemporary or historic. A dramatic monologue is like a speech from a play, but there is no dialogue to provide context, only an imaginary, silent listener. The reader has to infer the speaker's situation and character from what they say. This is the source of the drama.

Dramatis personae

The master of this form was English poet Robert Browning, whose focus was the psychology of the speaker. Often presented in blank verse, his monologues adopt a rationalizing tone, as the protagonist presents a case or argument. Browning uses imaginative empathy to enter the thought processes of the subject. The reader, making deductions from clues given, uses their own imagination to understand the scenario. Some questions may remain unanswered, since the clues are often suggestive rather than definitive.

Browning's poem "My Last Duchess," is an example of his great skill and method. The subject was inspired by the fifth Duke of Ferrara (r. 1559–1597), whose young wife had died in suspicious

Lucrezia de' Medici, the Duchess of Ferrara, was 16 when she died. The official cause of death was tuberculosis but rumors suggested she had been poisoned on the orders of her husband.

See also: "Kubla Khan" 130–131 ▪ *In Memoriam A.H.H.* 148–149 ▪ "How Do I Love Thee?" 150–151 ▪ "Goblin Market" 161 ▪ *The Waste Land* 198–205

> ## Browning's dramatic monologues bring novelistic realism to poetry.

> The poet empathically inhabits **the mind of a flawed character**.

> This character is brought to life by **naturalistic speech** as he or she **presents a case** to an imaginary listener.

> The subject cannot help revealing their **moral failings or personal weaknesses** in the course of making their case.

Robert Browning

Born into a nonconformist household in Camberwell, London, in 1812, Robert Browning was the son of an abolitionist and book lover. An admirer of the Romantic poets, he followed Shelley in becoming an atheist and vegetarian. He studied Greek at University College, London, and lived with his family. His epic poem *Paracelsus*, on the Swiss physician and thinker, was praised by Tennyson after its publication in 1835.

In 1846, Browning married the renowned English poet Elizabeth Barrett. Until she died in 1861, the couple lived in Pisa and Florence, Italy, where he wrote the poems included in the collection *Men and Women*, which attracted few sales but is now admired. Back in London, Browning's reputation grew with *Dramatis Personae* and *The Ring and the Book*. A Liberal who supported the emancipation of women, he died in 1889.

Other key works

1842 *Dramatic Lyrics*
1855 *Men and Women*
1864 *Dramatis Personae*
1868–1869 *The Ring and the Book*

circumstances. The first line of the poem establishes the context: a duke is showing someone a painting of his "last duchess," now deceased. He points out the "spot of joy" in the woman's cheek and tells his unknown auditor that she was susceptible to flattery, from the painter and others. "Her looks went everywhere" carries an undercurrent of jealousy, which shifts to derision at her lack of discrimination. This quickly changes to resentment, "as if she ranked / My gift of a nine-hundred-years-old name / With anybody's gift." The proud duke explains he did not "stoop" to chastise her. Downstairs waits the count whose daughter the duke intends to marry for her dowry. Finally, another artwork is pointed out: a bronze of Neptune taming a seahorse, commissioned by the duke. The sea god's subjection of this wild creature is an implicit metaphor of the man's ruthlessness.

Damaged personalities

The poem's impact comes from the sense that it represents unguarded conversational speech. Enjambment and iambic pentameter create this naturalistic effect; but rhyming couplets also give structure, hinting at the cold, controlling personality of the duke. That this possessiveness has led him to kill his wife is implied by his delivery of the chilling phrase, "Then all smiles stopped together."

Browning's other monologues include "Porphyria's Lover," which muses on murder as a route to absolute possession. The poet reveled in portraying damaged, vicious personalities, rendered with irony and dark humor. ▪

DREAMING DREAMS NO MORTAL EVER DARED TO DREAM BEFORE

"THE RAVEN" (1845), EDGAR ALLAN POE

IN CONTEXT

FOCUS
American Gothic

OTHER KEY POETS
**Elizabeth Barrett Browning
Charles Baudelaire, Emily
Dickinson, Allen Ginsberg**

BEFORE
1798 American writer Charles
Brockden Brown imports the
European craze for Gothic
stories into the US when he
publishes his novel *Wieland*.

1843 Edgar Allan Poe's
"Lenore" features a young man
hoping to meet his dead lover
in Paradise—a dream that will
occur in "The Raven."

AFTER
1846 Dark themes feature in
Mosses From an Old Manse,
short stories by Nathaniel
Hawthorne, the other major
writer of American Gothic.

1890 Emily Dickinson's *Poems*
includes works on Gothic
themes, especially mortality.

What has been called
American Gothic or
Dark Romanticism in
American literature flourished
during the early to mid-19th century.
Largely expressed in fiction, in
somber tales of sin, death, and
horror, the movement was rooted
in earlier Romantic preoccupations
with portraying human experience.
However, American Gothic rejected
the idealist and spiritual aspirations
of Romanticism.

The genre's central figure, Edgar
Allan Poe, was as much a poet as
he was a writer of macabre stories.

'The Raven" is perhaps his most
famous, and quotable, poem. It took
the reading public by storm when
it was published in the February
1845 issue of the *American Review*.
It was not only the morbid subject
matter of the poem—the story of
a scholar's descent into madness
after the death of his beloved—that
captured the public's imagination,
but the manner of the poem's
execution, which is as much
parodied as it is admired nearly
two centuries later.

Dark mood and content
The tale begins "upon a midnight
dreary" when a scholar, dozing off
while reading, hears knocking at
his door. The atmosphere gets eerier
when no one appears to be there.
Then a raven enters by the window.
An omen of loss straight out of the
deep well of mythology, the bird
introduces characteristically Gothic
elements—the supernatural and a
sense of foreboding. A crescendo
of grief builds as the scholar

The home setting of "The Raven"
is typical of American Gothic poetry and
prose, which often portray psychological
terror within mundane events and
everyday surroundings.

See also: "Kubla Khan" 130–131 ▪ "How Do I Love Thee?" 150–151 ▪ "To the Reader" 162–165
▪ "Because I Could Not Stop for Death" 168–169

Edgar Allan Poe

Born in Boston in 1809, Edgar Allan Poe had a short and often unhappy life. Orphaned by the age of two, he was fostered in Richmond, Virginia, where he began writing poetry in his early teenage years. Despite excelling at the University of Virginia, he was forced to leave because of a lack of financial support, and later failed to complete military training at West Point academy.

From 1831, Poe turned to writing full time, supporting himself with a series of jobs on literary journals. In 1835, he moved to New York and became editor of the *Southern Literary Messenger.* Poe's creative output was dazzling, and he is credited with inventing the detective genre, and influencing science fiction and modern horror. The cause of his death in Baltimore in 1849, after being found delirious, remains a mystery.

Other key works

1827 *Tamerlane and Other Poems*
1831 "To Helen"
1843 "Lenore"
1849 "Annabel Lee"

questions the raven, which perches on a bust of Pallas Athene, the Greek goddess of wisdom. To all questions, including whether the scholar will be reunited with his beloved in heaven, the bird gives the answer: "Nevermore."

This word—the short refrain to each stanza—is the thematic key to the poem. It encapsulates the finality and anguish of loss, and represents the sinister, self-destructive, and pessimistic concerns of American Gothic writing, which sought to expose darker truths.

Original form

The raven's chant-like refrain is also integral to building tension and mood in the poem. All 18 stanzas have an abcbbb rhyme scheme— the last "b" being "Nevermore," the linchpin of the entire structure. The scheme is further complicated by internal rhymes ornamented by alliteration. The poem's meter, a trochaic octameter (eight two-beat feet per line, interleaved with six two-beat feet per line) provides a haunting, musical quality.

Poe records in his 1846 essay "The Philosophy of Composition" that his aims in "The Raven" were to achieve originality of form and to communicate the "effect" of beauty, which he believed was most truthfully expressed through "melancholy"—"the most legitimate of all the poetical tones." His success is evidenced by his influence on the writers of the later Symbolist and Surrealist movements, who seized on his journeys into the darker side of the human subconscious, and his use of symbol and expressive form, as inspiration for their own works. ▪

Poe's raven, which would become a trope in its own right, blazed a trail in the use of symbols to express emotional truths in the real world while recalling mythological associations.

Deep into that darkness peering, long I stood there wondering, fearing,
Doubting, dreaming dreams no mortal ever dared to dream before […]
"The Raven" (lines 25–26)

'TIS BETTER TO HAVE LOVED AND LOST

IN MEMORIAM A.H.H. (1850), ALFRED TENNYSON

IN CONTEXT

FOCUS
Elegy

OTHER KEY POETS
John Milton, Percy Bysshe Shelley, Walt Whitman, Paul Laurence Dunbar, W. H. Auden

BEFORE
1638 John Milton publishes *Lycidas*, an elegy written for his friend Edward King, who drowned in the Irish Sea.

1821 *Adonais*, Percy Bysshe Shelley's 55-stanza elegy to his fellow British poet John Keats, is published.

AFTER
1940 "In Memory of W. B. Yeats" is one of a number of elegies in the collection *Another Time* by British-American poet W. H. Auden.

1981 British poet Tony Harrison publishes "Time," an elegy in 16-line sonnet form, written on the death and cremation of his mother.

British poet Alfred Tennyson wrote *In Memoriam A.H.H.*, an extended elegy of 131 cantos, bookended by a prologue and an epilogue, over the course of 17 years. It was prompted by the sudden death in 1833 of his dearest friend, Arthur Hallam. Aged 22, Hallam had died of a brain aneurysm while traveling in continental Europe with his father.

An 1882 cartoon from *Punch* magazine portrays Tennyson as "Alfred the Great," mocking the poet's preoccupation with medieval subjects, such as the Arthurian legends.

The shock to Tennyson was extreme. The men had met as undergraduates at Cambridge University, and the bond between them was intense.

The elegiac form

Tennyson's poem draws on a long poetic tradition, dating back to the *elegos* ("song of mourning") of ancient Greece. Greek elegies were written in elegiac couplets—one line of six feet, followed by a line of five—and could be applied to a variety of subjects, including love and war, as well as death.

By the 16th century, in English literature, the elegy had become solely a lament, usually about a significant individual, in verse not confined to any particular meter. Some of the greatest elegies, including John Milton's *Lycidas* (1638) and Percy Bysshe Shelley's *Adonais* (1821), use a pastoral setting, where the narrator and deceased subject are both cast as shepherds in a rural idyll.

Ambitious work

Tennyson drew on the structure of the pastoral elegy, including its progress through expressions of grief, mourning, and praise to

See also: *Paradise Lost* 102–109 ▪ "I Wandered Lonely as a Cloud" 126–129 ▪ "To Autumn" 138–141 ▪ "My Last Duchess" 144–145 ▪ *The Waste Land* 198–205 ▪ "The First Elegy" 206 ▪ *Poem Without a Hero* 265 ▪ "Casualty" 290–293

transcendent resolution, but he used radical changes of style, from the lyrical to the everyday. In the seventh canto, the poet imagines himself haunting London's Wimpole Street, where the Hallam family lived. Here are the doors "where my heart was used to beat / So quickly, waiting for a hand, // A hand that can be clasp'd no more—." Bereft, the poet stands outside the house, where "ghastly thro' the drizzling rain / On the bald street breaks the blank day."

Beyond the shifting moods and anguish of a specific grief, Tennyson used *In Memoriam* to reflect on the spiritually disorienting developments within Victorian society. Advances in science and industry were shaking the foundations of Christian values, raising concerns about the immortality of the soul, faith in God, and the place of humanity in the universe. In the 56th canto, he depicts the Christian believer doggedly trusting that God is "love indeed / And love Creation's final law—,"

> My Arthur, whom I shall not see
> Till all my widow'd race be run;
> Dear as the mother to the son,
> More than my brothers are to me.
> **In Memoriam A.H.H. (canto IX, verse 5)**

while "Nature, red in tooth and claw / With ravine, shriek'd against his creed—."

To weave the poem sequence together, Tennyson used the same stanza form throughout—four eight-syllable lines, rhyming abba, now known as the *In Memoriam* stanza. The rhyme scheme creates a succession of tightly controlled closed stanzas that form a series of steps, like grief itself, toward understanding and acceptance.

Fluctuating fortunes

Tennyson was 40 when *In Memoriam* was published. His earlier collections had included some of his finest poetry, such as "The Lady of Shalott" (1832) and "Ulysses" (1842), but had failed to draw overwhelming praise. The impact of *In Memoriam*, however, was electric, bringing him popular and critical acclaim in a year when he also became British Poet Laureate. His became the resounding poetic voice of Victorian England, interweaving notes of yearning, melancholy, and beauty in works such as *Idylls of the King* (1859–1885), about the legends of King Arthur, and "Crossing the Bar," an elegy written when he was 80.

Tennyson's reputation dipped at the end of his life, but there have been many subsequent admirers, including T. S. Eliot, who revered his matchless command of poetic form, imagery, and the music of language. ∎

Alfred Tennyson

Born the son of an Anglican rector in 1809, at Somersby, Lincolnshire, UK, Alfred Tennyson attended the University of Cambridge from 1827. There he joined the Apostles, an elite intellectual society, and published his first volume of poetry, *Poems, Chiefly Lyrical*. When his father died in 1831, leaving debts, Tennyson had to quit Cambridge without earning his degree.

Although his life remained unsettled over the next decade, Tennyson received praise for his 1842 two-volume collection *Poems* and achieved some financial security in 1845 when the UK government granted him a £200 annual pension. Queen Victoria's husband, Prince Albert, was an admirer and in 1850 campaigned for Tennyson to succeed William Wordsworth as Poet Laureate. In 1884, Tennyson accepted a peerage, as Baron (Lord) Tennyson, and he remained Poet Laureate until his death, in 1892.

Other key works

1830 *Poems, Chiefly Lyrical*
1842 *Poems*
1855 *Maud, and Other Poems*

HOW DO I LOVE THEE? LET ME COUNT THE WAYS

"HOW DO I LOVE THEE?" (1850), ELIZABETH BARRETT BROWNING

IN CONTEXT

FOCUS
Love sonnet sequence

OTHER KEY POETS
Petrarch, Edmund Spenser, William Shakespeare, Anne Bradstreet, John Keats, Pablo Neruda

BEFORE
1591 Philip Sidney's *Astrophel and Stella*, a series of 108 Petrarchan sonnets, is published posthumously.

1609 Shakespeare publishes *Sonnets*, a collection of love sonnets believed to be inspired by various men and women.

AFTER
1862 English writer George Meredith's *Modern Love* subverts the sonnet sequence's amatory tradition, instead detailing a failing marriage.

1959 *One Hundred Love Sonnets*, by Chilean poet Pablo Neruda, is dedicated to his wife Matilde Urrutia.

After Petrarch popularized the sonnet in the 14th century, the love sonnet sequence became a popular poetic form during the Renaissance period, when writers such as Shakespeare and his fellow English poet Philip Sidney wrote a series of poems for a loved one or muse. Though the sonnet sequence gradually fell out of favor, the stand-alone sonnet became popular among Romantic writers, including William Wordsworth and John Keats.

The poet particularly credited with reviving the love sonnet sequence is Elizabeth Barrett Browning. The success of her *Sonnets from the Portuguese*, published in 1850, made her one of the most celebrated love poets in history. She was already famous when the sequence of 44 sonnets was written between 1845 and 1846, while she and her future husband, Robert Browning, were courting. Originally, the poet had

no intention of making the collection available to the public, but after she gifted the collection to Robert in 1849, he insisted on publishing the poems. In an attempt to hide their intimate and personal nature she pretended that they were merely translations from Portuguese originals.

Evolving relationship

Over the course of the sonnet sequence, Barrett Browning explores the couple's evolving relationship. Already 40 and suffering from various health issues, she was initially unsure about Robert Browning's advances, and this is reflected in the early poems. By the end of the sequence, however, she has fully embraced their love.

The penultimate poem in the sequence, "How Do I Love Thee?," is considered one of the world's great love poems. In the sonnet, she describes the intensity of her

> I love thee to the depth and breadth and height
> My soul can reach [...]
> **"How Do I Love Thee?" (lines 2–3)**

See also: Fragment 31 32–33 ▪ Sonnet 1 62–63 ▪ Sonnet 130 88–93
▪ "To My Dear and Loving Husband" 100 ▪ "To Autumn" 138–141

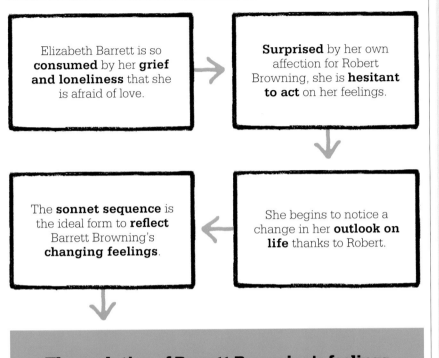

Elizabeth Barrett is so **consumed** by her **grief and loneliness** that she is afraid of love.

Surprised by her own affection for Robert Browning, she is **hesitant to act** on her feelings.

She begins to notice a change in her **outlook on life** thanks to Robert.

The **sonnet sequence** is the ideal form to **reflect** Barrett Browning's **changing feelings**.

The evolution of Barrett Browning's feelings is expressed in a love sonnet sequence.

Elizabeth Barrett Browning

Born in County Durham, UK, in 1806, Elizabeth Barrett was the eldest of 12 children. As the owners of plantations in Jamaica, the family lived comfortably during the poet's childhood. She had a classical education, learning Greek at the age of 11. In 1819, Barrett finished her first major poem, "The Battle of Marathon," which her father privately published the following year as a birthday present. Two years later, she fell sick with an illness that would have a lasting impact on her health.

Elizabeth published her first poetry collection in 1833. Three years later, she met William Wordsworth, who remained a close friend until his death. After her marriage to Robert Browning in 1846, the couple moved to Florence, Italy. In 1861, she died at Casa Guidi, their Italian home.

Other key works

1838 *The Seraphim, and Other Poems*
1847 "The Runaway Slave at Pilgrim's Point"
1856 *Aurora Leigh*

love for Robert, listing the ways in which she adores him. Through the anaphora (repetition) "I love thee" and sublime imagery, Barrett Browning presents their love as transcendental and all-consuming.

A woman's voice

The poem follows the typical Petrarchan rhyme scheme: it begins with an octave rhyming abbaabba, followed by a sestet rhyming cdcdcd. What separates Barrett Browning's sonnets from her predecessors' is the female voice. Women were typically the silent object of the sonnet, but here Barrett Browning is the speaker—her female gaze directed toward her husband.

Throughout the love sonnet sequence, Barrett Browning reckons with her own mortality and her history of loss and suffering. She initially turned to the sonnet form to process the grief she felt after her favorite brother, Edward, drowned in a sailing accident in 1840, not long after another brother had died. In "How Do I Love Thee?," she again acknowledges this profound loss in the lines "I love thee with the passion put to use / In my old griefs." And while she recognizes her own close proximity to death, the final lines of the poem suggest that she no longer fears it: "and, if God choose, / I shall but love thee better after death." ▪

I CELEBRATE MYSELF, AND SING MYSELF

"SONG OF MYSELF" (1855),
WALT WHITMAN

ANTANTO

IN CONTEXT

FOCUS
Free verse

OTHER KEY POETS
William Carlos Williams, Ezra Pound, T. S. Eliot, Allen Ginsberg, Adrienne Rich, Audre Lorde

BEFORE
1759–1763 English poet Christopher Smart writes *Jubilate Agno* (*Rejoice in the Lamb*), a 1,200-line free-verse poem with many lines starting "For" or "Let."

AFTER
1886 The French *vers libre* ("free verse") movement takes off with the foundation of the literary journal *La Vogue*.

1914 American poet Amy Lowell publishes the collection *Sword Blades and Poppy Seed*, featuring experiments with free verse and "polyphonic prose."

Traditionally, poetry in the English language is mostly structured by adherence to a regular pattern of meter and, usually, rhyme. Together, these two elements set up the "music" of a poem. A further organizing principle is stanzaic structure—there can be any number of stanzas, but each tends to have the same number of lines, like verses in a song. When poets such as John Milton (for example, in *Paradise Lost*) opted for blank verse instead of rhyming, they relied on iambic pentameter to create a strong rhythm of stresses (formed by the arrangement of syllables).

Speech rhythms

Free verse abandons traditional metrical conventions. Instead, it often follows natural or rhetorical speech rhythms for its musical impact. When particular words or phrases recur in free verse, they create a series of echoes that often give the poem a chanting, incantatory, or declamatory feel.

Unlike prose, free verse has fixed line endings. There are often line spaces, too, to signal to the reader where brief pauses occur.

[…] all language is vehicular and transitive, and is good, as ferries and horses are, for conveyance, not as farms and houses are, for homestead.
Ralph Waldo Emerson
"The Poet" in ***Essays: Second Series*, 1844**

The effect of these spaces is to create a set of "strophes," or sense units, which differ from stanzas in being of variable length. Free verse holds the reader's attention by creating musicality through the flow of sounds. One influence on the rhythms of English free verse was Bible translations, beginning with John Wycliffe's translations of the Psalms (1382–1395). The King James Version Bible (KJV) of 1611, which reached the US in 1630,

Walt Whitman

Born in 1819, on Long Island, New York, and brought up in Brooklyn, Walt Whitman was influenced by his father's Deism (rational theology that maintains religious truth should be subject to the authority of human reason) and by Quakerism. Whitman left school at 11 and had no further formal education. He worked as a newspaper compositor, traveling teacher, and journalist. As editor of the *Brooklyn Eagle* he campaigned against slavery.

In 1855, Whitman self-published *Leaves of Grass*. Ralph Waldo Emerson wrote: "I greet you at the beginning of a great career." Others were less positive, some denouncing the book's sexual content and egotism.

Whitman met Peter Doyle, the great love of his life, in 1865, and Doyle nursed him after his stroke in 1873. Whitman moved to Camden, New Jersey in 1874. He died there in 1892.

Other key works

1855 *Leaves of Grass*
1865 *Drum-Taps*
1891–1892 *Leaves of Grass* ("deathbed edition")

See also: "Psalm 57" 81 ▪ "The Road Not Taken" 182–187 ▪ *The Waste Land* 198–205 ▪ "The Sparrow" 216–217 ▪ Canto LXXXI 232–235 ▪ "Howl" 246–253

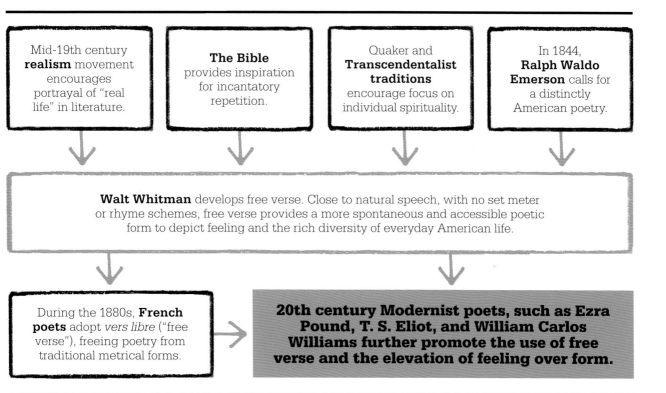

Mid-19th century **realism** movement encourages portrayal of "real life" in literature.

The Bible provides inspiration for incantatory repetition.

Quaker and **Transcendentalist traditions** encourage focus on individual spirituality.

In 1844, **Ralph Waldo Emerson** calls for a distinctly American poetry.

Walt Whitman develops free verse. Close to natural speech, with no set meter or rhyme schemes, free verse provides a more spontaneous and accessible poetic form to depict feeling and the rich diversity of everyday American life.

During the 1880s, **French poets** adopt *vers libre* ("free verse"), freeing poetry from traditional metrical forms.

20th century Modernist poets, such as Ezra Pound, T. S. Eliot, and William Carlos Williams further promote the use of free verse and the elevation of feeling over form.

exerted a powerful influence on American English and on specific American and British writers. Emily Dickinson's poetry and letters are scattered with allusions to the books of Genesis, Isaiah, Deuteronomy, and Revelation, and the Gospels, as well as the Psalms.

Walt Whitman also used the KJV Bible as his model for a characteristic style of free verse suited to his overall purpose: to convey the spirit of the United States as a nation, with all its unity and variety, as well as the miracle of life itself.

A celebration of joy

Leaves of Grass was Whitman's great work. He devoted his writing life to revising and reordering the collection in a succession of editions from 1855 to the much

longer "deathbed edition" of 1891–1892, which included around 400 poems. The book's longest and best known poem is "Song of Myself" (though that title was given only in the last edition). It is an uplifting celebration, in 1,336 lines, of the body and soul at ease, the equality and nobility of all human beings, the joy of the senses, and the miracle of nature. It sees death as a natural process that we should accept without fear as an essential component of life's cycles. Absorbed into nature at death—into the earth on which fresh grass grows—we attain earthly immortality.

God is given only a light presence in "Song of Myself," although Whitman describes how he leaves his signature on creation. Grass is "the flag of my

disposition, out of hopeful green stuff woven," but it is also "the handkerchief of the Lord."

American literary critic Harold Bloom called *Leaves of Grass* part of the "secular scripture" of the US. In his 1844 essay "The Poet," Whitman's fellow poet Ralph Waldo Emerson underlined the importance of forging a distinctively American style of poetry. "America," he wrote, "is a poem in our eyes; its ample geography dazzles the imagination, and it will not wait long for meters." Whitman provided the US with a style of long-line free verse that was unconstricted, and therefore capable of expressing the American sense of infinite potential for human fulfillment.

According to American writer Horace Traubel, Whitman once said: "The prairies typify America—our » land—these States—democracy— freedom, expanse, vista, magnificence, sweep, hospitality." The last seven words can be seen as keynotes for "Song of Myself." The "freedom," "expanse," "vista," and "sweep" reflect the form of the poem: free verse with long lines. "Democracy" and "hospitality" are found partly in the poem's content, but the long lines contribute to these values, too—they allow ample space within the poem for representations of Americans of all kinds, engaged in a range of activities, throughout the nation. Whitman is hospitable to all—virtuous and reprobate, male and female, enslaved and free. He is also hospitable to the reader: the ending of "Song of Myself" is one of the most inclusively welcoming in all poetry: "I stop somewhere waiting for you."

Purposeful repetition
One feature that gives "Song of Myself" its distinctive character is the rhetorical device of anaphora, the repetition of phrases at the start of neighboring clauses. In traditional rhetoric, anaphora is used for both emphasis and structure; in Whitman its use is purely structural. Often just one or two words are repeated, for example, in section 2, "Have you" (three times) and "You shall" (four). There are also many repetitions elsewhere in sentences, often overlapping: "I have heard what the talkers were talking, the talk of the beginning and the end, / But I do not talk of the beginning or the end." And 13 lines after this: "Clear and sweet is my soul, and clear and sweet is all that is not my soul." The technical term for repetition at the end of consecutive clauses is epistrophe. Whitman typically combines repetition and antithesis (particularly positive with negative) to create a unifying soundscape that reinforces the poem's impact. It is skillfully handled—always apparent but never tiresome, lifting the reader on the musical flow, like waves washing over a shore.

Folk of America
One anaphora Whitman frequently uses in "Song of Myself" is the definite or indefinite article, "The" or "A," especially to anchor a list. In section 15, for example, there are 55 instances of "The" starting a new line and clause, mostly in a list of people engaged in particular activities, from "The pure contralto sings in the organ loft" to "The old husband sleeps by his wife and the young husband sleeps by his wife." In

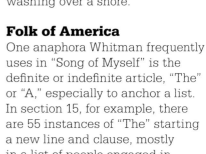

A 19th-century woodcut of a farmer praying for rain. Strong empathy for those—like farmers—who toiled hard for little reward runs through much of Whitman's poetry.

> And the secret of it all is, to write in the gush, the throb, the flood, of the moment [...] I always worked that way [...] By writing at the instant the very heart-beat of life is caught.
> **Walt Whitman**
> **July 1888**

between is a roster of different kinds of people: "carpenter," "children," "pilot," "mate" of a "whale-boat," "duck-shooter," "deacons," "spinning-girl," "farmer," "printer," "machinist," "conductor," "bride," and so on.

In presenting his mosaic of the whole spectrum of human activity, Whitman is re-creating and honoring America's teeming population, mostly without commentary. Occasionally,

however, he suggests where his sympathies might lie, clarifying his empathetic viewpoint. His description of "The lunatic" carried to the asylum, for example, is followed by a poignant vignette of past well-being that interrupts the anaphoric list: "(He will never sleep any more as he did in the cot in his mother's bed-room.)" Another sympathetic interruption comes after the sex worker is mentioned in the list: the crowd is laughing at her oaths and men are jeering at her, but Whitman exclaims in parentheses, addressing the woman directly, "(Miserable! I do not laugh at your oaths nor jeer you;)."

Echoes and contrasts within Whitman's list of human types enhance the poetry. For example, the bride who "unrumples" her white dress is linked with the sex worker who, two lines later "draggles" her shawl. In between comes the opium eater reclining "with rigid head," in contrast with the sex worker's bonnet bobbing on her "tipsy and pimpled neck." Such small visual connections are slender filaments in the poem's connective web, as well

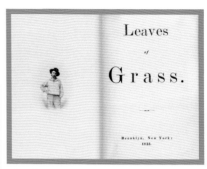

The first edition of *Leaves of Grass* was published in 1855 and contained just 12 poems. Whitman's last revision of the collection had more than 400.

as being symbolic of Whitman's sympathetic identification with all of humanity.

Selves and souls
The first edition of *Leaves of Grass* did not include the author's name on the title page; instead, an engraving of Whitman, bearded, tieless, in slanted hat and work clothes, served as a frontispiece. This was the persona of a proletarian bard that Whitman artfully cultivated. In section 24 of "Song of Myself" he provides a matching self-portrait in words: "Walt Whitman, a kosmos, of Manhattan the son, / Turbulent, fleshy, sensual, eating, drinking and breeding, / No sentimentalist, no stander above men and women or apart from them, / No more modest than immodest."

Available to all
The paradoxical assertion of democratic unpretentiousness and abundant self-esteem lies at the heart of "Song of Myself." In cataloging his powers, Whitman donates them to all. In love with the world, he introduces it to his readers like a matchmaker. He reassures them that all that matters—"the good of the earth »

The body and sex

Championing love in all its forms, Whitman was criticized for his sexual explicitness in *Leaves of Grass*. But the "Calamus" poems added in the 1860 edition, which celebrate "the manly love of comrades," did not attract the criticism directed at even mild treatments of heterosexual coupling. It was perceived as merely same gender affection, which was socially acceptable.

Whitman saw candid nudity as healthy, in art and life, but he hated pornography and lewdness. Honest acceptance of the body and its functions led, among other things, to equal valuation of men and women. He had sympathy for the Free Love movement of the time but did not accept its view that marriage was akin to legalized sex work. In Whitman's 1860 poem entitled "To a Common Prostitute," he expressed sympathy with those forced by poverty to sell their bodies: "Not till the sun excludes you do I exclude you."

> The bride unrumples her white dress, the minute-hand of the clock
>   moves slowly,
> The opium-eater reclines with rigid head and just-open'd lips [...]
> **"Song of Myself" (15, lines 40–41)**

and sun"—is readily available to himself and to them. His all-powerful "I" transcends limitation— "I [...] am not contain'd between my hat and boots"—and contains everyone within itself, like a universal spirit: "I am large, I contain multitudes". Every individual (symbolized as every leaf) expresses the whole (the grass).

Split identities

Whitman separates himself into three kinds of identity in "Song of Myself": my everyday self; my "real me" (or "Me myself"); and my soul. Least comprehensible is the soul, which requires a leap of faith to acknowledge its existence. It is part of nature, whereas "Me myself" goes back to the world's beginnings. The "I" of the poem juggles these ideas with apparent dexterity, but in fact there are philosophical enigmas that take many readings to recognize fully. Critics are divided on the meanings of Whitman's "I" in its various versions, and on the specific underlying ideas about selfhood.

However, Whitman's deepest self was not spirit alone, but a fusion of body (individual) and spirit (universal). The reader is told in section 3 of "Song of Myself" that "the unseen is proved by the seen, / Till that becomes unseen and receives proof in its turn." In other words, the tangible world has its own mystery, reflected back from the spiritual world, whose outward manifestation we perceive it as being.

In section 43 of "Song of Myself," Whitman touches upon the major religions, accepting their practices. Elsewhere he imagines himself crucified, with a crown of thorns. However, he was not preoccupied by either ritual or divinity: "And I say to mankind, Be not curious about God." Instead, he found inspiration in science—for example, 19th-century German scientist Justus von Liebig's ideas about chemical transformation in natural cycles. The poem's third line, "For every atom belonging to me as good belongs to you," hints at the natural immortality that such transformations might imply.

There are also strong Eastern overtones in the philosophical ideas informing the poem, though there is no evidence that Whitman had read Eastern mystical writings,

> It was then and is now an astonishment, perhaps the most unprecedented poem in the English language. It is also an important document in the history of American culture.
> **Robert Hass**
> **Former US Poet Laureate (1941–)**

and in some ways his thought processes were very different from the Indian sages. The notion of a deep self that shares its essence with the universal spirit echoes the *atman* ("self" in Sanskrit) of Eastern thought. However, he never entertains the Hindu concept that the world of the senses, and the cycle of births and deaths, are merely *maya*, or illusion. He did not believe in the idea of subjugating the senses, but in ecstatic union ("merge," as he called it) through surrender to the senses. Direct experience was valued over scholarship or other secondhand encounters.

It is likely that the poetry in "Song of Myself" stems from a personal mystical experience, perhaps the one that he describes in section 5, when he is saturated with "the peace and knowledge that pass all the argument of the earth." He discovers that "the spirit of God is the brother of my own"— and that "a kelson of the creation is love" (a kelson is the upper part of a boat's keel, conferring strength).

Heightened imagination

Whatever the source of Whitman's mystic experience, it turned him into a seer. It freed his imagination to encompass Earth and the heavens in fantastic flights, while never losing touch with ordinary American folk. On the one hand, he soared: "Speeding through space, speeding through heaven and the stars, / Speeding amid the seven satellites and the broad

Whitman's selves
The poet embraces a number of dualities of self in his poem: body—soul; individual—universal; actual—metaphysical; finite—infinite; and "I"—"kosmos".

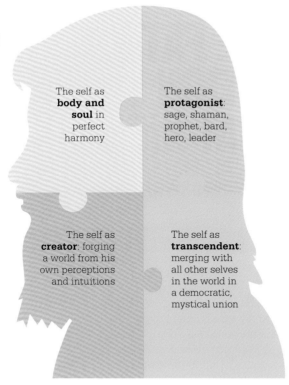

The self as **body and soul** in perfect harmony

The self as **protagonist**: sage, shaman, prophet, bard, hero, leader

The self as **creator**: forging a world from his own perceptions and intuitions

The self as **transcendent**: merging with all other selves in the world in a democratic, mystical union

Whitman and Lincoln

From the beginning of the Civil War (1861–1865), Whitman had great regard for President Abraham Lincoln. He was happy that "the commonest average of life," as he put it, had gained high office, becoming "the greatest, best, most characteristic, artistic, moral personality" in American life. He saw Lincoln's assassination in 1865 as a landmark in the shaping of the Republic.

Whitman's two elegies for the president are markedly different: "O Captain! My Captain" is formally traditional, with meter and rhyme, while "When Lilacs Last in the Dooryard Bloom'ed" is in free verse. In "Lilacs," Whitman drops his persona of all-knowing sage and focuses on death and the deceased, perceived as the "western star" (the planet Venus), mourned by the wood thrush, singing with "bleeding throat." The lilacs symbolize rebirth, Venus denotes Lincoln as immortal, and the singing thrush stands for Whitman himself. All three at the end of the poem are "twined with the chant of my soul, / There in the fragrant pines and the cedars dusk and dim."

A ticket to the lecture given by Whitman in Philadelphia on the 15th anniversary of the assassination of Abraham Lincoln.

ring, and the diameter of eighty thousand miles [...]." On the other, he brought into his poem "The mayor and councils, banks, tariffs, steamships, factories, stocks, stores, real estate and personal estate." The long lines of free verse gave him space to exercise his heightened imaginative vision to the fullest.

The free verse era

Whitman's free verse had an immense influence on subsequent poets. In the 1930s, Robert Frost commented that free verse was like "playing tennis without a net." For many poets, a rhyme scheme and regular meter act as a catalyst for the imagination, sending poetry in unexpected and rewarding directions. However, from Whitman onward, free verse established itself as a mainstream tradition. The poetry of T. S. Eliot

and Ezra Pound, for example, is indebted to Whitman. Eliot argued that fluidity in poetry was necessary to mirror the fast-changing, fluid nature of the modern world.

For many writers, free verse also seemed a prerequisite for sincerity in self-exploration. William Carlos Williams showed how formal freedom could be combined with a concise mode of expression. The old formal structures seemed to some to be authoritarian—an uncomfortable link with society's status quo. Allen Ginsberg's "Howl" (1956) is self-consciously Whitmanesque in its long, loping lines. A little more than a decade later, American poet C. K. Williams developed his characteristic long line and complex syntax. Simon J. Ortiz and Martín Espada are more recent American heirs of the "father of free verse." ∎

THE FATE OF A NATION WAS RIDING THAT NIGHT
"PAUL REVERE'S RIDE" (1861), HENRY WADSWORTH LONGFELLOW

IN CONTEXT

FOCUS
Fireside poetry

OTHER KEY POETS
**Edgar Allan Poe,
Walt Whitman, Emily
Dickinson, Robert Frost**

BEFORE
1821 In the US, William Cullen Bryant publishes the final version of "Thanatopsis"—Greek for "a view of death"—a meditation on mortality and "the love of Nature."

1837 American poet Ralph Waldo Emerson writes the "Concord Hymn" for the dedication of the Battle of Concord monument.

AFTER
1865 Walt Whitman writes "O Captain! My Captain!" in response to the assassination of President Abraham Lincoln in Washington, D.C.

1900 Longfellow is inducted into the Hall of Fame for Great Americans in New York City.

A merican poet Henry Wadsworth Longfellow's romantic account of "the midnight ride of Paul Revere" at the start of the American Revolution in 1775 is a celebration of action at a founding moment in a nation's history. Revere—historically a Boston silversmith—briefs a friend to keep watch for British troop movements and signal any activity. The friend sees British soldiers and alerts Revere who then gallops into the night to warn the American patriots in the towns of Lexington and Concord. The next day, the Americans drive back the British.

Warming the nation
The historical facts of Revere's ride are not quite as Longfellow described them, but the poet,

writing on the eve of the Civil War (1861–1865), wanted to create an inspiring national legend rather than a historic document. The author of hugely popular works, such as *The Song of Hiawatha* (1855), Longfellow was the first American poet to win major national and international acclaim, and along with American contemporaries such as William Cullen Bryant and James Russell Lowell was known as one of the "fireside poets." Their work, based on traditional values and written in conventional, easily recitable forms, found a natural home in middle-class domestic settings. Longfellow's reputation suffered from 20th-century criticism, but nothing diminishes the beauty of his finest work, including his 1867 translation of Dante's *The Divine Comedy*. ∎

A cry of defiance, and not of fear,—
A voice in the darkness, a knock at the door,
And a word that shall echo forevermore!
"Paul Revere's Ride" (lines 116–118)

See also: *The Divine Comedy* 58–61 ▪ "The Raven" 146–147 ▪ "Song of Myself" 152–159 ▪ "Because I Could Not Stop for Death" 168–169 ▪ "The Road Not Taken" 182–187

FRUITS LIKE HONEY TO THE THROAT / BUT POISON IN THE BLOOD

"GOBLIN MARKET" (1862), CHRISTINA ROSSETTI

C omposed in 1859, when British poet Christina Rossetti was 28, and published three years later, "Goblin Market" is a 567-line narrative tale of temptation, sacrifice, and redemption. Two young sisters, Laura and Lizzie, are offered seemingly irresistible fruit by male goblin merchants. Lizzie resists: the goblins' "offers should not charm us," she declares, their "evil gifts would harm us." But the more susceptible Laura succumbs. She tastes the goblin fruit and loses the zest for ordinary life. Deserted by the merchants and deprived of the fruit, she drifts toward death, saved only by her sister.

Breaking the pattern

In much of her poetry, Rossetti is a stickler for formal regularity, but in "Goblin Market" she permits herself an exuberant irregularity. Lines vary in length, rhyming patterns change constantly, meter shifts, and lists abound, packing in image after image to create an almost hallucinatory effect.

A chalk drawing from 1877 shows Christina Rossetti (left) with her mother, Frances Mary Lavinia Rossetti. The artist was Christina's brother, Pre-Raphaelite Dante Gabriel Rossetti.

By the time of her death, in 1894, Rossetti was one of Britain's most popular poets, talked of as a potential Poet Laureate. Her reputation suffered in the Modernist backlash against the Victorians, but from the 1970s feminist critics and others have reappraised her work, finding not only experiments with poetic form, but a previously undervalued radicalism. ∎

See also: Fragment 31 32–33 ▪ *The Divine Comedy* 58–61 ▪ "Kubla Khan" 130–131 ▪ "To Autumn" 138–141 ▪ "How Do I Love Thee?" 150–151 ▪ "The Windhover" 166–167

WE SNATCH IN PASSING AT CLANDESTINE JOYS

"TO THE READER" (1857), CHARLES BAUDELAIRE

IN CONTEXT

FOCUS
Symbolism

OTHER KEY POETS
**Stéphane Mallarmé,
Arthur Rimbaud, Paul
Valéry, Paul Verlaine**

BEFORE
1846 In his review of the Salon
art exhibition, Baudelaire urges
the need for modern subjects
and begins to formulate a
Symbolist aesthetic.

1848 Baudelaire publishes the
first of his translations of the
work of Edgar Allan Poe:
"Mesmeric Revelation."

AFTER
1866 Drawing on *Le Fleurs du
Mal*, Paul Verlaine publishes
his collection *Saturnian Poems*.

1876 Stéphane Mallarmé's
classic Symbolist poem "The
Afternoon of a Faun" blends
mythology with musicality.

In 1886 the term "Symbolism"
was first used by Greek-born
poet Jean Moréas in his
"Symbolist manifesto", published
in Parisian newspaper *Le Figaro*.
Rejecting Romanticism and the
realism that had dominated
Western culture from the end of
the 18th century, the piece cited
French poet Charles Baudelaire as
the originator of a new Symbolist
approach in literature and art.

Baudelaire lived in a world
being transformed—and often made
hideous—by industrialization, new
technologies, and the growth of
cities, yet he grasped *modernité*
("modernity": he was one of the
first writers to use the term) as

See also: "The Raven" 146–147 ▪ *The Waste Land* 198–205 ▪ "The Sparrow" 216–217 ▪ "A Postcard from the Volcano" 218–219 ▪ Canto LXXXI 232–235

Paris's modernizing cityscape, seen here in *Le Pont de l'Europe* (1876) by Gustave Caillebotte, was both a source of inspiration and a spur to escapism for Symbolist poets and artists.

something not to be repulsed, but positively sought out by artists. The true artist, he wrote, extracted from contemporary life "the mysterious beauty that can be contained in it, no matter how minimal or slight that beauty may be."

A new approach

Rather than realistic representations of the world, Baudelaire championed the importance of the internal landscape—the use of the senses, emotions, spirituality, and the imagination, expressed via symbols, myth, allegory, and metaphor—for conveying ideas and ultimate truths. He also redefined the role of the poet as an artist uniquely placed to reveal the incomprehensible or indefinable aspects of life through their personal feelings and insights.

"Au lecteur" ("To the Reader"), a poem that forms the preface to Baudelaire's only major poetry collection, *Les Fleurs du Mal* (*The Flowers of Evil*) of 1857, shows his transmutation of Romantic ideas into a distinctive new approach, soon adopted by other poets of the Symbolist movement. Baudelaire viewed the collection as an »

The whole visible universe is but a storehouse of images and signs to which imagination will give a relative place and value [...]
Charles Baudelaire
"Salon of 1859"
June 1859

French Symbolists

In his poem "Correspondences," Baudelaire speaks of a person passing through "forests of symbols," a state of mind where the senses mysteriously blend and merge, giving access to higher (or deeper) transcendent realities beyond the material, everyday world. Much influenced by him, Stéphane Mallarmé, Paul Verlaine, Arthur Rimbaud, Jules Laforgue, and other French Symbolist poets of the last decades of the 19th century sought to free poetry from the shackles of the literal, evoking instead the intuitions and emotional responses of the inner or transcendent life. Like Baudelaire, they exploited the musical, symbolic, and suggestive qualities of language and imagery; unlike him, they broke down traditional poetic forms, experimenting with free verse and disjointed typography on the page.

As a movement, Symbolism had mostly died by 1900, but the works of its poets and critics became a defining inspiration for experimental Modernist poets of the new century such as Ezra Pound, T. S. Eliot, Wallace Stevens, and William Carlos Williams.

"Flower Clouds" (1903) by Odilon Redon typifies the new era of sensory and expressive art inspired by the French Symbolist movement.

Allegorical imagery from *Les Fleurs du Mal* fed into Symbolist art: Carlos Schwabe (1866–1926) both illustrated Baudelaire's poems and absorbed their themes into his own work.

"architectural" whole: as he told his friend, poet Alfred de Vigny, *Les Fleurs du Mal* is not just an "album" arranged in order of composition, but a sequence with "a beginning and an end," in which many poems were written for specific places in the cycle. The place of "To the Reader," possibly drafted as early as the 1840s, when Baudelaire was in his twenties, is to introduce key themes and images, situating the reader in the world in which the succeeding poems will unfold.

The human condition

In its ten quatrains, "To the Reader" depicts Baudelaire's view of the human condition in a modernizing world, as well as showcasing the role of the poet. A believer in the Christian concept of original sin— humanity's innate propensity toward sin and vice—Baudelaire starts by analyzing the contradictory pull of good and evil. Stupidity,

error, sin, and avarice "possess our minds" and "torment our bodies." They control us, and although we feel remorse from time to time, we do so without true conviction: "Our sins are stubborn, our contrition lame [...] how cheerfully we crawl back to the mire." We are torn by our compulsions; objects we find repugnant also charm us. We steal "clandestine joys," squeezing them like an old orange.

Baudelaire's repeated use of the inclusive "we" establishes an empathetic and ironic tone. Rather

than moralizing, he is caught in the same bind of humanity as his readers. It is a Symbolist world in which legendary and mythic characters, such as "Satan Trismegistus," "serpents," and "monsters that howl and growl and squeal and crawl," coexist alongside beggars, sex workers, and rakes.

The ultimate monster

In the last quatrain of the poem, a monster fouler than all the others is revealed—one that would reduce the world to debris "and swallow all

Charles Baudelaire

Despite being born in Paris in 1821 into comfortable middle-class circumstances, Baudelaire spent much of his life in poverty and dissolution. His father died when he was six, and while Baudelaire adored his mother, he came to hate her second husband.

In his twenties, living the life of a dandy, Baudelaire ran through a large part of his inheritance from his father, which resulted in a lifetime of debt. He began a long, troubled affair with an actress, Jeanne Duval, during this time and began writing consistently to try to support himself, including

important art criticism, translations into French of the works of American writer Edgar Allan Poe, a novella, prose poems, and essays on wide-ranging topics.

A series of strokes in 1866 left him paralyzed and unable to speak, a long-term consequence of syphilis contracted in his teens. He died in Paris in 1867.

Other key works

1860 *Artificial Paradises*
1863 *The Painter of Modern Life*
1869 *Paris Spleen*

> I speak of Boredom which with ready tears
> dreams of hangings as it puffs its pipe.
> Reader, you know this squeamish monster well [...]
> **"To the Reader" (lines 37–39)**

creation in a yawn." This deathly thing is *"Ennui"* ("Boredom"). It is a monster to which all are prey—an inducement to experience life to the fullest, whether good or bad.

The final line of the poem both reaffirms the fellowship between poet and reader, and elevates the role of the poet as a conduit of hidden truths. You, Reader, you also know this creature: "—hypocrite reader,—my alias,—my twin!" Later quoted in T. S. Eliot's *The Waste Land* in 1922, the line is key to the rest of the poems in *Les Fleurs du Mal*.

Inner and outer worlds

Throughout *Les Fleurs du Mal* Baudelaire touches on the seedy sides of Parisian life; but what he encounters as he wanders the streets is a reflection of his own state of mind. Outer and inner worlds merge, and we, as readers, the poet's sisters and brothers, are drawn into the same interaction.

Closely allied with the *ennui* of "To the Reader," "spleen" is a recurring motif in the poems—a physical and moral malaise or sense of alienation that Baudelaire finds both in himself and in the world around him, degrading life. Against this, he brings the weapons of the artist—in his case a rigorous mastery of traditional poetic form. For Baudelaire, the transformation wrought by art is one of the few things that brings value to life.

This exploration of the philosophical purpose of poetry, the channeling of inner worlds,

and refusal to shy away from darker topics (some of the poems in *Les Fleurs du Mal* were banned until 1949 by Interior Ministry censors for offending religion and morality), are also features of the work of Edgar Allan Poe. Sensing a kindred spirit, Baudelaire made extensive translations of Poe's work which would influence Symbolist and Modernist poets along with his own.

Toward Modernism

Baudelaire's particular fusion of tradition and modernity inspired new ways of responding to the world. In guiding and fashioning the Symbolist movement he can be seen as the "midwife" of Modernism, forging a new path for poetry into the 20th century. He captured the essence of his contribution in an unfinished poem: "I have extracted from each thing its quintessence, / You gave me your mud and I've made gold from it." ∎

Armand Rassenfosse's illustration from the 1899 edition of *Les Fleurs du Mal* reflects Baudelaire's desire to reveal the hidden—often darker—thoughts and emotions behind a scene.

The development of Symbolism

Reacting against the rigid order and traditional subjects of Classicism, **Romanticism focuses on the response of the individual to nature**.

⬇

Baudelaire innovates a new style of poetry that uses symbol and metaphor to express the individual's response to the world.

⬇

French poets, such as Stéphane Mallarmé and Paul Verlaine, **react against the materialism** of society by **adopting Baudelaire's Symbolist lexicon**.

⬇

Modernist poets embrace Symbolism's **freedom of expression**, use of **sensory imagery**, and **search for alternative realities**.

I CAUGHT THIS MORNING MORNING'S MINION

"THE WINDHOVER" (1877), GERARD MANLEY HOPKINS

IN CONTEXT

FOCUS
Sprung rhythm

OTHER KEY POETS
William Langland, John Milton, Christina Rossetti, Emily Dickinson, Sylvia Plath

BEFORE
c. 1370s In his allegorical poem *Piers Plowman*, English poet William Langland uses stress in a way that Hopkins later admires and imitates.

1864 Hopkins meets Christina Rossetti, author of "Goblin Market" and an important influence on his work.

1875–1876 "The Wreck of the Deutschland," Hopkins' poem commemorating a shipwreck, employs sprung rhythm.

AFTER
1964 American poet John Berryman's *77 Dream Songs* collection shows a linguistic and metrical originality partly inspired by Hopkins.

One of the most innovative 19th-century poets, perhaps rivaled in this regard only by Emily Dickinson in the US, is British poet Gerard Manley Hopkins. His poetic style demonstrated mastery of a metrical mode he called "sprung rhythm." This counts the beat of a line solely according to stressed syllables, allowing for any number of unstressed syllables. As a result, the number of syllables can vary. As Hopkins explained, "any two stresses may either follow one another running or be divided by one, two, or three slack syllables." His justification for sprung rhythm was that it was found in common speech, music, and nursery rhymes, as well as old English poems.

Enigmatic elements

Describing the content of his poems, Hopkins used concepts that he termed "inscape" and "instress."

"Inscape" is a revelation of the inner essence of the subject, whether human, animal, or otherwise. The more complex quality of "instress" allows humans, thanks to their superior faculties, to recognize the inscapes of other beings and entities, differentiate between them, and interpret them. For the devoutly Catholic Hopkins, the instress of inscapes—taken to its logical conclusion—leads to the perception of Christ, since the true inner self of any phenomenon contains something of the divine.

Pure essence

Hopkins' poetic innovations are shown to their full effect in his sonnet "The Windhover"—a name in rural dialect for a kestrel, a falcon that hovers mid-air before diving on its prey. The first impression is of a strange and original idiom, far from any sense of Victorian restraint. Energy is generated by

> High there, how he rung upon the rein of a wimpling wing
> In his ecstasy! then off, off forth on swing,
> As a skate's heel sweeps smooth on a bow-bend […]
> **"The Windhover" (lines 4–6)**

See also: *Paradise Lost* 102–109 ▪ "Goblin Market" 161 ▪ "Because I Could Not Stop for Death" 168–169 ▪ "Do Not Go Gentle Into That Good Night" 240–241

Sprung rhythm animates the poem: **five stresses per line**; sometimes in **groups of two or three**.

Enjambed run-over—lines create forward momentum— as do **word repetitions** such as "off" and "of."

Ending the first line with just the **first syllable** of the hyphenated "king-dom" accelerates the poem's pace.

The soundscape of "The Windhover"

Exclamation marks end the octave and first tercet on an uplift, in contrast to the final line's gentle fall.

Capitalization of "**AND**" in line 10 adds emphasis to the **shift of subject**—to "thee" (Christ).

In the final line, **rhyme** and **alliteration** work densely together: "Fall, gall," and "gash gold-vermilion."

alliteration—"daylight's dauphin, dapple-dawn-drawn"—and by clusters of stressed syllables following sprung rhythm principles, such as "act, oh, air, pride, plume."

A sonnet typically consists of an eight-line octave followed by a six-line sestet. The octave in "The Windhover" describes the thrill of a morning sighting, capturing the bird's inscape as it hovers, then swings against the wind. In the first three lines—tercet—of the sestet, the subject shifts to Christ, to whom Hopkins addresses the poem. If the kestrel shows such marvellous inscape as it resists the air, then Christ's inscape—the fire that shines from his divinity— must be "a billion / Times told

lovelier, more dangerous." The final three lines suggest this is unsurprising. When a plow blade turns the soil, friction makes it "Shine"; similarly, when embers collapse, they show the "gold-vermilion" of their inner heat.

Christ is addressed in tender terms—"ah my dear." His inner heat, the poet implies, breaks out from his labor and sacrifice on behalf of humanity. Work and warmth are his keynotes. Christ's spirit also cuts through the hardships of life—the "shéer plód" of daily toil and the dying fire—"blue-bleak embers"— of aging. Out of the inscape of the kestrel and its wind-borne flight, Hopkins conjures the revelation— the instress—of Christ's divinity. ∎

Gerard Manley Hopkins

Born in Essex, England, in 1844, Gerard Manley Hopkins began writing poetry while at school, although his early ambition was to be a painter. He studied classics at Oxford University, where he converted to Catholicism. After deciding to train to become a Jesuit priest in 1868, Hopkins burned his poetry and vowed "to write no more."

In 1875, while studying in North Wales, Hopkins began to write poetry again—but most of his work remained unpublished in his lifetime. In 1877, he was ordained as a Jesuit priest, and in 1884 he became a professor of Latin and Greek at University College, Dublin. Illness blighted Hopkins' final years, and he died of typhoid fever in 1889. On his deathbed, he said: "I am so happy, I am so happy. I loved my life."

Key works

1875–1876 "The Wreck of the Deutschland"
1877 "Pied Beauty"
1879 "Binsey Poplars"
1918 *Poems of Gerard Manley Hopkins*

BECAUSE I COULD NOT STOP FOR DEATH—/ HE KINDLY STOPPED FOR ME

"BECAUSE I COULD NOT STOP FOR DEATH" (c.1863), EMILY DICKINSON

IN CONTEXT

FOCUS
The poem on the page

OTHER KEY POETS
George Herbert, Dylan Thomas

BEFORE
1633 George Herbert practices typographical patterning in "Easter Wings," shaping two stanzas like the outstretched wings of an angel.

AFTER
1918 In France, Guillaume Apollinaire's *Calligrammes* has poems with type arranged in pictorial forms.

1961 French poet Raymond Queneau publishes *Cent Mille Milliards de Poèmes*. It consists of 10 sonnets, each divided into strips that can be rearranged by readers.

2016 Canadian poet Anne Carson's *Float* consists of 22 booklets in a box, to be read in any order—an experiment with chance.

Some poets display an originality that extends beyond subject and style to the way their words appear on the page. Poetry traditionally resembles prose except in its rhythms, rhymes (if rhyming), and demarcated line endings. However, other differences are also possible. American poet e. e. cummings, for example, avoided capital letters in his work. Other poets have presented their work in highly individualistic formats, reflecting a more radical approach to the creative process. American poet Emily Dickinson took a unique approach to both punctuation (and therefore rhythm) and how her poems were presented.

An extraordinary method

From 1858 to 1864, Dickinson created 40 small, folded booklets, or fascicles, of 814 poems. They were transcribed by hand and arranged by theme, rather than chronologically. The few published in her lifetime were tidied up by others to match orthodox typographic styling. But originally (and in published editions from 1955), they used dashes in place of regular punctuation.

The dashes alter the reader's experience, and give cues to someone reciting a poem. Reflecting darting insights and emotions, they present a mind in motion, alive to every nuance. Typically, the meter is that of a ballad: most of the poems can be sung to the tune of "The Yellow Rose of Texas." However, the dashes break up that regularity and suggest an intimacy and immediacy, as in a notebook. This quality of being *unprocessed* adds to our impression of introspection. As American literary critic Harold

> Since then—'tis Centuries—and yet
> Feels shorter than the Day
> I first surmised the Horses' Heads
> Were toward Eternity—
> **"Because I Could Not Stop for Death" (lines 21–24)**

See also: "Prayer" 96–99 ▪ "Song of Myself" 152–159 ▪ "The Windhover" 166–167 ▪ "Do Not Go Gentle Into That Good Night" 240–241 ▪ "The Hill We Climb" 309

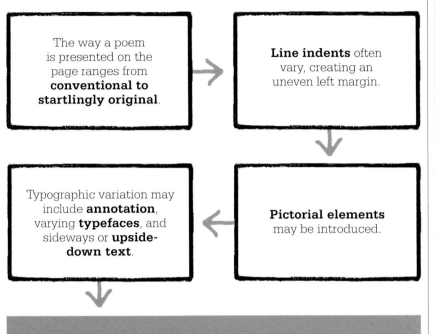

The way a poem is presented on the page ranges from **conventional to startlingly original**.

→

Line indents often vary, creating an uneven left margin.

↓

Typographic variation may include **annotation**, varying **typefaces**, and sideways or **upside-down text**.

←

Pictorial elements may be introduced.

↓

The format of the poem on the page may be unconventional.

Emily Dickinson

Born in 1830, Dickinson lived in Amherst, Massachusetts, all her life. Her father was a lawyer and trustee of Amherst College. At the age of 14, she was traumatized by the death of her second cousin and close friend Sophia Holland. Emily was a keen gardener and botanist. After leaving full-time education she mostly conducted her friendships through correspondence.

Dickinson never married but had close relationships with sister-in-law Susan Gilbert and with Thomas Wentworth Higginson, editor of *The Atlantic Monthly* magazine, from whom she sought literary guidance from 1862. After 1866, Dickinson became seriously reclusive.

Only 10 of Dickinson's nearly 1,800 poems were published in her own lifetime, and these were edited to make them more conventional. Typical subjects were nature, death, and eternity. It was not until 1890, four years after her death, that the first collection of her poems was published.

Other key works

1890 *Poems*
1891 *Poems: Second Series*

Bloom has pointed out, this represents her speed of thought: dashes accelerate.

The poem "Because I Could Not Stop for Death" shows her note-taking manner in action, imitating the lurches of rapidly passing time as well as the speed of her carriage. The poem begins with her riding comfortably, accompanied by distantly polite Death and assured Immortality. In the fifth of six quatrains, she passes a grave, seen as an underground house, which reminds her of the threat of impending extinction: "We paused before a House that seemed / A Swelling of the Ground—." Time gets collapsed in the last quatrain. With the chilling realization that bleak Eternity is her destination,

the idea of an afterlife falls away. The final dash, in place of a period, points to the abyss.

Patternings

Other poets have also sought visual effects. For example, Dylan Thomas used typographical patterning, shaping the stanzas in "Vision and Prayer" (1945) like diamonds and hourglasses. Going even further, "concrete poets" from French poet Guillaume Apollinaire (1880–1918) onward, have explored unorthodox typographic layout in a spirit of modernist iconoclasm. Many have exhibited their work alongside artists. There is an increasing vogue for making the page more vibrant through annotation, typographic variety, unusual page formats, or graphic or photographic images. ▪

WE WEAR THE MASK THAT GRINS AND LIES

"WE WEAR THE MASK" (1895), PAUL LAURENCE DUNBAR

IN CONTEXT

FOCUS
Double consciousness in Black American poetry

OTHER KEY POETS
Phillis Wheatley, Alice Dunbar-Nelson, Claude McKay, Langston Hughes, Maya Angelou, Amiri Baraka, Amanda Gorman

BEFORE
1829 Black American poet George Moses Horton protests against slavery in his collection *The Hope of Liberty*.

1865 The US Congress passes the 13th Amendment, which abolishes slavery.

AFTER
1896 The US Supreme Court upholds the principle of racial segregation in law.

1919 In "If We Must Die," Jamaican-American poet Claude McKay argues against living "behind the mask" and champions Black identity.

In "We Wear the Mask," Paul Laurence Dunbar uses the extended metaphor of a mask to explore the experience of being Black American in the late 19th century. While slavery had been abolished, daily life for Black Americans was still characterized by racism and deprivation. The act of "masking"—hiding true feelings, while presenting a false expression of contentment—is a survival tactic in an oppressive, white-dominated society. It also masks the internal struggle of validating both a Black and an American identity in a time

"We Wear the Mask" focuses on the **dual identity, or double consciousness**, inherent in living as a **Black American**.

Black Americans are forced to **suppress their culture** and view themselves from **a negative, white perspective**.

Dunbar presents a mask as a **symbol of double consciousness** and a **possible tool for change**.

The mask of double consciousness is a survival tactic in a white-dominated society but can also strengthen collective Black identity and signify resilience against oppression and prejudice.

See also: "On Being Brought from Africa to America" 118–119 ▪ "I, Too" 208–213 ▪ *Annie Allen* 236–239
▪ "Black Art" 268–269 ▪ "Power" 286–287 ▪ "The Hill We Climb" 309

Paul Laurence Dunbar

Born in Dayton, Ohio, in 1872, to formerly enslaved parents, Paul Laurence Dunbar began writing poetry at school and published his first poems when he was 16. Prevented from studying law by a lack of funds, he took a job as an elevator operator, which allowed him time to write and develop the Black American dialect style that would later win him acclaim.

By 1895, Dunbar had published two volumes of poetry and his work began to appear in national newspapers. In 1897, following a reading tour of England, he married American poet Alice Ruth Moore—later Alice Dunbar-Nelson—and took a clerkship at the Library of Congress in Washington, D.C. He left this job in 1898 to concentrate on full-time writing, which included a series of short stories, novels, and a play, as well as poems. After separating from his wife in 1902, Dunbar was plagued by ill-health. He died in 1906.

Other key works

1893 *Oak and Ivy*
1895 *Majors and Minors*
1896 *Lyrics of Lowly Life*

of inequality. Black American sociologist and civil rights activist W.E.B. Du Bois, writing in 1903, formalized this concept of living a dual existence by coining the term "double consciousness."

Using the mask

In the first line of his three-stanza poem, Dunbar introduces the notion of double consciousness with "the mask" that simultaneously "grins and lies." The deception needed for survival, and the skill required to uphold the mask, are made clear. The mask must hide both cheeks and eyes, which might betray true feelings, while expressing "myriad subtleties." Dunbar also describes the psychological cost of straddling two identities. The wearers of the mask have "bleeding hearts," experience "tears and sighs," and have "tortured souls."

Beyond the need to mask true feelings, "We Wear the Mask" also alludes to factors that add to double consciousness—the stereotypes and expectations upheld by white society—and how masking might subvert them. In stanza two, the rhetorical question "Why should the world be over-wise, / In counting all our tears and sighs?" is given the response "Nay, let them only see us, while / We wear the mask," which is reaffirmed in stanza three with "let the world dream otherwise." This suggests that the need to mask can be turned into an advantage; aside from offering protection, it binds the oppressed together, validating their hidden identity and dreams. The ability to "sing" and "smile" are not expressions of happiness, but of collective resilience.

Repetition of the inclusive "we" identifies the speaker as a member of the Black American community and the poem as its mouthpiece. In exposing the act of masking, Dunbar is both deploring its necessity and issuing a call to resistance.

Promoting Black identity

"We Wear the Mask" was just one of Dunbar's many poems to examine the tensions between resistance and assimilation—the lived experience of double consciousness. His work laid the foundations for the Harlem Renaissance of the early 20th century and encouraged later explorations of Black identity in poetry, including American poet Maya Angelou's own spoken-word adaptation of "We Wear the Mask," which expanded on its themes of race, oppression, and survival. ∎

We smile, but, O great Christ, our cries
To thee from tortured souls arise.
[…]
But let the world dream otherwise,
    We wear the mask!
"We Wear the Mask" (lines 10–11, 14–15)

FOR EACH MAN KILLS THE THING HE LOVES

THE BALLAD OF READING GAOL (1898), OSCAR WILDE

IN CONTEXT

FOCUS
Ballad

OTHER KEY POETS
Robert Burns, William Wordsworth, Samuel Taylor Coleridge, John Keats, Edgar Allen Poe

BEFORE
1798 Publication of William Wordsworth and Samuel Taylor Coleridge's *Lyrical Ballads* marks the arrival of the literary ballad as a poetic genre.

1820 John Keats publishes "La Belle Dame Sans Merci," a ballad about unrequited love.

AFTER
1899 Irish poet W. B. Yeats reworks a traditionally sung Gaelic ballad, "The Host of the Air," in literary form.

1940 British-American poet W. H. Auden's collection *Another Time* contains ballads on dark themes including aging and mortality.

In 1895, Irish playwright and poet Oscar Wilde was sentenced to two years hard labor for "gross indecency" (sex with other men, then illegal) and sent to prison. After his release, he wrote *The Ballad of Reading Gaol*, a poem describing his time there, and the chilling effect of the execution of fellow inmate Charles Thomas Wooldridge for murdering his wife.

Wilde initially published the poem anonymously under his prison identification number "C.3.3." (cell block C, landing 3, cell 3). The first printing sold out within a week and was quickly followed by several more. The seventh printing—the first to have Wilde's name on its cover—was the last edition to be published before he died in 1900.

Populist content and form

In the poem, Wilde recounts the crime committed by Wooldridge, as well as his trial and execution. Wilde then details the brutality of prison life, including the poor treatment of children—crimes that remained hidden behind the prison walls. Exploring the themes of guilt, compassion, forgiveness, and the possibility of redemption, the poem is an indictment of the cruelty of capital punishment and the whole prison system—a poetic plea for change. Wilde perhaps chose the ballad form to describe his time in prison because its style suited his new populist identity as a recent convict, and its rhythms evoked the repetitiveness of prison life.

Thought to date from the early Middle Ages, traditional or folk ballads are narrative poems, often

A newspaper report on the trial of Oscar Wilde from *The Illustrated Police News* in May 1895 shows his downfall from esteemed writer in 1882 to convicted prisoner in 1895.

See also: *Beowulf* 48–51 ▪ "London" 122–125 ▪ "The Raven" 146–147
▪ "Paul Revere's Ride" 160 ▪ "Skunk Hour" 242–245

Ballad

A ballad is a narrative song that is traditionally composed of rhymed abcb quatrains (four-line stanzas) made up of alternating four-stress and three-stress lines. Wilde's *The Ballad of Reading Gaol* retains the four-stress / three-stress line alternation, but has six-line stanzas and an abcbdb rhyme scheme:

1	2	3	4	
And **all**	men **kill**	the **thing**	they **love**,	A
By **all**	let **this**	be **heard**,		B
Some **do**	it **with**	a **bit-**	ter **look**,	C
Some **with**	a **flat-**	tering **word**,		B
The **co-**	ward **does**	it **with**	a **kiss**,	D
The **brave**	man **with**	a **sword**!		B

Traditionally, a verse in a ballad ends here.

A word that looks as if it should rhyme, but does not when it is spoken, is known as an "eye rhyme."

anonymous, and mostly set to music. During the 18th and early 19th centuries, well-known poets including the English Romantics increasingly adopted the ballad as a literary form, writing narrative poems that used some of the conventions of traditional ballads, while rejecting others. They became known as literary (or lyrical) ballads, many of which focused on political or social issues. At the time Wilde wrote *The Ballad of Reading Gaol*, folk ballads were again experiencing a popular revival with other contemporary writers, including W. B. Yeats, making use of the form.

Redefining the ballad

In *The Ballad of Reading Gaol* Wilde uses common, or ballad, meter with a regular abcbdb rhyme scheme. Combined with the use of refrain, repetition, and parallelism, this scheme builds a picture of prison life detail by detail. In other ways, Wilde's ballad is atypical. At 109 stanzas, it is much longer than a traditional ballad, and its stanzas have six rather than the usual four lines. Wilde also rejects the tradition of an impersonal narrator, and identifies with the other prisoners and the condemned man: he describes the two of them as "doomed ships that pass in storm."

Reviewers and fellow poets criticized Wilde for these democratic and nonconformist elements. They thought he showed too much sympathy for the inmates and used an excess of rhetorical flourishes and hyperbolic language to describe their plight. Paradoxically, the critics' complaints only confirmed Wilde's success—he had effectively used the ballad to instigate popular debate on penal reform. ■

Oscar Wilde

Born in Dublin, Ireland, in 1854, Oscar Wilde began to establish himself as a writer while at Oxford University. Here, he became a leading figure in the Aesthetic movement and his poem "Ravenna" won the 1878 Newdigate Prize for the best composition in English Verse. Wilde became famous for his flamboyant lifestyle as well as for his writing, which included essays, reviews, short stories, a novel, and plays.

In 1895, Wilde brought a libel case against the Marquess of Queensberry, father of his lover "Bosie," Lord Alfred Douglas. Wilde lost the case, and was tried and convicted of same sex acts. While in prison, Wilde wrote *De Profundis*, a long letter to Douglas that reflected on his life, art, the nature of forgiveness, and Christian faith. After his release in 1897, Wilde was bankrupt and in poor health. He settled in Paris and died in 1900.

Other key works

1878 "Ravenna"
1881 *Poems*
1894 "The Sphinx"

THE MO

AGE

1900–1940

DERN

Defender of the British empire **Rudyard Kipling** publishes "If—" which expounds the virtues of **steadfast stoicism**.

The **Nobel Prize in literature** is won by Bengali poet **Rabindranath Tagore**.

The Atlantic Monthly publishes Robert Frost's poem "The Road Not Taken"; it becomes **one of the US's best-loved poems**.

War poet Wilfred Owen portrays **the brutality of war** in "Dulce et Decorum Est," describing a gas attack on the Western front.

1910   1913   1915   1920

1912   1914–1918   1919   1920

"In the Bazaars of Hyderabad" by Sarojini Naidu expresses the energy and aspirations of the **movement for Indian independence**.

World War I, a conflict involving many great powers, spreads across large parts of the world.

American magazine *Others* prints Marianne Moore's "Poetry," in which **lines are organized by the number of syllables**.

W. B. Yeats presents an **apocalyptic vision for humanity** in his poem "The Second Coming."

The tumultuous events of the first four decades of the 20th century revolutionized the arts, including poetry. The scale of slaughter in World War I (1914–1918), followed by a global economic crash (1929), the breakup of long-standing European empires, and loss of faith in an interventionist God swept away old certainties and created feelings of confusion and alienation. For writers trying to capture this sense of anxiety, new forms of expression were needed.

Sense of doom
While a Modernist sensibility can be detected in the works of French poet Charles Baudelaire in the 19th century, and British writer Virginia Woolf famously placed the birth of Modernism in 1910, World War I is generally regarded as the point when traditional verse forms and themes began to seem outdated and inadequate. The war itself produced a rich seam of poetry, produced by young men fighting on the Western Front. Poets such as Wilfred Owen did not glorify honor and sacrifice in their works, as was traditionally expected, but wrote movingly about the personal impact and horrifying realities of the conflict.

After the war, the widespread sense of dislocation and despair at the waste of lives and resources, even among the victors, was encapsulated by American-British poet T. S. Eliot's *The Waste Land*. Published in 1922, it is generally considered the most influential poem in English of the 20th century. Its haunting cadences and fragmentary structure, including a cast of "voices," snatched references to popular culture, and cryptic allusions to literary tradition were bewildering yet thrilling.

Make it new
Modernism demanded a new spirit of inventiveness, reflecting a fast-changing urban world driven by technological innovation. In 1928, American poet Ezra Pound, the champion of many experimental poets, exhorted writers and artists to reject tradition and "make it new." While some poets, such as Eliot and American Marianne Moore, who organized her free verse by the number of syllables in each line, embraced this rallying cry with gusto, others reinvented old forms or put them to a new purpose. One such poet was American Robert Frost, who used natural settings

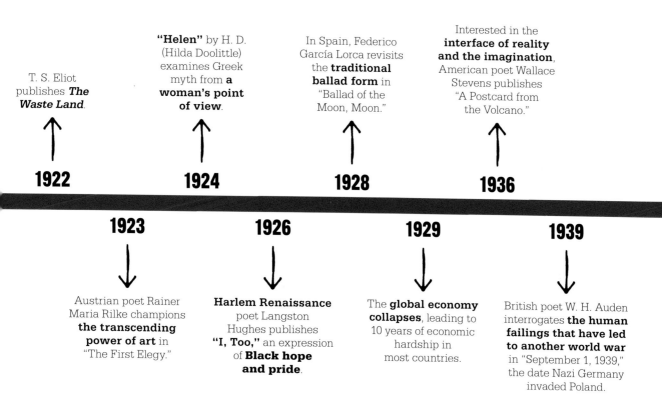

T. S. Eliot publishes *The Waste Land*.

1922

"Helen" by H. D. (Hilda Doolittle) examines Greek myth from **a woman's point of view**.

1924

In Spain, Federico García Lorca revisits the **traditional ballad form** in "Ballad of the Moon, Moon."

1928

Interested in the **interface of reality and the imagination**, American poet Wallace Stevens publishes "A Postcard from the Volcano."

1936

1923

Austrian poet Rainer Maria Rilke champions **the transcending power of art** in "The First Elegy."

1926

Harlem Renaissance poet Langston Hughes publishes "**I, Too**," an expression of **Black hope and pride**.

1929

The **global economy collapses**, leading to 10 years of economic hardship in most countries.

1939

British poet W. H. Auden interrogates **the human failings that have led to another world war** in "September 1, 1939," the date Nazi Germany invaded Poland.

and the familiar rhythms of everyday speech to tackle bleak themes such as personal doubt and extinction.

The revolution in poetry was not just about what was being produced by white male poets in the US and Europe. As the old world crumbled, a new one quickly sprang up. The enfranchisement of women in many countries during or just after World War I, the rise of socialism, and demands for self-determination, led to new voices and subject matter, especially from marginalized groups.

In New York City during the 1920s and '30s, Black poets such as Langston Hughes flourished as part of the cultural flowering later known as the Harlem Renaissance. The writers of this movement, many of whom used Black vernacular and the rhythms of jazz and blues, confronted racism and celebrated Black American lives. Also writing in the US, H. D. (Hilda Doolittle) was among a number of women who brought a feminist perspective to their work, and who became some of the first poets to examine the meaning of gender.

In other places, poetry was integral to a resurgence of local culture and identity. W. B. Yeats led an Irish Literary Revival linked to the flourishing of Irish nationalism; in Spain, Federico García Lorca, a member of the group of avant-garde writers and artists known as the Generation of '27, used the traditional forms of his native Andalusia to challenge state oppression. Indian poets, such as Sarojini Naidu also drew on their heritage and the rich traditions of their culture to express growing calls for independence from British colonial control.

History repeats

In the 1930s, the residual trauma of World War I was replaced by a new anxiety centered on the growth of Fascism in Europe and the prospect of another war. These concerns are found in the work of American poet Wallace Stevens, who expressed fears of a global apocalypse but also hope that poetic imagination might provide an antidote to the pain and suffering in the world. When Nazi Germany invaded Poland in 1939, triggering World War II (1939–1945), British-American poet W. H. Auden wrote "September 1, 1939," a deeply foreboding poem that also suggests there can only be hope if we begin to act out of love. ■

I AM HERE TO SING THEE SONGS

GITANJALI 15 (1912), RABINDRANATH TAGORE

IN CONTEXT

FOCUS
Devotional poetry

OTHER KEY POETS
**W. B. Yeats, Sarojini Naidu,
Ezra Pound, T. S. Eliot**

BEFORE
1861 Bengali poet Michael
Madhusudan Dutt's nine-
canto epic poem, *Meghnad
Badh Kavya* (*The Slaying
of Meghanada*), draws
inspiration from the ancient
Hindu epic *Ramayana*.

AFTER
1921 Kazi Nazrul Islam, an
Indian nationalist, writes
his anti-British revolutionary
poem, *"Bidrohi"* ("The Rebel").

1942 The 31 poems of
Jibanananda Das's *Banalata
Sen* explore themes of love,
loss, and freedom.

1943 British-American poet
T. S. Eliot's *Four Quartets*
blends his Anglo-Catholicism
with works from Eastern and
Western religious traditions.

The theme of spirituality, rooted in Indian traditions but with a Western influence, runs throughout the work of Bengali poet Rabindranath Tagore. "I am here to sing thee songs," the poet asserts in the English-language version of his *Gitanjali* (*Song Offerings*). While most of the 103 poems of the collection are devotional—offerings addressed to God—they also deal with topics such as love, nature, emptiness, and loss, and many of them have a satirical edge.

In the 15th poem, Tagore speaks of his own role, as poet or artist. There is not a place for him at the busy heart of everyday life. Rather, "In this hall of thine," he tells the deity, "I have a corner seat." He has "no work to do"; his life is "useless" and "can only break out in tunes without a

Jorasanko Thakur Bari, Kolkata, is the ancestral home of Tagore's family and where he was born. The 18th-century house is now the campus of Rabindra Bharati University.

See also: Sonnet 130 88–93 ▪ *Don Juan* 136–137 ▪ "My Last Duchess" 144–145 ▪ "In the Bazaars of Hyderabad" 181
▪ "The Second Coming" 194–197 ▪ Canto LXXXI 232–235

Rabindranath Tagore

Born into a wealthy landowning family in Kolkata, India, in 1861, Tagore began publishing poetry in Bangla when he was in his twenties. He also wrote short stories, plays and, later, novels. In addition, he founded a school, which later became Visva-Bharati University, West Bengal, seeking to integrate the best of Asian and Western culture. From 1913, he traveled widely, lecturing and speaking out in support of Indian independence.

Despite his renown, much of Tagore's best work has never been translated and remains unknown outside Bengal. He wrote more than 4,000 poems, of which around half are songs set to music. As well as using traditional Bengali poetic forms, he wrote Western-style sonnets and blank verse. Following publication of the English poems, Tagore became the first non-Westerner to win the Nobel Prize in Literature in 1913. He died in Kolkata in 1941.

Other key works

1894 *Sonar Tori*
1900 *Khanika*

purpose." Yet shift the context—when "the hour strikes for thy silent worship at the dark temple of midnight"—and the marginal figure becomes central. In this deeper, darker realm of mystery and spiritual meaning, the poet can cry out boldly to the deity: "command me, my master, to stand before thee to sing." No longer tucked in a corner, he and his songs are commanded, necessary, expecting "honor."

Bangla to English

Tagore was in his fifties when he made the prose translations that became the English *Gitanjali* (1912)—translations of poems from both his earlier Bangla volume *Gitanjali* (first published in India in 1910) and other collections. While recuperating from an illness, he made English translations of some of the Bangla originals. On a visit to London, he showed them to British artist William Rothenstein, who set about sharing them with other friends, including W. B. Yeats and Ezra Pound.

Published in London, with an introduction by Yeats, the English *Gitanjali* brought Tagore—already well known in Bengal—worldwide fame, and in 1913 he became the first non-European to win the Nobel Prize in Literature. Many of the poems had their roots in his grief at the death of his wife and two children within a few years of each other, and the poet's relationship with God, the core preoccupation of the sequence, is seen through this lens. "Thou hast made me endless, such is thy pleasure," the first poem begins, addressing the deity. "This frail vessel thou emptiest again and again, and fillest it ever with fresh life."

The second poem celebrates the loving intensity of the speaker's relationship with the deity: "When thou commandest me to sing it seems that my heart would break with pride; and I look to thy face, and tears come to my eyes." But as with all love bonds, there are times when the loved one seems far away, even absent. "If thou speakest not," the poet exclaims in the 19th poem, "I will fill my heart with thy silence and endure it. I will keep still and wait like the night […]."

Final appeal

The final poems speak of death, not as an ending but as a possible liberation or homecoming. In the poet's final appeal to God, he evokes an image of migrating birds: "Like a flock of homesick cranes flying night and day back to their mountain nests let all my life take its voyage to its eternal home in one salutation to thee." ▪

When in the morning air the golden harp is tuned, honor me, commanding my presence.
Gitanjali **15** (lines 8–9)

YOURS IS THE EARTH AND EVERYTHING THAT'S IN IT
IF— (1910), RUDYARD KIPLING

IN CONTEXT

FOCUS
Poetry and empire

OTHER KEY POETS
Alfred Tennyson, Rupert Brooke, T. S. Eliot, Wilfred Owen, Derek Walcott

BEFORE
1818 "Ozymandias" by English Romantic poet Percy Bysshe Shelley evokes the fragility of empire building.

1842 Alfred Tennyson publishes "The Vision of Sin," an inspiration for Kipling's early poems depicting the dark side of imperial life in India.

AFTER
1939 *Notebook of a Return to My Native Land* by Martinican poet Aimé Césaire examines the formation of Black cultural identity in a colonial setting.

2010 St. Lucian poet Derek Walcott revisits discussions on empire and colonial control in "The Lost Empire."

orn in Bombay (Mumbai), India, in 1865 to British parents, Rudyard Kipling was both a product and staunch supporter of the British Empire. His poem "If—" is a tribute to the British "stiff upper lip"—an exhortation to duty, courage, and stoicism in the face of adversity. While an instant success, "If—" marked a tipping point in changing times. A gradual transition from the Victorian values associated with empire-building to a more modern post-colonial outlook was underway, and Kipling was increasingly criticized for his imperialist opinions and jingoism. The continuing popularity of "If—," despite the controversies around Kipling's views, is a testament to the quality of his writings.

Written as a single long sentence, the poem lists the characteristics needed to navigate life successfully and with dignity. The poet-speaker appears to be advising his son, but the direct form of his address, and the repetition of words at the start of successive clauses turns the poem into a mantra for life directed to any reader. Celebrating aspiration while acknowledging that life does not always go according to plan, "If—" perhaps unwittingly prefigures the fall of empire with its message that even if you cannot achieve your hopes, you will have experienced the essence of what it is to be human—"a Man." ∎

Kipling stands next to his father, John Lockwood Kipling, an artist, teacher, and museum curator, who did much to promote arts and crafts in India, where he raised his family.

See also: "On Being Brought from Africa to America" 118–119 ▪ "Ozymandias" 132–135 ▪ *The Waste Land* 198–205 ▪ *Omeros* 300–303

WHAT DO YOU SELL, O YE MERCHANTS? / RICHLY YOUR WARES ARE DISPLAYED

"IN THE BAZAARS OF HYDERABAD" (1912), SAROJINI NAIDU

Included in her 1912 collection *The Bird of Time*, Sarojini Naidu's poem "In the Bazaars of Hyderabad" signifies an important stage in the development of Indo-Anglian poetry—work written by Indian poets in English. The English language arrived in India with colonialism, and was first used by Indian poets during the early 19th century. Understood globally, English became a powerful way for Indian writers to communicate their nation's strengths during the struggle for independence in the early 20th century.

Behind the bazaar

Over five stanzas, Naidu creates the experience of bargaining at a bazaar, using rhythm and rhyme to evoke the call and response of trading. A cascade of sensuous imagery depicts a wealth of goods, such as "Daggers," "Saffron," and "Sandalwood," while a catalog of bazaar people— "pedlars," "goldsmiths," "merchants," "musicians," "magicians," and "flower-girls"—conjures up the energy and breadth of Indian society.

The poem evokes the vibrancy of India's markets, but it is also a political work. A key figure in the Indian nationalist movement, Naidu supported the boycott of European goods to prove India could become self-sufficient. Only merchandise of Indian origin is described in the poem—implying that India need not rely on foreign products. The final image of flower-girls weaving garlands "to perfume the sleep of the dead" also hints that the price of independence may be bloodshed. ∎

One needs a Seer's Vision and an Angel's voice to be of any avail.
Sarojini Naidu
**Letter to Indian politician
G. K. Gokhale, 1914**

See also: *Mahabharata* 22–23 ▪ *Gitanjali* 15 178–179 ▪ "If—" 180 ▪ "The Looking Glass" 270–271

TWO ROADS DIVERGED IN A WOOD, AND I – / I TOOK THE ONE LESS TRAVELED BY

"THE ROAD NOT TAKEN" (1916), ROBERT FROST

Robert Frost followed in a long tradition of poets who wrote using the everyday, or vernacular, language of their time and place. In Western literature, vernacular language has been used since at least the Middle Ages, when one of its first advocates, Dante, chose to write in Italian rather than Latin. This precedent would influence later European writers from Geoffrey Chaucer in the 14th century to the Romantics in the 19th century.

An authentic form

Like many of his contemporaries in the early 20th century, such as the Modernists T. S. Eliot and Ezra Pound, Frost wanted to break away from the smooth tones and artificial devices found in the work of late Victorian poets such as Alfred Tennyson. Unlike the Modernists, however, Frost had no desire to invent new verse forms, and he rejected the irregularities of free verse, comparing the writing of free verse to playing tennis "with the net down." He wished, instead, to combine everyday language and speech rhythms with traditional verse forms and meter as a way of injecting poetry with both energy and authenticity.

Frost wrote of wanting to bring the regularity of a pre-stressed meter and the irregularity of everyday speech and intonation into a "strained relation" with each other, aiming to "drag and break" the intonation across the meter "as waves first comb and break stumbling on the shingle." In practice, this meant adding extra syllables where required to accommodate the irregular rhythms and emphasis of natural speech, rather than adhering to a strict meter. Frost wrote much of his poetry in an iambic meter (two-syllable feet with the stress on the second syllable), and he referred to lines with extra syllables as "loose iambic," as against the "strict iambic" of a regular meter.

For Frost, the sound of everyday speech—that is, tone of voice, or intonation—was a vital component of his verse. He was a keen talker; and also listened intently to the way others talked. As his friend, American poet Raymond Holden noted, in conversation "[Frost] was also attending to the patterns of

Robert Frost

Born in San Francisco in 1874, Robert Frost moved with his mother and sister to New England at the age of 11. He began writing poetry in high school, where he met his future wife, Elinor White, whom he married in 1895. The couple lived in New Hampshire, where Frost bought a farm and took teaching jobs while continuing to write.

Unable to find a US publisher for his poems, Frost took his family to England in 1912. Here, his first two collections were issued in 1913 and 1914. Frost returned to the US in 1915, settling in New England. His first two volumes of poetry were soon published in the US to critical acclaim. In 1924, Frost's collection *New Hampshire* won the first of his four Pulitzer Prizes. Despite a series of family tragedies, Frost kept up a heavy workload of writing and teaching for the rest of his life. He died in Boston in 1963.

Other key works

1913 *A Boy's Will*
1914 *North of Boston*
1923 *New Hampshire*

See also: "To a Mouse" 120–121 ▪ "I Wandered Lonely as a Cloud" 126–129 ▪ "Song of Myself" 152–159 ▪ "Because I Could Not Stop for Death" 168–169 ▪ "Poetry" 188–191 ▪ "Casualty" 290–293

The landscape of New Hampshire, with its isolated farms, small villages, and woodlands, provided Frost with a vocabulary of familiar images that he used to explore universal themes.

your speech, listening for a poetic rhythm." In normal speech, pitch, stress, and tone of voice are key to understanding what is being said. Frost called this the "sound of sense"—as when you hear people arguing on the far side of a closed door and know what is being said without hearing the words.

Familiar subjects

"The Road Not Taken" first appeared in Frost's third collection, *Mountain Interval*, published in 1916. Frost often wrote about the landscape of rural New England, where he lived for much of his life, and about the lives of its inhabitants, in poems that address themes of love, beauty, and the natural world, but also death, struggle, and loneliness. Frost takes a more meditative approach in "The Road Not Taken," which was inspired by his friend, British poet Edward Thomas, whom he got to know in England. Nevertheless, the poem addresses an experience that is familiar to everyone.

At the start, the speaker recalls standing in a wood confronted by two roads that lead in different directions. He studies one to the point where it disappears around a corner, then chooses the other because it looks less used—though he concedes that, really, both roads are equally worn. Neither have been used that morning. The speaker keeps the first road for another day, though he doubts that he will be back, knowing the way one decision leads on to another. In the final stanza, he imagines himself telling this story in the future. Faced with a choice between two roads, he took the less-used one, and "that has made all the difference."

A host of ambiguities

At first glance, "The Road Not Taken" seems to have a very straightforward message: choose your own path regardless of what other people do. But on closer reading, it is full of contradictions and ambiguities. When reading his work in public, Frost would warn his audiences to beware of taking it on face value, describing it as "a tricky poem."

The contradictions in the poem begin with the title, "The Road Not Taken," as the poem is really about the road actually taken. In the final stanza, the speaker recalls his choice of road "with a sigh," suggesting a hint of regret over his decision: did the road not taken represent a missed opportunity? A bleaker reading is that the choice made no difference at all, and the speaker is trying to convince himself that it did. The sigh of regret may be a reference to Edward Thomas. The two poets went for country walks together, with Thomas planning what he hoped would be interesting routes, but then regretting his choices. "No matter which road you take," Frost wrote to him, "you'll always »

I alone of English writers have consciously set myself to make music out of what I may call the sound of sense.
Robert Frost
Letter to his friend John Bartlett, 1913

The Georgian poets

A group of English poets known as the Georgians, after King George V, were the most influential force in poetic life in England in the run-up to World War I (1914–1918). Including A. E. Housman, John Masefield, D. H. Lawrence, Edmund Blunden, Rupert Brooke, and Edward Thomas, they wrote traditional poetry about nature and country life. Frost, who shared many of the same poetic concerns, got to know several of the group while he was living in England. Some of the Georgian poets, including Brooke and Thomas, lived in the village of Dymock in Gloucestershire, and Thomas persuaded Frost to settle there while in England. Both Brooke and Thomas were killed in World War I.

The village of Dymock was an inspirational place for the Georgian poets. In 1914, however, the idyll was shattered as World War I scattered the poets far and wide.

sigh, and wish you'd taken another." Frost wrote the poem after his return to the US and sent it to Thomas, who was aware of his hesitant nature and did not appreciate Frost making fun of him.

Structure and meter

The poem's loose iambic meter encourages the reader to linger on certain syllables, reflecting the speaker's hesitancy and doubt as he tries to make his decision. Frost also used a strict iambic meter at times, as in his well-known poem, "Stopping by Woods on a Snowy Evening." In that poem, the relentless beat pushes the poem along in defiance of the speaker's sense of fatigue and desire to rest— a decision that could have fatal consequences in a freezing New England winter.

In "The Road Not Taken," the way in which Frost sets sentences against stanzas contributes to the poem's impression of naturalness, while keeping to a traditional form. The poem consists of four five-line stanzas. The long first sentence, in which the speaker muses about whether he should go this way or that way, runs through two and a half of the four stanzas. This is followed by a short, one-line sentence: decision made. The third sentence, in which certainty wobbles, is covered in two lines, and the final sentence, a hypothetical reflection on the decision, takes up a whole stanza. The structure of the poem seems to reflect natural

We must go out into the vernacular for tones that haven't been brought to book.
Robert Frost
Letter to American writer and critic William Stanley Braithwaite, 1915

thought processes, which are set against a regular abaab rhyme scheme that holds the varying syntactical units together.

The rhythms of life

Frost's vernacular rhythms are also much in evidence in his narrative poems, which explore the everyday activities of rural life—clearing land, mending walls, picking apples, climbing trees, and coping with loss and death. These poems, mostly written in loose iambic pentameter blank verse, include direct speech, conversations, and even arguments, in which the voice sometimes switches from one character to the other midline, creating a convincingly conversational tone.

The best known narrative poems are "Home Burial," which consists of an argument between a couple whose young child has just died, and "Wild Grapes," in which a woman recalls an incident from her youth when she dangled helplessly from a tree branch while her brother encouraged her to let go, something she was unable to do.

Although Frost wanted to capture the sounds of everyday speech, he made use of several

Oh, I kept the first for another day!
Yet knowing how way leads on to way,
I doubted if I should ever come back.
"The Road Not Taken" (lines 13–15)

poetic devices in order to depict recognizable experience. Nature is a constant theme in his work. Woods, trees, paths, flowers, seasons, and snow regularly appear, but as metaphors or symbols for moods and states of mind, rather than as subjects in their own right. Caesurae (mid-line pauses) and enjambments (lines that run over) are also used, particularly in his blank verse poems, to add to the impression of natural speech. Various sound patterns, such as rhyme schemes and alliteration, also add to the mood and meaning.

Components of vernacular poetry (intonation, language, and syntax).

Traditional poetic devices (meter and rhyme scheme).

The "sound of sense," or conversational language in a structured form.

Critical reaction

The early poems written by Frost were first published in England during his time there between 1913 and 1915, and were well received. Ezra Pound, whom Frost met in England, gave Frost's first collection, *A Boy's Will*, a good review in the American magazine *Poetry*, commenting that to read Frost's work was to learn about life. Other poets who shared Frost's interest in creating work based on ordinary lives—especially poetry rooted in their own locales or experiences—also admired his work. W. H. Auden acknowledged Frost as "a kindred spirit" in his approach to the natural world, and praised the "quiet and sensible voice" he used to express a range of emotion and experience.

To Irish poet Seamus Heaney, Frost's work suggested new ways of combining local dialects and idioms with the features of formal verse; he particularly admired the naturalness and spontaneity of Frost's characters in poems written in formal meter. However, not everyone shared this opinion: some literary critics attacked Frost's use of traditional form as backward-looking, and his use of colloquial speech as too simplistic.

The people's poet

By the time of his death in 1963, Frost's work was widely known and popular with the public, not least because he gave numerous public readings throughout his life—he liked to say that he was his own best salesman. Supporters praised his poems' values of self-reliance and independence, and their democratic use of language as it is spoken. Others recognized a Modernist sensibility in the psychological complexities of his characters, and in the ambiguities that require the reader to dig down into his work to discover its meaning. While the accessibility and popularity of Frost's writing continued to divide opinion in some parts of the literary world, in 2000 the US public voted "The Road Not Taken" to be the nation's favorite poem. ∎

Robert Frost recites a poem before John F. Kennedy at the US Capitol, Washington, D.C., in January 1961—the first time a poet is invited to read for a presidential inauguration.

SO ACCURATELY WRITTEN, AND WITH SUCH DISCIPLINED PLEASURE*

"POETRY" (1919), MARIANNE MOORE

* Frank Kermode

In the early 20th century, American poet Marianne Moore was a leading figure in Modernism—a literary movement that arose as a response to the broad, rapid changes created by industrialization. By the time Moore published the first version of her poem "Poetry" in *Others: A Magazine of the New Verse* in 1919, she was living in New York City, and her work was generating interest among fellow American poets such as Ezra Pound and William Carlos Williams.

In 1921, the poet H. D. (Hilda Doolittle), a friend of Moore, included "Poetry" in a small collection, *Poems*, published by

The Egoist Press in England, albeit without Moore's permission. The poem—with minor revisions—first appeared in book form in the US in the collection *Observations* (1924).

A variation on free verse

Like her fellow modernists, Moore sought to break free from the strictures of 19th-century poetry, such as formal meter and regular line lengths. She did this by using a type of free verse known as syllabics, which is based on the number of syllables contained in a line rather than the number of stresses. The haiku, a poetic form developed in Japan in the 17th century, has three lines of five, seven, and five syllables and is a form of syllabics; syllabic verse was also commonly used for poems in European languages such as French, Italian, and Spanish. The form was not often used as the basis for English verse, however, before writers such as Moore took it up in the 20th century.

Spoken English, which relies on a combination of stressed and unstressed syllables, falls easily into a regular metrical pattern, such as iambic (where the first syllable is unstressed, the second stressed) or trochaic feet (where the first syllable is stressed, the second unstressed), and most poetry was traditionally based on this system. In the case of syllabic verse, the poet decides on the line lengths for each poem, rather than following a preexisting metrical pattern. Syllabic lines can vary in length within a poem, and stresses can fall randomly.

Using syllabics presents a complex writing challenge, but it offers poets a number of linguistic

Despite her reputation for difficulty, Moore championed precision; her images, while mysterious in their meaning, are often clear, almost cinematic, as visuals.
Gabrielle Bellot
Caribbean editor and writer for *Literary Hub*, 2019

opportunities. Lines can be fitted to natural speech patterns—something that was particularly important to Moore—and readers' expectations of a line that has a regular pattern and stressed and unstressed syllables can be disrupted. The syllabic discipline can also draw attention to the artificiality of poetic form while still giving the verse shape and a sense of structure.

In search of good poetry

"Poetry" expresses Moore's views on poetry itself and, in particular, what constitutes good and bad poetry. She published several different versions of the poem over her lifetime, and all have the same ironic opening statement—that she dislikes poetry. This initially seems a strange remark for a poet to make, but Moore goes on to say that it is bad poetry she dislikes, and then explains in more detail what she means by good and bad poetry.

The poem lists potential poetic subject matter, including hands grasping, bats hanging upside down, wild horses, wolves, and even everyday items such as business documents and schoolbooks. Moore clarifies, however, that when writers load their chosen subject matter with meanings it does not have, or make comparisons that do not ring true, the result is not poetry.

Good poetry, Moore says, will exist only when poets fulfil two criteria: when they can strike the difficult—and paradoxical—balance between reality and the imagination and, when using the imagination, they can make their subject matter appear absolutely real and the imagery authentic to the reader. For this to happen, the basic matter of poetry should be presented in all its raw, original, and genuine form. Whatever the material, Moore maintains, poets must visualize it in their imagination so intently that they can bring it alive in the reader's mind.

Poetic methodology

Moore worked by making a collage of images and ideas taken from a range of sources, including newspapers, magazines, and brochures. She also incorporated a broad selection of literary and nonliterary references and quotations. In explanation, she once commented: "If I wanted to say something and somebody had said it ideally, then I'd take it but give the person credit for it."

Her eclectic subjects included a porcelain swan, the way a pangolin moves, the tentacle-like glaciers on the summit of Mount Rainier in Washington state, or watching a baseball game—although the »

At a reception in New York, in 1948, Marianne Moore (seated center right) is joined by other eminent poets, including Elizabeth Bishop (behind Moore) and W. H. Auden—perching on a ladder.

diversity of the natural world was her most common subject. Moore did not treat these things as abstract ideas, but described them in great detail, using vivid but precise language and visually rich imagery. In so doing, she revealed and explored a vast web of associations between the natural and human worlds that seem completely authentic. William Carlos Williams recognized this quality in her work early on when he wrote in the *Quarterly Review of Literature* (1948) about feeling "the swirl of great events" even when Moore was writing about something seemingly insignificant.

Every syllable counts
In poems written in syllabic verse, there is no limit to how long the lines can be—and those lines do not need to match each other for length. In her poems, Moore varies the number of syllables per line within a stanza, but the pattern of line lengths repeats from stanza to stanza. The 1919 version of "Poetry" has five six-line stanzas, and the number of syllables per line in each stanza is 19, 22, 11, 5, 8, and 13.

For someone listening to a reading of "Poetry," it can be challenging to keep track of the syllabic patterns, as sentences flow on from line to line and stanza to stanza. It is not vital, however, to think about the number of syllables in each line since Moore employs an abbccd rhyme scheme that suggests where the line endings fall. Some lines end on unstressed syllables or unstressed words, such as prepositions, but they carry the rhyme nevertheless. This creates an unobtrusive rhyme scheme that is known as light rhyme. The stanza pattern and the light rhyme scheme between them provide just enough structure

to hold together the lengthy sentences, in which images and ideas come thick and fast.

The lives of a poem
Like many poets, Moore revised her poems after their original publication, but she took the practice to unusual extremes. Four major revisions of "Poetry" exist. The first made small but significant changes and two small cuts that upset the syllabic pattern and left the third stanza a line short. In 1924, a much shorter version of "Poetry," consisting of 13 lines and no stanzas, appeared in *Observations*. *The New Poetry*, an anthology published in 1932, includes a version of the poem that more closely resembles the original, but it is still shorter, having three five-line stanzas with a syllabic pattern of 8, 14, 11, 19, and 16 syllables, and internal rather than end rhymes.

In *The Complete Poems of Marianne Moore*, published in 1967, "Poetry" appeared chopped

In the best modern verse, room has been made for the best of modern thought and Miss Moore thinks straight.
William Carlos Williams
"Marianne Moore," 1925

Syllabic verse

In the poetic form of syllabic verse, the syllables in a line are not—or need not be—stressed. All that matters is that each line has a specific number of syllables—such as the six syllables per line in Thomas Nashe's *A Litany in Time of Plague* (1592):

Adieu, farewell, earth's bliss;

This world uncertain is;

Fond are life's lustful joys;

Death proves them all but toys;

None from his darts can fly;

I am sick, I must die.

---

down to just three lines, to the consternation of many of Moore's admirers, who implored her not to discard her earlier work. One of her supporters, Canadian critic Hugh Kenner, saw the revisions as violent acts. Despite publishing the revised versions, Moore did not prevent the reprinting of earlier versions and seemed happy to let all versions coexist.

"Poetry" was not the only poem Moore revised. She altered many early works, possibly wanting to bring them more in line with her later poetry or to reassert authorial control over poems that had become much analyzed and reviewed. The original versions of the works may have ceased to be "genuine" to her because they had become too familiar, or her own exacting standards may have demanded repeated reassesment and revision over time. Moore also left out many previously published earlier poems from her collection *The Complete Poems*, commenting in the preface that "omissions are not accidents." This revisionist approach was an aspect of her work that she wished neither to discuss nor explain.

A lasting legacy

Moore's influence on the poetry of her time was extensive, and she also became a celebrated cultural figure. While employed as acting editor of *The Dial* magazine in the 1920s, she published work by many leading poets, including Ezra Pound, William Carlos Williams, and T.S. Eliot. Later, Elizabeth Bishop was introduced to Moore, who became her a mentor and a close friend.

Moore's work also influenced other young poets such as John Ashbery, who studied her poems and incorporated quotes from them into his own. When reviewing *The Complete Poems* in the *New York Times Book Review*, he wrote that he was tempted "to call her simply our greatest modern poet". This status was affirmed by her many literary awards; however, her role as a cultural icon and literary celebrity perhaps found its most populist expression in a request by a Ford Motor Company executive in 1955, who asked if she could apply her poetic talent to naming the company's latest car model. ∎

Not overworked.
Not dominated by
a male voice.
A secret music.
Robyn Schiff
American poet, 2016

Marianne Moore

Born near St. Louis, Missouri, in 1887, Marianne Moore grew up in Pennsylvania, where she went to Bryn Mawr College and started writing short stories for its magazine. In 1918, she moved to New York City, by which time her first published poem, "To the Soul of Military Progress," had appeared in *The Egoist*, a London literary magazine. She became acting editor of *The Dial* magazine in 1925 after winning its 1924 Dial Award for her first American collection, *Observations*.

Moore won the Pulitzer Prize, the National Book Award, and the Bollingen Prize for her 1951 *Collected Poems*. Further small collections followed, as did more literary awards and an honorary doctorate from Harvard University. She also wrote prose pieces on many subjects, including sports— she was an avid baseball fan. Moore died in 1972.

Other key works

1921 *Poems*
1924 *Observations*
1935 *Selected Poems*
1951 *Collected Poems*

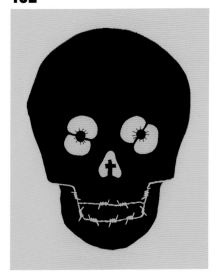

THE OLD LIE: DULCE ET DECORUM EST / PRO PATRIA MORI
"DULCE ET DECORUM EST" (1920), WILFRED OWEN

IN CONTEXT

FOCUS
War poetry

OTHER KEY POETS
W. B. Yeats, Rudyard Kipling, W. H. Auden, Dylan Thomas, Anna Akhmatova

BEFORE
1913 The motto "Dulce et decorum est pro patria mori" is inscribed on the chapel wall at Sandhurst, the British Royal Military College.

1914 British poet Laurence Binyon writes "For the Fallen," honoring the dead but also lamenting the deaths yet to come in World War I.

AFTER
1940 In "For Wilfred Owen," American poet Josephine Jacobsen highlights the new horrors of World War II.

1964 British poet Philip Larkin writes "MCMXIV", inspired by photographs of idealistic young men queuing to enlist for World War I.

The Latin phrase, *dulce et decorum est pro patria mori*—"it is sweet and proper to die for your country"—comes from the *Odes* of Horace, the Roman lyricist, written in the 1st century BCE. It is inscribed on the graves of many soldiers who died fighting in World War I (1914–1918), to honor their sacrifice for their country. The words are now more commonly associated with antiwar sentiment, due to British poet–soldier Wilfred Owen using them both for the title and closing line of his most famous poem. Owen's "Dulce et Decorum Est" is a frank recounting of the horrors of war, ending with a clear condemnation of Horace's motto as "The old Lie."

Owen wrote the first draft of the poem in Craiglockhart Hospital in Edinburgh, Scotland, in October 1917, while receiving treatment for "shell shock"—a neurological condition associated with exposure to artillery explosions. He revised the poem in early 1918 after his discharge from hospital, with some input from his fellow British war poet Siegfried Sassoon, whom he had met in Craiglockhart.

Harrowing detail
"Dulce et Decorum Est" describes a gas attack on the Western front, in France. The speaker sees a fellow soldier fail to put on a gas mask in time and die a grisly death as a result, "blood / […] gargling from the froth-corrupted lungs." The first stanza describes the weary soldiers, tired and coughing, some having lost their boots. This immense fatigue makes them slow to react to the attack announced in the second stanza: "Gas! GAS! Quick, boys!"

Owen describes the gas as thick and misty, "a green sea" for the man to drown in. The color suggests it is chlorine gas, first used on a large scale by German forces at Ypres in April 1915. By 1917, two other gasses were also used: the invisible and

> In all my dreams before my helpless sight,
> He plunges at me, guttering, choking, drowning.
> **"Dulce et Decorum Est" (third stanza, lines 1–2)**

See also: Sonnet 1 62–63 ▪ Sonnet 130 88–93 ▪ "Ozymandias" 132–135 ▪ "If—" 180 ▪ "The Second Coming" 194–197 ▪ "September 1, 1939" 220–223 ▪ *Poem Without a Hero* 265

more deadly phosgene and mustard gas—the most common. Only about 3 percent of people exposed to gas died, but its effects were agonizing enough to generate terror.

The two-line third stanza evokes the nightmarish sight of the gassed man, before the fourth stanza vividly describes his death. At 12 lines, the fourth is the longest stanza, two lines short of a sonnet but following that form in its use of iambic pentameters and abab rhyming scheme. Although, at 28 lines, the poem could divide into two sonnets, Owen subverts the form by varying line and stanza lengths and using abrupt punctuation and random enjambment (running on of lines) to emphasize the panic and confusion of the attack.

Truth and propaganda

Owen addressed the first draft of his poem to "Jessie Pope etc.," referring to the author of *Jessie Pope's War Poems* (1915); he later amended this to "a certain Poetess" before removing it entirely. Pope's poems were pro-war and patriotic,

first published in Britain's *Daily Mail* to encourage young men to enlist in the army. "Dulce et Decorum Est" was an impassioned rebuttal of this kind of propaganda, which associated enlisting with masculinity and courage. Owen's antiwar poetry portrayed war as brutal and inglorious. British poet Ted Hughes, writing in 1964, compared it to taking TV cameras into a war zone to show its horrors.

Views of war

Owen was part of a wider group of soldier–poets writing candidly about their experiences in World

The epitaph on Owen's gravestone (center), in Ors, France, is taken from his poem "The End," and reads "Shall Life renew these bodies? Of a truth / All death will he annul."

War I. Among British serving men, Isaac Rosenberg wrote "Break of Day in the Trenches" as a grim reflection on the absurdity of being stuck in a trench, while Robert Graves's "A Dead Boche" shares the experience of stumbling upon a German soldier's corpse.

Other poets wrote more idealistically about World War I. Rupert Brooke's "The Soldier," which describes the foreign places where English soldiers are buried as being part of England, was criticized for romanticizing the war, and Canadian soldier John McCrae's "In Flanders Fields" featured in pro-war propaganda and inspired the wearing of the poppy as a symbol of remembrance. The war, however, was no respecter of differing stances and took the lives of Owen and Rosenberg, Brooke and McCrae alike. ▪

Wilfred Owen

Born in 1893 in the Shropshire town of Oswestry, UK, Wilfred Owen worked as a tutor in France for two years from 1913. There, he experimented with poetry, heavily influenced by the English Romantic poets, especially John Keats. He enlisted in the army in 1915 and was commissioned as a second lieutenant in the Manchester Regiment in 1916.

In April 1917, Owen was injured in France and sent to Craiglockhart Hospital in Scotland, to recover. There he met Siegfried Sassoon, who had a great impact on his poetry. Owen also edited

Hydra, the hospital's magazine. He returned to the Western front in August 1918 and was awarded the Military Cross for resisting an enemy attack. A week before the Armistice, in November 1918, Owen was killed crossing the Sambre-Oise canal in northern France. Most of his poems were published posthumously by Sassoon.

Other key works

1919 "Strange Meeting"
1920 "Anthem for Doomed Youth"

THINGS FALL APART; THE CENTER CANNOT HOLD

"THE SECOND COMING" (1920), W. B. YEATS

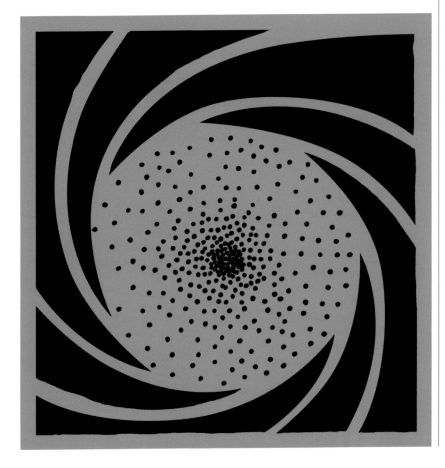

IN CONTEXT

FOCUS
Spiritualism

OTHER KEY POETS
Rumi, William Blake, Gerard Manley Hopkins

BEFORE
1820 Percy Bysshe Shelley publishes *Prometheus Unbound*, described by Yeats as "among the sacred books of the world."

1893 Yeats edits an edition of the writings of visionary poet William Blake.

AFTER
1958 Nigerian novelist Chinua Achebe publishes *Things Fall Apart*, using a phrase from "The Second Coming" as its title.

1968 American author Joan Didion names her *Slouching Towards Bethlehem* essay collection after the final line from "The Second Coming."

Although a metaphorically complex poem, "The Second Coming" carries a clear message. For its author, W. B. Yeats, Western civilization, which had grown and expanded for 2,000 years, is close to collapse, with potentially horrible consequences.

In January 1919, at age 54, Yeats was seeing all around him the signs of imminent apocalypse. World War I (1914–1918), ending only two months earlier, had left more than 20 million people dead and toppled three long-standing empires; the Russian Revolution was also threatening to engulf Europe in a tidal wave of atheistic Communism that might even

See also: "London" 122–125 ▪ "Ozymandias" 132–135 ▪ *The Waste Land* 198–205 ▪ "Do Not Go Gentle Into That Good Night" 240–241 ▪ "Casualty" 290–293

For Yeats, **chaos and destruction** linked to **personal, Irish, and world events** suggest an imminent **apocalypse**.

Yeats's **mystical interpretation** is that the end of a 2,000-year Christian era is approaching.

He believes that a new **cycle of history** is emerging that will be the **antithesis** of the expansive, progressive, and ethical Christian era.

"The Second Coming" predicts that this new era will bring an Antichrist, a bestial and cruel being bereft of all virtues.

reach Yeats's beloved Ireland, which was tumbling into a violent civil war.

At home, the poet's young wife, Georgie, and unborn child had barely survived the 1918–1919 influenza pandemic, which saw the deaths of at least 50 million people worldwide. Driven by these cataclysmic signs, Yeats set to work on the two-stanza, 22-line blank verse "The Second Coming."

End of civilization

"The Second Coming" can be read on two levels, both as a warning and as a prediction of the end of Christian civilization. It begins with a falcon, out of reach of its

falconer's call, tracing the path of an imagined swirling spiral—what Yeats called a "gyre." The falcon or gyre is so out of control that the "center cannot hold" and "mere anarchy" is loosed upon the world ("mere" being used in its original meaning of "total" or "complete"). A bloody tide of war is unleashed, overwhelming enlightened values, as good men lose their convictions, leaving the field to extremist fanatics.

The second stanza begins with the hope that "surely" there must be a means to prevent civilization's imminent collapse. This is couched in the biblical imagery of the Second Coming of Christ. But the »

W. B. Yeats

Born in Dublin in 1865, poet, playwright, author, editor, and essayist William Butler Yeats was the foremost literary figure in Ireland during his lifetime. Although an Anglo-Irish Protestant and resident of London for decades, he remained an Irish nationalist.

While a Dublin art student, Yeats developed a lifelong interest in spiritualism and occultism and he later joined London's Hermetic Order of the Golden Dawn—a secret society devoted to occultism.

In 1917, after a series of thwarted proposals of marriage to several other women, Yeats married Georgie Hyde-Lees, with whom he had a daughter and a son. In 1922, he became a senator in the new Irish Free State parliament and two years later he won the Nobel Prize in Literature. Yeats died in France in 1939.

Other key works

1903 *In the Seven Woods*
1914 *Responsibilities*
1919 *The Wild Swans at Coole*
1921 *Michael Robartes and the Dancer*
1928 *The Tower*
1933 *The Winding Stair*

poet quickly turns from the New Testament vision of "revelation" to the pagan *Spiritus Mundi*, or "World Soul"—and from this new point of view he sees that the Second Coming might instead be the visitation of something terrifying, a monstrosity or "rough beast" spawned by the failure of civilization to cohere.

Yeats, however, is doing more than issuing a warning about Western civilization's potential fate. The poem also references his fundamental beliefs in the mystical and spiritual forces that lie behind the workings of the world and every aspect of life. For Yeats, "The Second Coming" is also his grim prediction. The "rough beast" *will* come, and there is nothing civilization can do about it.

Spiritual guidance

In a letter written to Irish writer John O'Leary in 1892, Yeats states, "The mystical life is at the center

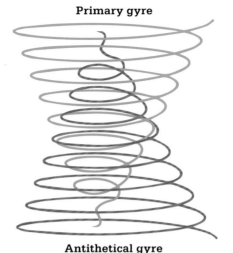

Primary gyre

Antithetical gyre

Cycles of history

Yeats's view of history takes the form of a double gyre— two conical spirals, each representing a historical cycle, that intersect to form the shape of an hourglass. One gyre is open at the top, the other open at the bottom. The place where they meet is a point of equilibrium between two eras, before one slowly becomes the dominant civilization while the other weakens.

of all that I do and all that I think and all that I write." The belief that reality was ultimately spiritual in nature and harbored numerous unseen beings and secret patterns continued to grow throughout his life. Yeats had taken part in seances since 1888, and in 1919, when he composed "The Second Coming," he was almost two years into a spirit-led "automatic writing" experiment with his wife. She acted as a medium, receiving spirit messages and writing them down. Spirits would also speak through her when she slept, while Yeats acted as the interpreter of the strange messages.

The mysterious "controls" and "instructors," as Yeats called them, also appeared to be revealing the complex spiritual dynamics at work behind all phenomenal appearances—the interlocking phases and cycles that Yeats would later elaborate in his philosophical work *A Vision*, published in 1925.

Yeats is photographed with his wife, Georgie, on a lecture tour of the US in the 1920s. On the tour, he described himself as "an Irish Nationalist" and Ireland as "a country of oppression."

These phases and cycles operated at every scale, from a single atom to a human life, and even to whole eras of history—the portentous aspect that provided the inspiration for "The Second Coming."

Mystical patterns

Yeats used a double-gyre diagram to illustrate his theory of the cycles of historical change. Each gyre is a swirling vortex, which is born, expands, and inevitably falls apart in a cycle lasting about 2,000 years, marking an era of human history. As a cycle expands, the apex of the gyre that will replace it has already penetrated through its stem. The new gyre is always antithetical— opposite—in movement and character. As Yeats says in *A Vision*: "Each age unwinds the thread another age has wound."

The cycle of history reflected in "The Second Coming" is the Christian era, nearing the end of its 2,000-year reign and having in turn usurped the preceding Classical era. It is now a "widening gyre," traced out by the falcon in the poem's opening line. Each historical cycle dies a violent death, hence the poem's imagery of centers ripping apart and bloody tides engulfing men. In Yeats's vision, the new era is already arriving—"after twenty centuries of stony sleep"—its apex driving into the midst of the dying Christian era and carrying "the rocking cradle" that awaits the birth of a new age.

According to Yeats's theory, the coming age must be the opposite or inverse of what it usurps—the Western culture that has always expanded upward and outward, carrying science and progress and morality and high ideals with it. Yeats foresees the drowning of the "ceremony of innocence"—the customs, structure, order, and decency embodied in Christian civilization, the perfection of all virtues.

Being antithetical, the new cycle must be typified by an Antichrist, lacking any virtue. To reveal its nature, Yeats consults the *Spiritus Mundi*—his storehouse of poetic images—and recoils in horror. He glimpses a terrible sphinx-like creature stirring, with "gaze blank and pitiless as the sun." This vision is still hazy, but Yeats knows the new order is unstoppable, and wonders in dread what it will be.

> And what rough beast, its hour come round at last,
> Slouches towards Bethlehem to be born?
> **"The Second Coming"** (lines 21–22)

"The Second Coming" was first published in the journal *The Dial* in 1920 before appearing the following year in the volume *Michael Robartes and the Dancer*. In the latter, it follows the poem "Demon and Beast," and immediately precedes "A Prayer for My Daughter," an especially appropriate pairing because the "daughter" is Yeats's child, born in the aftermath of his wife's near-death from influenza. The metaphorical storm at the opening of "A Prayer for my Daughter" also acts as an echo of the apocalyptic vision of "The Second Coming."

Prophetic articulation

Beyond his mystical obsessions and complexity of thought, Yeats remained a master poetic craftsman. The carefully honed weight and economy of his words and imagery have resonated across the century since "The Second Coming" was written. New generations turn to the poem during wars or periods of political unrest, finding in lines such as "the center cannot hold" and "The best lack all conviction, while the worst / Are full of passionate intensity" the perfect prophetic articulation of world events where "things" really do seem to "fall apart."

Yeats stands like a mountain looming over the landscape of spiritualist poetry. Few except Blake—who creates his own mythology—rival his ability to combine an occult philosophy with a lyric expression. Persian poet Rumi (1207–1273) and polymath Omar Khayyam (1048–1131) reflect the mystical side of Islam; Gerard Manley Hopkins that of Christianity. But that is not quite the same thing. The thoroughly delineated universe of the spiritualist or occultist movement does not seem to chime with poetry—except with Yeats. ∎

An illustration for Yeats's poem "The Lake Isle of Innisfree" (1890) suggests the "peace" the poet longs for on the lonely Irish island.

The Irish Renaissance

When W. B. Yeats and his friend and fellow mystic George Russell (pseudonym "AE") attempted to "marry" the Irish imagination to the holy places and sacred sites of Ireland in their writings, they were promoting what would soon be called the Irish Literary Revival or Irish Renaissance. This vigorously successful campaign to revive Irish writing in the late 19th and early 20th centuries was linked to the rise of Irish nationalism and a revival of interest in Ireland's Gaelic culture.

Joined by Irish writer and folklorist Lady Augusta Gregory, Yeats helped found several Irish literary societies and, in 1904, the Abbey Theatre in Dublin—the first Irish national theater. Both he and Gregory wrote plays for the Abbey, as did Dublin playwrights John Millington Synge—whose *The Playboy of the Western World* (1907) celebrated the west coast peasantry—and Seán O'Casey, who ennobled the Dublin working class in *The Plough and the Stars* (1926).

THESE FRAGMENTS I HAVE SHORED AGAINST MY RUINS

THE WASTE LAND (1922), T. S. ELIOT

IN CONTEXT

FOCUS
Modernism

OTHER KEY POETS
e. e. cummings, Marianne Moore, H. D., Wallace Stevens, W. H. Auden, Ezra Pound

BEFORE
1857 Charles Baudelaire, often seen as the first Modernist, publishes *Les Fleurs du Mal* (*The Flowers of Evil*).

1914 Ezra Pound publishes *Des Imagistes*, an anthology of poems from the Imagist movement, an early subtype of Modernism.

AFTER
1930 London publisher Faber and Faber releases *Poems* by the young W. H. Auden. Over the next decade, Faber champions many Modernist poets.

1957 Ted Hughes publishes his first collection, *The Hawk in the Rain*. His work is both influenced by, and a departure from, Modernism.

> Unreal City,
> Under the brown fog of a winter dawn,
> A crowd flowed over London Bridge, so many,
> I had not thought death had undone so many.
> **The Waste Land (lines 60–63, "I. The Burial of the Dead")**

In 1922, *The Waste Land* erupted into the literary world like few other long poems before it. Innovative in almost every sense, the 433-line poem bewildered, infuriated, and delighted readers, often simultaneously. Published a few months after another mold-shattering masterwork, Irish writer James Joyce's novel *Ulysses*, *The Waste Land* came to be seen as a landmark of Modernism.

The birth of Modernism

Modernism wasn't a self-conscious or organized movement. The term refers to parallel responses, emerging around the 1870s, to a Western world that was dramatically transformed by mass production, new inventions, improved communications, and insights into humanity provided by evolutionist Charles Darwin and psychoanalyst Sigmund Freud.

While the extent and rapid pace of change were exciting, they were also highly destabilizing. Across the arts, traditional modes of expression involving coherent narrative and structure no longer seemed adequate or truthful, and artists, writers, and composers looked for new ways to capture what they were experiencing. In painting, the experimentation that began in the 19th century with Impressionism and Post-impressionism led in the 20th century to the bold colors of Fauvism and the geometric shapes of Cubism; in music, in 1913, the ballet *The Rite of Spring* by Russian composer Igor Stravinsky scandalized Paris audiences with its raw energy and dissonance.

This sense of dislocation culminated in World War I (1914–1918), a conflict defined by slaughter on an unprecedented scale made possible by the mass production of weapons.

Poetic revolution

The Waste Land first appeared in print in October 1922, in the inaugural issue of *The Criterion*,

---

The five sections of *The Waste Land*

"The Burial of the Dead"

Spring's cruel awakening in an arid wasteland

"A Game of Chess"

Unsatisfactory relationships in marriage

"The Fire Sermon"

Bleak sexual encounters and spiritual degeneration

"Death by Water"

The triumph of death, rendering life inconsequential

"What the Thunder Said"

Desperate yearning and the possibility of peace

See also: "Poetry" 188–191 ▪ "The Second Coming" 194–197 ▪ "Helen" 207
▪ "A Postcard from the Volcano" 218–219 ▪ Canto LXXXI 232–235

> [...] it sounds for the first time in all their intensity, untempered by irony or disguise, the hunger for beauty and the anguish at living which lie at the bottom of all his work.
> **Edmund Wilson**
> American writer and critic
> (1895–1972)

a newly founded London literary magazine edited by Eliot himself. The poem soon arrived in the US, first in a magazine called *The Dial* in November, and then, in December, in book form. The following year, Eliot's friends, writers Virginia and Leonard Woolf, printed it at their Hogarth Press in London.

Collage-like, *The Waste Land* is built up from an accumulation of fragmentary images and texts, many of them snippets of the works of others, from Dante, Shakespeare, and Chaucer to German composer Richard Wagner, as well as popular songs and nursery rhymes. The poem juxtaposes numerous different voices, from the high-blown to the sardonic and the colloquial. Lacking any clear overall narrative,

Marie Lloyd performed popular songs in music halls; Eliot described Lloyd as expressing the part of England with "the greatest vitality" and alluded to several of her songs in *The Waste Land*.

the text is imbued with a sense of anxiety and the potential cruelty of life, underpinned by a powerful feeling of doom.

Themes and structure
Divided into five unequal parts, *The Waste Land* has two underlying themes: death and sex (or fertility). Eliot drew poetic inspiration from his wide reading in European and Indian literature and philosophy, as well as from the works of two British scholars: anthropologist James Frazer and folklorist Jessie Weston.

The poem's first section, "The Burial of the Dead," opens with the statement, "April is the cruellest month," a deliberate parody of the opening of Geoffrey Chaucer's Prologue to *The Canterbury Tales*, in which April is the bringer of renewal and fertility, symbolized by spring rain showers. In Eliot's poem, this very stirring into life is what makes April "cruel," forcing people out »

T. S. Eliot
Born into an upper-class family in 1888, Thomas Stearns ("Tom") Eliot grew up in St. Louis, Missouri. He began writing poetry at an early age. After studying at Harvard in the US and the Sorbonne in Paris, he attended Oxford University in the UK and then moved to London in 1915.

In 1927, Eliot became a British citizen and was baptized into the Church of England. He later described some of his work as being "Anglo-Catholic in religion."

After success with poetry, Eliot turned his hand to poetic drama, starting with *Murder in the Cathedral* in 1935. Also written that year, his poem "Burnt Norton" led to three others, published together as *Four Quartets* in 1943.

Eliot was awarded the 1948 Nobel Prize in Literature. In 1957—10 years after the death of Vivienne, his first wife, by then estranged—he embarked on a happy marriage with Valerie Fletcher. He died in 1965.

Other key works

1930 *Ash Wednesday*
1935 *Murder in the Cathedral*
1943 *Four Quartets*

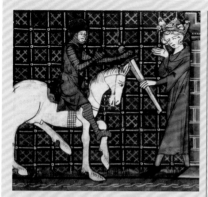

The Fisher King (right) greets Perceval in a 14th-century manuscript of Chrétien de Troyes' *Perceval, The Story of the Grail*.

The Fisher King

Running through *The Waste Land* is the myth of the Fisher King, a character who first appears in literature in *Perceval*, an Arthurian romance by French poet Chrétien de Troyes, around 1190. Wounded in his groin in battle, the king is no longer capable of riding, and his only diversion is to sit and fish. He is associated with the Holy Grail, a stone or dish of miraculous power (later identified with the chalice said to have been used at Christ's Last Supper), which is kept in his castle. The king's wound will only heal when a knightly hero accomplishes certain tasks. These are eventually performed by Perceval.

Some scholars have linked the legend of the Fisher King with ancient fertility rituals, because the king's wound has rendered him and his realm infertile: a "waste land." The tale has inspired many works of art, including Richard Wagner's opera *Parsifal* (1882) and British director Terry Gilliam's film *The Fisher King* (1991).

of the forgetfulness of winter into the often painful renewal of "Memory and desire."

In Part II of the poem, "A Game of Chess," the focus shifts to sex and the anguish of frustration when married couples, trapped in dysfunctional relationships, cannot find satisfactory connection. Part III, "The Fire Sermon," brings further loveless sexual encounters, including the assault of a typist by a "young man carbuncular." The short Part IV, "Death by Water," reverts to the theme of death. In Part V, "What the Thunder Said," drought symbolizes both death and spiritual drought; the final arrival of lightning and "a damp gust / Bringing rain" suggests the possibility of peace, at least at a personal level. The whole poem ends with a threefold repetition: "Shantih shantih shantih" (Sanskrit for "peace").

Rooted in tradition

The Waste Land was hailed as revolutionary, yet Eliot himself, as many of his friends and contemporaries enjoyed pointing out, was highly conservative. An American transplanted to literary London, he seemed to become more English than the English. Virginia Woolf observed, teasingly, that it was as if he were wearing not just a conventional three-piece suit, but a four-piece one. Such jokes hid a serious point. Tradition, not revolution, lay at the heart of Eliot's conception of poetry and art. In an essay published three years before *The Waste Land*, he stressed the importance of the "historical sense." The true poet, he believed, had a sense of past as well as present, the "timeless" as well as the "temporal". Poetic works,

[…] an impression of an intensely modern, intensely literary consciousness which perceives itself to be not a unit but a chance correlation […]
Conrad Aiken
American poet and friend of Eliot
(1889–1973)

he believed, can only exist in relation to works by other poets and artists, including those who are long dead.

In *The Waste Land*, Eliot weaves together fragmented references spread out through space and time, from the fifth-century theologian St. Augustine to the Buddha, from the Bible to the Hindu scriptures, and from the Arthurian legend of the Fisher King to the works of Dickens, with allusions to modern popular culture in between.

Influential experiences

Eliot's poetry was influenced by both wider literary developments and events in his own life. In France, an early manifestation of Modernism had occurred when a group known as the *Symbolistes*, inspired by French poet Charles Baudelaire and US writer Edgar Allan Poe, rejected the conventions of Realism. Poets Paul Verlaine, Arthur Rimbaud, and Jules Laforgue, among others, aimed to communicate mood and feeling through the inner music of language and use of symbols. Eliot came across British critic Arthur Symons's book *The Symbolist Movement in Literature* (1899) while an undergraduate at Harvard. He later claimed that the book changed the direction of his life from philosophy to poetry, and from the US to Europe.

A second decisive encounter came a few years later in London, when Eliot visited his fellow American poet Ezra Pound. Already an established figure in European literary circles, Pound was a leader of the briefly flowering Imagist movement, another early strand of Modernism. Its followers advocated using precise language and imagery, and discarding all that was superfluous.

Impressed by Eliot's "The Love Song of J. Alfred Prufrock," Pound took Eliot under his wing. He would later play a crucial role in the final shaping of *The Waste Land*. He also encouraged Eliot's relationship with Vivienne Haigh-Wood and in 1915, courtship turned into marriage.

Eliot in the City

In 1917, Eliot found work in the City of London, the capital's financial district, an experience that fed

Virginia Woolf, pictured here between Eliot and Vivienne in 1932, suggested that Anglo-American Modernism began in 1910: "On or about December 1910, human character changed."

into *The Waste Land*. Bleak images of the City—its people, streets, and buildings—recur throughout the poem, conveying the ceaseless activity of the metropolitan machine. At the time, Europe and the US were gripped by galloping inflation, leading to both destitution and greedy profiteering.

Writing *The Waste Land*

Eliot continued to write poetry while working in finance, and in 1917 published his first poetry collection, *Prufrock and Other Observations*. In a letter home to his mother at the end of 1919 he mentioned a "long poem" he planned to write—and his resolution to settle down to work on it.

Nearly three years later, when *The Waste Land* finally appeared, many would see it as encapsulating the desolation of a generation still recovering from World War I, raddled by the loss of old beliefs and values, and facing social and economic uncertainties. While this view holds some validity, it is equally true that the poem emerged from Eliot's own personal hell at this time. The recent death of his father in the US engendered feelings of guilt for not having pursued a career in philosophy, as his father had wanted, and the failures of his marriage to Vivienne were painful. Although the widely read Vivienne helped nurture the poet in Eliot, her fragile mental health drained his energy. With expensive medical bills to pay, he was obliged to work long hours, not just at his office in the City, but in the evenings and at weekends as a literary journalist and lecturer.

By the summer of 1921, Eliot was working in earnest on his long poem. But the pressures on him were becoming unbearable, and »

London Bridge is depicted in *The Waste Land* as a place where the dead walk. Eliot may have been referring to the soullessness of the City or to the multitudes killed in World War I.

> There is shadow under this red rock,
> (Come in under the shadow of this red rock),
> And I will show you something different from either
> Your shadow at morning striding behind you
> Or your shadow at evening rising to meet you;
> I will show you fear in a handful of dust.
> **The Waste Land (lines 25–30, "I. The Burial of the Dead")**

he was on the edge of a breakdown. With his wife's and doctor's encouragement, he negotiated a three-month leave of absence from his job in the bank. He spent October in the English seaside resort of Margate and then, at the recommendation of a literary friend, British artist and aristocrat Ottoline Morrell, two months at a clinic for nervous disorders in Lausanne, Switzerland. Like many other details from Eliot's personal life, both Margate and Switzerland crop up in *The Waste Land*. In Switzerland, Eliot completed *The Waste Land*'s final two sections—"Death by Water" and "What the Thunder Said."

The better craftsman
On his way back to England in January 1922, Eliot stopped over in Paris to leave a typescript of his work with Pound. At that stage, the poem ran to more than 600 lines and was entitled "He Do the Police in Different Voices"—a quotation from a character in Charles Dickens's *Our Mutual Friend*. Pound's response was generous and enthusiastic—"I am wracked by the seven jealousies"— and ruthless. To release its genius,

the poem needed radical cuts; Pound recommended losing more than 200 lines. It was Pound who recognized that the lines at the top of the second page of Eliot's typescript—"April is the cruellest month"—should become the opening lines of the poem.

Eliot went along with almost all of Pound's edits, and he also changed the title of the poem to *The Waste Land*, a reference to the Arthurian legend of the wounded Fisher King, whose wound brings sterility to his people and his land. Eliot's esteem for his mentor is seen in his dedication to Pound at the front of *The Waste Land*, where

he calls him "*il miglior fabbro*" ("the better craftsman"), a line borrowed from Dante's *Divine Comedy*.

Eliot's contemporaries
The Waste Land's status as the single most iconic Modernist poem of the 1920s is unchallenged, but many contemporaries of Eliot's were also probing the limits of poetic possibility around the same time, embracing the exhortation (attributed to Pound) to "Make it new." They included American poets Gertrude Stein, H. D. (Hilda Doolittle), William Carlos Williams, and e. e. cummings. One of the greatest American Modernists was poet Wallace Stevens. Stevens' first collection, *Harmonium*, published in 1923, included "Thirteen Ways of Looking at a Blackbird." Its 54 short, stark lines are divided into 13 mini-poems, comparable to haiku in their pared-back intensity.

Pound's own *Hugh Selwyn Mauberley*, a cycle of 18 short poems, was published in 1920.

Modernist writers in Paris in 1923 included (left to right) Ford Madox Ford, James Joyce, and Ezra Pound. Lawyer John Quinn (far right) defended Joyce's *Ulysses* against censorship.

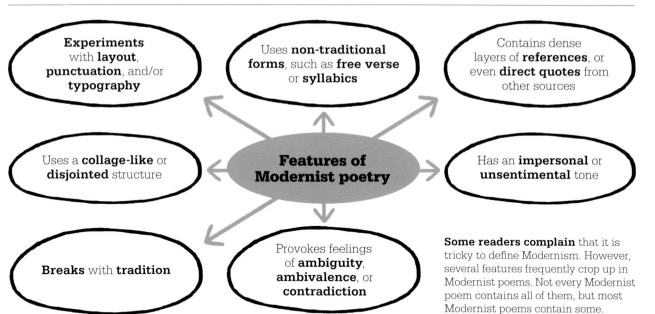

Experiments with **layout, punctuation,** and/or **typography**

Uses **non-traditional forms,** such as **free verse** or **syllabics**

Contains dense layers of **references**, or even **direct quotes** from other sources

Uses a **collage-like** or **disjointed** structure

Features of Modernist poetry

Has an **impersonal** or **unsentimental** tone

Breaks with **tradition**

Provokes feelings of **ambiguity, ambivalence,** or **contradiction**

Some readers complain that it is tricky to define Modernism. However, several features frequently crop up in Modernist poems. Not every Modernist poem contains all of them, but most Modernist poems contain some.

A foreshadowing of *Cantos*, his Modernist epic, it depicts a minor poet looking back on his life and work and commenting ruefully on his earlier fruitless attempts at writing conventionally "sublime" verse, "Bent resolutely on wringing lilies from the acorn."

In Paris, Pound and Stein nurtured innovative writers and artists: organizing soirées where they could meet, introducing them to publishers and patrons interested in supporting avant-garde work, and even lending them money. James Joyce—whose novel *Ulysses* was the other masterpiece of Modernism published in book form in 1922—was among those championed by Pound and Stein. In 1925, critic Andrew Warnod called their breeding ground for talent the *École de Paris* (School of Paris).

The poem's legacy
The Waste Land propelled Eliot into the ranks of the most highly esteemed English-language poets of the age, alongside older figures such as W. B. Yeats. For writers emerging in the interwar years, the influence of *The Waste Land* was inescapable. William Carlos Williams said of the poem, "It wiped out our world as if an atom bomb had been dropped upon it."

Novelists, including Americans F. Scott Fitzgerald and Ernest Hemingway, were also profoundly influenced by *The Waste Land*. In Britain, writer Evelyn Waugh took

[…] I could not tell you exactly what every word and line mean, but that is not necessary for an understanding and appreciation of the poems.
Leonard Woolf
"'Jug Jug' to Dirty Ears,"
***The Nation and Athenaeum*, 1925**

a quotation from the poem for the title of his fourth novel *A Handful of Dust* (1934), a reminder that death lurks even in the midst of life. In Waugh's seventh novel, *Brideshead Revisited* (1945), the character Anthony Blanche recites *The Waste Land* through a megaphone to undergraduate Oxford oarsmen on their way to rowing practice.

Eliot as editor
For young poets from the UK and Ireland, such as W. H. Auden, Stephen Spender, and Louis MacNeice, *The Waste Land* had exposed new ways of using the English language. When Eliot left the City to join the publishing house Faber and Faber in 1925, he became Auden's and Spender's editor. Eliot also nurtured new poets, including in the 1950s Ted Hughes, who described *The Waste Land*—which he acknowledged is often perplexing—as "a drama of voices." Hughes exhorted people to listen to the music of these voices. Then, he said, *The Waste Land* becomes "wide open." ∎

ONE'S GENTLY WEANED FROM TERRESTRIAL THINGS
"THE FIRST ELEGY" (1923), RAINER MARIA RILKE

In 1912, Bohemian-Austrian poet Rainer Maria Rilke was on a cliff-top walk in Italy, when a line came to him, as if a revelation: "Who, if I cried, would hear me among the angelic / orders?" This philosophical question would form the opening line of the first of his *Duino Elegies*. Ten religious and metaphysical poems, written over a decade, the elegies grapple with the anxieties of human existence in a war-torn world.

How to be human
Rilke's plea in "The First Elegy" is followed by a discourse on the limitations of the human condition. Measured against angels—self-contained, fully conscious symbols of strength and a "higher order" of reality—we only half understand and experience the world. But despite our inadequacies, Rilke offers some consolation: suffering, as in unrequited love, can allow us to access "something more than itself." Suffering opens a space in which art can emerge—art that "lifts us and comforts and helps." In addressing

Rilke's muse, psychoanalyst Lou Andreas-Salomé (center), shown here with Rilke (left), introduced him to the work of philosopher Friedrich Nietzsche and psychoanalyst Sigmund Freud.

the tension between art, beauty, and suffering, Rilke presents a modern approach to spirituality and a seminal philosophy on how to live as imperfect humans in an imperfect world. Its expression in the elegies would make them some of the most influential writing of their time. ∎

See also: *Eugene Onegin* 142–143 ▪ "How Do I Love Thee?" 150–151 ▪ "To the Reader" 162–165 ▪ *The Waste Land* 198–205

REMEMBERING PAST ENCHANTMENTS / AND PAST ILLS

"HELEN" (1924), H. D. (HILDA DOOLITTLE)

IN CONTEXT

FOCUS
Reimagining the Classics

OTHER KEY POETS
Percy Bysshe Shelley, John Keats, W. B. Yeats, Ezra Pound, Derek Walcott

BEFORE
1831 American poet Edgar Allan Poe alludes to Classical myth to praise a contemporary woman in "To Helen."

1910 In "No Second Troy," W. B. Yeats frames the story of his own unrequited love in the context of Greek mythology.

1912 The Imagist movement is launched, its celebration of direct expression was inspired by Classical forms.

AFTER
1961 H. D. publishes *Helen in Egypt*, an epic poem based on the myth of Helen and Achilles.

1990 St. Lucian poet Derek Walcott references Homer in his modern epic *Omeros*.

P oets have always used Classical mythology to give shape and significance to human emotions. In the early 20th century, this became a popular device among Modernist writers, who turned to Greek writing to express states of mind such as love and rage. However, such myths were often still told from the perspective of their male protagonists. The 20th-century Imagist poet Hilda Doolittle, who wrote under the pen name H. D., reimagined these stories from the woman's point of view. A Greek scholar and admirer of the poet Sappho, she mostly wrote in lyric rather than epic form.

Beautiful scapegoat
The "Helen" of H. D.'s poem is Helen of Troy—wife of Menelaus, the Greek king of Sparta—famed for her beauty. Helen was taken to Troy by Paris, son of the Trojan king—whether willingly or unwillingly depends on the source chosen. The Greeks laid siege to Troy for 10 years to get her back. In the poem, Helen has returned to a Greece that hates her, holding her responsible for the loss of so many Greek lives. They hate her face and looks of sorrow. They could only love her if she were dead. But the poem is ambiguous about her culpability: do the Greeks hate her for being the cause of the Trojan War or for her beauty?

H. D.'s flesh-and-blood Helen is a rejoinder to Edgar Allan Poe's statue-like figure in "To Helen" (1831), and to W. B. Yeats's "No Second Troy" (1910), in which she represents beauty as a destructive force in the personal and political worlds. ∎

All Greece hates
the still eyes in the white face [...]
"Helen" (lines 1–2)

I, TOO, AM AMERICA

"I, TOO" (1926),
LANGSTON HUGHES

IN CONTEXT

FOCUS
Harlem Renaissance

OTHER KEY POETS
**Paul Laurence Dunbar,
Alice Dunbar Nelson,
Georgia Douglas Johnson**

BEFORE
1895 The poems in Paul
Laurence Dunbar's *Majors and
Minors* use both dialect and
standard English to reflect the
Black American experience.

1922 Black American poet
Georgia Douglas Johnson
tackles race issues in her
collection *Bronze*.

AFTER
1927 The poems in James
Weldon Johnson's *God's
Trombones* are based on the
Black American sermon.

1929 Countee Cullen, a Black
American poet, compares the
suffering of Christ to that of
Black Americans in his
collection *The Black Christ*.

The Harlem Renaissance
was a golden age of Black
American culture, starting
around 1918 and continuing until
1937. Literature, jazz, theater, film,
and the visual arts all played a part.
Creative individuals and groups in
the Harlem district of New York
City sought to explode the white
stereotype of the "Negro" and
restore to Black Americans a truer
sense of their identity and heritage.
At the same time, there was an
effort to free Black Americans
from the shame many felt when
perceiving themselves through
the lens of white bourgeois moral
values. This creative movement
was more about debate than
the promotion of a particular
program. Its impact on later Black
culture was huge.

Social background
The Great Migration of Black
Americans from the rural South to
the conurbations of the north and
northwest of the US—for more than
five decades from 1916—was an
important strand of US social
history. It was driven by labor
shortages that had resulted from
new immigration laws in the 1920s

> Tomorrow,
> I'll be at the table
> When company comes.
> **"I, Too" (lines 8–10)**

and the subsequent reduction
in European migrants. Black
Americans flocked to employers
desperate to fill job vacancies.

There were other good reasons
to flee the South, too. After the
post–Civil War Reconstruction
(ending in 1877), racism had been
institutionally sanctioned by the
Jim Crow laws, which enforced
segregation right up to the start of
the Civil Rights movement in the
1950s. Extrajudicial lynchings were
the most violent manifestation of
racial hostility, and in 1937,
American songwriter Abel
Meeropol composed the poem
"Strange Fruit" about such a
lynching. Two years later, singer
Billie Holiday recorded it as a song.
The lynching of 14-year-old Emmett
Till in Mississippi in 1955 and the
subsequent acquittal of two
defendants by an all-white jury
heightened the outrage felt by Black

Langston Hughes

Born in 1901, in Joplin, Missouri,
Langston Hughes was brought up
by his mother and grandmother.
He started writing poetry at
high school in Cleveland, Ohio.
After dropping out of Columbia
University, New York, feeling racist
exclusion (he later completed a
degree at Lincoln University,
Pennsylvania), he worked his
passage on a freighter to Africa,
then traveled around Europe.

After publication of his first
collection *The Weary Blues* in
1926, Hughes's output was prolific,
including eight books of poetry,
four of fiction, numerous plays and

essays, two autobiographies,
and studies of Black history. He
also founded theater companies
in Harlem and Los Angeles. A
prime figure in the Black Civil
Rights movement, Hughes was
the first Black American to
make a living from writing
and lecturing. He died in 1967.

Other key works

1926 *The Weary Blues*
1932 *The Dream Keeper and
Other Poems*
1951 *Montage of a Dream
Deferred*

See also: "London" 122–125 ▪ "Song of Myself" 152–159 ▪ "We Wear the Mask" 170–171 ▪ "Black Art" 268–269

A 1919 issue of *The Crisis*, the magazine of the National Association for the Advancement of Colored People, which played an important role in publicizing the Harlem Renaissance.

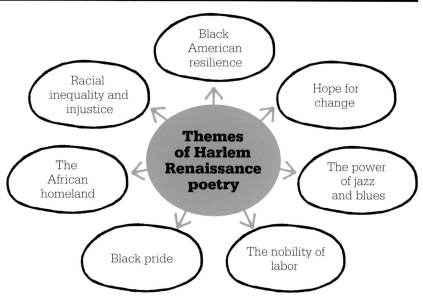

Themes of Harlem Renaissance poetry

- Black American resilience
- Hope for change
- The power of jazz and blues
- The nobility of labor
- Black pride
- The African homeland
- Racial inequality and injustice

Americans and all decent people. Lynchings continued into the 1960s.

Many Black Americans from the southern states moved to New York City but found their "promised land" was compromised. Life could be harsh in city ghettos. Migrants from the South were often treated as inferior by the Black establishment in the north. During the Great Depression of the 1930s, poverty led to a rise in crime rates, but creativity, particularly in Central and West Harlem, enjoyed an extraordinary flourishing. An increase in literacy also fed the Harlem Renaissance. At the same time, the creation of national bodies concerned with Black American civil rights added to the momentum of protest. Race pride and pan-African awareness were consciously cultivated.

Renaissance bard

Langston Hughes was one of the leading poets of the Harlem Renaissance. Naming his poetic influences as Walt Whitman, Carl Sandburg, and Paul Laurence Dunbar, he wrote in free verse for the people, specifically his Black compatriots, in work that could be understood by any literate person. Connection with a wide readership, in terms of both language and subject matter, was crucial to him.

Hughes described his subject as an urban demographic: "workers, roustabouts, and singers, and job hunters" in the cities, insecure in their jobs, paying for their furniture in installments, and stretching their wages by pawning possessions.

Hughes's poem "I, Too" illustrates his characteristic style and message at their simplest, though composed with an artful balance of assertion and understatement. Verbosity was anathema to Hughes, and three of the poem's 18 lines have just one word: "Tomorrow," "Then," and "Besides"—ordinary everyday words.

The first line, however, sounds a note of economical oratory: "I, too, sing America." The use of singing as a verb whose object is not the song but the *subject* of the song harks back to the usual translation of the first line of Virgil's *Aeneid*: "Arms, and the man I sing [...]." Walt Whitman did the same in his poems, "I Sing the Body Electric" and "One's-Self I »

> They'll see how beautiful I am
> And be ashamed—
> **"I, Too" (lines 16–17)**

> Down on Lenox Avenue the other night
> By the pale dull pallor of an old gas light
>   He did a lazy sway. . . .
>   He did a lazy sway. . . .
> To the tune o' those Weary Blues.
> **"The Weary Blues" (lines 4–8), 1926**

Sing." What Hughes is doing here is expropriating the grandeur of white speech idiom, as well as offering himself—by subtle implication—as a Black American Whitman. The word "Too," of course, has no antecedent, so readers have to supply their own—whether Virgil, Whitman, or, more generally and recently, the tradition of those white people who have claimed, in oratory or poetry, to glorify America.

The next line, after a line space, is simple self-identification: "I am the darker brother." Implied in "brother" is social equality. Although he is sent to the kitchen "When company comes," he laughs and eats well and grows strong. This description continues the idea of a rich parallel life, despite segregation from the dining room, and at the same time uses creative ambiguity, since "grow strong" could be taken as relating to Black America generally, not just this individual.

"Tomorrow" takes us to a liberated future, expressed with total confidence. "Nobody'll dare [. . .]" recognizes how complete this redemption will be: not just a new convention, but a change of mindset that nobody with any self-respect will resist—again note the sweeping confidence. "Besides" prepares for heightened self-esteem: the Black self as beautiful. That beauty, projected with absolute conviction, will be so obvious that white onlookers will be ashamed of previous prejudice. The poem concludes with a direct echo of the first line, so that the two lines form a frame, for a radiant self-portrait: "I, too, am America."

The broken stair

"I, Too" is an extended metaphor: the scene is vividly realized but also represents segregation and pride in general terms. We extrapolate from the domestic to the national. Hughes used a similar metaphorical technique in his earlier (1922) poem "Mother to Son." Again, the vernacular voice is crucial: "Life for me ain't been no crystal stair." In other poems, blues and jazz intonations come to the fore, but the focus remains true to working-class lifestyles. Some Black intellectuals

Attended by up to 50,000 people, the 1920 parade of the Universal Negro Improvement Association in Harlem signified the increasing confidence of Black Americans.

The Savoy jazz club (depicted here in a 1989 mural) was on Lenox Avenue, a street mentioned by Hughes in several of his poems, including "Juke Box Love Song" and "The Weary Blues."

believed this emphasis did a disservice to Black potential. Hughes's core audience, however, responded more positively. In verse molded to both the sounds of local speech and the rhythms of blues and jazz, he expressed a vision of "Black pride" without militancy and often with humor—powered by a firm belief in the goodness of the human heart.

Harlem dynamo

Black American women were central and influential in the Harlem Renaissance, and their work was widely read. The poetry of Jessie Fauset, Georgia Douglas Johnson, Angelina Weld Grimké, Anne Spencer, and others was featured in magazines such as *The Crisis*.

Other key poets of the movement included Jamaican-born Claude McKay. His work, collected in *Harlem Shadows* (1922), celebrated Jamaican farming life and protested against racial inequality. His sonnet,

"If We Must Die," with its defiant final couplet—"Pressed to the wall, dying, but fighting back!"—does not specifically refer to skin color or race and has been valued as a resistance cry against oppression of every kind, everywhere. Another key figure, Countee Cullen, found inspiration in Keats and, to some extent, English poet A. E. Housman, and generally championed a Black American style that gained authority from English precedents. It was in part the creative conservatism of McKay and Cullen that prompted Hughes to forge his own more vernacular style, rooted formally, as well as in subject matter, in the Black experience. Cullen is a poet of contradictions, committed to protest and the serious exploration of race, while trying to earn for Black poetry a place within existing traditions.

James Weldon Johnson was a versatile American poet who used dialect in a way that aligned him with Hughes. In 1922, he won critical plaudits for editing a major anthology of Black verse, *The Book of American Negro Poetry*. He went on to compile collections of the song form known as the spiritual. ∎

But in spite of the Nordicized Negro intelligentsia and the desires of some white editors we have an honest American Negro literature already with us.
Langston Hughes
"The Negro Artist and the Racial Mountain," 1926

Poetry and jazz

The quintessential music of 1920s Harlem was jazz, which evolved from enslaved people's work songs, spirituals (religious folk songs), blues, brass band music, and ragtime (the forerunner of jazz music). It was played in speakeasies, where illegal liquor was sold. Louis Armstrong, Duke Ellington, Bessie Smith, and Fats Waller often performed in the Cotton Club, which Hughes—a rare Black visitor—criticized as "a Jim Crow club for gangsters and monied whites." Working-class speakeasies frequented by Black Americans included the Sugar Cane. Police estimated that every block in Harlem had around ten of them.

Poets such as American Vachel Lindsay and UK-born Mina Loy included references to jazz instruments and venues in their work. Hughes went further, writing poems that imitate jazz rhythms and refrains to create a distinctive Black American voice.

Louis Armstrong (kneeling) playing with "King" Oliver's Creole Jazz Band at a speakeasy in 1922. There were more than 30,000 speakeasies in New York City alone in the 1920s.

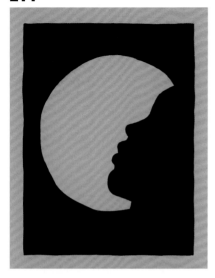

LUBRICIOUS AND PURE

"BALLAD OF THE MOON, MOON" (1928), FEDERICO GARCÍA LORCA

IN CONTEXT

FOCUS
Duality

OTHER KEY POETS
Edgar Allan Poe, Walt Whitman, Charles Baudelaire, Rainer Maria Rilke, Ted Hughes, Seamus Heaney, Derek Walcott

BEFORE
1898 Spain's defeat in the Spanish-American War in the Caribbean prompts Miguel de Unamuno and other influential Spanish writers—the Generation of '27—to work for national literary and intellectual renewal.

AFTER
1944 Generation of '27 poet Dámaso Alonso publishes *Children of Wrath*, capturing the mood of Spain after its civil war (1936–1939).

1977 Surrealist poet Vicente Aleixandre, one of the Generation of '27, is awarded the Nobel Prize in Literature.

The first of 18 poems in Spanish poet Federico García Lorca's *Romancero gitano* (Gypsy Ballads), "Ballad of the Moon, Moon" sets the tone for a collection that mingles myth and realism. It tells a story in which the moon comes down to a Romani forge one night, appearing as a woman dressed in creamy white. She finds only a young boy, who stares at her. The boy warns her to flee in case the other Romani people come back and

find her, and turn her heart "into necklaces and white [silver] rings." The moon, however, is not afraid. When the Romani do, indeed, return, they find the forge empty. The moon-woman has kidnapped the boy—the "moon crosses the sky / with a child by the hand."

Dispassionately told and yet haunting, the narrative is completed in 36 lines. The duality of the poem's title is repeated within the poem. The moon-woman is both "lubricious and pure" (unchaste and chaste); she is fluid, swaying her arms, yet bares "breasts of hard tin." The Romani people are victims, screaming and weeping for their lost child, yet they would have made the moon their victim, and profited from her, had they caught her. In the end, it seems to be the night "air [...] keeping watch" that embraces all and somehow holds the dualities together.

The traditional Spanish ballad, with its roots in the 14th century, appealed to Lorca as a kind of mini-

Gypsy Ballads was first published in the Spanish magazine *Revista de Occidente* (*Magazine of the West*), which provided a platform for the Generation of '27 writers and poets.

See also: "The Raven" 146–147 ▪ "Song of Myself" 152–159 ▪ "To the Reader" 162–165 ▪ "The First Elegy" 206 ▪ "Pike" 260–263 ▪ *Omeros* 300–303

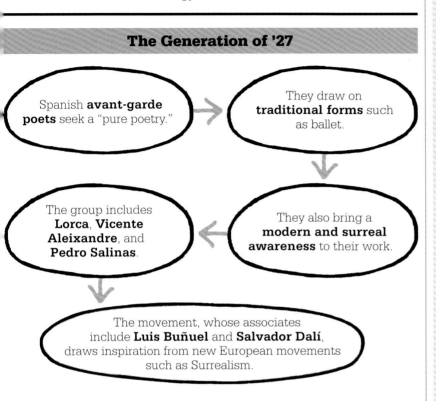

The Generation of '27

Spanish **avant-garde poets** seek a "pure poetry."

They draw on **traditional forms** such as ballet.

The group includes **Lorca**, **Vicente Aleixandre**, and **Pedro Salinas**.

They also bring a **modern and surreal awareness** to their work.

The movement, whose associates include **Luis Buñuel** and **Salvador Dalí**, draws inspiration from new European movements such as Surrealism.

Federico García Lorca

Born near Granada, Spain, in 1898, Federico García Lorca moved to Madrid in 1919, where he became friends with future filmmaker Luis Buñuel and surrealist artist Salvador Dalí. Lorca was a member of the Generation of '27 group of influential Spanish poets in the mid-1920s. Following the success of *Gypsy Ballads*, he visited the US and Cuba in 1929–1930. This experience opened new worlds for him, including the Black culture of Harlem in New York City.

After returning to Spain in 1930, Lorca's first major success as a playwright was the verse drama *Blood Wedding*, (1933), which was followed by *Yerma* and *The House of Bernarda Alba*. He completed the last in June 1936, just as the Spanish Civil War was starting. Two months later, on August 18, right-wing Nationalist forces shot his brother-in-law and arrested Lorca, who were both known for their socialist views. He is believed to have been shot the following day.

Other key works

1928 *Gypsy Ballads*
1940 *Poet in New York*

epic, combining storytelling with a short lyrical form. Its sense of mystery—abrupt openings, events told with minimal contextual explanation, and sudden endings—was also attractive to Lorca. The Romani inspiration came from his native Andalusia, home of *cante jondo* ("deep song") and flamenco. Although he was keen to avoid the merely folkloric, he nonetheless had a romantic view of Andalusia's Romani. The "gypsy," he wrote, "is

the loftiest, most profound and aristocratic element of my country." Routinely persecuted, they had a resonance for Lorca, a gay man in a society where homosexuals might suffer similarly.

Chilling realism

Combining Romani themes with the ballad form allowed Lorca to create a *retablo*—a word meaning both "altarpiece" and "puppet show"— of his birthplace. The realism he also sought recurs through *Gypsy Ballads*, but most chillingly in the 15th poem, "Ballad of the Spanish Civil Guard," where he evokes the Civil Guard, at the time widely regarded as an instrument of oppression, setting out to raid a Romani quarter with their "skulls of lead," "their soul of patent leather." ▪

> How the owl sings,
> ay, how it sings in the tree!
> **"Ballad of the Moon, Moon"**
> **(lines 29–30)**

THIS SPARROW / WHO COMES TO SIT AT MY WINDOW / IS A POETIC TRUTH
"THE SPARROW" (1955), WILLIAM CARLOS WILLIAMS

IN CONTEXT

FOCUS
Stepped-line poetry

OTHER KEY POETS
Walt Whitman, Denise Levertov, Allen Ginsberg

BEFORE
1855 In *Leaves of Grass*, American poet Walt Whitman innovates a free verse form based on the cadence and rhythms of speech.

1914 "Oread," a six-line Imagist poem by American poet H. D. uses a free verse form with concise, distilled language.

AFTER
1956 Encouraged by William Carlos Williams to find his own voice, Allen Ginsberg writes "Howl" in long-line free verse.

1957 In *Here and Now*, UK-born American poet Denise Levertov rejects traditional forms in favor of a more experimental vernacular idiom and the use of direct, objective descriptions.

American poet William Carlos Williams' "The Sparrow" opens with a surprising assertion: that the sparrow sitting on his windowsill represents not just a "natural" truth (about its own corporeal existence) but a "poetic" one. The poem playfully teases out this statement, pointing, for example, to the way the sparrow "loves to / flutter his wings / in the dust." At one level, this represents a practical truth—the bird "does it / to rid himself of lice." At another level, the sparrow's relief makes it "cry out lustily." This is "a trait / more related to music / than otherwise," placing it in the realm of artistic or poetic truth.

The poem's exploration continues, presenting aspects of sparrow behavior objectively, semi-scientifically (Williams was a practicing family doctor throughout his working life, used to observing physical and scientific phenomena),

The industrial city of Paterson, New Jersey, here pictured in 1937, was instrumental in inspiring Williams to develop an American poetic form that could express everyday experience.

See also: "The Old Pond" 110-111 ▪ "Song of Myself" 152–159 ▪ *The Waste Land* 198–205 ▪ "Helen" 207 ▪ Canto LXXXI 232–235 ▪ "Skunk Hour" 242–245 ▪ "Howl" 246–253

William Carlos Williams

Born in Rutherford, New Jersey, in 1883, William Carlos Williams had a British-born father and a Puerto Rican mother. He began writing poetry while at school, but in 1902 enrolled to study medicine at the University of Pennsylvania, where he also formed lifelong and influential poetic friendships with Ezra Pound and H. D.

After medical studies abroad, Williams returned to Rutherford in 1912, where he lived for the rest of his life. He practiced as a doctor while writing poetry, fiction, plays, essays, and articles in his spare time. Widespread recognition came only from the late 1940s. A heart attack in 1948, followed by strokes and cancer, did little to impair his creative energy. Williams died in 1963 and was posthumously awarded the Pulitzer Prize for his final collection of poetry.

Other key works

1923 *Spring and All*
1946–1958 *Paterson*
1954 *The Desert Music and Other Poems*
1962 *Pictures from Brueghel and Other Poems*

---

yet also relating it to a broader imaginative context. Williams' attempt to express a poetic quality in objective form is also bound into the innovative structure of the poem, which uses a type of free verse in a "triadic" or stepped line.

Finding new form

Written in 1955, "The Sparrow" is one of Williams' later works. When he was young, a decisive influence was the Imagist poetry of his friends Ezra Pound and Hilda Doolittle (H. D.). Their core principles included "direct treatment" or scrutiny of the thing written about in a poem and lean, stripped-back language, inspired by Japanese forms such as the haiku. To this, Williams added the difficult task of "lifting to the imagination those things which lie under the direct scrutiny of the senses"—bringing the thing scrutinized into the zone of "poetic" or imaginative truth.

A tireless experimenter with poetic form, Williams was eager to evolve a distinctly American way of expressing American experience—including poetic truth. The stepped line consisted of one long line, split into three fragmentary "sub-lines," each placed below the previous one and then indented.

Williams called these sub-line fragments "variable feet," a "foot" being the basic rhythmic unit within a line of verse. Each "foot" or fragment—varying from a single syllable in some cases to ten or more—is a step in the unfolding of the line's meaning. In their organization, they also aim to evoke the quality of spoken language— and in particular, the intonations of American speech.

In Williams' hands, the triadic line became a way of shaping and directing the flow of free verse. It was typical of the stylistic boldness that made him, from the late 1940s, a hero and inspiration for the emerging post-war generation of American poets. Notable among these was the young Beat poet Allen Ginsberg, whom Williams mentored and who described Williams' rhythmic units as the "squiggly tunes of speech." ▪

Imagist poets react **against** the rigidity and order of **traditional forms of poetry**.

⬇

Williams takes their ideas further and **seeks to invent a new, authentically American poetic form**.

⬇

Williams' stepped-line form divides text into even, rhythmical units.

⬇

Williams' new verse form (and everyday subject matter), **influences the work of the Beat poets**.

WHAT WE SAID OF IT BECAME // A PART OF WHAT IT IS

"A POSTCARD FROM THE VOLCANO" (1936), WALLACE STEVENS

IN CONTEXT

FOCUS
The aesthetic imagination

OTHER KEY POETS
Marianne Moore, T. S. Eliot, William Carlos Williams

BEFORE
1880–1900 French Symbolists Arthur Rimbaud and Stéphane Mallarmé focus on dreams and the power of imagination.

AFTER
1937 "The Man with the Blue Guitar," a poem by Wallace Stevens on the uniqueness of the individual's imagination, is inspired by Picasso's painting *The Old Guitarist* (1903).

1942 Stevens' 630-line masterpiece *Notes Toward a Supreme Fiction* declares that the quest for poetic perfection is never-ending.

1956 American poet John Ashbery's first collection, *Some Trees*, debuts a new style of abstract aestheticism, tinged with melancholy.

Poems about poetry are a Wallace Stevens speciality. He forged an erudite music of deep philosophical ideas, entwined with delectable imagery in the quest toward a "supreme fiction"—pure poetry examining the interplay between reality and imagination. This was an alternative, often exotic world, detached from everything mundane but accessed through sensation. Since sound is sensory, too, Latinate polysyllables, such as "opulent" and "aureoles" (both in "A Postcard from the Volcano") also

played a part. His strategy was to catch the flow of life in a weave of words both truthful and pleasing. Ideas and objects occupied the same dimension of being.

In "Anecdote of the Jar" (1919) Stevens describes how he placed a jar on the ground, the wilderness rising around it. The three four-line stanzas amount to a still life with landscape. The jar is round, gray, and bare, and holds "dominion." Two implications are held in balance, one positive, one negative: the function of art is to keep confusion at bay or to keep nature

Wallace Stevens

Born in 1879, in Reading, Pennsylvania, Stevens had Dutch heritage on both sides of his family. His father was a lawyer, his mother a teacher. He started writing poetry in his teens. At Harvard University, he studied with humanist philosopher George Santayana. After graduating from New York Law School, he was admitted to the bar in 1904. In 1909, he married Elsie Kachel. His father opposed the match, which led to a lasting rift between them.

Stevens was unusual among poets in having a full-time office career, as an executive for an insurance company, eventually becoming vice-president. He was 44 when his first book of poems, *Harmonium*, was published in 1923. Stevens' *Collected Poems* won the Pulitzer Prize in 1955, the year he died.

Other key works

1923 *Harmonium*
1936 *Ideas of Order*
1950 *The Auroras of Autumn*

See also: "To the Reader" 162–165 ▪ "Poetry" 188–191 ▪ *The Waste Land* 198–205 ▪ "The Sparrow" 216–217

under submission. The subject, at one level, is poetry itself; the imagined horizons are vast (the state of Tennessee), yet the poem turns in on itself to consider its own aesthetics.

Gifts to the future

"A Postcard from the Volcano" follows a clearer line of argument than many Stevens' poems. It begins with children picking up "our bones" and ends with a view of "A dirty house in a gutted world." The dead, we deduce, are victims of the eruption of Vesuvius, in antiquity. The reference to a "postcard" is a touch of the comic irreverence often encountered in Stevens' poems.

Yet the poem is serious. The dead have left behind "what still is / The look of things, left what we felt // At what we saw." A run

The Dream by Henri Rousseau (1910). Stevens admired the French Post-Impressionist's jungle paintings, and his landscape descriptions carry traces of the painter's influence.

of 24 monosyllables in one stanza expresses a subtle idea with deceptive simplicity: that an ancestral way of thinking infiltrates the psyche of future generations of humanity.

In the penultimate stanza, the dead change from being plural and near to singular and far, from "we" to "he"—the owner of a ruined mansion. Its ghost is Stevens, rich in posthumous wisdom, but condemned to angrily haunt a ruin. The only sign of natural vitality is the "opulent" sun shining on the devastated building—its splendor offensive to one who can benefit no more from its rays.

So distinctive was Stevens' poetry that any imitation would have been read as pastiche. Those who were influenced later in the 20th century by his style include English poets David Gascoyne and Charles Tomlinson, and American poets Mark Strand and Jorie Graham. However, none of them has been so uncompromising in their aestheticism. ▪

Exotic place names, like Catawa and Cythère—**derived from reading**, rather than from personal experience.

Decorative words, such as "sombreros" and "duenna"—Stevens used a **vast vocabulary**.

Nonsense syllables with echoes of nursery rhymes to **offset the examination of aesthetics**.

Hallmarks of Wallace Stevens' language

Measured cadences, dispensing with rhyme—sometimes with overtones of **Miltonic blank verse**.

Foreign words and phrases, particularly French—although Stevens **never left the US**.

Unlikely juxtapositions, such as "literate despair" and "budded aureoles"—both in "A Postcard from the Volcano."

ALL I HAVE IS A VOICE / TO UNDO THE FOLDED LIE

"SEPTEMBER 1, 1939" (1939), W. H. AUDEN

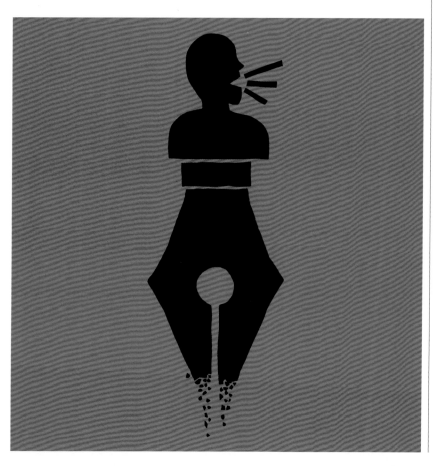

IN CONTEXT

FOCUS
Anti-Romanticism

OTHER KEY POETS
Wilfred Owen, T. S. Eliot, Philip Larkin

BEFORE
1938 W. H. Auden, Cecil Day-Lewis, Louis MacNeice, and Stephen Spender—the Auden Group—come together for the only time in the 1930s, in a BBC radio broadcast.

AFTER
1948 Auden wins the Pulitzer Prize for *The Age of Anxiety: A Baroque Eclogue*—a six-part poem in a modern version of Old English alliterative verse.

1994 Auden's 1938 poem "Funeral Blues" becomes a popular elegy after being recited in the film *Four Weddings and a Funeral*.

Modernist poet T. S. Eliot marked the end of Romanticism with *The Waste Land* in 1922. Its disjointed poetry tinged with neurosis mirrored the social disorientation triggered by World War I. In the 1930s, with war looming again, another anti-Romantic poet came to the fore: W. H. Auden.

The major British and Irish poets of the 1930s—Louis MacNeice, Stephen Spender, W. H. Auden, and Cecil Day-Lewis (collectively known as the Auden Group or by the nickname "MacSpaunday")—were less radical in their forms than Eliot. Auden often wrote sonnets, sestinas, and ballads. However, he was keen

See also: "I Wandered Lonely as a Cloud" 126–129 ▪ "Dulce et Decorum Est" 192–193 ▪ "The Second Coming" 194–197 ▪ *The Waste Land* 198–205 ▪ "Do Not Go Gentle Into That Good Night" 240–241 ▪ "An Arundel Tomb" 256–257

W. H. Auden

Born in York, in 1907, Wystan Hugh Auden was brought up in the English North and Midlands. After graduating from Oxford University, he spent time in Berlin, before serving as a stretcher bearer in the Spanish Civil War (1936–1939). In 1930, his first book of verse was published by Faber and Faber, where T. S. Eliot was an editor. Auden's early love poems use cryptic language to veil his homosexuality.

In 1938, Auden emigrated to the United States after marrying Erika Mann, the daughter of German novelist Thomas Mann to provide her with a passport. He became a US citizen and met long-term partner Chester Kallman. His beliefs shifted from Freudian and Marxist to Episcopalian. Auden wrote prolifically in many forms, including comic verse letters, sonnets, and limericks. He died in 1973.

Other key works

1932 *The Orators*
1936 *Look, Stranger!*
1940 *Another Time*
1947 *The Age of Anxiety*

to avoid outdated platitudes, and to move away from the influence of the great late Romantic, W. B. Yeats. Features of Auden's poetry that make it anti-Romantic include a concern with modern issues and phenomena, a detachment from feelings, an abandonment of 19th-century tropes about nature and sublimity, and an emphasis on reason rather than emotion.

Anti-Romantic yet lyrical

All the MacSpaunday group could be said, in their different ways and degrees, to be anti-Romantic, though that did not mean they discarded lyricism. MacNeice's lines in "Trilogy for X" (1941), "We think of love bound over, / The mortgage on the meadow," has a nostalgic cadence, despite its sobering message, while Auden's love poems, notably "Lullaby" (1937), are among the most treasured in the genre. The Romantics had dwelt on death and despair as well as love, but what makes Auden's love lullaby unorthodox are its strokes of harsh realism. While a lover lies asleep in their embrace, the poem's speaker alludes to their own faithlessness and acknowledges —albeit tenderly—their lover's mortality and guilt.

War, despair, and hope

Auden's "September 1, 1939" shows another anti-Romantic characteristic: a restless, nuanced engagement with the seismic changes of the times. The title is the date when Nazi Germany invaded Poland, the event that triggered World War II (1939–1945). The poet sits in a New York bar pondering how "the clever hopes" of "a low dishonest decade" have expired: the reference is to the misplaced faith in appeasement with Hitler.

The poem passes through four stages: despair, explanation, moral conclusion, and affirmation. The explanation examines how the "whole offense" of Nazism came about—through a craving for not universal love but satisfaction of the ego. Hitler's psychopathic greed is traced back to the vengeful harm done to Germany in the 1919 Treaty of Versailles, which brought World War I to a close. The moral lesson, when it comes, is clearly stated: "We must love one another or die." The labyrinthine argument that precedes this maxim, over eight 11-line stanzas, prevents it from seeming too glib. Yet Auden later, with characteristic moral »

[…] modernism has provided the automobile of literature with a fifth gear, but […] post-modernism also likes to get out the old road maps. In this sense, Auden is […] our first post-modernist poet.
John Fuller
British poet and critic, 2000

rectitude, felt the maxim showed "incurable dishonesty": he revised "or" to "and," since we all die in the end. He suppressed the whole stanza in 1945, and finally removed the poem from his *Collected Shorter Poems* when it was published in 1966.

The last stanza returns to the present, nighttime moment. "Our world in stupor lies"; yet points of light flash all around where responsible people exchange their messages—individuals, journalists, writers. It implies that there is a fine balance between the dark New York cityscape and a larger symbolic world, and between citizens going about their business and poets trying to meet the era's demands. The positive note is left to the last of the 99 lines, when Auden exhorts himself to "Show an affirming flame." Significantly, this flame is pure symbol—with no

practical context of hearth, lamp, or purgation. This reminds us of the earlier admission that all the speaker has "is a voice."

The limitations of poetry

Auden alluded to the passivity of poetry—the idea that it might simply exist, without having any great social impact—in works such as "In Memory of W. B. Yeats," as well as in "September 1, 1939." His approach appears to contrast with the Romantic view expressed by Shelley in his essay, *A Defence of Poetry*, written in 1821, that "poets are the unacknowledged legislators of the world." However, all that Shelley is claiming is moral authority, and Auden would not have disagreed. His "affirming flame" is a moral beacon.

Auden would have parted company with Shelley on the question of poetic talent. Shelley

(despite his atheism) wrote that the worth of poets and poetry was "indeed divine." Romantic aesthetics valued *afflatus*, a mystic form of poetic inspiration linked with genius. Another 1930s poet, Dylan Thomas, had sufficient self-belief to see poetry in these terms. For Auden, though, the poetic gift was a matter of work and luck. In his essay *The Dyer's Hand* (1962), Auden asserted that the writings we describe as inspired are the ones that turn out better than we might reasonably have hoped—nothing more.

Subjects and styles

Auden's erudition was vast, although there are only glimpses of this in "September 1, 1939." He viewed life through the lens of Freudian psychology, hence his description of himself in the poem as composed of "Eros and dust." Eros was the desirous, consuming form of love, in contrast to Agape, or universal, neighborly love. For Auden, poetry was the laboratory in which such ideas could be rigorously tested. He had studied science and engineering before switching to English, and he retained a strong attraction to the scientific approach. The Russian-American poet Joseph

In the late 1930s, 52nd Street in New York City was home to jazz venues such as The Famous Door (pictured, 1938). In "September 1, 1939," Auden locates himself in one of them.

Brodsky commented that Auden had "the greatest mind of the 20th century."

Embracing modernity

Auden worked conscientiously to explore his themes in depth, whatever the focus—the evils of war, the injustices of capitalism, the relation of art to life, the nature of suffering, the individual's role in history, and the relationship between body and spirit. Nothing about modern life seemed anti-poetic to him, and every one of these themes is characteristic of anti-Romanticism.

In language, too, Auden had little use for the archaic: after the obscurities of his early poems and despite the complex syntax of his later ones, his diction was mostly modern, often colloquial. Occasional poetic inversions, especially in more lyrical pieces, gave way to a plain-speaking mode that at times became prosaic.

Some critics have complained of obscurity in the early poems, verbosity in the later ones, and incoherence in both. At times, Auden lapsed into whimsy. The language he used became more convoluted and garrulous as he aged, and British poet and

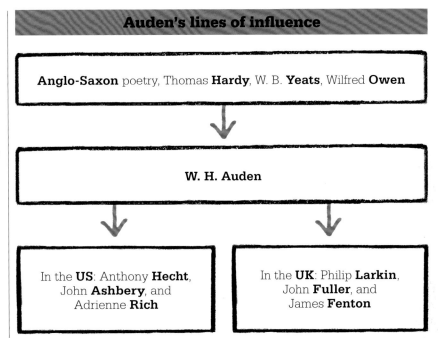

Auden's lines of influence

Anglo-Saxon poetry, Thomas **Hardy**, W. B. **Yeats**, Wilfred **Owen**

W. H. Auden

In the **US**: Anthony **Hecht**, John **Ashbery**, and Adrienne **Rich**

In the **UK**: Philip **Larkin**, John **Fuller**, and James **Fenton**

critic James Fenton has even detected the influence of novelist Henry James.

A platform for a purpose

Abstraction, such as references to love, death, law, order, will, and similar concepts, often with capital initials, is another charge levelled against Auden. In "September 1, 1939" he mentions "Collective Man" and "Authority." Alluding to the power of the majority and that of those who govern, these references are in line with the Marxist philosophy that informed Auden's thinking (and that of other '30s poets, with the notable exception of MacNeice, who was left-wing but never Marxist). Auden's reason for leaving England for the US was the burden he felt as a highly

W. H. Auden and friend, lover, and coauthor Christopher Isherwood (left) start their 1938 journey to China to document the Sino-Japanese War. This inspired their work *Journey to a War.*

visible poet with a responsibility to guide the public through the perils of the age: he needed to escape the pressure to propagandize.

In the US, Auden felt liberated but, at first, lonely—even after connecting with Chester Kallman, his lover, who strayed toward other men. Auden's loneliness comes through powerfully in "September 1, 1939," adding a personal counterpoint to the poem's sociopolitical anxieties. There is also a sense of being unable to participate in ordinary life: the "dive" bar is a haven of comfort that Auden cannot share, any more than he shares the narrow aspirations of "dense commuters."

The US, however, seemed to Auden the ideal setting in which to pursue his mission as a moral voice for humankind—and in the process to find ways of resisting both existential despair and consumerist decadence. Back home in England, the threat of devastating evil was near and dangerous. ∎

POST-WAR
CONTEMPO
1940–PRESENT

AND
RARY

"Middle Passage" by Black American poet Robert Hayden **exposes the realities** of the Transatlantic Slave Trade.

Gwendolyn Brooks's *Annie Allen*, a poem about the ordinary but heroic struggles of a young Black woman, **reinvents the Classical epic**.

Five young **countercultural poets**, later dubbed the Beats, read their poetry at Six Gallery in San Francisco.

The **violence of nature** is one of the themes explored in Ted Hughes's collection *Lupercal*, containing the poem "Pike."

Indigenous Australian **poet and activist** Oodgeroo Noonuccal publishes *We Are Going*, her first poetry collection.

1945   **1949**   **1955**   **1960**   **1964**

1945   **1951**   **1959**   **1962**

Modernist icon Ezra Pound completes *The Pisan Cantos* in a US military detention center near Pisa, Italy.

Dylan Thomas uses **the villanelle verse form** in "Do Not Go Gentle Into That Good Night," a protest against death.

In the US, **"confessional poet"** Robert Lowell publishes his autobiographical collection *Life Studies*.

Sylvia Plath writes "Daddy," about her **troubled relationship with her father**. The poem is included in the collection *Ariel*, later published posthumously.

When World War II ended in 1945, war-shattered Europe took time to rebuild, but the US recovered quickly. Factories that had been making weapons and military planes switched to producing consumer goods, and the economy boomed as people bought cars and furnished new homes. However, not all Americans embraced or benefitted from this consumerist society, and the conservative values that went with it. In the 1950s, a growing counterculture took shape, spearheaded in poetry by Allen Ginsberg, leader of a coterie of other antiestablishment writers and artists who became known as the Beats. Ginsberg's poem "Howl," written and performed in 1955, was a freewheeling tirade against everything the US stood for.

Less outrageous and performative but far from conventional, veteran American Modernists such as Ezra Pound, William Carlos Williams, Marianne Moore, and Wallace Stevens continued to create notable work, with Moore and Stevens picking up Pulitzer Prizes when they were in their seventies.

Identity poetry

Post-war poetry in the US began to focus increasingly on identity. Black Americans who had contributed to the Allied victory in Europe only to face racial inequality back home wanted spokespeople to articulate their rage. Robert Hayden and Gwendolyn Brooks wrote image-rich poems correcting the history of enslavement and drawing attention to the injustices and violence that Black Americans still faced.

By the 1960s, poetry had become a powerful tool in the pursuit of civil rights. The Black Arts movement (BAM), founded in 1965 by poet, playwright, and activist Amiri Baraka as the cultural wing of the Black Power movement, produced a stream of innovative poets. Sonia Sanchez explored improvisational jazz-like poetry in "a/coltrane/poem" (1975) and Ntozake Shange, whose experimental "choreopoem" *for colored girls who have considered suicide/ when the rainbow is enuf* (1970) combined poetry, music, movement, and dance.

While Black American poets tended to focus on group identity in the search for empowerment, Theodore Roethke and fellow white "confessional poets" Robert Lowell and Sylvia Plath were preoccupied with the self, recalling in painful

American Elizabeth Bishop, a late Modernist, **breathes new life** into the sestina, an old verse form, with her poem "Sestina."

Chinua Achebe's "Refugee Mother and Child" is **a lament for people dying of starvation** after the Biafran War (1967–1970).

American poet Michael Donaghy's "Machines" is **inspired by the metaphysical forms** of 17th century poet John Donne.

Carol Ann Duffy becomes Britain's Poet Laureate.

↑
1965

↑
1971

↑
1988

↑
2009

1965
↓

1967
↓

1978
↓

1990
↓

2021
↓

The **brutalities of Stalinist Russia** are laid bare in Anna Akhmatova's *Poem Without a Hero*, a work begun 23 years earlier.

In India, Kamala Das's poem "The Looking Glass" explores the taboo subject of **female sexual desire**.

In **response to the acquittal** of a white police officer who murdered an unarmed Black child, Audre Lord writes "Power."

St. Lucian poet Derek Walcott publishes *Omeros*, (1990), a **richly lyrical poem** about his Caribbean homeland inspired by Homer's epics.

Black American poet Amanda Gorman recites "The Hill We Climb" at the **inauguration ceremony** for President Biden.

---

detail the poet's own traumatic experiences and breaking the convention of poetic detachment.

Outside the US

In Britain, post-war poets tended to focus on profound understandings rather than great political and social issues, though Seamus Heaney sometimes wrote nuanced poems about conflict in his native Northern Ireland. Ted Hughes, a protégé of T. S. Eliot, was particularly admired for his anti-Romantic animal poems, such as "Pike" (1959), which exposed the dark violence of nature. His peer Philip Larkin was a master in perhaps the most essential job of the poet—expressing what other people feel, and Welsh writer Dylan Thomas delighted readers and listeners with the sheer lyricism of his verse. Irony was also a common feature of British

poetry during this period, as in Stevie Smith's popular poem "Not Waving but Drowning" (1957).

In parts of the world experiencing war, unrest, and state oppression, poets continued to take up their pens in response. Anna Akhmatova confronted the horrors of Stalinist Russia in *"Poema bez geroya"* ("Poem Without a Hero"), a work that took her more than 20 years to complete, and Nigerian Chinua Achebe wrote movingly about famine in the wake of the Biafran War (1967–1970). Reflection on the effects of colonialism was also a common theme.

Intersectional poetry

The rise of the women's movement in the 1970s produced a significant body of work about gender, sexuality, and female empowerment. Adrienne

Rich was a major voice in the US, as were Black Americans Audre Lord and Maya Angelou. These Black poets, and those in post-colonial societies, also sought to address the multiple layers of discrimination and marginalization that women of color often faced— what feminist Kimberlé Crenshaw called intersectionality.

The trends continued into the late 20th century and into the new millennium. Scottish poet Carol Ann Duffy often subverts traditional forms and themes to address feminist and queer issues, and American poet Sheila Black writes about disability. Explored and celebrated, nonconformity is also a common theme of "poetry slams"— live performances of spoken word poetry, a form that stretches all the way back to ancient Greece. ∎

SUCH WALTZING WAS NOT EASY

"MY PAPA'S WALTZ" (1942), THEODORE ROETHKE

British poet and critic William Empson's book *Seven Types of Ambiguity* (1930) alerted readers of poetry to hidden double meanings that can enrich the reader's experience by pointing to parallel meanings, held in suspension.

Ambivalence is something else: the term refers to different implications of significance, sometimes affecting a whole poem or passage in a poem. As W. H. Auden wrote in 1941, poetry might be defined as the "clear expression of mixed feelings." Anyone can love and dislike at the same time, or be attracted and repelled. Such contradictions reflect complexity of personality. To speak of different sides of a person's character would be a simplification, for the self has no mappable topography. The ambivalent poem does more justice to life's richness.

A boisterous waltz

American poet Theodore Roethke's "My Papa's Waltz," a poem in four four-line stanzas about a boy dancing with his drunken father in a kitchen, is a fine example of ambivalence in poetry. The boy hangs on "like death," which sounds ominous from the start, as his mother looks on disapprovingly. Pans slide off the shelf, so we know the waltz is boisterous. Words like "battered" and "scraped" are troubling, even though not, in their context, violent. Then we learn the father is beating time on the boy's head (with a hand "caked hard by dirt," perhaps from gardening), raising ambiguity with the word "beat." The last lines describe how the boy clings to his papa's shirt as he is waltzed off to bed, suggesting

The greenhouse belonging to Roethke's father, a German immigrant market gardener, left a deep impression on Theodore. "My Papa's Waltz" suggests that "papa" is a gardener.

See also: "London" 122–125 ▪ "The Road Not Taken" 182–187 ▪ "The Second Coming" 194–197 ▪ "Do Not Go Gentle Into That Good Night" 240–241

Poems commonly show **ambivalence** in one of these areas:

Relationships, which can prompt mixed feelings about a person or group.

Symbols and images, which can carry both positive and negative overtones simultaneously.

Events, which can cause conflicting emotions—as they happen, or in memory or prospect.

Theodore Roethke

Born in Saginaw, Michigan, in 1908, Theodore Roethke described his father Oscar's greenhouse as "my symbol for the whole of life, a womb, a heaven-on-earth." When Roethke was 14, his father died of cancer and his uncle by suicide, tragedies that deeply influenced his work.

After studying English at Michigan and Harvard universities, he established himself as a gifted poetry teacher, notably at the University of Washington in Seattle between 1947 and 1963. W. H. Auden praised his first book of poetry, *Open House*. Roethke's introspective style influenced many, including Sylvia Plath, and he was awarded the Pulitzer Prize for Poetry for "The Waking" in 1954. He battled with depression for much of his life and was a heavy drinker. In 1963, while swimming in a friend's pool, Roethke died of a heart attack.

Other key works

1941 *Open House*
1948 *The Lost Son and Other Poems*
1953 *The Waking, Poems 1933–1953*

loving attachment. But there might be something sinister afoot; we cannot be sure. A waltz, with its zigzagging movement, can symbolize a shifting relationship. At the same time, this playful waltzing romp, with drunken missed steps, is a parody of graceful dancing. We are left uneasy, anxious for the boy's welfare.

Universal questions

Instances of ambivalence abound in poets as different from each other as Englishman William Blake and American Robert Frost. In "The Fly," Blake realizes that he is as vulnerable to death as the insect he has just killed but slips into an evasive conclusion: "Then am I / A happy fly, / If I live, / Or if I die." Frost, in his sonnet "Meeting and Passing," shows neither hope nor lack of hope after he has talked with a lady he met on a walk: "Afterward I went past what you had passed / Before we met, and you what I had passed."

Ambivalence became hardwired in poets who devised their own cryptic idioms after the precedent set by T. S. Eliot in *The Waste Land*. American poet John Ashbery also offers a classic example of ambivalence. His "Two Scenes" (1956) begins with a line both ambiguous *and* ambivalent: "We see us as we truly behave." It ends with the comment, "In the evening / Everything has a schedule, if you can find out what it is." Is this notion reassuring (knowledge brings power) or troubling (the shared schedule being the finite nature of existence)? ▪

At every step you missed
My right ear scraped a buckle.
"My Papa's Waltz" (lines 11–12)

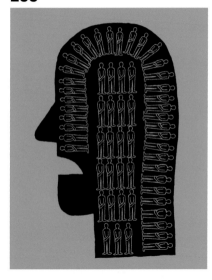

DEEP IN THE FESTERING HOLD THY FATHER LIES
"MIDDLE PASSAGE" (1945), ROBERT HAYDEN

IN CONTEXT

FOCUS
History poetry

OTHER KEY POETS
T. S. Eliot, Wilfred Owen, Langston Hughes, W. H. Auden, Derek Walcott

BEFORE
1920 Published posthumously, Wilfred Owen's *Poems* records the horrors of World War I, changing prevailing public perception of the war.

1922 T. S. Eliot's *The Waste Land* revolutionizes history poetry in its use of varied sources and voices.

AFTER
1962 Robert Hayden radically revises "Middle Passage," making cuts to move it further from the traditional narrative of European history.

1990 *Omeros*, by St. Lucian poet Derek Walcott, weaves together complex narrative threads to explore Caribbean colonial history in an epic form.

Robert Hayden was keen for "Middle Passage," his groundbreaking poem on the slave trade, to be read in the context of US history, not just Black American history, and this desire shapes its form. Written in three parts, the poem offers a radical and uncomfortable tribute to the enslaved. Hayden uses multifarious voices of enslavers, incorporating extracts from diaries, shipping logs, historical accounts, and hymns, to discredit many of the traditional narratives of US history and force the reader to confront its horrors. In this regard, the poem fulfills a historical function—the reporting of past events—while also highlighting important themes

In narrating history through fragments, Hayden shows **the difficulty of accurately representing traumatic events**.

⬇

Questioning the objectivity of **past narratives challenges present perceptions** and beliefs.

⬇

By **subverting traditional narratives**, the poet gives the enslaved a voice in the poem.

⬇

The poem acts as a counter-text to traditional historical narratives.

See also: "On Being Brought from Africa to America" 118–119 ▪ *The Waste Land* 198–205 ▪ "I, Too" 208–213 ▪ "Black Art" 268–269 ▪ *Omeros* 300–303

Robert Hayden

Born Asa Bundy Sheffey in 1913, Robert Hayden experienced a difficult childhood in foster care in a poor neighborhood in Detroit, Michigan. Ostracized by his peers for his thick glasses, Hayden sought solace in books, winning a scholarship to college.

In 1940, Hayden published his first poetry collection and married Erma Inez Morris, whose Bahá'í faith would influence his work. The following year, he enrolled at Michigan University, where W. H. Auden was an important mentor. Hayden published several volumes of poetry in the 1940s and '50s, but only enjoyed widespread acclaim with the publication of *Selected Poems* in 1966. Three years later, after many years teaching at Fisk University in Tennessee, Hayden joined the faculty at Michigan. From 1976, he was Consultant in Poetry to the Library of Congress (now known as US Poet Laureate), the first Black American to hold the position. Hayden died in 1980.

Other key works

1940 *Heart-Shape in the Dust*
1962 *A Ballad of Remembrance*

that history poems continue to explore, such as whose perspective history validates and why.

At the start of the poem, an unidentified voice pitches us into the midst of the action and introduces a fragmented discourse: "*Jesús, Estrella, Esperanza, Mercy*: / Sails flashing to the wind like weapons / sharks following the moans the fever and the dying." Stripped of context, the opening sounds like a prayer, but later in the poem, we learn that these are the names of slave ships. The words also echo pleas from the ships' captives. By layering these multiple meanings, Hayden questions the dominant narrative of history.

Constructing narratives

In the poem's second section, a man shares his experiences of being a slave trader in Africa with an unseen younger listener in a dramatic monologue. Although relayed by a single voice, the story is a composite one, constructed by Hayden from several slavers' accounts. In this, and in its content, the section highlights how history is formed, with stories woven into its narrative. The speaker also symbolizes the exclusive nature of history—it is invariably told through the voice of victors—which calls the reader to consider who is being left out of this account.

Shaping the future

In the final part of the poem, Hayden offers an account of a rebellion on the slave ship *La Amistad* given by one of its crew. Based on real events, and including a reference to President John Quincy Adams (an opponent of slavery), its sense of reportage reminds us that historical "truth" is subjective. Who history designates a hero is called into question. The sailor describes his fellow enslavers as "true Christians" and the leader of the rebellion as a "surly brute who calls himself a prince"—exposing history's fickle attributions and the unreliability of its narrators.

The poem's final lines offer some hope, but this is tempered by the reader's awareness of the enduring struggle of the enslaved. The final part of the poem also shows the role of history poetry in recording and reconfiguring its narratives. In immortalizing stories while starting new discussions, poetry redefines the past as well as informing the future. ▪

Sengbe Pieh, also known as Joseph Cinqué, or Cinquez—as in Hayden's poem—became a hero after he led a successful revolt on the Spanish slave ship *La Amistad* in July 1839.

WHAT THOU LOVEST WELL REMAINS, / THE REST IS DROSS

CANTO LXXXI (1948), EZRA POUND

IN CONTEXT

FOCUS
Imagism

OTHER KEY POETS
William Carlos Williams, Marianne Moore, T. S. Eliot, Allen Ginsberg

BEFORE
1908 "Lecture on Modern Poetry" by British poet and philosopher T. E. Hulme lays the foundations for Imagism.

1912 Pound coins the term "Imagiste" for American poet H. D. (Hilda Doolittle).

1922 American poet T. S. Eliot publishes *The Waste Land*, including revisions by Pound.

AFTER
1966 British poet Basil Bunting publishes "Briggflatts" in the style of Pound's *Cantos*.

1968 Pound's remaining work on the *Cantos* is published as *Drafts and Fragments*.

The long and controversial career of American poet Ezra Pound spanned the first seven decades of the 20th century, most of it spent in Europe. His early work looked to Victorian poets such as Robert Browning, but during 12 years in London, England, from 1908, Pound changed into a "modern" poet, championing a new clarity and directness.

The image is all
Pound pioneered the modernist literary movement known as Imagism, which focused on presenting the "image" (the subject of the poem) in precise terms stripped of unnecessary elements.

[…] it's a mosaic or cut-up, or a weave or a tapestry, or a collage, the *Cantos*, therefore none of us are expected to understand it, particularly, first off […]
Allen Ginsberg
teaching *The Cantos*, 1980

In March 1913, he published a treatise on Imagism—"A Few Don'ts by an Imagiste"—in *Poetry* magazine, outlining what he considered to be the rules of this aesthetic, urging poets to "Use no superfluous word, no adjective, which does not reveal something." The next month, Pound illustrated his theory by publishing the poem "In a Station of the Metro," which consists of just two lines, one subject, and one simple image of a crowded subway station and petals on a bough.

In 1915, Pound embarked on what was to become a vastly longer poem, *The Cantos*—an unfinished 800-page project of more than 100 sections, or cantos, from the Italian word for "song." In his 1913 treatise, Pound had suggested that the Imagist should "fill his mind with

Pound (top right) poses with fellow writers and artists outside the Jockey Club, Paris, in 1923. The *Pisan Cantos* includes references to his time in the French capital and the people he met.

the finest cadences he can discover, preferably in a foreign language so that the meaning of the words may be less likely to divert his attention from the movement." The many languages used by Pound in *The Cantos*, including Italian, French, and Greek, Old English, and modern English, as well as his use of colloquial idioms and fragments of speech, are a testament to his much-praised ear for lyrical rhythms.

Italy and controversy

In 1924, Pound moved from Paris, France, to Rapallo, Italy, where he collaborated with the fascist regime of Benito Mussolini and supported the rise of Adolf Hitler in Germany. From 1941 to 1945, he made more than 100 broadcasts for Italian radio, filled with antisemitic and pro-fascist propaganda. At the end of World War II (1939–1945), he was arrested in Pisa and then detained at the nearby American

Disciplinary Training Center for six months. Due to be charged with treason, Pound was sent instead to a psychiatric hospital in the US, his lawyer claiming that he was unfit to stand trial because he had suffered a mental breakdown.

During his stay at the detention center, Pound was allowed to use a typewriter, and it was here—in isolation—that he produced cantos LXXIV–LXXXIV, which became known as the *Pisan Cantos*. They are the most personal—and perhaps coherent—of the cantos, based largely on Pound's memories of his life before World War II and his recollections of the people he once knew—what American poet Allen Ginsberg, speaking in 1980, referred to as Pound's "prison mental gossip."

The *Pisan Cantos* were published in the US in 1948, and the following year Pound won the first Bollingen Prize for American Poetry, conferred by the »

Library of Congress. His peers were divided over the appropriateness of the honor. Some believed that Pound's work could not be separated from his beliefs, and that an avowed antisemite and apparent fascist should be barred from winning such a prestigious award. Others thought that his poetry should be evaluated on its own merits, separately from the man's views. American poet and critic Louis Untermeyer, writing in the *New York Herald Tribune*, called the poems "a ragbag and tail end of Pound at his worst." He wrote that the *Pisan Cantos* were evidence of "a very disordered mind, one affected by the seeds of Fascism."

Lyrical libretto

In his Imagism treatise, Pound draws parallels between the rhythm of music and that of poetry, saying the best verse contains "a sort of residue of sound which remains in the ear of the hearer." Pound underlies the inspiration he takes from musical structure in Canto LXXXI of the *Pisan Cantos*, where line 96 marks the start of a section entitled "libretto"— meaning words to be sung. The tone and style change again in line 133, with the words "What thou lovest [...]," which introduce a more lyrical section, using archaic language to convey a message of humility over vanity. The line and what follows suggest that love is the most worthwhile thing in life—success and material wealth will not last.

The libretto continues with a repeated invocation to "pull down thy vanity," acting like a prayer or chant. In one repetition, Pound directs the plea to French fashion couturier Jeanne Paquin, whose green dresses he says are outdone in elegance by the natural world. Just as Paquin may be an example of vanity, Pound also finds an example of humility in a writer he admired: anti-imperialist British poet Wilfrid Scawen Blunt, whose collected poems were published in 1914.

It is unclear whether Pound is directing the message of "What thou lovest [...]" toward himself or toward others. Some critics have interpreted it as Pound's first post-war reckoning with his own beliefs. Pound is perhaps comparing himself to the delusional ant in the libretto, who believes himself "a centaur in his dragon world"—ungenerous in his previous beliefs.

A collage of references

Allen Ginsberg described *The Cantos* as "collage"—an apt description of the many and

An illustration from a French fashion magazine of 1914 shows a dress designed by Jeanne Paquin, who is referenced by Pound in Canto LXXXI as an emblem of vanity.

> The sum of human wisdom is not contained in any one language, and no single language is capable of expressing all forms and degrees of human comprehension.
> **Ezra Pound**
> *ABC of Reading*, 1934

varied references that Pound stitched together to form his work. Pound himself confessed to a friend in 1966 that his method was not conducive to creating great art, saying: "I picked out this and that thing that interested me, and then jumbled them into a bag."

While Pound is considered a modernist, many of his references and language choices come from medieval English. In particular, he was influenced by 14th-century English writer Geoffrey Chaucer, whom he considered had a better understanding of people than even Shakespeare. Pound praised Chaucer's "leisurely" prose in his 1913 Imagism manifesto. In the libretto, for example, Chaucer's exhortations from the "Ballad of Good Counsel" to "Reule weel thiself, that other folk canst reede"

("rule well yourself, who others advise") are mimicked as "Master thyself, then others shall thee beare."

Like the rest of *The Cantos* project, the *Pisan Cantos* cycle rapidly through numerous words, phrases, and allusions to different people and times in a number of languages with no obvious unifying thread. Pound's technique makes finding meaning a challenge for the reader, but the richness and depth of historical and cultural references are a fitting reflection of what can be seen as an epic chronicle of Pound's own chaotic life.

Poetic legacy

Pound heavily influenced many of the most significant modernist writers. He facilitated the publication of Irish writer James Joyce's novels *A Portrait of the Artist as a Young Man* and *Ulysses*, and promoted American poets such as Robert Frost, William Carlos Williams, and Marianne Moore. T. S. Eliot, in particular, took inspiration from *The Cantos* and relied on Pound as both editor and reviser when finalizing the manuscript of *The Waste Land*.

Despite the controversy that attaches to Pound, and the difficulty of his verse, he is admired by many as one of the greatest American poets, and *The Cantos* is considered one of the 20th century's most important poems. It continues to draw the attention of poets and critics, for praise and censure. ∎

Ezra Pound

Born in Hailey, Idaho, in 1885, Ezra Loomis Pound moved at a young age to Wyncote, near Philadelphia. After graduating from college with a philosophy degree, he left for Europe and published his first book of poetry, *A Lume Spento* (*With Tapers Quenched*), in Venice in 1908. Later that year, Pound arrived in London— with £3 in his pocket—and was introduced to Irish poet W. B. Yeats. Success and fame followed over the next decade with the publication of poetry collections and essays.

Pound married British artist Dorothy Shakespear in 1914, and the couple moved to Paris in 1920 and then Italy in 1924. In Italy, Pound turned his attention to *The Cantos*— and to fascist politics, which led to his arrest in 1945. He was committed to St. Elizabeths psychiatric hospital in Washington, D.C., where he remained until 1958. On his release, Pound returned to Italy, where he died in 1972.

Other key works

1912 *Ripostes*
1915 *Cathay*
1920 "Hugh Selwyn Mauberley"

Pull down thy vanity
      How mean thy hates
Fostered in falsity […]
Canto LXXXI (lines 158–159)

WHOM THE HIGHER GODS FORGOT, / WHOM THE LOWER GODS BERATE

ANNIE ALLEN (1949), GWENDOLYN BROOKS

IN CONTEXT

FOCUS
A new heroic

OTHER KEY POETS
**Walt Whitman,
Derek Walcott**

BEFORE
c. 8th century BCE Homer's
The Iliad and *The Odyssey*
establish the heroic epic genre
in Western literature.

1855 American poet Walt
Whitman's "Song of Myself"
reconfigures the epic hero
as a universal "everyman."

AFTER
1963 The complete version
of American poet William
Carlos Williams' five-volume
epic *Paterson* is published in
one edition. The hero is not
a person but a city.

1990 Derek Walcott publishes
Omeros, a blend of the heroic
epic and personal experience.

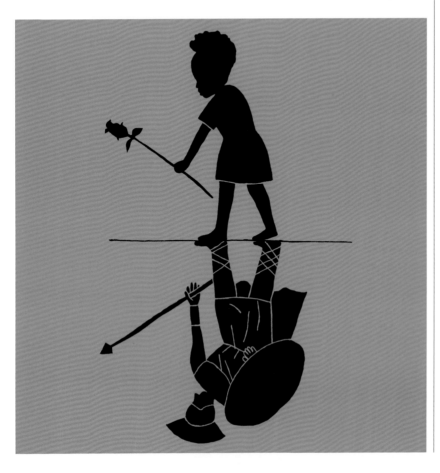

S ince ancient times, the
preferred starting point for
the heroic epic, as noted by
the 1st-century Roman lyric poet
Horace, was *in medias res*—"in
the middle of things"—rather than
ab ovo—literally "from the egg," or
"from the beginning." Homer's *The
Odyssey* and *The Iliad*, and Virgil's
The Aeneid follow this tradition of
getting straight to the action, as
does Dante's *Divine Comedy* in the
14th century. But when American
poet Gwendolyn Brooks planned
Annie Allen, she wanted to start
as close to the "egg" as she could,
because her work is an internalized
epic that would redefine the concept
of what it means to be heroic.

Gwendolyn Brooks

> I think it is the task or job or responsibility or pleasure or pride of any writer to respond to his climate.
> **Gwendolyn Brooks**
> Interview in *Contemporary Literature*, 1970

Brooks's collection does not involve a Classical quest for fulfillment undertaken by a legendary male hero, but follows the adventures of a gifted Black American girl, growing up on the South Side of Chicago, in 20th-century America.

Brooks divided her book into three parts, reflecting three stages in the life journey of the work's eponymous hero. Unlike the ordered progression of a traditional epic, the form and arrangement of the poems within each section vary greatly. The overall effect is of loosely aligned shards of experience that provide glimpses into Annie's thoughts and emotions as she proceeds through life.

A child's innocence

The first part of *Annie Allen*, "Notes from the Childhood and Girlhood," consists of 11 poems of mixed form, meter, and rhyme. Beginning with the poem "the birth in a narrow room," we see Annie start life as a child full of dreams, prancing around everyday items in the home. One poem introduces Annie's parents,

Maxie and Andrew Allen; but like other characters in the collection, they are described obliquely and never in detail.

It gradually becomes clear that Brooks's narrative will diverge from the Classic path. The detail of daily life sets the tone and pace, and the possibility of a triumphant ending already seems unlikely. Hinting at the hopelessness that follows the innocence of childhood, Annie's parents' eyes are no longer alight, and adult concerns such as death, injustice, and lack of opportunity hover in the background. When one of the family's backyard chickens is slaughtered in "Sunday chicken," Annie feels the injustice. In "throwing out the flowers," she grapples with growing realizations about the unfair and transitory nature of life.

Bitter experience

In "The Anniad," a long narrative poem that forms the second part of Brooks's collection, the shaping of a new heroic form is more explicit. The title playfully alludes to *The Aeneid* by Virgil and, at first glance, its 43 stanzas resemble a traditional form. The poem uses a scheme based on "rhyme royal," a seven-line rhyming stanza form introduced by English poet Geoffrey Chaucer in the 14th century and used in his Classically inspired epic *Troilus and Criseyde*. However, Brooks does not use iambic pentameter rhythm and subtly varies the rhyme scheme.

Brooks further subverts heroic models in the poem's narrative arc. In Virgil's *The Aeneid*, the hero Aeneas leads his people from the shambles of defeat to a new and promised land that will become Rome under Emperor Augustus. »

Born in Topeka, Kansas, in 1917, Gwendolyn Brooks moved with her family to the South Side of Chicago as a baby. This part of the city, especially the Bronzeville neighborhood, would inspire much of her work. Brooks began writing poetry in childhood, and by her teenage years was already a published poet. Her first collections—*A Street in Bronzeville* and *Annie Allen*—used Bronzeville as their setting.

In the 1960s, Brooks turned to what she called "verse journalism," teaching and mentoring young Black poets in her own community and across the US. She continued writing poetry into the 1990s and received many honors, including the Poetry Society of America's Frost Medal (1989) and the National Medal of Arts (1995). Brooks also served a term as the US Poet Laureate and as Poet Laureate of Illinois from 1968 until her death in 2000.

Other key works

1945 *A Street in Bronzeville*
1960 *The Bean Eaters*
1968 *In the Mecca*

In "The Anniad," we begin with hope, only to steer a downward course as Annie becomes caught in a cycle of degradation and despair.

Not the stand-out (male) hero of traditional epics, Annie is drawn as an "everywoman"—heroic in her survival of low expectations, racial discrimination, poverty, and dashed hopes. Lying on her "featherbed," still young, she dreams of "What was never and is not" and "What is ever and is not." There is no opportunity for epic glory, just hopes for small gains against the odds. Annie deems marriage her best option and fantasizes about a "paladin," the knightly champion of medieval romances, who she hopes will sweep her off her feet. Yet the "man of tan" who seduces Annie is more flawed than heroic. Called into military service and sent overseas during World War II,

he contracts a venereal disease that will enfeeble, if not kill, him. Abandoned, Annie remains behind, a "Little lady" lost. Increasingly promiscuous, she sees her "culprit magics fade," sinking into despair in moments "When the desert terrifies." By the end of the second edition, she is "Derelict and dim and done," left kissing the only thing remaining—the "minuets of memory."

Realizations of maturity

Brooks follows "The Anniad" with an appendix—a poem in three parts that acts as a gloss to the epic story just told: the lover-soldier who goes off to war and does not come back, or not as the same man. It finishes on another note of despair, with a sad, searching refrain.

The third section of *Annie Allen*, "The Womanhood," contains 15 poems using a variety of forms,

meters, and rhymes. The narrator has reached maturity and is disillusioned with a post-war world driven by the "American Dream." No gilded future awaits Annie's children, "the children of the poor"; they are "adjudged the leastwise of the land," her "sweetest lepers," because of the color of their skin.

The racial divide becomes a prominent theme in the poems in this section, and the concept of heroism takes on a more explicitly social and political character. In the 1940s, institutionalized segregation was nearly universal in the US. With few exceptions, neighborhoods, schools, stores, restaurants, toilets, buses, and

A North Carolina bus station in 1940 advertises its racially segregated waiting areas, evidence of the grinding daily inequalities and racial prejudice exposed by Brooks in *Annie Allen*.

trains were all rigidly segregated by race. This was the "color line" that could not be breached. It was enshrined in law as "separate but equal" opportunities, but in practice the emphasis was always on "separate" and rarely on "equal." In the poem "Beverly Hills, Chicago," Black people can drive around the wealthy white suburbs but can only admire the spacious lawns and handsome houses from a distance. The poem acknowledges that white people have problems, too; but points out that even their troubles are luxurious ones.

Living heroically

Annie's children will have few options. They can turn to the Church, which to Brooks is the equivalent of wearing a blindfold. Or they can fight for the space to "fiddle" and enjoy life, if only for a little while before they, too, cross the threshold of the "university of death," where all applicants are accepted equally.

No matter how determined Annie is to be admitted to "our mutual estate" of just being human, to "enjoy my height among you," there is always someone reminding her that the color line is "Long and electric" and

She [Brooks] easily catches the pathos of petty destinies; the whimper of the wounded [...]
Richard Wright
African American novelist
(1908–1960)

The life journey of *Annie Allen*

Childhood
An idyllic world of **dreams and imagination** is dominated by **parents and relatives**, but there are **the first intimations of death and decay**.

Youth
Full of expectation, there are daydreams about a **romantic future**, but **encounters with the real world**—many of them sexual—**cause disillusionment** to the point of despair.

Womanhood
In maturity, **worn-out dreams are cast aside** and **new quests pursued**, among them the **fight against racial prejudice** and the search for a **better future for all**.

---

that "prejudice is native" and "ineradicable." Annie cannot abide that; but, having lost all her childhood illusions, she can, in the final lines of the book, only urge her people to "Rise." At the end, Annie is still standing— not a warrior hero like Homer's Odysseus or Virgil's Aeneas, but an ordinary person living a heroic life who understands that sometimes there is bravery in simply engaging with the world.

Widely acclaimed

Brooks initially encountered resistance to *Annie Allen* from publishers, some of whom thought the poems too opaque. Persistence paid off, however, and when the collection was published in August 1949, it received glowing reviews in the Chicago newspapers and the

adulation of crowds at launch and signing events. The following year, *Annie Allen* won the Pulitzer Prize for Poetry. At the age of 32, Gwendolyn Brooks became the first Black American to win a Pulitzer in any category. Many more awards would follow.

Situated on the cusp of social and political change (and prefiguring the more militant works of the 1960s Black Arts Movement), Brooks's reworking of the traditional epic to expose the plight of contemporary Black women created a new type of American epic narrative, and a new form of hero. In 1954, just five years after the publication of *Annie Allen*, the US Supreme Court began to dismantle the oppressive segregation so powerfully evoked by Brooks. ∎

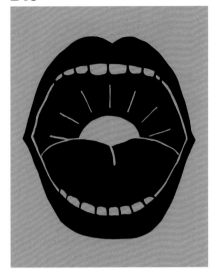

RAGE, RAGE AGAINST THE DYING OF THE LIGHT
"DO NOT GO GENTLE INTO THAT GOOD NIGHT" (1951), DYLAN THOMAS

Although the villanelle originated in France in the late 16th century, it is not known again until the 19th century, when it came into fashion thanks in part to being championed by English poets and literary critics Edmund Gosse and Austin Dobson. In the 1930s, the form was revived again by English poet William Empson. Dylan Thomas's "Do Not Go Gentle Into That Good Night" is one of the best-known examples of the form.

Rhyming scheme
The structure of the villanelle is repetitive; it has only two rhyming sounds, and includes two lines that are alternately repeated at the end of each stanza (refrains). Modern poets often use it to convey an obsession, unshakable realization, or threat. The challenge for the poet is to achieve natural diction within the strict form, and to prevent the repetitions from weakening the poem's vitality.

Losing momentum is a particular risk in the last four lines (quatrain) of a villanelle, where there needs to be some tension or propulsive logic when the two refrains finally come together. For the refrain endings, the poet will need six extra rhymes, and for the non-refrain endings, five, so it is important there are enough rhymes available. Elizabeth Bishop, in her villanelle about loss, "One Art," takes a risk by choosing "master" and "disaster" as the rhyming end-words of her refrains. "Faster" and "vaster" work well, but she also cleverly uses the half-rhyming phrase "last or."

The rhyming in "Do Not Go Gentle Into That Good Night" is more straightforward, since the

The Bard (1774), by Welsh painter Thomas Jones, depicts a Welsh bard cursing English invaders. Dylan Thomas's verse was credited with reviving the Welsh bardic tradition.

Villanelle

A villanelle is a 19-line poem that has five tercets (three-line stanzas) followed by a quatrain (four-line stanza), with aba and abaa rhyme schemes respectively. Lines 1 and 3 of the first stanza are repeated three times each: line 1 at lines 6, 12, and 18, and line 3 at lines 9, 15, and 19.

1	Line 1	A	10		A
2		B	11		B
3	Line 3	A	12	Repeat line 1	A
4		A	13		A
5		B	14		B
6	Repeat line 1	A	15	Repeat line 3	A
7		A	16		A
8		B	17		B
9	Repeat line 3	A	18	Repeat line 1	A
			19	Repeat line 3	A

Dylan Thomas

Born in Swansea, Wales, in 1914, Dylan Thomas attended the grammar school where his father taught English. He left school at 16 to become a local reporter. His first poetry collection, published in 1934, wove strands of sex, sin, and scripture into vivid imagery. In 1937, living in London, he married dancer Caitlin Macnamara. Exempted from military service, he wrote documentary scripts for the BBC during World War II.

Thomas's life was beset by drinking and money problems. For four years, from 1949, he lived with his family in The Boathouse, Laugharne—the town that inspired Llareggub in his radio play *Under Milk Wood*, broadcast in 1954. He was admired for his short stories, and his *Collected Poems* (1952) also met with acclaim. Thomas died in New York, aged 39, on a 1953 tour of the US that was overshadowed by his heavy drinking.

Other key works

1934 *Eighteen Poems*
1936 *Twenty-Five Poems*
1939 *The Map of Love*
1946 *Deaths and Entrances*

---

final words of the first two lines, "night" and "day" respectively, are both rich in rhymes. The refrains— the title line and "Rage, rage against the dying of the light"— are used without modification, but the effect is by no means monotonous. Rhythmically, there is variety, with some enjambment (running over of lines) and the use of the refrain on two occasions as a descriptive statement breaking the run of imperatives. The repeat of "Rage, rage" causes the poem to build in intensity as it moves forward. The two refrains converge in the final couplet; although a period separates them, they form a logical unit.

Essentially, Thomas's villanelle is a protest against death. The poem is an address to the poet's father David John (D. J.), who died several years later. The refrains urge him to fight against mortality, even with his dying breath. Within the framework of this clear message are flourishes that are typical of the poet's bardic high style.

Empson's wasteland

While Thomas used the repetitions to convey fierce energy, British literary critic and poet William Empson did the opposite in "Missing Dates" (1937), also about regret and death. For him they mimic a diminution, like a retreating tide. The waste that "remains and kills" is the neglect of opportunities, including creative ones. The two poems show contrasting ways in which modern writers have used the villanelle's repetitions: to convey urgent effort or to express attritional loss. ■

I HEAR / MY ILL-SPIRIT SOB

"SKUNK HOUR" (1958), ROBERT LOWELL

IN CONTEXT

FOCUS
Verse autobiography

OTHER KEY POETS
Elizabeth Bishop, Allen Ginsberg, Sylvia Plath

BEFORE
1798 In *Lyrical Ballads* English poet William Wordsworth uses his own experience of suffering as material for his work.

1922 T. S. Eliot addresses personal unhappiness and a fragmenting world in *The Waste Land*.

AFTER
1960 Sylvia Plath's first collection, *The Colossus*, is published.

2012 *Dear Elizabeth*, a play by Sarah Ruhl about the friendship between Lowell and Elizabeth Bishop, premieres in New York.

American poet Robert Lowell's fourth collection, *Life Studies*, published in 1959, included "Skunk Hour" and gave rise to a new category of poetry, named "confessional" by the American critic M. L. Rosenthal due to the autobiographical nature of the poems' subject matter. This thread would run through Lowell's work for the rest of his life.

Family tensions

Lowell was born into a prominent and privileged Boston family. Some of his mother's ancestors had arrived from England on the *Mayflower*, while his father came from a family of poets and

Robert Lowell

Born in Boston, Massachusetts, in 1917, Lowell entered Harvard but switched to Kenyon College in Ohio, where he met Jean Stafford, his first wife. In 1943, he was imprisoned for objecting to US participation in World War II. His first collection of poems, *The Land of Unlikeness* (1944) was followed by *Lord Weary's Castle* in 1946, which won the Pulitzer Prize for Poetry. Having separated from Stafford, he married writer Elizabeth Hardwick in 1949.

In the 1960s and '70s, Lowell was active in the American Civil Rights movement and protested against the Vietnam War. Both formed the background for poems in his next collections, *For the Union Dead* and *Near the Ocean*. Lowell won a second Pulitzer Prize with *The Dolphin*. He died in New York in 1977.

Other key works

1946 "The Quaker Graveyard in Nantucket"
1959 "Memories of West Street and Lepke"
1964 *For the Union Dead*
1973 *The Dolphin*
1977 "Epilogue"

academics, a background that Lowell was at odds with from a young age. During his short time at Harvard, he suffered the first in a lifelong series of bouts of manic depression due to bipolar disorder. He then moved to Kenyon College in Ohio, a liberal arts college where he met John Crowe Ransom, joint founder of New Criticism. This dominated literary theory in the US at the time and stressed the self-contained, self-referential nature of poetry.

Lowell's early poems adhere to the strictures of New Criticism. The tone is impersonal, the style formal and imposing, keeping to a strict meter and measure, and the poems are skillfully crafted. But by the time Lowell wrote the poems in *Life Studies* in the 1950s he had changed tack. He began using elements of his life as raw material for his poetry. At the same time, the work of American contemporaries such as Allen Ginsberg and William Carlos Williams inspired him to write in a freer style, with a loose meter and informal rhyme schemes that allowed him to express his inner turmoil. Most importantly, whereas New Criticism required a separation between the poet and the speaker in a poem, Lowell and the voice in the poems are one. It is an approach that allowed him to dramatize personal experience.

Loneliness and self-disgust

Life Studies contains "91 Revere Street," an autobiographical essay in which Lowell describes his parents and wider family in unflattering terms. The collection also includes poems that draw on his relationship with his parents, the breakdown of his first marriage, and his experiences in prison for being a conscientious objector during World War II and in a psychiatric hospital due to a period of manic depression. They also display the religious sensibility that led him to convert to Catholicism in the early 1940s.

"Skunk Hour" addresses a particularly painful moment in Lowell's life, when he was beset with feelings of loneliness and self-disgust. He begins by describing some of his fellow residents in the once exclusive and prosperous community living on Nautilus Island in Massachusetts. They include a rich, aged widow, a member of the area's dwindling social elite, who lives in a spartan cottage and gradually buys up all the properties that spoil her view; and the local millionaire, who »

What I write almost always comes out of the pressure of some inner concern, temptation, or obsessive puzzle.
Robert Lowell
"After Enjoying Six or Seven Essays On Me," 1977

has departed the island now that summer is over. This former enclave of the wealthy is now a declining resort.

At this point the narrator switches to the first-person, "I." To assuage his loneliness, he goes out at night to watch cars parked along the local lovers' lane—"I watched for love-cars"—and hates himself for his voyeurism. His "I myself am hell" echoes the words of English poet John Milton's Satan in *Paradise Lost* after his ejection from Heaven.

One dark night,
My Tudor Ford climbed the hill's skull;
I watched for love-cars. [...]
"Skunk Hour" (lines 25–27)

New Criticism

A style of literary criticism, New Criticism was in vogue from the 1930s to the 1960s, particularly in the US. It advocated studying the text of a poem as an autonomous entity, without reference to outside events or sources, or biographical information about the poet. Everything the reader needed to be able to understand the text was contained within the poem.

The New Criticism movement was initiated by American critics and poets Allen Tate and John Crowe Ransom, and American academics Robert Penn Warren and Cleanth Brooks developed it for university teaching. Advocates of New Criticism in the UK included poets T. S. Eliot and William Empson, and literary critics F. R. Leavis, and I. A. Richards.

In some hands, New Criticism took an almost scientific approach to analyzing and quantifying the formal elements in a poem and the use of poetic devices such as imagery.

The speaker's loneliness during the hours of darkness also echo the dark night of the soul described by 16th-century Spanish priest and poet St. John of the Cross. Then the town's skunks come out to scavenge for food: "They march on their soles up Main Street." They are his only company.

Maternal redemption

The image of a town in decline and the reference to Satan's fall from grace both reflect the speaker's sense of his own moral

Lowell dedicated "Skunk Hour" to his friend Elizabeth Bishop (right), saying that it was influenced by her poem "The Armadillo." In 1965, Bishop in return dedicated "The Armadillo" to Lowell.

decline. In a letter to his friend, American poet Elizabeth Bishop, Lowell referred to himself as a moral skunk. However, the mother skunk's determined search for nourishment may point to a route out of the speaker's own predicament, and a glimmer of redemption. Some commentators see in the two matriarchal figures at the beginning and end of the poem—"Nautilus Island's hermit / heiress" and the "mother skunk with her column of kittens"—a reference to Lowell's own mother, who was the dominant force in his parents' relationship. The mother skunk "swills the garbage pail / She jabs her wedge-head in a cup / of sour cream," and "will not scare," her determination and

> The poet's naked confrontation of his own pain […] should strike any reader to the heart.
> **Erica Wagner**
> **American author and critic**
> **(1967–)**

fierceness providing a foil to the speaker's feelings of inadequacy and self-hatred.

Making art from life

Lowell's work is usually described as autobiographical rather than confessional—he used real people, events, and his own experiences, however painful, as raw material for his work but his poems are not self-exploratory. He did not make the personal and secret inner world public in the way that later poets such as Sylvia Plath and Anne Sexton did. And Lowell's work was never just autobiographical. He addressed both history and the turbulent politics of his own time. He remained highly critical of US materialism and imperialism.

Elizabeth Hardwick, an American novelist, short story writer, and literary critic, was hurt by Lowell's poems describing the breakdown of their often tumultuous marriage.

In 1973, Lowell published three volumes based on an earlier single collection, *Notebook*, which first appeared in 1968. One volume, *History*, is made up of sonnets about historical and contemporary figures. The poems in *For Lizzie and Harriet* describe the breakdown of his marriage to his second wife, Elizabeth Hardwick, and are written in the voices of Hardwick and their daughter Harriet. The third volume, *The Dolphin*, contains more poems about Elizabeth and Harriet, and others about Lowell's third wife, author Caroline Blackwood.

In *The Dolphin*, Lowell included some of Hardwick's letters, turned into verse and altered in the process, for which he was heavily criticized by Bishop and American feminist poet Adrienne Rich among others. Lowell's defense was that his autobiographical verse included fiction as well as fact. In his final collection, *Day by Day* (1977), Lowell looked back on his life and work.

Far-reaching impact

Lowell's poems in *Life Studies* and his teaching had a profound effect on a group of younger poets, including Plath, Sexton, and

American poet John Berryman. In the late 1950s, Plath and Sexton attended Lowell's poetry workshops at Boston University and learned how to use deeply personal experiences such as depression and breakdown in their work. Also, Lowell's poems had legitimized the use of raw feeling as subject matter, something that Plath, Sexton, and others were already beginning to do. American literary critic Helen Vendler said that he gave his students "the sense of a life, a spirit, a mind, and a set of occasions from which writing issues." Plath acknowledged Lowell's influence early on, praising his breakthrough into "very serious, very personal, emotional experience." ∎

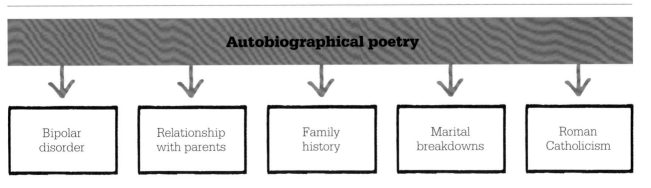

Autobiographical poetry

| Bipolar disorder | Relationship with parents | Family history | Marital breakdowns | Roman Catholicism |

I SAW THE BEST MINDS OF MY GENERATION DESTROYED BY MADNESS

"HOWL" (1956), ALLEN GINSBERG

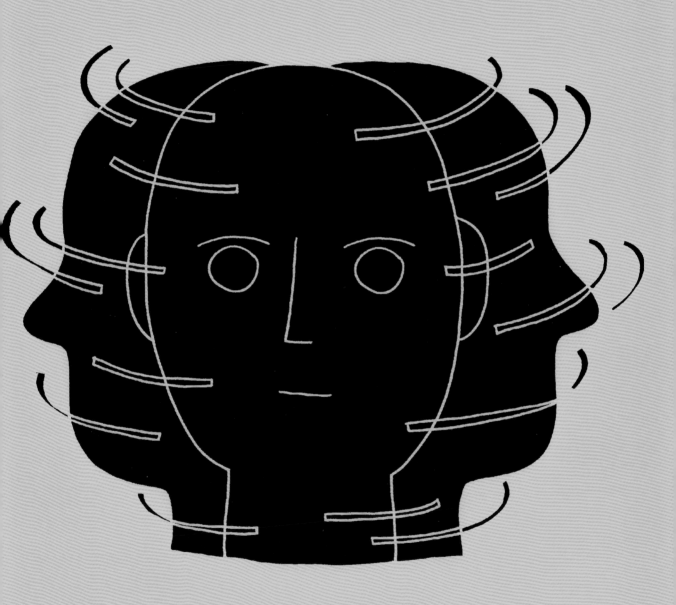

IN CONTEXT

FOCUS
Beat poetry

OTHER KEY POETS
Matsuo Bashō, William Blake, Samuel Taylor Coleridge, Walt Whitman, William Carlos Williams

BEFORE
1670 American pastor and poet Samuel Danforth's sermon "Errand into the Wilderness" establishes the tradition of Puritanical "jeremiads."

1953 American writer William S. Burroughs publishes his semiautobiographical first novel, *Junkie: Confessions of an Unredeemed Drug Addict*.

AFTER
1958 Lawrence Ferlinghetti publishes the best-selling antiestablishment poetry collection *A Coney Island of the Mind*.

1981 Ginsberg's punk anthem "Birdbrain" is recorded.

To the new generation of poets emerging in the US in the 1940s and '50s—the "Beat" poets or the "Beats"—American society seemed fossilized and damaged. The Nazi Holocaust of World War II (1939–1945) and the nuclear bombing of the Japanese cities Hiroshima and Nagasaki by the US in 1945 had created a landscape of moral degradation. Post-war recovery in the US had prompted materialistic aspirations, the consumerist pursuit of the "American Dream". At the same time, the early years of the Cold War with Russia (1947–1991) had led to an atmosphere of paranoia and political repression in public life. Law enforcement was seen as an instrument of authoritarianism.

Questioning mainstream attitudes and institutions, the young Beat poets reacted strongly against social convention. Initially, they were active in New York City, Los Angeles, and especially San Francisco, where they gravitated to the City Lights bookstore, founded by poet and publisher Lawrence Ferlinghetti. Later, they also lived and worked in Paris, France, and the Moroccan city of Tangier.

The term "Beat" has numerous associations. It relates to popular musical rhythms—especially jazz "beats"—but there is also a gloomy undercurrent—"downbeat"—as well as one of enlightenment, as in "beatific." The Beat poets saw themselves as streetwise and unspoiled. As American writer John Clellon Holmes—chronicler of the Beats and popularizer of the term "Beat Generation"—stated, "To be beat is to be at the bottom of your personality looking up."

Testing the boundaries

The Beat way of writing was free of social and literary restrictions and prized the authenticity of personal experience. Allen Ginsberg, the movement's main figurehead, popularized the mantra "First thought, best thought." With this emphasis on spontaneity came a new free-verse style of poetry and a spectrum of experimental approaches to life, encompassing hallucinogenic drugs, sexual liberation, left-wing political radicalism, and Eastern mysticism.

Another key strand of Beat theory was an affinity with the essential, natural self, echoing

Allen Ginsberg

Born in Newark, New Jersey, in 1926, Allen Ginsberg grew up in Paterson, where his father, also a poet, taught English. His mother—a committed Marxist—endured recurring mental illness. Ginsberg studied at Columbia University in New York City, from 1943, where he experimented with mind-altering drugs and befriended William S. Burroughs and Jack Kerouac, who became the leading Beat prose writers.

After leaving Columbia in 1948, Ginsberg pursued various jobs, including café cleaning and market research. In 1954, he moved to San Francisco, where physician and writer William Carlos Williams introduced him to the poet Kenneth Rexroth and the wider city poetry scene. From the early 1960s Ginsberg traveled widely, gave poetry readings, took part in left-wing politics, and marched against the Vietnam war. He died in 1997.

Key works

1961 *Kaddish and Other Poems*
1963 *Reality Sandwiches*
1973 *The Fall of America: Poems of These States*

Allen Ginsberg (center) stands outside the City Lights bookstore in 1956 with fellow "Beats" (left to right) Bob Donlon, Neal Cassady, Robert LaVigne, and Lawrence Ferlinghetti.

the philosophy of 18th-century French thinker Jean-Jacques Rousseau, who believed that human beings are intrinsically good until corrupted by society's evils. Inspiration was provided in art by the Surrealism movement of the 1920s and '30s, and in poetry by the English early Romantic visionary William Blake and by Matsuo Bashō, the 17th-century master of the Japanese haiku verse form with its conciseness and emphasis on the passing moment.

Poetic new dawn

On October 7, 1955, the first notable public performance by Beat poets took place at the 6 Gallery in San Francisco. The idea, a precursor of the conceptual art movement, was hatched by American artist Wally Hedrick. Five young poets—all in their twenties or thirties—were

Like Whitman, [Ginsberg] was a bard in the old manner—outsized, darkly prophetic, part exuberance, part prayer, part rant.
J. D. McClatchy
American poet and editor of *The Yale Review*, 1997

showcased: Allen Ginsberg, Philip Lamantia, Michael McClure, Gary Snyder, and Philip Whalen. They were introduced by 49-year-old Kenneth Rexroth, himself a San Francisco poet and later dubbed "Father of the Beats" by *Time* magazine—a title he rejected.

Ginsberg used the occasion to read his unpublished 112-line incantatory poem "Howl." Its impact was immediate, described by McClure as leaving the listeners "standing in wonder [...] knowing at the deepest level that a barrier had been broken, that a human voice and body had been hurled against the harsh wall of America."

Within a year, Lawrence Ferlinghetti had published 10 Ginsberg poems, including "Howl," in the collection *Howl and Other Poems*—part of his Pocket Poets series. Ferlinghetti was then tried in 1957 for distributing obscene material—notably the passages in the poem about homosexual

coupling—but the case was dismissed by the judge on the grounds that the poem had "redeeming social importance."

Lament and resistance

"Howl" is, in part, a modern "jeremiad"—a literary piece that laments the woes of an era. The term comes from the Book of Jeremiah in the Bible, where the 7th-century BCE prophet Jeremiah declares the calamities affecting Israel are punishment for breaking its covenant with Jehovah and lapsing into pagan idolatry.

In the 17th century, jeremiad-like election sermons became a feature of the annual opening of the Massachusetts General Court. For the Puritan pastors of the time, colonial New England was in moral decline, with preachers seeing God's anger in crop failures, extreme weather, and "monstrous births"—children born with deformities. Typically, a jeremiad had three »

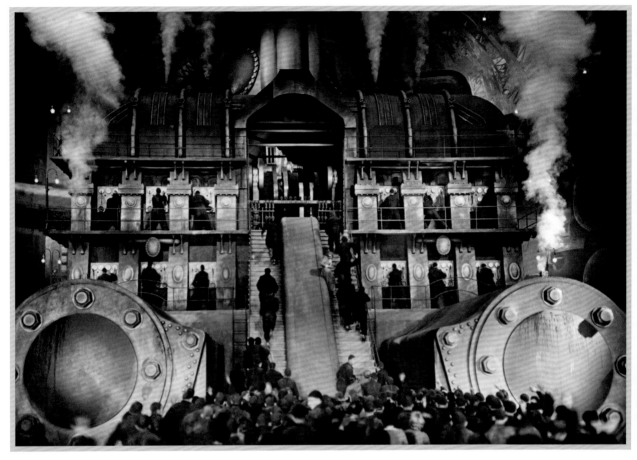

The Moloch Machine in the film *Metropolis*, which turns into a nightmarish mechanical monster, is heavily referenced in part II of "Howl."

stages: a catalog of moral failures; the contrasting values of the most idealistic first colonists; and a call for repentance and renewal.

Although "Howl" is also composed in three parts, these do not coincide with the traditional jeremiad structure. In part I of the poem, the focus is on American counterculture heroes—such as Beat poet Neal Cassady, who appears as "NC," and painter Robert LaVigne—and the catalog of harms they faced. In part II, instead of looking at abandoned values, Ginsberg intensifies the focus on dysfunction. In part III, rather than calling for social healing, he sounds a note of personal connection.

Rhythms and bases

"Howl" is infused with the chant-like style of the epic "Song of Myself" by American poet Walt Whitman, particularly in its long lines and use of anaphora—a repeated phrase that starts consecutive sentences. Ginsberg also cited jazz as an inspiration for the poem's repetitions and extended lines. He likened this to "a bop refrain—chorus after chorus after chorus—the ideal being, say, Lester Young in Kansas City in 1938, blowing 72 choruses of 'The Man I Love' until everyone in the hall was out of his head." Ideally, Ginsberg said, each line should be treated as a single breath unit: "one physical-mental inspiration of thought contained in the elastic of a breath."

All three parts of "Howl" use repetition to provide what Ginsberg called a "base"—a repeated word or phrase that serves as the launchpad for each line's poetic invention and collectively as a unifying frame for the freewheeling poetry. The base in part I is "who," referring to the "best minds of my generation": the outcasts—poets, artists, radicals, and jazz musicians—damaged by toxic trends in culture and society. In part II, that structural role is taken over by "Moloch"—the name of the robotic giant demon in the

1927 German film *Metropolis*, directed by Fritz Lang. Moloch was also the devilish idol in the Old Testament book of Leviticus, to whom the Canaanites sacrificed children. In part III, the base is a simple phrase of reassurance addressed to American writer and friend of Ginsberg Carl Solomon: "I'm with you in Rockland"—a mental institution where Solomon is imagined to be staying.

Visionary moments

Interwoven with the harsh, feverish lamentations of "Howl" is a solidarity with creative souls who inhabit the gutter—those who take drugs, indulge in free love, and pitch themselves against repression from industrial-militaristic vested interests. There is also a thread of visionary fantasy. This flows not so much from the many references to drugs but more from Ginsberg's experiences of "imaginative" visions after reading the poetry of William Blake at the suggestion of his mentor, American writer William S. Burroughs. In 1948, Blake's poem "Ah! Sun-Flower" caused Ginsberg to live for a week "on the edge of a cliff of eternity"; while in "The Sick Rose" he heard "the doom of the universe."

Some of Ginsberg's poems allude to the impact of specific lyrics in Blake's works. The reference in the third line of "Howl" to "angelheaded hipsters burning for the ancient heavenly connection to the starry dynamo in the machinery of night" sets a visionary tone that occasionally

resurfaces, usually in more muted language. Other recurring notes are the comically incongruous— "O victory forget your underwear we're free"—and the brazenly shocking. Despite the passionate, hyperbolic intensity of the poem, the language uses carefully crafted imagery and diction.

Word bending

At times in "Howl," Ginsberg breaks linguistic norms—"crazy" is used as a noun and "purgatoried" as a verb, for example. Words are also strung together in Cubist-like collages—"teahead joyride neon blinking traffic light"—or in incongruous pairs—"pubic beards" or "waving genitals and manuscripts." Creative wordplay abounds, as when "junk" appears two words after "China," evoking both garbage and Chinese sailboats. Within the free-verse structure, the poet still finds room for the lyrical in imaginative phrasing such as "apartment cliff-banks of the Hudson" or "those human seraphim, the sailors."

Ginsberg also employed a poetic shock tactic in startling word juxtapositions that he called "eyeball kicks." This allowed him to make surprising leaps between low and high tones, as in "cocksman and Adonis of Denver" (from street language to Roman myth) or "pingpong of the abyss" (from an innocent game to the terror of hell). Ginsberg's inspiration for what he called the "electrochemical effect" of eyeball kicks came both from the haiku poetry form and sudden »

The three parts of "Howl"

Part I
Subject: Creative heroes opposed by repression, materialism, and the military
Base: "Who" iterated 58 times
Mode: One long sentence

Part II
Subject: Society's evils personified as "Moloch," the monstrous robotic giant
Base: "Moloch" iterated 38 times
Mode: Short exclamations

Part III
Subject: Empathy for hospitalized Carl Solomon
Base: "I'm with you in Rockland where […]" iterated 19 times
Mode: Direct address

> who burned cigarette holes in their arms protesting the narcotic tobacco haze of Capitalism […]
> **"Howl" (part I, line 31)**

Buddhism and the Beats

The Beat poets found spiritual nourishment in Buddhism and other Eastern faiths. They were drawn to the Zen form of Buddhism—with its emphasis on personal enlightenment, or *satori*—popularized in the US by Japanese monk D. T. Suzuki. Ginsberg met Suzuki in 1958, and in 1962 traveled to India, where he met the Dalai Lama, Tibet's Buddhist spiritual leader. In 1972, he took Buddhist vows and received his dharma (Buddhist) title, Dharma Lion.

Ginsberg also embraced the Hindu Hare Krishna movement, introducing chanting into his poetry performances and in 1967 welcoming its leader, Bhaktivedanta Swami, at a San Francisco music festival. Ginsberg expressed his spirituality in poems such as "Angkor Wat" (1963) and the collection *Mind Breaths* (1977).

["Howl"] was a seismic event on the landscape of Western culture, shaping the counterculture and influencing artists for generations to come.
David Wills
American critic and editor of *Beatdom*, 2006

Moloch whose mind is pure machinery! Moloch whose blood is running money! Moloch whose fingers are ten armies! [...]
"Howl" (part II, line 5)

shifts he had observed in the brushwork of the 19th-century French painter Paul Cézanne.

From scream to elegy

Despite the wild twists and turns in its language, "Howl" has a straightforward trajectory. Part I—a single sentence consisting of 78 extended lines, more prose than poetry—is a catalog of heroism by unnamed souls "destroyed by madness." They take drugs, listen to jazz, see angels, burn money, copulate, ride the subway, talk, scream, vomit, study literature, wander America, campaign for communism, bite detectives, howl, forage for food, attempt suicide, and become hospitalized. At the end of part I, the souls blow the suffering of America's mind into an ecstatic saxophone cry—the "howl" of the title—"with the absolute heart of the poem of life butchered out of their own bodies good to eat a thousand years"—a visceral take on the traditional idea of poetry as a path to immortality.

Part II begins with a rhetorical question: "What sphinx of cement and aluminum bashed open their skulls and ate up their brains and imagination?" This is answered with various elaborations on Moloch, the monster that personifies greed, lovelessness, cruelty, militarism, and destruction. Part III becomes more personal as it switches the pronouns from "they" to "you" (addressing Carl Solomon) and "I." After scenarios of Solomon's days imagined in Rockland State Hospital in New York, the poem ends with a quieter

passage of Ginsberg dreaming of his friend walking "dripping from a sea-journey on the highway across America in tears to the door of my cottage in the Western night," echoing the end of Walt Whitman's "Song of Myself": "I stop somewhere, waiting for you."

Ginsberg was to give the personal elegiac note even more attention and power in a later poem "Kaddish" (1961), written to commemorate his mother, Naomi. In contrast to the incantations of "Howl," "Kaddish"—from *kaddish*, a mourner's prayer or blessing in Judaism—follows regular speech patterns in a weave of specific and often tender reminiscence that combines the three strands of guilt, memory, and death.

The wider scene

A generation of American poets who had grown up during World War II and its aftermath, including Gregory Corso, Doug McClure, Philip Lamantia, and Philip Whalen, aspired, like Ginsberg, to use poetry as a countercultural force for good. Collectively they attempted to open minds to a greater understanding of drugs, the possibilities for both sexual and spiritual liberation, the importance of ecological awareness, and the threats posed by the military–industrial complex. Also, in a manner that echoed Romantic poets such as John Keats and Percy Bysshe Shelley, the Beats helped to shift attention from social conformism to the fulfillment of the individual, using linguistic shock tactics to blast away at what they saw as mind-limiting inhibitions. Some critics thought that this approach was marred by a ranting, overexcited tone, whereas others praised the writing as raw, candid, and powerful.

Gregory Corso, praised by Ginsberg who was his friend and traveling companion, as an "awakener of youth," exhibited Ginsberg's influence in his choice of the long line and bold diction. The poems in his 1958 collection *Gasoline* display an incantatory and spoken word style reminiscent of "Howl." Michael McClure favored typographic manipulation, using lines of varying length (often simply a single word) to create verse patterns. He focused on spontaneity, Buddhist values, and environmental issues—once reading passages from his 1964 *Ghost Tantras* series to the caged lions of San Francisco Zoo.

Philip Lamantia was a surrealist poet, inspired by the Spanish artists Salvador Dalí and Joan Miró and described as a "visionary" by Lawrence Ferlinghetti. His poetry

Paterson poets: Ginsberg and Williams

Ginsberg's home city, Paterson, New Jersey, was also the inspiration for William Carlos Williams's epic five-volume poem *Paterson* (1946–1958) about an archetypal American industrial center. Ginsberg saw Williams, more than 40 years his senior, as a poetry mentor. In their correspondence, Williams urged the young poet to stop trying to emulate past masters such as William Blake, write in his own voice, use strong visual imagery, and move from formal to free verse. Ginsberg showed enough promise for two of his letters to be included in Book IV

of *Paterson*, published in 1951, although Williams was later to say in an interview: "I am disgusted with him [Ginsberg] and his long lines."

Despite his reservations, Williams contributed an introduction to Ginsberg's *Howl and Other Poems* (1956), expressing admiration for a poet who had gone through horrifying experiences and yet found love. Williams's statement there, "Poets are damned but they are not blind, they see with the eyes of the angels," is an implicit endorsement of Ginsberg's imaginative powers.

influenced Ginsberg, who shared Lamantia's love of William Blake's art and poetry.

Like Ginsberg, both Philip Whalen and Gary Snyder embraced Zen Buddhism—Whalen so much so that he became a Zen priest in 1973. Their poetry, however, lies at the less strident end of Beat, with Whalen embracing humor and the

mundane, and Snyder exhibiting a closeness to wild landscape and nature.

A musical legacy

In their rebellion against convention and their advocacy for freedom and experimentation, the Beats placed poetry center stage as a countercultural force. They also paved the way for permissive 1960s and '70s rock music culture. Michael McClure was a close friend of Jim Morrison—lead singer and lyricist of The Doors—and encouraged his efforts as a poet. Ginsberg's language influenced American songwriters such as Bob Dylan, Lou Reed, and Patti Smith. Punk rock and Ginsberg also embraced each other. The poet shared a stage with The Clash in 1981 and appeared on the band's 1982 album *Combat Rock*. ∎

The bearded figure of Allen Ginsberg (left) joins more than 10,000 people at a "Be In" counterculture event in New York City's Central Park on Easter Sunday in 1967.

254

A RIGID HOUSE / AND A WINDING PATHWAY
"SESTINA" (1965), ELIZABETH BISHOP

IN CONTEXT

FOCUS
The sestina

OTHER KEY POETS
Dante, Edmund Spenser, W. H. Auden

BEFORE
1579 "Ye Wastefull Woodes," the first sestina in English, appears in Edmund Spenser's *The Shepheardes Calender*.

c. 1848 Dante Gabriel Rossetti translates Dante's "Sestina of the Lady Pietra degli Scrovigni."

AFTER
1966 John Ashbery publishes the comic sestina "Farm Implements and Rutabagas in a Landscape" in *The Double Dream of Spring*.

1996 In "Two Lorries," from the collection *The Spirit Level*, Seamus Heaney plays with the end-word rules of a sestina.

When American poet Elizabeth Bishop wrote "Sestina," she was embracing a poetic form with a history stretching back almost 800 years. The sestina is a complicated, 39-line verse pattern that contains no rhymes but features six repeated end-words used in a rotating sequence in each of six stanzas, finished off by a three-line envoi (end stanza) that reuses all six words.

Arnaut Daniel, a French nobleman and troubadour—a traveling lyrical poet—invented the sestina at the end of the 12th

[…] rather like riding downhill on a bicycle and having the pedals push your feet […] into places they wouldn't normally have taken.
John Ashbery
Interview in *The Craft of Poetry*, 1974

century. The inherent musical quality of the form, with its chorus-like repetitions, endeared it to court circles in the south of France, where troubadours performed love songs as entertainment.

Revivals of the form
In the 13th and 14th centuries, the sestina was taken up by Italian poets Dante and Petrarch. The form was then reimported to France in the 16th century, when it also first appeared in English.

Although never as attractive to poets as the less complex sonnet, the sestina has enjoyed a number of further revivals. The 19th-century British poets Dante Gabriel Rossetti and Algernon Charles Swinburne dabbled in the form, followed in the 20th century by British-American W. H. Auden and Americans Ezra Pound and John Ashbery. Irish poet Seamus Heaney breathed new life into the sestina by picking unlikely key words or using homophones, (words that sound the same but are spelled differently) and pararhyme.

Mood music of loss
In "Sestina," from her collection *Questions of Travel*, Elizabeth Bishop uses the repetition of the

See also: *The Divine Comedy* 58–61 ▪ *The Faerie Queen* 82–85 ▪ "Poetry" 188–191 ▪ "September 1, 1939" 220–223 ▪ Canto LXXXI 232–235

end-words "house," "grandmother," "child," "stove," "almanac," and "tears" to create an unsettling mood of claustrophobia within a seemingly normal domestic setting. A child and its grandmother sit beside the stove. The grandmother laughs at jokes she reads aloud from the almanac as she tries not to cry. Her upset is probably connected to the absence of the child's parents. The child draws a picture of the house, and an anthropomorphized almanac drops "little moons" from its pages, saying "Time to plant tears."

The repetition of the key words reinforces their resonance. "House" is the "rigid," uneasy setting—the child draws its garden but does not venture outside. "Grandmother" is the soothing parent-substitute. "Child" is the main subject—being inventive in changed circumstances. "Stove" offers a poor surrogate for true family comfort. "Almanac" is the inevitability of time passing. "Tears" is the repeated emotional response that manifests itself even in the drops spilling from a kettle.

Bishop's poetry is known for enigmatic understatement. Her "Sestina" is not a virtuoso performance, with flashy variations on the key words, but a quiet meditation on loss that subtly acknowledges the everyday wonders of a child's imagination. ▪

The sestina formula

The end-words of a sestina's first stanza are repeated in a different order in each of the subsequent five stanzas, according to a strict set of rules. For the key words, the poet goes to line 6 of the previous stanza to make line 1 of the new stanza, then to line 1 to make line 2, and so on.

The order in which the end-words are rearranged follows a spiral pattern, starting at the end of the stanza.

Stanza 1	Altered to	Stanza 2	3	4	5	6
End-word 1	2nd	6	3	5	4	2
End-word 2	4th	1	6	3	5	4
End-word 3	6th	5	4	2	1	6
End-word 4	5th	2	1	6	3	5
End-word 5	3rd	4	2	1	6	3
End-word 6	1st	3	5	4	2	1

The end-word of line 6 (of stanza 1) becomes the end-word of line 1 (of stanza 2). Then the end-word of line 1 becomes the end-word of line 2, and so on.

Once the end-words of stanza 2 are arranged, the rules repeat for the next four stanzas. The numbers show where the end-word for each line appears in stanza 1.

Elizabeth Bishop

Born in 1911 in Worcester, Massachusetts, Elizabeth Bishop was eight months old when her father died and five years old when her mother was committed to a mental institution. Bishop was then raised by her grandparents in Nova Scotia, Canada, and later by an aunt in Massachusetts. She studied at Vassar College in New York state, and met American poet Marianne Moore in 1934. Moore became an important mentor to Bishop.

Bishop moved to Florida in 1937, where she wrote much of her first poetry volume, *North & South*. Between 1951 and 1964, she lived in Brazil with her lover, Lota de Macedo Soares, who died in 1967. Until 1974, Bishop divided her time between Brazil and the US. Initially regarded as a "poet's poet," she gained a wider readership with *Geography III*. By the time of her death, in 1979, Bishop had won virtually every major American literary award, including the Pulitzer Prize in 1956.

Key works

1946 *North & South*
1965 *Questions of Travel*
1976 *Geography III*

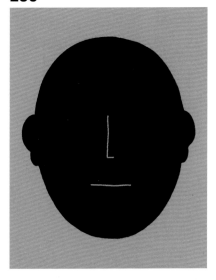

HOW SOON SUCCEEDING EYES BEGIN / TO LOOK, NOT READ
"AN ARUNDEL TOMB" (1956), PHILIP LARKIN

IN CONTEXT

FOCUS
Disillusion

OTHER KEY POETS
Thomas Hardy, W. B. Yeats, W. H. Auden, Carole Ann Duffy

BEFORE
1857 The poems in Charles Baudelaire's *Les Fleurs du Mal* (*The Flowers of Evil*) address depression, lost innocence, alcohol, and urban corruption.

1914 Thomas Hardy's *Satires of Circumstance* includes poems of regret and guilt after the death of his estranged wife Emma.

1954 British poet Thom Gunn's "Carnal Knowledge" addresses distance within intimacy.

AFTER
1971 Larkin's "This Be the Verse" is a sardonic reflection on the passing on of unhappiness from one generation to the next.

In 1867, English poet Matthew Arnold in "Dover Beach" heard in the sound of the ocean the retreat of the comforts of religious faith. In reflecting on the contraction of religion, he anticipated the work of his fellow countryman, Philip Larkin. Larkin's 1955 poem "Church Going" addresses the subject eloquently.

The church Larkin visits in the poem is an "accoutred frowsty barn [...] In whose blent air all our compulsions meet, / Are recognised, and robed as destinies." Faith has evaporated. Yet tradition urges even the faithless to visit churches as a place for contemplation—"If only that so many dead lie round." The poet uses small consolations to convey a resigned disappointment in all that religion once offered.

Stone cold truths
The year after "Church Going" was published, Larkin wrote and published "An Arundel Tomb,"

about a tomb he comes across in Chichester Cathedral. "An Arundel Tomb" is another disillusioned church poem. The tomb dates from the 14th century: the Earl of Arundel and his wife lie side by side in stone, holding hands. Larkin contemplates changes wrought by time—the hand-holding seen now as sentimental rather than conventional; the air polluting and eroding; chivalric values disappearing; the Latin motto losing significance; and the commemorated couple out of place in modernity. All they have left is an emblem of fidelity that proves "Our almost-instinct almost-true: / What will survive of us is love."

Larkin's concluding idea is couched in a double qualification. John Keats ended his "Ode on a Grecian Urn" (1819) with another questionable aphorism: that beauty is truth, truth beauty. Larkin, however, tells us his maxim is not

> They would not guess how early in
> Their supine stationary voyage
> The air would change to soundless damage [...]
> **"An Arundel Tomb" (lines 19–21)**

See also: "Dulce et Decorum Est" 192–193 ▪ "The Second Coming" 194–197 ▪ "September 1, 1939" 220–223 ▪ "Standing Female Nude" 294–295

quite true and not quite believed, as the focus shifts, from the couple in effigy to himself and his kind.

Double qualification also appears to good effect in "Talking in Bed" (1964). The setting should encourage intimacy, but Larkin wonders why it is so difficult, even when physically so close, to find words "not untrue and not unkind." Artfully fitted into a triple rhyme scheme, the line suggests that even the imperfect best we might have hoped for is beyond our reach.

Other poems

Disillusion characterizes many of Larkin's poems. For example, "Toads" (1955) focuses on the daily grind of work, while "Mr. Bleaney" (1955) presents a view of a lonely life in a bedsit (studio apartment). "The Whitsun Weddings" (1964), though, shows him in lighter mood, as he balances condescending observation of wedding couples boarding a train against a glimpse into their destinies, symbolized by an arrow shower "somewhere becoming rain"—a resonant image of fertility.

Larkin's more typical discontent surfaces in later British poets such as Don Paterson. Carol Ann Duffy's note-perfect sonnet "Prayer" has Larkinesque plangency in its reference to a sad lodger and someone calling a child's name "as though they named their loss." ▪

Philip Larkin

Born in Coventry, England, in 1922, Larkin graduated from Oxford University with a first-class degree in English. There he met British novelist and poet Kingsley Amis, who became a close friend. Larkin did most of his writing during a 30-year tenure as librarian at the University of Hull, England. His first book of poetry, *The North Ship* (1945), showed Yeats's influence; it was followed by two novels, *Jill* and *A Girl in Winter*. His second poetry book, *The Less Deceived*, brought critical and public attention, which grew with the next two collections. In 1984, Larkin was offered, but declined, the position of Britain's Poet Laureate.

From 1950 until his death, he had a relationship with the academic Monica Jones. The publication of Larkin's *Selected Letters* in 1992 caused controversy and a reassessment of Larkin's career at least in part because they exposed his overt racism and sexism. He died in 1985.

Other key works

1955 *The Less Deceived*
1964 *The Whitsun Weddings*
1974 *High Windows*

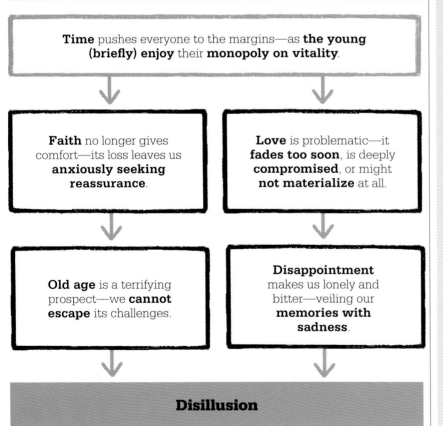

Time pushes everyone to the margins—as **the young (briefly) enjoy** their **monopoly on vitality**.

Faith no longer gives comfort—its loss leaves us **anxiously seeking reassurance**.

Love is problematic—it **fades too soon**, is deeply **compromised**, or might **not materialize** at all.

Old age is a terrifying prospect—we **cannot escape** its challenges.

Disappointment makes us lonely and bitter—veiling our **memories with sadness**.

Disillusion

I WAS MUCH TOO FAR OUT ALL MY LIFE / AND NOT WAVING BUT DROWNING

"NOT WAVING BUT DROWNING" (1957), STEVIE SMITH

A drowned man speaks in Stevie Smith's "Not Waving but Drowning," but nobody hears him—except the narrator of the poem and us, its readers. The tragicomic tale unfolds in just three four-line stanzas, told in three voices: the narrator, the drowned man, and an indeterminate "you" or "they"— people acquainted with the man in his lifetime, but clearly not as well as they thought.

In the first stanza, the narrator sets out the (impossible) situation, with the dead man, presumably brought back to shore, moaning

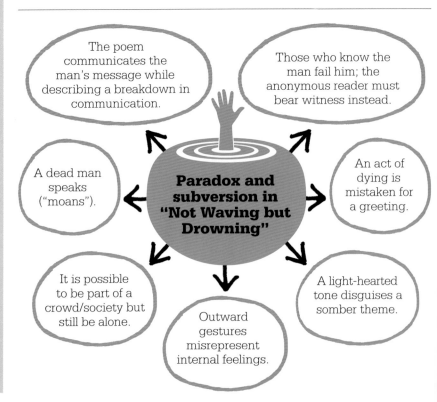

The poem communicates the man's message while describing a breakdown in communication.

Those who know the man fail him; the anonymous reader must bear witness instead.

A dead man speaks ("moans").

Paradox and subversion in "Not Waving but Drowning"

An act of dying is mistaken for a greeting.

It is possible to be part of a crowd/society but still be alone.

Outward gestures misrepresent internal feelings.

A light-hearted tone disguises a somber theme.

See also: "London" 122–125 ■ "Ozymandias" 132–135 ■ "My Last Duchess" 144–145 ■ "An Arundel Tomb" 256–257 ■ "Daddy" 266–267

Stevie Smith

Florence Margaret ("Stevie") Smith was born in Hull, England, in 1902. In 1906, her father abandoned the family, and Smith moved with her mother and sister to Palmers Green in north London. After her mother died in 1918, Smith was cared for by her aunt, who would become one of the most important figures in her life.

Smith took work as a secretary for a magazine publisher in 1922, a job she held for more than 30 years. She began writing during this time. Her first book, *Novel on Yellow Paper* (1936), was an instant hit, followed the next year by her first volume of poetry. Her popularity waned in the 1940s, but revived with "Not Waving but Drowning" in the late '50s. In the 1960s, she became a literary star with dramatic live and broadcast readings of her poems. In 1968, Smith's aunt died at the age of 96; the two women were still living in the same house in Palmers Green. Smith died in 1971.

Other key works

1937 *A Good Time Was Had by All*

the plaintive words: "I was much further out than you thought / And not waving but drowning." In the second stanza, the people who knew him speak about the man and his death: "Poor chap, he always loved larking [...] / It must have been too cold for him his heart gave way." The last stanza intensifies the micro-tragedy, as the dead man (seemingly able to hear his former acquaintances, although they cannot hear him) protests: "Oh, no no no". It is not what these people think; it never was. This man, whom they perceived as a merry jester had always been "too far out" for all of his life, "not waving but drowning."

Darkness and light

Poignant, deftly sketched, both simple and subtle, the poem reaches into painful human experience, coming close, in the words of critic Michael Tatham, to "saying all that need be said about our isolation from one another." Loneliness, isolation, and death often feature in Smith's work. She was unafraid to penetrate the dark corners of life, places she knew from personal experience; she had a history of depression and three months after writing "Not Waving but Drowning" attempted suicide. Yet, as with the drowned man of her most famous poem, humor and a light touch are present and vital in her poems.

A tradition of subversion

The use of subversive humor to address dark subjects, often too painful to contemplate head-on, has ancient roots. Satire developed in tandem with tragedy in Greco-Roman literature to hold society and human nature to account.

Steeped in the Greek and Roman classics, Smith referenced these forebears, often tweaking or upending poetic traditions for her own ends. Many of her poems also drew on oral forms—ballads, folk songs, hymns, and nursery rhymes. She put these to subversive use in "The Frog Prince," a poem in which a fairy-tale character contemplates death as a friend to be welcomed.

Her fellow poet Philip Larkin coined the term "*faux-naif*" ("false naive") for her style: simple and childlike, on the one hand; utterly unsentimental and acerbic, on the other. As in "Not Waving but Drowning," the effect is darkly comic—simultaneously achieving ironic social commentary while giving expression to Smith's distinctive, idiosyncratic voice. ■

Miss Smith [...] sees something poetic move where we do not, takes a potshot at it, and when she holds it up forces us to admit that there was something there [...]
Philip Larkin
Reviewing Smith in
***The New Statesman*, 1962**

THE DREAM / DARKNESS BENEATH NIGHT'S DARKNESS HAD FREED

"PIKE" (1959), TED HUGHES

IN CONTEXT

FOCUS
New naturalism

OTHER KEY POETS
William Shakespeare, William Wordsworth, John Keats, Gerard Manley Hopkins, W. B. Yeats, T. S. Eliot

BEFORE
1889 Yeats publishes *The Wanderings of Oisin and Other Poems*; the poems' rhythms and use of folklore influence Hughes.

1918 Hopkins' Poems is published. Hughes's English teacher introduces him to its experiments with rhythm and meter.

AFTER
2009 Poet Laureate Carol Ann Duffy establishes the Ted Hughes Award for New Work in Poetry.

British poet Ted Hughes once wrote: "I think of poems as a sort of animal. They have their own life, like animals, by which I mean that they seem quite separate from any person, even from their author, and nothing can be added to them or taken away without maiming and perhaps even killing them."

For Hughes, nature and creativity were fundamentally interwoven. If poems were, for him, like animals, it is also true that animals inspired some of his boldest, most original poems. Close observation of nature stood at the heart of his work. The nature Hughes celebrated had nothing mild or picturesque about

See also: Sonnet 130 88–93 ▪ "I Wandered Lonely as a Cloud" 126–129 ▪ "Kubla Khan" 130–131 ▪ "To Autumn" 138–141 ▪ "The Windhover" 166–167 ▪ "The Second Coming" 194–197 ▪ *The Waste Land* 198–205

> Pike obsessed great stretches of my adolescence and were central to my recurrent dream life […]
> **Ted Hughes**
> *Letters of Ted Hughes,* 2007

it. As one critic noted of his first poetry collection, *The Hawk in the Rain* (1957), his poems displayed " an admirable violence." In Hughes's vision, violence lay hidden within the beauty of nature, and beauty within the violence. The wild animals he wrote about were just that—wild, untamed.

At the same time, animals symbolized things larger than themselves. For Hughes, energies at work in animals, the wind, rain, and all other aspects of nature were the same energies at work in the depths of the human psyche. To observe nature intently was, ultimately, to learn about oneself, and the role of the poet was something like the role of the shaman in Indigenous societies (one of Hughes's lifelong interests): to make perilous journeys into the unconscious depths of the self and return with wisdom for the wider world.

In helping to bring a raw naturalism back into poetry, Hughes cited influences including Anglo-Saxon and Middle English poets, and Shakespeare, Blake, Donne, Yeats, Hopkins, and Eliot.

Ted Hughes (center) with his fellow "Faber Poets" at the offices of London publisher Faber and Faber in 1960. Left to right: Stephen Spender, W. H. Auden, Hughes, T. S. Eliot, and Louis MacNeice.

A famously predatory freshwater fish is the subject of "Pike" from Hughes's second collection, *Lupercal.* Short, like many of his best poems, with 11 four-line stanzas, "Pike" takes the reader on a strange, almost shamanic journey: from the shallows to the depths; from small, measurable things to those that loom large and fearsome, at least in the imagination; from a detached objectivity to a visceral dread. All of this is achieved by a precise, attentive rendering of physical objects, including living objects such as pike and, later in the poem, the poet's state of mind. As Hughes would write of another creature

in the early animal poem "The Thought-Fox": "I made it [he said of the fox]. And all through imagining it clearly enough and finding the living words" to express what he had imagined.

In "Pike," the stabbing precision of the language is striking from the start and gives a clear sense of the poet finding "the living words" to communicate what exists in both the physical outer world and his »

Pike, three inches long, perfect
Pike in all parts, green tigering the gold.
Killers from the egg: the malevolent aged grin.
They dance on the surface among the flies.
"Pike" (lines 1–4)

Ted Hughes

Born in Yorkshire, England, in 1930, Ted Hughes spent much of his childhood exploring the moors around his home with his older brother Gerald. Ted won a scholarship to Cambridge University, graduating in anthropology and archaeology in 1954.

While working in London in 1956, he met and married American poet Sylvia Plath. They had two children, but after the family moved to Devon in 1961, Hughes began an affair with German-born Assia Wevill. He and Plath separated, and in 1963 she asphyxiated herself in a gas oven. Six years later, Wevill took her own life and that of their daughter in the same way. Hughes found domestic peace with his second wife, Carol, whom he married in 1970. Hughes was appointed Poet Laureate in 1984, and weeks before his death in 1998, Queen Elizabeth II appointed him to the Order of Merit.

Other key works

1957 *The Hawk in the Rain*
1960 *Lupercal*
1970 *Crow*
1998 *Birthday Letters*

imaginative recall. "Pike, three inches long, perfect / Pike in all parts, green tigering the gold," it begins. The tone is detached, almost scientific (including a measurement: "three inches long"), yet the facts are mediated through a human imagination, bringing a hint of admiration—"perfect / Pike in all parts"—and the sense of an exotic, albeit dangerous beauty: "green tigering the gold." The danger then becomes explicit. Pike are predators ("Killers from the egg"); to predate is the essence of their perfection as pike. At this stage, though, they are still comparatively small, dancing "on the surface among the flies"—scarcely more threatening than flies.

Images of horror

The second stanza begins the journey into the depths. A jewel-like beauty survives—the pike move over "a bed of emerald," presumably green waterweed—but down here in the pikes' own realm the human measurement of the poem's first line no longer applies. The scales are different. Here, the pike, a "silhouette / Of submarine delicacy and horror," are a "hundred feet long." The fourth stanza creates the first of three alarming images—of pike as prisoners of their evolutionary advantage. They have evolved as supremely efficient predators, symbolized by their "jaws' hooked clamp and fangs" that can no longer change. The jaws are an "instrument" that makes them

effective killers, and the instrument now rules the creature: the pike's life is "subdued to its instrument."

The image in the next stanza is based, apparently, on Hughes's own recollection of his school days, when he and his classmates kept baby pike in a glass tank. At first, there were three, then two, finally "one. // With a sag belly and the grin it was born with." The third image, the most horrific, continues the theme of predatory aggression unable to correct itself even in the face of self-destruction. Two adult pike, each having preyed upon the other, are dead in the willow-herb, one "jammed past its gills down the other's gullet."

A switch of perspective

The seventh stanza concludes with the grim image of the "outside eye," the eye of the pike that has attempted to swallow the other, staring, "as a vice locks," with the "same iron" in its glare. At this

Owls hushing the floating woods
Frail on my ear against the dream
Darkness beneath night's darkness had freed,
That rose slowly towards me, watching.
"Pike" (lines 41–44)

point, the poem's perspective shifts, opening up into a scene by a large pond where the poet once fished. The pond is ancient, having "outlasted" the stones of the nearby monastery, and deep, "as deep as England"; pike—"immense and old"—inhabit its depths.

Evoking Englishness and the pond's history expands the scope of the imagery. There is the sense that the depths now being referred to include metaphorical ones, such as the depths of human culture, with the pike emblematic of "creatures" that lurk in the human unconscious. The poet recalls the terror pike induced in him when he fished there, particularly at nightfall. In the last two stanzas the scene dissolves into dreamlike strangeness. Night falls and for all his terror, the poet fishes on, with "the hair frozen on my head / For what might move, for what eye might move." Owls hoot in the surrounding woods, but he scarcely hears them. He has entered a semi-hallucinatory state, where

darkness "beneath night's darkness" has "freed" a "dream" in him. It rises from the depths toward him, "watching"—the poem's final word.

Mystery and dread

The ending of "Pike" is mysterious, and meant to be. Even so, for Hughes—who was a passionate real-life angler—fishing was symbolic of the creative process. In *Poetry in the Making*, he describes a person fishing, alert to "the least twitch" of their float, aware of the "fish below there in the dark," the "whole purpose of this concentrated excitement [… being] to bring up some lovely solid thing […]"—the fish. In the same way, the poet by attention and alertness brings up the beauty of a poem from the depths of the unconscious. "Pike" suggests that a certain dread often accompanies this beauty.

The elemental themes of Hughes's poetry have influenced many, from Seamus Heaney to 20th-century Welsh poet R. S. Thomas. ∎

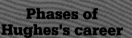

Phases of Hughes's career

1957–1963
The Hawk in the Rain;
Lupercal

1963–1966
Following Plath's death, Hughes writes no poetry for three years

1967–1979
Wodwo; Crow: From the Life and Songs of the Crow; Season Songs; Cave Birds

1980–1998
River; Shakespeare and the Goddess of Complete Being; Birthday Letters

Hughes grew up in the Yorkshire village of Mytholmroyd. As boys, he and his friends fished from the canal. His poetry was influenced by what he saw while playing in the local countryside.

WE BELONG HERE, WE ARE OF THE OLD WAYS

"WE ARE GOING" (1964), OODGEROO NOONUCCAL

IN CONTEXT

FOCUS
Indigenous voice

OTHER KEY POETS
Robert Burns, Federico García Lorca, Joy Harjo

BEFORE
1940s–1960s White Australian poet and First Australians' advocate Judith Wright writes about the effects of British colonialism in Australia.

1964 Judith Wright urges Jacaranda Press to publish *We Are Going*, a collection of poetry by Kath Walker (later Oodgeroo Noonuccal).

AFTER
1970 Noongar poet Jack Davis publishes *The First-Born and Other Poems*.

1988 Kath Walker changes her name to Oodgeroo (meaning "paperbark tree") of the Noonuccal of Minjerribah, as part of her protest over celebrations planned for the Australian Bicentenary.

With the publication of *We Are Going* in 1964, political activist and poet Oodgeroo Noonuccal (then known as Kath Walker) became a household name in Australia—and the first First Australian to publish a book of poetic verse. Selling over 10,000 copies, the collection's success made Walker a key voice for Indigenous communities within Australia, with her work receiving several literary awards. Initially, Noonuccal's verse was criticized for dismissing

I see my books as the voice of the Aboriginal people, not my own personal voice. They dictate what I write [...]
Oodgeroo Noonuccal
Interview in *Meanjin*, 1977

traditional poetic forms and for being too propagandistic, yet her words stood out for expressing the impact of colonialism on Indigenous lands, languages, and cultures.

Past, present, and future

The poem that gives Noonuccal's first collection its name moves between past and present to reflect on what Indigenous peoples have lost and what remains. It begins in the past tense as a small group of First Australian people enter a town now inhabited by "many white men." When one of the people begins to speak, the poem shifts into the present tense. The speaker conveys the deep connection between Indigenous peoples, nature, and the land. The repetition of "gone" emphasizes loss and the culture destroyed, while that of "we are" tells of a community still present. The poem's final line— "and we are going"—echoes this duality; it may reference the forced removal of First Australian peoples, but it is also a testament to their resilience and survival. ∎

See also: "Ballad of the Moon, Moon" 214–215 ▪ "Black Art" 268–269 ▪ "Don't Bother the Earth Spirit" 298–299 ▪ *Sonata Mulattica* 305

I HAVE LIT THE SACRED CANDLES, / SO THAT THIS EVENING MIGHT SHINE
POEM WITHOUT A HERO (1965), ANNA AKHMATOVA

IN CONTEXT

FOCUS
Acmeism

OTHER KEY POETS
Charles Baudelaire, Ezra Pound, H. D., T. S. Eliot

BEFORE
1911 Russian poets Sergey Gorodetsky and Nikolai Gumilev establish the Guild of Poets. Advocating precision, clarity, and craftsmanship in writing, its members will form the Acmeist movement.

1913 Russian poet Osip Mandelstam writes "The Morning of Acmeism," a manifesto that sets out the movement's doctrine.

AFTER
1976 *Poem Without A Hero* is published for the first time in the Soviet Union.

1987 Exiled Russian poet and Akhmatova protégé Joseph Brodsky is awarded the Nobel Prize in Literature.

Begun in 1940 and finished nearly 25 years later, Russian poet Anna Akhmatova's *"Poema bez geroya"* (*Poem Without a Hero*) represents her reckoning with the horrors that defined the early years of the Soviet Union. In the poem, the poet, alone on New Year's Eve, is visited by the ghosts of friends and acquaintances from the year 1913—a time of peace and artistic freedom before war, the Russian revolution, and Stalinist terror demolished their world. Recalling this era in the light of the suffering that followed, Akhmatova attempts to unpick the "riddle" of her life.

Acmeist masterpiece
The content, form, and language of the poem reflect Akhmatova's role in the Acmeist movement, a group of young Russian poets, who met in St. Petersburg around 1910. The Acmeists rejected the vagueness and mysticism of the predominant Symbolist movement, favoring instead the precise rendering of real objects and experiences, and

Anna Akhmatova, painted in 1922 by Soviet artist Kuzma Petrov-Vodkin, chose to remain in the Soviet Union despite censorship of her work.

rigor in poetic form. This focus on emotional honesty and concrete realities, which often shone a light on the brutalities of the Soviet regime, resulted in the persecution of many of the group. *Poem Without a Hero* was published in 1965, by which time Akhmatova was considered one of the century's great poetic voices. ■

See also: Fragment 31 32–33 ▪ "Ozymandias" 132–135 ▪ *Don Juan* 136–137 ▪ *Eugene Onegin* 142–143 ▪ *The Waste Land* 198–205

DADDY, I HAVE HAD TO KILL YOU

"DADDY" (1965), SYLVIA PLATH

IN CONTEXT

FOCUS
Confessional poetry

OTHER KEY POETS
Robert Lowell, Ted Hughes

BEFORE
1959 American poets Sylvia Plath and Anne Sexton meet in Robert Lowell's writing class at Boston University.

1959 W. D. Snodgrass, an American poet, brings out *Heart's Needle*, a pioneering confessional collection.

AFTER
1966 Anne Sexton's *Live or Die* includes a confessional poem about Plath's suicide.

2012 In *Stag's Leap*, American poet Sharon Olds draws on the personal experience of marital breakdown. This collection wins the T. S. Eliot Prize for Poetry and the 2013 Pulitzer Prize for Poetry.

From classical times, the "I" of a poem is interpreted as a **mask put on by the poet** to talk of **universal subjects** such as love.

The concerns of the poetic "I" might be **more troubled** or **less troubled** than those of the poet.

"Confessional poetry" **removes the poet's mask** to show more of **the suffering self**.

The poet's family and relationship issues, addictions, and mental state are laid bare.

The expression of feelings in verse through the first-person voice has a long history. In the 16th century, English poets such as Philip Sidney and John Donne often complained about being ill-served or unlucky in love, a tradition that stretched back to Roman poets such as Propertius and Horace. Although addressing the reader directly, these poets were not necessarily speaking for themselves but rather using poetry as a way to examine universal truths.

In the second half of the 20th century, the existing convention of the poet-speaker was overturned by a new form of brutally honest

See also: "Skunk Hour" 242–245 ■ "Sestina" 254–255 ■ "Pike" 260–263 ■ "The Looking Glass" 270–271 ■ "Diving Into the Wreck" 278–283 ■ *Hair* 306–307

Sylvia Plath

Born in Boston, Massachusetts, in 1932, Sylvia Plath lost her father to gangrene when she was eight. While a student at Smith College, Massachusetts, she had a breakdown and attempted to take her own life.

Plath went on to study English at the University of Cambridge, England. There, in 1956, she met fellow poet Ted Hughes and married him a few months later. They moved to the US in 1957, then back to England in 1959, separating in 1962 after Hughes refused to end his affair with German poet Assia Wevill.

In 1963, Plath died by suicide, aged 30, in the kitchen of her London apartment. Her collection *Ariel*, containing "Daddy" and edited by Hughes, was published posthumously in 1965. Plath was awarded the Pulitzer Prize for poetry in 1982 following the publication of *The Collected Poems*.

Key works

1960 *The Colossus and Other Poems*
1965 *Ariel*
1981 *The Collected Poems*

poetry—born of the writer's personal experience—that opened deep psychic wounds in an attempt to purge strong emotions and life traumas. Described in 1959 by American poet and critic M. L. Rosenthal as "confessional poetry," this style emerged in the US against the unsettled backdrop of the Cold War and civil rights activism. To make sense of their place in a rapidly shifting society, poets looked inward, removing the distinction between the "I" of lyric poetry and the poet's true self; something Rosenthal referred to as removing "the mask."

The poetry of anguish

At the vanguard of confessional poetry was American writer Robert Lowell. One of his students, Sylvia Plath, wrote confessional poetry of shockingly forceful directness, often expressed in dramatic symbols and imagery. Her subjects were unresolved issues with her parents, her precarious mental health, and tensions with her husband, British poet Ted Hughes.

Plath's poem "Daddy" was written in 1962 and published posthumously in the 1965 *Ariel* collection. In it, she directly addresses her father, Otto Plath, combining facts—such as his German heritage—with deliberate hyperbole (exaggeration). The poem's imagery, set within a loose pattern of rhyming, is nightmarish: a shoe as a prison; Otto as a seal's head in the Atlantic; Plath as a Holocaust victim; Otto as a Nazi, a devil, and a torturer. "Daddy" expresses deep emotions, exposing the draw that Plath—and, more broadly, humanity—seems to feel toward authoritarian men, despite the fear and trauma that they cause. She speaks of her struggle to kill off Otto's influence, and refers both to her masochistic attraction to Hughes, and to a non-fatal suicide attempt. The poem

turns the tradition of the elegy on its head, expressing relief, not sorrow, at death: "Daddy, daddy, you bastard, I'm through."

Later perspectives

From the 1960s, the popularity of confessional poetry led to public readings, which in the 1980s morphed into performance poetry events, including "slams." Plath's influence has continued in the intensely personal work of more recent American poets such as Sharon Olds and Louise Glück, while feminist and LGBTQ+ poets have used the confessional approach to draw attention to abuses and inequalities. Others, such as Northern Irish poet Medbh McGuckian, explore their experiences in a more lyrical style. ■

At twenty I tried to die
And get back, back, back to you.
I thought even the bones would do.
"Daddy" (lines 58–60)

WE WANT A BLACK POEM. AND A / BLACK WORLD

"BLACK ART" (1965), AMIRI BARAKA

IN CONTEXT

FOCUS
Black Arts Movement

OTHER KEY POETS
Gwendolyn Brooks, James Baldwin, Audre Lorde, Sonia Sanchez, June Jordan, Lucille Clifton, Ntozake Shange

BEFORE
1920s–'30s The Harlem area of New York City becomes a social and cultural hub for African American artists exploring the Black experience. This period is later referred to as the Harlem Renaissance.

1965 On February 21, civil rights activist and Nation of Islam spokesperson Malcolm X is assassinated in Manhattan.

AFTER
1970s Black women poets, including Sonia Sanchez, begin the Black feminist movement as a counterbalance to the Black Arts Movement's (BAM) male-dominated rhetoric.

In April 1965, writer and political activist Amiri Baraka (then known as LeRoi Jones) opened the Black Arts Repertory Theatre/School (BARTS) in Harlem in New York City. Baraka envisioned BARTS as a creative and educational space where intellectuals and artists, including writers, musicians, and actors, could come together to change perceptions of "Blackness." Although it would close within a year, the school marked the start of the Black Arts Movement (BAM), which remained at the forefront of Black cultural activism in the US into the 1970s.

Building on the legacy of the earlier Harlem Renaissance, BAM sought to explore and spread ideologies of Black empowerment through art and literature to create a new "Black aesthetic" based on Black identity, experience, and cultural traditions. However, what separated BAM from its predecessors, and at times alienated other artists, was its strong nationalistic and militaristic overtones. Members of BAM were politically engaged in the Black Power movement and Nation of Islam, both collectives at the more revolutionary extreme of civil rights campaigning. Baraka articulated elements of their militant ideologies in his poem "Black Art," which was written in 1965 and first appeared in *Liberator* magazine in 1966.

Poetry as power

Originally titled "Black Arts," Baraka's two-stanza, 55-line poem was written as a manifesto for BARTS and for BAM. In its first section, Baraka explores the role

Baraka spoke and co-chaired the National Black Political Convention in Gary, Indiana, in 1972. It was attended by more than 10,000 Black activists, politicians, and artists.

The goals of Amiri Baraka for BARTS and BAM

To make **"art for the sake of the world."**

To **educate the Black community**, so they can better judge the politics of the world around them.

To **encourage the Black community to establish their own identity** and place in the world.

of poetry as a force for change in society. At first, he seems to imply that poems are useless, beginning with the bold statement "Poems are bullshit." However, this dramatic opening gives way to the poem's real thrust: that poetry must have a meaningful message, or stand for someone or something.

Baraka expands on this point with an explosive list of the types of writing he wants to see—a raw poetic voice with "live / words of the hip world live flesh & / coursing blood." Extra force is provided by

using violent imagery: "We want 'poems that kill.' / Assassin poems, Poems that shoot / guns." A feature of some, but not all BAM writing, this type of controversial language made Baraka a polarizing figure within the movement. In his poem, Baraka encourages graphic assaults on specific racial and ethnic communities, and many criticized his misogynistic, antisemitic, and homophobic rhetoric.

Rallying cry

"Black Art" claims that it is only through violence that the Black community can find real freedom, the opportunity to flourish, and the space to love: "Let there be no love poems written / until love can exist freely and / cleanly." In the second, six-line stanza of the poem, the anti-white rhetoric of the first stanza gives way to a Black nationalistic tone—one that calls for a distinct Black identity and political voice. These final lines are Baraka's rallying cry, not only to BAM, but to the whole of the Black American community—"Let All Black People Speak This Poem / Silently / or LOUD." ▪

We wanted Black Art. We felt it could move our people, the Afro American people, to revolutionary positions [...]
Amiri Baraka
"The Black Arts Movement: Its Meaning and Potential," 2011

Amiri Baraka

Born Everett Leroy Jones in Newark, New Jersey, in 1934, Amiri Baraka's interest in poetry began at school, and he won a college scholarship to study English. In 1957, after three years in the US Air Force, he moved to Greenwich Village in New York City. Here (now known as LeRoi Jones), he befriended the Beat poets, publishing their work through Totem Press and the avant-garde poetry magazine *Yugen*, both of which he ran with his wife Hettie Cohen.

From 1965, Baraka became increasingly involved in the Black Arts Movement. A vocal member of the Nation of Islam political movement, he changed his name to Imamu Ameer Baraka in 1968 (later Amiri Baraka) to reflect his Islamic affiliations. In the 1970s, he embraced Marxist-Leninism and began a series of teaching appointments at American universities. He won several awards, including the PEN/Faulkner Award in 1989. Baraka died in 2014.

Other key works

1969 *Black Magic*
1970 *It's Nation Time*

ALL YOUR / ENDLESS FEMALE HUNGERS
"THE LOOKING GLASS" (1967), KAMALA DAS

IN CONTEXT

FOCUS
Female sexual desire

OTHER KEY POETS
Sappho, Elizabeth Barrett Browning, Emily Dickinson, Adrienne Rich, Carol Ann Duffy

BEFORE
7th century BCE Greek poet Sappho writes poems describing intense emotions and desire for another woman.

1891 American poet Emily Dickinson's "Wild nights— Wild nights!," which conveys her sexual desires, is published after her death, despite her editor's misgivings.

AFTER
1977 Adrienne Rich publishes *Twenty-One Love Poems*, a pamphlet of poems that openly portray lesbian desire.

1999 Carol Ann Duffy explores both heterosexual and lesbian women's desires in her poetry collection *The World's Wife*.

One of the most significant writers of India's post-colonial era, Kamala Das examined the marginalization and oppression of women in modern India in works that brought personal experience into the public sphere. Through her confessional style, she gained notoriety for writing candidly about women's lives, and particularly for exploring love, passion, and female sexual desire in a way not articulated by female writers before—especially in India.

Reflecting desires

Das's poem "The Looking Glass" is an example of her uninhibited depiction of sex and womanhood. It begins with Das exhorting women to "be honest about your wants as / Woman"; she then urges women to embrace their sexual femininity and openly share their bodies and "Endless female hungers" with their partners. Sexual desire is described unashamedly as an essential component of being a woman—as much a part of the whole, and the everyday, as "Long hair," "sweat," or "menstrual blood."

"The Looking Glass" validates female sexual desire, but Das's advice on how it is best satisfied reveals the constraints on Indian women in an unequal, patriarchal society. The poem acknowledges with irony that while women have agency—"Getting a man to love you is easy"—the only way to satisfy their own desires is to allow the man to see "himself as the stronger one" and to "Admit your / Admiration." The mirror provides a means of both feeding the male ego and recognizing the objectification of women and what British feminist Laura Mulvey later called the "male gaze." But a sexualized way of looking is permitted to women, too.

[…] Oh yes, getting
A man to love is easy, but living
Without him afterward may have to be
Faced. […]
"The Looking Glass" (lines 16–19)

See also: Fragment 31 32–33 ▪ "Letter of the God of Love" 72–73 ▪ "To My Dear and Loving Husband" 100 ▪ "Diving Into the Wreck" 278–283

"The Looking Glass" represents the start of a new era of candor in discussing women's experiences and desires.

Historically, **women avoided discussing their sexual experiences** in deference to social mores.

Kamala Das draws on her own life to reveal the collective experiences that women have been too afraid to express.

"The Looking Glass" argues for the **free expression of female sexuality** despite the limitations of society.

Female poets begin to **disclose their passions, emotions, and frustrations** in feminist writing from the 1970s onward.

Das urges women to appreciate their partner's "fond details" and to seek out love—though she admits, "with eyes that / Gave up their search," not always successfully.

Reality and feminism

Das does not shy away from the complexities of love and lust, and the poem's ending provides a warning that relationships may not last, while also reiterating the power of sexual desire. Living without passion, a body that once "gleamed / Like burnished brass" is "now drab and destitute."

Some critics have viewed the poem's closing melancholic tone as a direct reflection of Das's own search for love and sexual pleasure. She had been forced to marry while a teenager, and openly discussed not having the sort of intimate relationship with her husband that she argues for in her work. Whether the love in Das's poem directly represents her lived experience or just her aspirations to vocalize female sexual desire, "The Looking Glass" moved poetry into a new feminist realm.

Das's honest approach gave women writers permission—and the language—to express themselves more freely and to value their voice. Her incisive appraisal of women's daily lives, choices, and thoughts chipped away at patriarchal assumptions and romantic tropes. In giving voice to the previously unspoken, Das claimed poetry as a decisively female space. ∎

Kamala Das

Also known by her Malayalam pen name, Madhavikutty, and her adopted Muslim name, Kamala Surayya, Kamala Das was born in 1934 in the Indian village of Punnayurkulam, in the Thrissur district of the Malabar Coast, now part of Kerala. Her high-status literary family—her uncle and mother were both respected writers—encouraged her writing from a young age. At 15, she married a much older man, Madhava Das, a bank executive. The couple moved to Bombay (now Mumbai) where they had three children.

Das had started writing poetry as a child, but she only began to publish her work in the 1960s to supplement the family income. In 1963, she was awarded the PEN Asian Poetry Prize—the first of her many honors. As well as poetry in English, Das wrote various prose works in Malayalam (her mother tongue) including an autobiography *Ente Kahta* (1973), published in English as *My Story* in 1976.

After her husband died in 1992, Das began a relationship with Sadiq Ali, an Islamic scholar. Rejecting Hinduism, she embraced his faith and assumed the Muslim name she kept until she died—in Pune, India, in 2009.

Other key works

1965 *Summer in Calcutta*
1967 *The Descendants*
1973 *The Old Playhouse and Other Poems*
1996 *Only the Soul Knows How to Sing*

u blew away our passsst / and showed us our futureeeeee

"a/coltrane/poem" (1970), SONIA SANCHEZ

escribed by the Harlem Renaissance poet Langston Hughes as "one of the inherent expressions of Negro life in America," jazz music has held a fundamental place in American culture since its inception. For Hughes, it proved so integral to his understanding of Black identity that he began to meld it with his poetry, inviting jazz musicians to accompany him as he performed his work in New York City. His poems "Flatted Fifths" and "Jam Session" are early examples of the style and form of jazz poetry.

Although Hughes is credited with developing the genre in the 1920s, it was only in the 1960s and

Sonia Sanchez

Born Wilsonia Benita Driver in Birmingham, Alabama, in 1934, Sonia Sanchez was only one year old when her mother died, after which she was cared for by various relatives. In 1943, she moved to live with her father in Harlem in New York City, where she later completed a degree in political science at Hunter College.

Postgraduate studies in poetry were followed by teaching posts at various universities and colleges in the US. In the early 1960s, a short-lived marriage to Albert Sanchez provided the poet with her professional name.

An influential member of the Civil Rights, Black Arts, and Black feminist movements, Sanchez continues to advocate for disadvantaged groups. She has written plays and children's books and won many awards, including the Langston Hughes Poetry Award in 1999, and the Academy of American Poets' Wallace Stevens Award in 2018.

Other key works

1974 *A Blues Book for Blue Black Magical Women*
1984 *Homegirls & Handgrenades*

'70s, during the flowering of the Black Arts Movement (BAM), that African American artists began to fully explore jazz poetry's capabilities. Prominent BAM member and Black feminist poet Sonia Sanchez is one of a number of writers who popularized jazz poetry during this period. Describing her work as a mixture of "poetry, motion, and sound," she celebrated and harnessed the rhythms and tone of jazz music, while also exploring themes linked to identity and racial and social injustice.

Rhythmic roots

Sanchez was exposed to jazz and blues music from an early age. Often taken to jazz clubs around New York City by her father, an established jazz drummer, she met influential artists, including singer Billie Holiday and pianists Count Basie and Art Tatum. These formative years would have a significant impact on Sanchez's own lyrical works. She began writing poetry in childhood as a means of overcoming a stutter, which

she developed at age six following her grandmother's death. As a teenager, Sanchez was reluctant to share her work, but during her college years she began to make an impression with public poetry readings in Harlem bars, where she also met artists linked to the emerging BAM.

A new significance

The publication of her first poetry collection, *Homecoming*, in 1969, followed by *We a BaddDDD People* a year later, established Sanchez as an exciting new poetic voice. Her work showcased attempts to emulate the sounds of different instruments as well as the rhythms of jazz improvisation. She also explored new forms, such as the compact three-line, 17-syllable Japanese haiku, which she used to create blues or jazz haiku.

Jazz saxophonist John Coltrane, pictured in 1965, became a muse and cultural icon for many BAM poets of the 1960s and '70s, who were inspired by his compositions and playing style.

A flourishing American jazz scene in the late 1950s and early '60s provided poets with ample inspiration. The unexpected or premature death, from drug overdose or illness, of many of the era's most prominent jazz musicians in the late 1960s would also inspire a flurry of poetic dedications. The loss of great performers and culturally significant figures, such as the saxophonist John Coltrane, who »

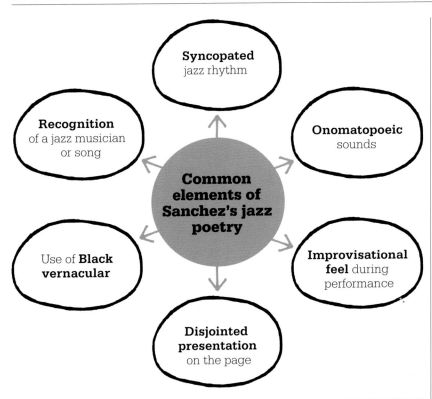

Syncopated
jazz rhythm

Onomatopoeic
sounds

Recognition
of a jazz musician
or song

Common elements of Sanchez's jazz poetry

Use of **Black vernacular**

Improvisational
feel during
performance

Disjointed presentation
on the page

died in 1967, had a huge impact on the rising artists of BAM and resulted in a great outpouring of affection. This was manifested in so many tributes to his memory that a new jazz poetry sub-genre developed—the "Coltrane poem."

The jazz elegy

Sanchez's "a/coltrane/poem" reflects the emergence and style of what is now referred to as the "jazz elegy." Throughout the piece, Sanchez imitates the form and rhythm of jazz music on the page, while also commemorating Coltrane as a pioneer of free jazz.

The poem begins with Sanchez's declaration of admiration: "my favorite things / is u/blowen." She discusses the power of free jazz— how it can "stretchen the mind / till it bursts past the con/fines of / solo / en melodies." She also alludes to the sudden loss of other important

jazz figures, describing their deaths as a "massacre / of all blk/ musicians." This is the first of a number of violent images used by Sanchez, and conjures the intense emotion—"A LOVE SUPREME"— that jazz music represents for Black culture and the African American community. It also foreshadows the fury that will replace the melancholic tones of reminiscence at the start of the poem. Sanchez soon goes on to reproach the white people "WHO HAVE KILLED / WILL CONTINUE TO / KILL US WITH / THEY CAPITALISM."

Challenging injustice

Jazz poetry provided members of BAM with an outlet to express their anger at societal injustice and a channel for issuing calls to action. In "a/coltrane/poem," Sanchez reflects some of the genre's politically militant aspirations, echoing the

Black nationalist sentiment found in poems such as "Black Art," written by civil rights activist and BAM founder Amiri Baraka.

Sanchez denounces "WITE/ AMURICA," including its false promises to the Black community and the oppression it has meted out. Like Baraka, she views violence as a necessary element of activism and exhorts "PUSHem/ PUNCHem/STOMPem." Later in the poem, she instructs readers to "step over the wite/ness / that is yesssss terrrrrr day / weeeeeeee are tooooooooday," a call to usher in a new age of self-determination and equality. Jazz is also conscripted to the political cause, with Sanchez appearing to weaponize the screech of Coltrane's saxophone and the genre of jazz music itself: "THE SOLO / SOUND OF YO/FIGHT IS MY FIGHT / SAXOPHONE."

Eventually, explosive rage segues into a wordless rhythm of "da dum da," with the instruction to sing (and stomp) to the "tune of my favorite things." The overlapping beats slowly transition into a chant, in which Sanchez exhorts the Black community to "RISE. & BE. what u can." In the last lines of the poem, this rhythmic thread draws the subject back to Coltrane and

Her career is one of the most breathtaking and vast of any of the Black Arts poets […]
Paula Hayes
American visual artist
(1958–)

> a love supreme.
> for each
> other
> if we just
> lissssssSSSTEN.
>
> **"a/coltrane/poem" (lines 126–130)**

the unifying and uplifting power of his music. Sanchez praises him for "showen us life/ / liven" and, again echoing the sentiments of Baraka's "Black Art," states that the love conveyed in Coltrane's music can be experienced by everyone "if we just / lissssssSSSTEN."

Musical aesthetic

Despite the performing origins of jazz poetry, many of the genre's works were not intended for live performance. Sanchez's poem is among these—viewed on the page, it is difficult to imagine how it is meant to be read aloud. In an interview in 2014, Sanchez stated that she performed the poem only after a group of students asked her to do so (and had waited for three hours to listen to the work). Sanchez found herself channeling the improvisational nature of jazz music for the reading.

The difficulty in understanding the rhythm of the poem comes from its textured arrangement on the page: some of the words are arranged like musical notes descending the stave of a score. Sanchez has said that she wished to imitate Coltrane, "breaking down the melody," with the intention of encouraging the reader to "engage

between the lines, between the music." The use of onomatopoeia—found in much jazz poetry—adds to the musical feel. Sanchez even emulates the sound of Coltrane's saxophone, stretching the word "screech" into multiple letter repeats—"scrEEEccCHHHHH"—to convey the sustained wailing power of the musical instrument. The aesthetics of jazz, and music composition, are continued in the use of multiple slashes within verses, enforcing a syncopated rhythm, and shifts between lower- and uppercase typography for dramatic effect.

A distinctly Black voice

Jazz poetry played an important role in validating and spreading the voice of the African American community, and challenging the dominance of white male voices in the written arts. In "a/coltrane/poem," Sanchez uses the diction of what African American writer James Baldwin termed "Black English" (now often referred to as African American Vernacular English). This gives the poem its distinctive cultural identity, and reflects the role of jazz music in giving "voice" to the African American community.

This voice (including its unique ability to relate Black experience), the exploration of Black rhythms, and the improvisational elements drawn from music into jazz poems continue to find expression in poetry today. Exhibited particularly in the work of Black American performance poets, rappers, and the work of slam poets, it shows the ongoing legacy of jazz poets such as Sanchez, and the power of combining music with words. ■

Sonia Sanchez gives a performance of her poetry in March 2011 at a tribute event in Philadelphia, Pennsylvania, to support her friend, legendary jazz saxophonist Odean Pope.

OUR HISTORIES CLING TO US*
"REFUGEE MOTHER AND CHILD" (1971), CHINUA ACHEBE
* Chimamanda Ngozi Adichie, 2012

Mourning is a universal human experience and the lament, or grieving song, is one of its oldest poetic expressions. Such laments have evolved in two principal forms. One is the elegy, from the Greek word *elegos* for "lament," usually a long, complex, and elegant meditation on loss in general, as well as bereavement, written from a personal perspective. The other, probably older, form is the dirge, its English name derived from the first word of the Latin chant used in the Church's Office for the Dead—*"dirge."* Often sung or chanted at ceremonies, the dirge is shorter, more mournful, and its subject is always the dead, or those who are about to die.

The dead and the dying
In the aftermath of the Biafran War (1967–1970) in southeastern Nigeria, Chinua Achebe wrote a poem honoring his good friend, the Nigerian poet Christopher Okigbo, who was killed in the fighting. Called "Wake for Okigbo," it was based on the traditional dirges of the Igbo people, Achebe's Nigerian ethnic group. The same year, observing the war-induced famine that killed two million Biafrans, overwhelmingly children, Achebe wrote a different type of lament—"Refugee Mother and Child"—a poem memorializing one who was about to die.

The poem consists of just four sentences: if they were not divided into five stanzas they would read like prose. There is no "poetizing," no use of rhyme, and no meter. Achebe begins by considering and rejecting religious consolation—a traditional source of solace in the poetry of loss. Referencing the iconic image of the Virgin Mary caring for the child Christ, a symbol of Christian

[...] poetry that had surged from the depths to bring pain-soaked solace in the breach and darkness of civil war.
Chinua Achebe
"In Lieu of a Preface: A Parable,"
Collected Poems, 2004

See also: "The Raven" 146–147 ▪ *In Memoriam A.H.H.* 148–149 ▪ "The First Elegy" 206 ▪ "Do Not Go Gentle Into That Good Night" 240–241

maternal love and God's ministration for humanity, he discards this trope. It is useless and no match for the refugee mother of his poem. This living mother is superior, epitomizing motherhood in the tender care of her child in a real and broken world.

Universal resonance

Achebe's mother and child are not contextualized in a specific time or place, but the poet's use of direct description, without metaphor or allusion, leaves no doubt that we are observing a real scene. At the nameless camp, listless mothers have given up hope as their children stagger with the distended bellies of starvation and malnutrition; unable to wash, they are filthy with the remnants of old excrement.

These shocking images could serve to distance the reader from the events described, but the poem shifts its focus to one mother, whose feelings and actions have a universal resonance. This mother can still evince pride in her dying son: she has bathed him and combs what remains of his hair. However, her mournful trace of a smile and the use of ghostly imagery imply she knows what lies ahead. She is described as having eyes that sing, evoking both a funeral song—the dirge of a burial rite—and a lullaby. This conflation serves to highlight the brevity of life, and the finality of death, familiar themes in the poetry of loss.

Meditations on life and death continue in the poem's final lines, where Achebe focuses on the rituals that shape human lives. A wistful reference to small everyday routines recalls the daily comforts we may still experience, but which the mother and child have lost, or never enjoyed. The mother's final tender gesture—a ceremonial last rite in the process of loss—involves parting her child's hair, which is likened to laying flowers on a grave. ▪

A mother comforts her child in 1968 at one of the refugee camps that inspired Achebe's poem. The camps housed more than one million refugees displaced by the Biafran War.

Chinua Achebe

Born Albert Chinualumogu Achebe in Ogidi, British Nigeria, in 1930, Chinua Achebe was brought up by Christian convert parents. The mixture of British colonial culture and ancient Igbo traditions that characterized his childhood would inform his later literary work. Having excelled at university, he worked for the Nigerian Broadcasting Service while starting his writing career.

In 1958, Achebe published his novel *Things Fall Apart* to great acclaim; it was followed by four more novels as well as numerous short stories, essays, and poems. Achebe served as Biafran foreign minister during the short-lived Biafran Republic (1967–1970). He spent much of his later life teaching in the US, especially at Bard College in New York state. Achebe died in 2013, six years after being awarded the Man Booker International Prize for lifetime achievement.

Other key works

1971 *Beware, Soul-Brother, and Other Poems*
1973 *Christmas in Biafra and Other Poems*

A BOOK OF MYTHS / IN WHICH / OUR NAMES DO NOT APPEAR

"DIVING INTO THE WRECK" (1973), ADRIENNE RICH

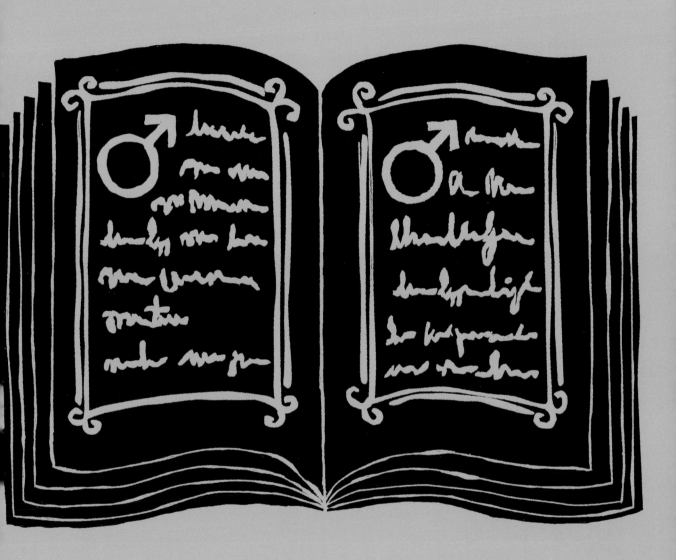

IN CONTEXT

FOCUS
Feminist poetry

OTHER KEY POETS
Christine de Pizan, Emily Dickinson, Maya Angelou, Sylvia Plath, Audre Lorde, June Jordan

BEFORE
1949 *Le Deuxième Sexe* (*The Second Sex*) is published by French feminist philosopher Simone de Beauvoir.

1968 Black American feminist poet Audre Lorde publishes her first collection, *The First Cities*.

AFTER
1983 *Writing Like a Woman*, by Jewish-American poet Alicia Ostriker, is the first major critical work to explore American feminist poetry.

2014 Canadian feminist Instapoet Rupi Kaur's debut published collection, *Milk and Honey*, becomes a bestseller in the United States.

A drienne Rich was one of the most provoking and influential writers to emerge during the Women's Liberation movement of the 1960s and '70s. Over six decades, she published more than 20 poetry collections and multiple volumes of essays, exploring issues around identity, sexuality, gender, religion, and politics through a feminist lens. This intersectional approach and her vocal participation in the women's rights movement resulted in some of the most progressive views found within the literature of her generation. Rich's 1973 collection *Diving Into the Wreck*, including the poem of the same name, is considered her first great feminist work.

Women's fight for rights

After World War II (1939–1945), women who had been supporting the war effort by running farms and factories were expected to return to the home and act as dutiful wives and devoted mothers. By the 1960s, many were questioning the restrictions imposed on their livelihoods and turned to feminist organizations for answers.

The search for gender equality in private and public spheres became a core theme for a number of women poets, including Rich. While some feminist writers used their poetry to convey personal experiences and frustrations, others directly challenged the legal injustices faced by women. Rich and other American poets, including Sylvia Plath and June Jordan, used poetry, for example, to condemn men's ability to force themselves upon their wives or partners without it being labeled rape.

The feminist community allowed Rich to develop her identity as a poet and a woman, without the two conflicting. She also actively supported other social justice movements, such as civil rights and protests against the Vietnam War in the late 1960s and early 1970s.

Transitional works

Through Rich's poetry, readers can trace the writer's personal growth and the development of her feminist thought. Although her first collection, *A Change of World* (1951), was well received, Rich's early poetry was heavily influenced

---

Adrienne Rich

Born in 1929 to an upper-middle-class family in Baltimore, Maryland, Adrienne Rich was raised Christian, although her father's heritage was Jewish. In 1951, while attending Radcliffe College in Massachusetts, she was selected for the Yale Younger Poets Award by W. H. Auden, for her first collection, *A Change of World*.

In 1953, Rich married American economist Alfred H. Conrad, with whom she had three sons. The couple separated in 1970, and later that year Conrad died by suicide.

In 1976, soon after coming out as a lesbian, Rich met Jamaican-American writer Michelle Cliff, who became her life partner. Rich died in 2012, a year after her final collection, *Tonight No Poetry Will Serve*, was published.

Other key works

1963 *Snapshots of a Daughter-in-Law*
1976 *Twenty-One Love Poems*
1978 *The Dream of a Common Language*
1983 *Sources*

See also: "Letter of the God of Love" 72–73 ▪ "Because I Could Not Stop for Death" 168–169 ▪ "Daddy" 266–267 ▪ "Power" 286–287 ▪ "Still I Rise" 288–289 ▪ "a survival plan of sorts" 308

The women's rights movement, which Rich strongly backed, grew massively in the late 1960s. Here, protesters participate in a pro-choice rally in New York City in 1968.

by the ideals and structures of male poets such as W. H. Auden and W. B. Yeats.

It was not until she married and had children during the 1950s that Rich began to question the role assigned to women within society. She had devoted herself to her husband and three sons at the expense of her work as a poet, and the resentment she began to feel as a wife and mother became the basis of *Snapshots of a Daughter-in-Law*, published in 1963.

For many critics, *Snapshots* marks the beginning of Rich's transition from conventional poet to forward feminist thinker, influenced by feminist philosophers such as her contemporary Simone de Beauvoir in France and 18th-century British women's rights champion Mary Wollstonecraft. Nevertheless, the total transformation of Rich's thought and style came only with the publication of her collection *Diving Into the Wreck* in 1973.

A break with patriarchy

Diving Into the Wreck represents Rich escaping from the traditional, patriarchal world of poetry. Throughout, she reconciles with the effect male dominance has

> The words are purposes.
> The words are maps.
> **"Diving Into the Wreck"**
> **(lines 53–54)**

had on women and their history, and searches for some means of reparation or reconciliation. While some male critics were struck by the anger expressed in Rich's writing, particularly toward men, what stands out is her radical, vivid imagery and the rejection of conventional poetic forms.

In the titular poem "Diving Into the Wreck," Rich imagines a lone diver's journey down to a sunken ship. Written as a first-person narrative, the poem begins with the speaker—presumably a woman, although Rich avoids any reference to gender—preparing for the expedition. Their mission is a personal one that must be done alone; as well as literally descending into the depths of the ocean, the diver is delving into their own psyche and history. Although this notion of isolation

and solitude is repeated throughout the poem, Rich recognizes that other women, including other poets, have made a similar journey. Approaching the ladder on the side of the boat, the diver says: "We know what it is for, / we who have used it."

Although divided into stanzas, "Diving Into the Wreck" has no formal structure. Each stanza is a different length and written in free verse. In the fourth stanza, as Rich's narrator goes deeper underwater, the poet's liberal use of enjambment reflects the diver's anticipation and fear of what will be found. The wreck represents the trauma endured by women living in a patriarchal society. The narrator has come to see the damage firsthand, to bear witness to "the wreck and not the story of the wreck / the thing itself and » not the myth." As noted by Canadian author Margaret Atwood, the myths referenced by Rich within the poem are the myths around the roles of men and women and their relationship to one another, themes explored in Beauvoir's feminist book *The Second Sex*. The wreckage discovered resembles a corpse, as Rich describes the curved "ribs of the disaster." Rich is interested in what can be salvaged from the wreckage of women's trauma and

A scuba diver explores a shipwreck in the Caribbean Sea. In "Diving Into the Wreck," the dive is an act of self-exploration and the wreck the damaged history of womankind.

> we are the half-destroyed instruments
> **"Diving Into the Wreck" (line 83)**

what lessons can be learned from the past. While "Diving Into the Wreck" primarily explores the damaging effects of male dominance on women, it also conveys the ability of poetry to explore difficult subjects or challenging experiences.

For many feminist writers like Rich, poetry was a way of processing and overcoming personal suffering and injustice. Rich describes words as the "purposes" and "maps" that have

helped guide the diver to the shipwreck and the discovery of the damage done to women.

Embracing the androgyne
One of the many radical ideas presented by Rich in her poetry is the search for the "androgyne"— the blending of two sexes. As the speaker in "Diving Into the Wreck" approaches the sunken ship, two merpeople swim around the wreckage: "And I am here, the mermaid whose dark hair /

streams black, the merman in his armored body." Yet as the three figures circle the wreckage, they begin to blur into one: "I am she: I am he."

Here and elsewhere in the *Diving Into the Wreck* collection, Rich presents the androgyne as a solution to inequality between men and women. Derived from the Greek words *andros* ("male") and *gynos* ("female"), androgyny is seen as the elimination of gender difference and opposition. Despite her rejection of myths earlier in "Diving Into the Wreck," Rich appears to find refuge in this new mythical creature.

Rich would eventually dismiss the controversial idea of androgyny in her 1978 collection *The Dream of a Common Language*. The poem "Natural Resources" states that "There are words I cannot choose again: / humanism / androgyny." As in a number of her poems, Rich was unafraid to present radical ideas in her work and later admit that she no longer believed in them.

Intersectional feminism

While the women's rights movement faced criticism for being solely interested in the experiences and needs of white, middle-class,

> Rich's feminist poetics is a fluid, dynamic, and, above all, historicized one.
> **Alice Templeton**
> American author
> (1956–)

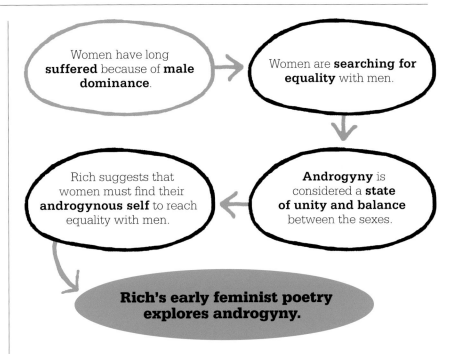

Women have long **suffered** because of **male dominance**.

Women are **searching for equality** with men.

Rich suggests that women must find their **androgynous self** to reach equality with men.

Androgyny is considered a **state of unity and balance** between the sexes.

Rich's early feminist poetry explores androgyny.

heterosexual feminists, Rich sought to advocate for the interests of women from minority communities. After the publication of her collection *Twenty-One Love Poems* in 1976, she also became more open about her sexuality, discussing in both prose and poetry the rights and experiences of lesbian women.

Rich's intersectional approach to feminism—embracing differences in gender, race, and sexuality—brought her into contact with other prominent feminist poets, including Audre Lorde. When Rich won the National Book Award for Poetry in 1974, she stated that she would accept the award only alongside Lorde and her other fellow nominee, Black American writer Alice Walker, "in the name of all women whose voices have gone and still go unheard in a patriarchal world." Rich went on to win many other awards for her work, although in 1997 she famously became the first writer to refuse the National Medal

of Arts—awarded to celebrated artists by the US government. Rich said her decision to reject the award was due to widening of the "radical disparities of wealth and power in America."

A memorable legacy

Rich constantly reinvented herself through her poetry, but she was consistent in challenging inequality and injustice—be it between men and women, Black and white feminists, or heterosexual and lesbian women. As the women's rights movement gave way to a new wave of feminism in the 1990s, Rich continued to be a prominent figure within discussions on women's position in modern society. Recognized as one of the most original poetic minds in the US, her exploration of identity embodied the experiences of the various marginalized communities she represented, and continues to speak volumes today. ■

somebody/ anybody sing a black girl's song

for colored girls who have considered suicide/ when the rainbow is enuf (1975), NTOZAKE SHANGE

IN CONTEXT

FOCUS
Choreopoem

OTHER KEY POETS
Gwendolyn Brooks, Amiri Baraka, Sonia Sanchez

BEFORE
1950 Gwendolyn Brooks wins the Pulitzer Prize in poetry for *Annie Allen*, portraying Black American urban life.

1959 *A Raisin in the Sun*, Lorraine Hansberry's play about housing discrimination in south Chicago, Illinois, debuts in New York City.

AFTER
1981 The Nuyorican Poets Cafe, which counts Shange as a founding member, moves to larger New York City premises due to its expanding audience.

2020 *How to Exterminate the Black Woman*, Monica Prince's choreopoem about Black women's battle to thrive, premieres in the US.

Beginning in 1965, the Black Arts Movement (BAM) formed the cultural wing of the Black Power movement in the US: a revolutionary organization that rejected racial integration and sought Black self-determination. The artistic works generated by

Ntozake Shange (right) performs in her choreopoem *for colored girls who have considered suicide/ when the rainbow is enuf* in 1976. The production was nominated for a Tony Award in 1977.

the BAM were innovative and profound, but often hyper-masculine—a response to the historical degradation of Black American men. Female artists and writers felt marginalized in the BAM, and sexism was widely debated within its publications.

In the 1970s, poet and playwright Ntozake Shange began to address issues of race, Black power, and sexism with a fresh, distinctive voice. Both criticizing and extending the BAM, she created a specifically

Ntozake Shange

Born Paulette Linda Williams in 1948, Ntozake Shange grew up in a middle-class Black home in Trenton, New Jersey. Her father and mother mixed with well-known Black musicians and writers, and Shange cultivated an interest in poetry at an early age.

In 1971, while studying at the University of Southern California for a master's degree in American Studies, Shange rejected both "Paulette" and "Williams" as being, respectively, patriarchal and a slave name. Instead, she adopted the Zulu name Ntozake Shange, suggested by friends.

Shange went on to write highly acclaimed poetry collections, plays, novels, and essays centering the experiences of Black women and girls. She died in 2018 following a series of strokes. Her choreopoem *for colored girls* […] continues to be performed, and a film adaptation, directed by Tyler Perry, was released in 2010.

Other key works

1978 *Nappy Edges*
1987 *Ridin' the Moon in Texas*
1991 *The Love Space Demands*

female aesthetic that openly discussed Black women's realities, their bodies, and the cycles of their lives: topics that had often been trivialized or ignored.

The first choreopoem

Shange's most ambitious work is *for colored girls who have considered suicide/ when the rainbow is enuf.* A 20-piece "choreopoem"—a word coined by Shange to describe a blend of poetry, dance, movement, and song—it chronicles the lives of seven Black women, identified only by the color of their clothes. When it opened on Broadway in 1976, the work was hailed as groundbreaking by critics and audiences alike. It departed from

> dark phrases of womanhood of never havin been a girl half-notes scattered without rhythm/ no tune
> **for colored girls […] ("dark phrases," lines 1–4)**

traditional Western poetry and storytelling to create a new art form that rejected expected plot elements and characters, and chimed with the lived experience of Black women. The work also acknowledged the deep oral roots of Black feminist writing. Its interweaving strands highlighted the relationship between voice and body and how they cannot be disentangled, especially when dealing with topics such as violence, incest, and rape.

Challenging convention

Like Shange's other poetry, *for colored girls* […] used nonstandard spelling and vernacular language, and rejected capitalization. Shange also employed the forward slash (/), not to indicate a line break but as an act of "cutting across" with a new thought or hesitation: "carin/ struggle/ hard times." This overthrow of poetic convention seized the attention of readers, while also challenging the ways in which the white aesthetic was seen as the universal norm.

Shange's innovations with form and language broke vital new ground. As well as inspiring Black American poets and playwrights, such as Monica Prince and Suzan-Lori Parks, Shange paved the way for writers in other marginalized groups, including those of Latin and Indigenous descent and members of the LGBTQ+ community, to find new, creative ways to express their pain and longing and move forward with hope "to the ends of their own rainbows." ▪

> She did not sound like anybody else, ever.
> **Michael Denneny**
> **Shange's editor (1943–)**

TO MAKE POWER OUT OF HATRED

"POWER" (1978), AUDRE LORDE

IN CONTEXT

FOCUS
Intersectional poetry

OTHER KEY POETS
Claude McKay, Langston Hughes, Gwendolyn Brooks, Maya Angelou, Adrienne Rich

BEFORE
1936 Black American poet Sterling Brown publishes "Southern Cop" about a Black victim killed by a policeman.

AFTER
1978 After the police murder of Arthur Miller in New York City, Black American poet June Jordan writes "Poem about Police Violence."

1992 "4/30/92 for rodney king" by Black American poet Lucille Clifton explores the death of King at the hands of the police.

2016 American poetry slam team Nayo Jones, Kai Davis, and Jasmine Combs perform a poem for Sandra Bland, who died in police custody.

Clifford Glover, a 10-year-old Black boy, was killed by an undercover police officer, Thomas Shea, in New York City in 1973. The officer claimed that Glover had run away after being approached on an—unfounded—suspicion of robbery. He shot Glover in the back as he ran, believing that the child was carrying a weapon.

Shea was tried for murder in 1974 but acquitted by a jury of 11 white men and one Black woman.

American Audre Lorde wrote "Power" after hearing about Shea's acquittal on her car radio. She later said that, filled with rage, she had to pull the car over and write the poem. Like much of her poetry, it reflects Lorde's commitment to activism—

"Power" begins with the poet speculating on the difference between "poetry" and "rhetoric."

Poetry is the sharing of an individual's truth, from an equal position.

Rhetoric is speaking from a position of power and persuasion.

Poetry requires the speaker to be **vulnerable** and to **participate** in the action.

Those who use rhetoric take **no responsibility** for the actions they incite.

Poetry is an alternative to rhetoric

See also: "We Wear the Mask" 170–171 ■ "I, Too" 208–213 ■ "Middle Passage" 230–231 ■ *Annie Allen* 236–239 ■ "Black Art" 268–269 ■ *for colored girls who have considered suicide / when the rainbow is enuf* 284–285 ■ "Still I Rise" 288–289

Audre Lorde

Born to Caribbean immigrant parents in 1934, Audrey Lorde was raised in Harlem. As a child, she chose to drop the last letter of her given name. Her first poem was published by *Seventeen* magazine when she was still in college.

In the 1960s, Lorde worked as a librarian, married a white gay man, and had two children. She joined the Civil Rights, anti–Vietnam War, and feminist movements and continued to write poetry, leading to her first collection, *The First Cities*, in 1968. In 1970, she divorced her husband and began to explore her lesbianism in her collection *Cables to Rage*.

Lorde was diagnosed with breast cancer in 1977 and chronicled her illness in the book *The Cancer Journals* (1980). She continued to pursue activism, teaching, and writing, serving as the New York State Poet Laureate until her death in 1992.

Other key works

1976 *Coal*
1978 *The Black Unicorn*
1986 *Our Dead Behind Us*

---

tackling racism, patriarchal power, and homophobia. She introduced herself as "Black, lesbian, mother, warrior, poet" and believed that her poetry was born of intersections between these different worlds.

Horror and shame

"Power" quotes excerpts from the trial, including Shea's recorded racist shout as he shot Glover and his claim that he did not notice that Glover was a child—only that he was Black. The poem details the physical effects of Shea's crime, as Lorde describes Glover's "shattered" face and "punctured [...] shoulders." And she focuses on the role of the Black female juror, forced to give up the small power of her position and join the white men around her in acquitting Shea. Lorde reflects on this woman's role as a fellow mother, describing her actions as making a "graveyard" for Black children.

The power to change

American poet–activist Lexi Rudnitsky has pointed to Lorde's description, in the second stanza of "Power," of being lost in a desert and unable to write poetry. This desert is a place of violence and "whiteness," where there is no "imagery or magic." Rudnitsky refers to Lorde's 1977 essay "Poetry Is Not a Luxury," in which she describes Black women writing from a dark, deep, and ancient place and identifies poetry with magic. To Lorde, whiteness negates poetry, like a blank page. In "Power," that figurative white desert is soaked red by Glover's blood.

At the start of "Power," Lorde is pondering how she should respond to injustice. One option, which her rage leads her toward, is what she describes as "rhetoric"—using the power of her angry, persuasive language to incite young people to violence, which she herself will not have to be involved in. The other option is to write "poetry"—a personal truth in which she becomes an active participant.

Lorde saw poetry as a potential new language for change. In "Poetry Is Not a Luxury," she wrote that where this "language does not yet exist, it is our poetry which helps to fashion it." She condemned the "sterile word play" of "white fathers" that made up older poetry, contrasting it with the passionate work of her own contemporaries, which served as "a revelation or distillation of experience." For Lorde, "Power" was an in-the-moment expression of anger, which she later chose to perform as an act of political protest; taken as a poem, she considered it to be entirely "without craft." ■

I am trapped on a desert of raw gunshot wounds
and a dead child dragging his shattered black
face off the edge of my sleep
"Power" (lines 5–7)

BUT STILL, LIKE DUST, I'LL RISE

"STILL I RISE" (1978), MAYA ANGELOU

IN CONTEXT

FOCUS
Poem as memoir

OTHER KEY POETS
**William Shakespeare,
Paul Laurence Dunbar,
Langston Hughes,
Amanda Gorman**

BEFORE.
1903 In the US, pan-African activist W.E.B. Du Bois publishes his seminal book of essays *The Souls of Black Folk*.

1926 Poet Langston Hughes publishes *The Weary Blues*.

1950 Gwendolyn Brooks wins the Pulitzer Prize in Poetry for her collection *Annie Allen*.

AFTER
1999 The posthumous album *Still I Rise*, by American rapper Tupac Shakur, is released three years after he is fatally shot.

2013 Angelou's "His Day Is Done" is a tribute on the death of former South African president Nelson Mandela.

The subversive power of hope and self-belief drives Black American poet Maya Angelou's "Still I Rise." From the first line—"You may write me down in history"—the poem's speaker (standing for the wider community of oppressed Black people) addresses and challenges the supposedly powerful "You" of the white oppressors. With their "bitter, twisted lies," these oppressors tread down the speaker "in the very dirt." Yet, through defiant self-belief, this "dirt" of oppression becomes the "dust" of the speaker's transcendence of it: "But still, like dust, I'll rise."

Inner strength

"Does my sassiness upset you?" the second stanza begins, a question echoed with variations twice more in the poem: "Does my haughtiness offend you?" and "Does my sexiness upset you?" Against these manifestations of inner strength—sassiness, haughtiness, sexiness—all the oppressors can bring to bear is economic clout, and even that turns ludicrously against them in the swagger and attitude of the speaker: "I walk like I've got oil wells / Pumping in my living room"; "I laugh like I've got gold mines / Diggin' in my own backyard"; "I dance like I've got diamonds / At the meeting of my thighs."

In the last two stanzas, the meter and rhyming patterns shift, the beat, becoming faster, more insistent: "I'm a black ocean, leaping and wide, / Welling and swelling I bear in the tide." At the same time, the previous refrain, "I'll rise"—future tense—becomes present: "I rise." What was foreshadowed in the defiance of the earlier stanzas becomes

> Leaving behind nights of terror and fear
> I rise
> Into a daybreak that's wondrously clear
> I rise
> **"Still I Rise" (lines 35–38)**

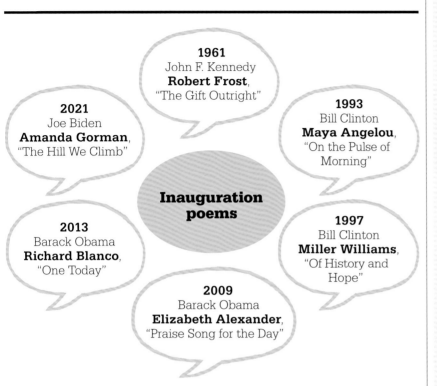

1961
John F. Kennedy
Robert Frost,
"The Gift Outright"

2021
Joe Biden
Amanda Gorman,
"The Hill We Climb"

1993
Bill Clinton
Maya Angelou,
"On the Pulse of
Morning"

**Inauguration
poems**

2013
Barack Obama
Richard Blanco,
"One Today"

1997
Bill Clinton
Miller Williams,
"Of History and
Hope"

2009
Barack Obama
Elizabeth Alexander,
"Praise Song for the Day"

Maya Angelou

Born Marguerite Annie Johnson in St. Louis, Missouri, in 1928, Angelou was initially raised by her grandmother in rural Arkansas. At age seven, during a stay with her mother, she was raped by her mother's lover. The man was later killed by her uncles, the trauma of which caused Angelou to stop speaking for four years.

In 1940, Angelou moved to California to live with her mother, and won a scholarship to study dance and acting. She moved to New York in 1959, where she joined the Harlem Writers' Guild, set up to encourage Black writers. She was involved with the Civil Rights movement, and during the 1960s lived for a while in Africa. In 1981, she was appointed Professor of American Studies at Wake Forest University, North Carolina. The seventh of her autobiographical books, *Mom & Me & Mom*, was published in 2013. She died in 2014.

Other key works

1971 *Just Give Me a Cool Drink of Water 'fore I Diiie*
1983 *Shaker, Why Don't You Sing?*

present and actual, culminating in an emphatic triple assertion: "I rise / I rise / I rise."

Defiance of racism

The poem comes from Angelou's third poetry collection, of almost the same title, *And Still I Rise*, published in 1978. The themes of racism and the defiance of it run through all her work. Her own literary development had three strands: the musical and oral traditions of her youth, including spirituals, blues, and preaching; the Black literary tradition of figures such as the 19th-century American anti-slavery campaigner Frederick Douglass; and the classical English-language tradition, including Shakespeare, Robert Burns, and Edgar Allan Poe. Of these, the oral remained vital for Angelou. Written and spoken, private and public, were

complementary for her. Her poetry was meant for performing, a goal superbly achieved when she was invited to write a poem for President Clinton's inauguration in 1993.

In the resulting work, "On the Pulse of Morning," the call to inner, private strength and outer, public confidence were in explicit balance. "Give birth again / To the dream," she told the watching millions in a clear reference to her late friend Martin Luther King, Jr.'s famous "dream" of a fairer world. "Women, children, men, / Take it into the palms of your hands, / Mold it into the shape of your most / Private need. Sculpt it into / The image of your most public self." For her, these two, private need and public self, were aspects of one thing—a bold, positive presence or voice in the world. ▪

DAWN-SNIFFING REVENANT, / PLODDER THROUGH MIDNIGHT RAIN

"CASUALTY" (1979), SEAMUS HEANEY

IN CONTEXT

FOCUS
Cultural geography

OTHER KEY POETS
**William Wordsworth,
Gerard Manley Hopkins,
W. B. Yeats, Ted Hughes**

BEFORE
1798 William Wordsworth
and Samuel Taylor Coleridge
publish *Lyrical Ballads*,
which is rooted in the
English Lake District.

1942 Irish poet Patrick
Kavanagh bases *The Great
Hunger* on the harsh rural life
of County Monaghan.

AFTER
1991 In *Gorse Fires*, Michael
Longley uses precise imagery
from his native West of Ireland.

2008 *Stepping Stones*, a
collection of interviews with
Seamus Heaney, provides
insight into his inspirations.

Poetry often reflects a close
relationship with place—
not only a particular rural
or urban landscape, but also its
history, and its political and cultural
significance. These are evident in
its buildings, monuments, and open
spaces, and in the behavior and
attitudes of its citizens. Cultural
geography is the layering and
interlacing of these connections—
binding a poet such as Seamus
Heaney to his social setting and
enriching his writings.

At the geographic heart of
Heaney's poetry is Northern
Ireland, specifically its experience
of the Troubles—the civil unrest
that lasted from the late 1960s until

See also: *Beowulf* 48–51 ▪ "I Wandered Lonely as a Cloud" 126–129 ▪ "The Windhover"166–167 ▪ "The Second Coming" 194–197 ▪ "Sestina" 254–255 ▪ "Pike" 260–263

Seamus Heaney

Born in County Derry, Northern Ireland, in 1939, Seamus Heaney was the eldest of nine children. His father owned a small farm and was also a cattle dealer. After studying English at Queen's University in Belfast, Heaney worked as a teacher and a lecturer in the city. An early influence was Ted Hughes, with whom he later collaborated on a verse anthology, *The Rattle Bag* (1982).

Heaney won acclaim for his first major collection, *Death of a Naturalist* (1966), and in 1972 he moved to County Wicklow in the Republic of Ireland to write

full-time. From 1981, he taught at Harvard University in the US, and in 1989 became Professor of Poetry at the University of Oxford. Heaney won the Nobel Prize in Literature in 1995, praised for works that "exalt everyday miracles and the living past." He died in 2013, three years after *Human Chain*, his final collection, was published.

Other key works

1975 *North*
1979 *Field Work*
1996 *The Spirit Level*

the 1998 Good Friday Agreement. Violence, erupting through sudden terrorist action, vengeful reprisals, or brutal repression, was woven into the landscape of Heaney's life, even in the rural community where he had spent his boyhood.

Uneasy times

The struggle was between Protestant Loyalists—who wanted Northern Ireland to remain part of the UK—and Catholic Republicans seeking an independent Ireland, free of British rule. The religious factor added an element of die-hard extremism, and sectarian tit-for-tat aggression raised the tension among the population. Heaney's powerful three-part elegy "Casualty" captures the unease of the times while also celebrating the human spirit's indomitable integrity.

Mourners attend the funeral procession for 11 of the 13 people killed by British soldiers on Bloody Sunday. The funeral is one of many references to the Troubles in Heaney's work.

The subject of the elegy is a Catholic eel fisherman, Louis O'Neill (unnamed in the poem), "blown to bits" while out drinking one night in a pub frequented by Protestants. He breaks two taboos: ignoring the curfew imposed after Bloody Sunday—January 30, 1972, when British soldiers killed 13 unarmed Catholics in Derry—and mixing socially with Protestants.

In "Casualty," Heaney looks beyond social and religious divisions to insist on the value of unassuming humanity: the dignity of the self-contained individual. The first part of the poem begins by remembering O'Neill—in a different pub—in verse that deflects attention from itself by joining up the rhyming (sometimes half-rhyming) abab quatrains into one column, rather than arranging »

Heaney and the mythic past

Heaney's respect for Irish identity is linked to an interest in the mythic past. This encompasses Irish and Greek myth and the northern European goddess Nerthus, referred to as "Mother Earth" by the 1st-century Roman historian Tacitus. In the *North* collection, several poems use the Greek myth of Hercules and the giant Antaeus to mirror the English colonization of Ireland. Antaeus gains strength from contact with the ground—a reference to Ireland drawing spiritual nourishment from its rightful homeland. In "Punishment" and Heaney's other "bog" poems, the remains of victims possibly sacrificed to Nerthus and found preserved in Danish and German bogs evoke the brutalities of the Irish sectarianism of the Troubles. "Casualty," despite its matter-of-fact language, ends with a lyrical folkloric echo: the idea of a ghost melting away as dawn breaks.

How culpable was he
That last night when he broke
Our tribe's complicity?
"Casualty" (Part II, lines 32–34)

them as four-line stanzas. Heaney, who knew O'Neill, admires the fisherman's "deadpan sidling tact" but—self-conscious—steers their conversation away from the subject of poetry.

Internal conflict

Part two of the poem pictures the funeral of 11 of the Catholic victims of Bloody Sunday, attended by tens of thousands, and then moves on to the bombing that killed O'Neill. Heaney's core concern is whether he should put his poetic gift at the service of politics or stand for love, peace, forgiveness, and reconciliation. His heart leans toward love, but this leaves him with a guilty conscience.

A sense of betrayal or desertion of a just cause is a recurrent theme in Heaney's poetry. In "Exposure," published in *North* in 1975, he describes himself as "an inner émigré, grown long-haired / And thoughtful; a wood-kerne // Escaped from the massacre[…]." A pacifist stance taken among those who commit to the struggle for freedom feels uncomfortable, but Heaney explores such tensions within himself with sincerity and subtlety.

The mysterious beyond

The third part of "Casualty" starts with an imagined view of O'Neill's funeral, which moves seamlessly into a fishing scene: "that morning / I was taken in his boat." Unwilling to end the elegy with comfortable reminiscences, Heaney invites the ghost of his friend to question him again, from his "proper haunt / Somewhere, well out, beyond…." Though not exactly mystical, this concluding vignette gestures toward the infinite unknown, a kind of secular heaven, beyond the limits of the everyday.

Symbols drawn from Irish myth, history, and landscape.

The **Irish language** and **local dialects**.

Place evoked through **cultural contrasts**, such as **home and crafts** versus **guns and bombs**.

The **clash between loyalty and peace**—and other values **shaped by geography**.

Recurring elements in Seamus Heaney's poetry

The examination of **cultural norms**, such as the **value of poetry** compared to **physical work**.

Irish farming family, taught in the US, and served as Oxford Professor of Poetry, brought to the Irish experience a more teasing, enigmatic imagination, as evidenced in his early poems. "Dancers at the Moy" from *New Weather* (1973), is a tightly written parable that conflates Ireland with ancient Rome to foresee how conflict might one day be turned into festive harmony. The Moy is a village on the Blackwater River that separates the counties of Armagh and Tyrone—for Muldoon a place "burned into the retina."

By contrast, the geography of English poet—and Heaney's friend—Tony Harrison is mostly urban. His long poem *V* (1985), follows a group of soccer supporters in Leeds, UK, allowing him to explore class divisions and tribal affiliation as he maps his home city's cultural landscapes. ∎

In Heaney's later poetry, the interplay between the marvellous and the everyday becomes a key theme. "The Wishing Tree," an elegy for his mother, from *The Haw Lantern* (1987), describes upturned faces watching the tree lift into heaven, trailing a shower of nails and coins driven into its trunk by locals making wishes; and "Lightenings viii," from *Seeing Things* (1991), repeats an ancient tale about a magical ship appearing above monks at prayer.

Profound simplicity

The focus in "Casualty" on a characterful individual known only to their own community, yet with qualities of universal value, places the poem in a long tradition that links it with Gerard Manley Hopkins' "Felix Randal" (a farrier), written in 1880, and "Harry Ploughman" (1918). The dignity of skilled labor looms large within this tradition. Heaney's anonymous casualty is unemployed (on the "dole") but his fisherman's skills, as well as his independent spirit, entitle him to respect.

Heaney esteems the everyday craft and practicality of country people. In "Mossbawn: Sunlight,"

from *North*, a memorable simile for love—"like a tinsmith's scoop / sunk past its gleam / in the meal-bin"—suggests that love acquires its sometimes hidden gleam from repeated practice. It is working at commitment, over and over, that makes love shine bright.

Heaney refers in "Casualty" to his "tentative art," but he also equates this in other poems with humble but energetic and skillful rural activity. "Digging," from *Death of a Naturalist* (1966), likens writing to spadework—particularly that of the poet's father—a comparison both for the labor of the writer's unwavering commitment and the profundity of digging down to find hard truths. The poet has only a pen, not a spade, but he determines nevertheless to do some good with the tool of his trade.

Ripples in the stream

Heaney's interweaving of personal memory and communal history, using plain, accessible language heightened by vivid imagery, exerted a powerful influence on contemporaries and later writers. His student Paul Muldoon, who like Heaney came from a Northern

The shine of morning light on the lough [...] reminded me of the dawn scene in *Hamlet*, when the ghost fades on the crowing of the cock—so in 'Casualty' Louis then turns into a 'dawn-sniffing revenant.'
Seamus Heaney
Stepping Stones, 2008

HE POSSESSES ME ON CANVAS

"STANDING FEMALE NUDE" (1985), CAROL ANN DUFFY

IN CONTEXT

FOCUS
Ekphrastic poetry

OTHER KEY POETS
John Keats, Rainer Maria Rilke, W. H. Auden, Elizabeth Bishop

BEFORE
1819 Keats writes his "Ode on a Grecian Urn" after reading articles about Greek sacrifice and worship in *The Examiner*, a radical British newspaper.

1855 "Fra Lippo Lippi," by Robert Browning, questions whether art should be true to life or to an ideal.

1940 Elizabeth Bishop's poem "Cirque d'hiver" describes a toy circus horse that reminds her of the work of Surrealist painter Giorgio de Chirico.

1978 "Not My Best Side," by British poet U. A. Fanthorpe, offers a comical dramatization of Paolo Uccello's 1470 painting *St. George and the Dragon*.

Just as art can take a poem as its subject, conversely some poems focus on a work of art. The term used to describe them is *ekphrastic*—from a Greek word meaning "description." Often the poet uses the scene depicted as a prompt for their own ideas, perhaps imagining (or asking) what might have just happened or what might happen next. There may be an element of philosophical thought. The argument sometimes moves far from the art that inspired it. The resulting poem, especially if highly crafted, stands in an intriguing relationship with the original: instead of one work of art there are now two, in competing media. It is left to the reader to decide whether a debate is taking place between the two works.

Museum of Fine Arts

W. H. Auden's "Musée des Beaux Arts" (French for "Museum of Fine Arts"), written in 1938, is an ekphrastic poem inspired by a number of paintings attributed to 16th-century Flemish artist Pieter Bruegel the Elder, culminating with *Landscape with the Fall of Icarus*.

The brilliance of Auden's poem is that generalization is confined to the first four lines: suffering takes place while others go unmoved about their business. Then the reader learns of important events (borrowed from art) happening at the margins. Icarus, falling from the sky after attempting to fly using wings of feathers and wax, crashes into the sea. Two farmers work busily, unaware of the nearby drama. The vivid conclusion is a detail from the painting—Icarus

An early copy of Pieter Bruegel's *Landscape with the Fall of Icarus* is still on display in Brussels at the *Musées royaux des Beaux-Arts*, after which Auden's poem is named.

See also: *The Odyssey* 24–31 ▪ "To Autumn" 138–141 ▪ "The First Elegy" 206 ▪ "September 1, 1939" 220–223

half-sunk under the waves after his fall, no doubt observed by sailors on a ship, which nevertheless calmly continues its voyage. In this poem Auden cleverly uses the world of painting to contrast the lives of people who continue to pursue their mundane everyday routines while others are suffering.

Subverting genre

British poet Carol Ann Duffy in "Standing Female Nude" addresses the circumstances, not the content, of a painting. She shows empathy with an exploited sex worker who is posing nude for much-needed cash: "Six hours like this for a few francs." All we learn of the picture itself is the model's bitter comment: "It does not look like me."

By ironically using a title that the artist might have chosen, Duffy subverts the genre of nude portraiture, at the same time as auditing the human cost of subjection to the male gaze. The language is plain and blunt, and so another subversion is taking place here—of the kind of mild-mannered ekphrastic poem that treats a painting admiringly or perhaps philosophizes airily about its subject.

A contrasting approach

Austrian poet Rainer Maria Rilke's "Archaic Torso of Apollo" (1908) describes the headless torso of the sun god radiating energy like a starburst. We *imagine* the missing head and feel a dazzling power— a nobility we have failed to honor. The poem concludes: "You must change your life." In contrast to Duffy's standing nude, this art is said to elevate life rather than degrade it. ∎

The shield of Achilles

An early example of ekphrastic poetry is Homer's detailed description of the shield of Achilles in his c. 8th century BCE epic *The Iliad* (Book 18). Used in combat with Hector, the chief warrior of the Trojan army, the shield was fashioned for Achilles by the god of craftsmanship, Hephaestus.

Its ornamentation depicts Earth and the heavens, two cities (one in which a wedding and a law case are being held, the other besieged), farming and a festival, a lion attacking a bull, and the encircling ocean. The passage is a microcosm of Greek society, with the implication of life as a balance of opposites. W. H. Auden's 1952 poem *The Shield of Achilles* presents a 20th-century interpretation of Homer's epic poem.

Interpretative—examining what the art might mean, especially if enigmatic.

Amplifying—elaborating on the subject depicted (for example, spinning a narrative from a scene).

Philosophical— exploring the relationship between art and reality, or some other philosophical idea.

An ekphrastic poem may take one or several approaches, sometimes mixing one with another.

Circumstantial— looking at the context of creation, such as the artist's studio.

Responsive—expressing the poet's feelings about the art, sometimes in relation to his or her own life.

SO MUCH IS CHANCE, / SO MUCH AGILITY, DESIRE, AND FEVERISH CARE
"MACHINES" (1988), MICHAEL DONAGHY

IN CONTEXT

FOCUS
The New Metaphysicals

OTHER KEY POETS
John Donne, George Herbert, Andrew Marvell, T. S. Eliot

BEFORE
1949 William Empson's "Thanks for a Wedding Present" includes typical Metaphysical elements, such as puns, references to science, and original conceits.

1957 Helen Gardner cites Shakespeare as a precursor to Donne and Herbert.

1987 British poet Tony Harrison, in his sonnet "Marked with D," uses Metaphysical wit in an elegy for his father.

AFTER
2000 Donaghy's third poetry collection *Conjure* shows his customary Metaphysical emphasis on ideas in the context of everyday life.

Metaphysical poetry, a style established in the 17th century by English poets such as John Donne and George Herbert, favored the "conceit." This is a stretched comparison, "whose ingenuity," as British literary critic Helen Gardner put it, "is more striking than its justness." Another defining characteristic was the fusion of intellectual thought and feeling. T. S. Eliot, who admired the Metaphysical poets' inventiveness, linked this with a capacity for "devouring all kinds of experience." The planetary motions or a pair of compasses were just as appropriate for poetic images as a sunrise or flowers. Typically, a Metaphysical poem follows a witty, concentrated argument, and the reader's pleasure derives in part from understanding its twists and turns.

Metaphysical traits surfaced intermittently in the poetry of subsequent poets, such as in the paradoxes of British poet Edward FitzGerald's *The Rubaiyat of Omar Khayyam* (1859): "I sometimes think that never blows so red / The Rose as where some buried Caesar bled." From the mid-20th century, a new kind of Metaphysical poetry emerged, especially in the UK, where poets William Empson, Tony Harrison, Don Paterson, and American-in-London Michael Donaghy all explored its potential.

Metaphysical heritage
Donaghy's "Machines," from his collection *Shibboleth*, displays the Metaphysical influences of Donne and Empson. This is a love poem—"Dearest," Donaghy begins—but our expectations are immediately undermined by mock seriousness (his next words are "note how"), as he points to the similarity between a harpsichord pavane (a short processional dance) by Purcell and a 12-speed bike.

> Dearest, note how these two are alike:
> This harpsichord pavane by Purcell
> And the racer's twelve-speed bike.
> **"Machines" (lines 1–3)**

See also: Sonnet 130 88–93 ▪ "Death, Be Not Proud" 94–95 ▪ "Prayer" 96–99
▪ "To His Coy Mistress" 101 ▪ *The Waste Land* 198–205

The essence of New Metaphysical poetry

> Poets use **wit and erudition** to create poetry that fuses **thought and feeling**.

> **Unexpected contrasts** are a stock-in-trade—especially **conceits** juxtaposing **local and cosmic** scales.

> Thought-provoking **paradox** is a common characteristic.

> A poem's **argument** often shows great **condensing of ideas**.

Describing the bicycle's gears, with reference to Ptolemy and the US bicycle company Schwinn, Donaghy takes us by surprise with a simple enjambed participle: the gearing "Is gone"—just as Purcell's chords are gone, with the passage of time. Ridden away, the bike has disappeared.

Wit and contradiction

The argument in Donaghy's "Machines" echoes a line in Empson's "Invitation to Juno" (1928). The line in question is commonsensical: "Johnson could see no bicycle would go: / 'You bear yourself, and the machine as well.'" This is a piece of witty intellectual persuasion aimed at getting a loved one into bed. Empson's implicit argument is that all around us are examples of apparent impossibility that have proved possible; so the impossibility of Ixion, a mortal king, and Juno, wife of the god Jupiter, coming together is no less possible.

Donaghy compares the bicycle to his talk of love: both should move him to a new place, both paradisal ("Dante's heaven") and evanescent ("melt into the air"). Donaghy admits the risk of falling from his seat, the pain of separation linked with the difficulty of finding equilibrium through poetry. The poem ends with what bicyclists and harpsichordists prove, "Who only by moving can balance, / Only by balancing move." The Metaphysical paradox has dizzying implications about life and love. The poet can only be himself through his bond with another; absence reinforces closeness; and life is perpetual motion. ∎

Michael Donaghy

Born in New York City in 1954 to Irish immigrant parents, who both died in their thirties, Donaghy grew up with his sister in the Bronx. He later studied at Fordham University and the University of Chicago, where he edited *Chicago Review*, a literary magazine.

As a teenager, Donaghy developed a keen interest in traditional Irish music, playing the flute, tin whistle, and bodhrán. Music was a recurrent theme in his poetry, and in 1985 he moved to the UK to join his partner, a fellow musician, and played in various Irish music groups. Donaghy quickly established himself as a leading figure on the British poetry scene. *Shibboleth*, his first published collection, won the Whitbread Prize for Poetry in 1989. Further collections, awards, and accolades followed before his sudden death in 2004. Donaghy's fourth collection of poetry, *Safest*, was published posthumously in 2005.

Other key works

1990 *Errata*
2000 *Conjure*

A JOURNEY TOWARD A RENEWAL OF LIFE*
"DON'T BOTHER THE EARTH SPIRIT" (1989), JOY HARJO
* Mary Leen

IN CONTEXT

FOCUS
Modern narrative poetry

OTHER KEY POETS
**Oodgeroo Noonuccal,
Elizabeth Acevedo**

BEFORE
1983 American literary critic
Kenneth Lincoln coins the term
Native American Renaissance.

AFTER
1997 Shoshone writer nila
northSun's *A snake in her
mouth: poems 1974–96* uses
what she calls "reservation
English" in poems about
working-class Indigenous life.

2017 Oglala Lakota poet
Layli Long Soldier's *Whereas*
responds to S. J. Res. 14, a
Congressional apology to
Indigenous Americans.

2021 The Pulitzer Prize is
awarded to Mojave poet
Natalie Diaz for *Postcolonial
Love Poem*, which centers
Indigenous experiences and
explores colonial violence.

I n the 1960s, Indigenous peoples
across the US mobilized to
demand equal rights to white
Americans. The movement also
bore creative fruit, with an upsurge
of Indigenous people creating art
and song, and writing about their
experiences and struggles. Key
figures of what was later dubbed
the "Native American Renaissance"

The dramatic landscapes of New
Mexico and the American Southwest,
which are home to many Indigenous
nations, inspired much of Harjo's
poetry and prose.

included Joy Harjo, a member
of the Muscogee (Creek) Nation.
In the decades that followed, she
wrote several books of poems
dedicated to her community, their
sacred lands, and their renewed
cultural confidence.

One of Harjo's best-known
poems is "Don't Bother the Earth
Spirit," from *Secrets from the
Center of the World* (1989). The
collection consists of short prose
poems—narrative poems without
line breaks, which take a form
similar to prose—interspersed
with photographs of landscapes

See also: "We Are Going" 264 ▪ "Power" 286–287 ▪ "Still I Rise" 288–289 ▪ "Hair" 306–307

Joy Harjo

Born in Tulsa, Oklahoma, in 1951, Joy Harjo is a member of the Muscogee (Creek) Nation. At first, influenced by her great-aunt, Muscogee painter Lois Harjo Ball, she intended to become a visual artist. At age 16, she attended the Institute of American Indian Arts in New Mexico. Later, as an undergraduate at the University of New Mexico, Albuquerque, she switched her focus to creative writing, which she later taught at several universities.

Since the publication of her first poetry collection, *The Last Song*, in 1975, Harjo has won numerous awards for her poetry, memoirs, and children's books. In 2019, she became the first US Poet Laureate of Indigenous descent. A musician as well as a poet, Harjo plays the saxophone and flute: she has released several albums, and often performs music alongside her poetry.

Other key works

1983 *She Had Some Horses*
1994 *The Woman Who Fell from the Sky*
2019 *An American Sunrise: Poems*

taken by American astronomer Stephen Strom in Navajo country, in the southwestern United States.

In "Don't Bother the Earth Spirit," Harjo frames the natural world as a sacred and sentient being, and as the creator of human life. To many Indigenous cultures, the land is sacred, and spiritual connections with the landscape are a major part of Indigenous religion. The "center" in Harjo's *Secrets from the Center of the World* is not a major city, but the earth of the American Southwest.

Storytelling traditions

Harjo's poem uses the metaphor of a spirit of the earth telling an ancient story—the story of life. With offers of food and drink, the spirit draws a listener in to hear this tale, which includes all of the joy and suffering of human life, and is inescapable. American scholar Mary Leen argues that the poem takes us to what Black American theorist Gloria Jean Watkins (better known as "bell hooks") called "the homeplace"—a place of spiritual growth and nurturing.

The story in this poem is perhaps Indigenous life itself. Storytelling is important to Indigenous peoples' sense of identity, community, and history, and most Indigenous nations have oral history traditions that inform how poets see their work. For example, Simon J. Ortiz, an Acoma Pueblo poet also active during the Native American Renaissance, explicitly uses the term "storyteller" rather than "poet" when referring to himself.

It is possible to look at the poems in *Secrets from the Center of the World* as a running dialogue with and about the land. While broken up by Strom's photographs, the pieces have no titles (they are referenced elsewhere by their first phrase), and run on from each other. The poems are narrative and instructive, using stories to pass on their message.

Past and future

"Don't Bother the Earth Spirit" introduces ideas of both cultural continuity and change. The story told by the spirit represents the oldest tale ever told, while also describing how this narrative must continue to evolve due to larger or universal forces outside our control, such as natural disasters and the inevitability of death.

One of Harjo's major concerns as a poet is the ongoing survival of Indigenous cultures. Despite colonizers' attempts to eradicate these cultures, Harjo's poem espouses hope for survival—by growing and adapting—as long as people continue to listen to and tell their ancient stories. ▪

[…] that's what humans always do: we make and tell stories about who we are […]
Joy Harjo
Discussing storytelling, 2021

ART IS HISTORY'S NOSTALGIA

OMEROS (1990), DEREK WALCOTT

IN CONTEXT

FOCUS
Modern epic

OTHER KEY POETS
Homer, Virgil, Dante, Ezra Pound, Pablo Neruda

BEFORE
1911 Saint-John Perse, a French poet, publishes *Pour fêter une enfance* (*To Celebrate a Childhood*), about his Caribbean childhood.

1939 Martinican writer Aimé Césaire publishes *Cahier d'un retour au pays natal* (*Notebook of a Return to My Native Land*), an inspiration for *Omeros*.

AFTER
2010 Barbadian poet Kamau Brathwaite publishes *Elegguas*, poems for the departed.

2013 British poet Kae Tempest publishes *Brand New Ancients*, an epic focussing on the experiences of modern life.

In his 325-page poem *Omeros*, St. Lucian poet Derek Walcott created a modern epic. Omeros is the Greek name for Homer, author of *The Iliad* and *The Odyssey*, the great epics of ancient Greece. But while Walcott's poem clearly references the Homeric works, his allusions to Greek legend are just one strand in the poem, which he wrote to try to encapsulate the diversity of the modern Caribbean, including the variety of pre-colonial, colonial, and post-colonial cultural influences that partly shaped it. There was beauty in this picture along with pain, notably the trauma of slavery. In his 1974 essay "The Muse of

See also: *The Odyssey* 24–31 ▪ *The Aeneid* 34–39 ▪ *The Divine Comedy* 58–61 ▪ "Song of Myself" 152–159 ▪ *Annie Allen* 236–239

St. Lucia's fishermen and their world are central to *Omeros*. The poem opens with a vivid description of a group of fishermen felling trees to make pirogues (canoes) like the one seen here.

History," Walcott wrote of the "Caribbean sensibility [which] is not marinated in the past [...] It is new. But it is its complexity, not its historically explained simplicities, which is new." The representation of this sensibility lies at the heart of *Omeros*.

Form and plot

Running to more than 7,000 lines, *Omeros* is divided into seven books, subdivided into chapters (64 in all), each further divided into three cantos of differing lengths. Within the cantos, most of the stanzas have three lines, modeled on the *terza rima* pioneered by medieval Italian poet Dante in *The Divine Comedy*. Unlike Dante, however, Walcott allowed himself latitude with the rhyming schemes, making different lines rhyme in different stanzas or across stanzas, and using half-rhymes and humorous rhymes. Lines have six stresses, a type of meter called hexameter.

Classic epic poetry is known for its "elevated" style, which in Walcott's case is manifested by rich lyricism and use of metaphor and myth. In Book One, for instance, the poet describes the season when hurricanes batter the Caribbean,

a time when all people can do is "listen to the gods in session, // playing any instruments that came into their craniums, / the harp-sighing ripple of a hither-and-zithering sea, / the knucklebone pebbles, the abrupt Shango drums // made Neptune rock in the caves." The bringing together of the West African Yoruba deity Shango and the Roman god of the sea, Neptune, is typical of how Walcott integrates cultural influences. An example of his wordplay is the use of "rock." Is the image of Neptune "rocking" backward and forward? Or has Neptune been turned to stone? Or does "rock" have a more slangy, contemporary meaning, as in

dancing and having a boisterous time? The next words are: "Fête start!" And the gods are, indeed, described as having a noisy get-together—"a hurricane-party in their cloud-house."

Borrowed names

A love triangle drives the narrative. Helen is a bewitchingly beautiful young island woman; two fishermen, Hector and Achille, are infatuated with her and rivals for her love. The names are clear borrowings from Homer's *Iliad* but, typically of Walcott, the associations are not entirely simple. During slavery it was not uncommon for plantation owners to rename their workers after characters from classical literature. Some of the names were passed down the generations, even to the present day. As with the names, the young people and all the characters in the poem are both archetypal (universal, drawn from myth) and intensely individual »

> I sang our wide country, the Caribbean Sea.
> Who hated shoes, whose soles were as cracked as a stone,
> who was gentle with ropes, who had one suit alone […]
> **Omeros (Book Seven, Chapter LXIV, Section I, lines 10–12)**

Derek Walcott

Born in Castries, St. Lucia (then a British colony), in 1930, Walcott was brought up by his mother, trained as a painter, and began writing poetry and plays as a teenager. He self-published his first poetry collection, *25 Poems*, at the age of 18.

After completing university studies in Jamaica, Walcott moved to Trinidad in 1959, where he worked as a teacher and literary critic. His first poetry collection to receive international acclaim was *In a Green Night*, which explored themes linked to the history, culture, and colonial legacy of the Caribbean. These themes also infused his plays. From 1959, Walcott moved between Trinidad, New York, and Boston, where he taught creative writing and literature at Boston University for more than 20 years. Walcott was awarded the Nobel Prize in Literature in 1992. When he died in 2017, he was given a state funeral in St. Lucia.

Other key works

1962 *In a Green Night*
1970 *Dream on Monkey Mountain and Other Plays*
1973 *Another Life*

and realistic. Other Black islanders are Philoctete (another Homeric borrowing), a former fisherman with a gangrenous wound on his shin; Ma Kilman, a shop owner and healer; and Seven Seas, a one-time sailor, now old and blind. Alongside them are a white couple, Dennis and Maud Plunkett, who settled on the island after World War II and once employed Helen as their maid. The poet himself is another presence— he is the narrator, reflecting upon the poem and his life.

Dream journey

Injury and healing are recurring and intertwined themes in the poem, as is journeying. One of the poem's most moving episodes comes in Book Three, where Achille, spurned by Helen for his rival Hector, makes a dream journey (ostensibly a sunstroke-induced hallucination) back to

A 1783 painting by Thomas Luny depicts the Battle of the Saintes (1782), fought by the French and British in the Caribbean. In *Omeros*, ancestors of both Achille and Dennis Plunkett take part.

the Africa of his forebears. It starts (at the end of Book Two) with a fishing trip in his canoe in which he follows "the skipping of a sea-swift / over the waves' changing hills, as if the humming // horizon-bow had made Africa the target / of its tiny arrow."

The sea-swift plying the Atlantic between Africa and the Caribbean is one of the poem's recurring images, emblematic of a possible free exchange between the New World and the Old, the present and a past freighted with pain. In his dream, Achille finds himself with fishers by an African river and encounters a father figure named Afolabe. The Africans welcome and embrace him, but there is also a vision of what is still to come for them—a "chain of men / linked by their wrists with vines." These are horrors Achille knows about and the image of the uprooted, dispossessed people being carried west across the Atlantic in slave ships carries him back to the Caribbean and the waking world. For all the anguish, however,

Visual surprise is
natural in the Caribbean;
it comes with the landscape,
and faced with its beauty,
the sigh of History dissolves.
Derek Walcott
What the Twilight Says, 1957

he knows himself to have been enriched by his dream encounters. As he and his mate steer the canoe back to shore, the beauty of a soaring frigate bird, a large black seabird of the Caribbean, captures his feelings of triumph and healing: "The black bugger beautiful, / though!" he cries.

Voice of the New World
After Walcott's death, Nigerian poet and novelist Wole Soyinka referred to the poet's "great feel for nature and history, within whose matrix he so lyrically situated and wove his island tapestry." In his own mind, Walcott saw himself in a lineage of New World poets that included Walt Whitman, his fellow Caribbean poet Aimé Césaire, Guadeloupe-born French poet Saint-John Perse, and the Chilean Pablo Neruda. For Walcott, such writers had a very particular path to tread. The "common experience of the New World" was colonialism—a fact of history that encompassed a toll of horrors, including slavery and the genocides of Indigenous peoples, along with the imposition of alien languages and their associated cultural traditions.

In "The Muse of History," Walcott warned against a "servitude" to this history, which led, he believed, to an unhealthy dualism between "a literature of revenge written by the descendants of slaves" and "a literature of remorse written by the descendants of masters." For Walcott, the authentic New World poet needed to transcend such positions. "The truly tough aesthetic of the New World neither explains nor forgives history," he wrote. "It refuses to recognize it as a creative or culpable force." The vision and calling was instead "Adamic"— for the poet to inhabit the hybrid, eclectic, wounded space that was the New World rather as the biblical Adam initially inhabited the Garden of Eden.

Adamic moment
Book Six of *Omeros* brings an explicitly Adamic moment. After Catholic mass, Ma Kilman follows a mountain trail, led by an ancestral instinct that a plant exists that can heal Philoctete's leg wound. As she climbs, she becomes more and more aware of the gods of her people. In a sense, she is making the journey that Achille made— back into the ancestral realm. She finds the healing plant, according to the poet a native of West Africa that was brought across the ocean centuries earlier as a seed in the stomach of a sea-swift. Returning to her village, Ma Kilman uses an old sugar-mill cauldron—an emblem of slavery—to set a hot bath in which she steeps the root of the plant. She obliges the initially reluctant Philoctete to get in. Maternally, she rubs his face. He surrenders and his wound heals.

Epics are traditionally about "first days"—the origins of national, cultural, or religious identities. Walcott's legacy in writing *Omeros* was to create a Caribbean epic, reflecting the mosaic of island reality. ∎

Major themes in *Omeros*

St. Lucia symbolized by Helen		The island was so hotly contested between the French and English that it was termed the "Helen of the West Indies." The Helens—woman and island—fulfill the role of heroine.
Homeric mythology		Epic themes of love and conflict are reinterpreted through the lives of ordinary people in a post-colonial society: Helen; the fishermen Achille and Hector; and Seven Seas, a blind man who represents Homer.
The legacy of slavery		Philoctete's festering leg wound symbolizes the suffering of his enslaved African ancestors. The poem discusses how the legacy of slavery impacts the lives of modern St. Lucians.
Spiritual and cultural ties to Africa		Ma Kilman uses her knowledge of traditional medicine to heal Philoctete, and Achille experiences a vision in which he visits his African ancestors.
The poet		Walcott, as narrator, confronts his own past and heritage and sets out his role as a poet—to preserve Caribbean language and to celebrate the identity and lives of ordinary St. Lucians.

THAT BODY / THEY TRIED SO HARD TO FIX
"WHAT YOU MOURN" (2007), SHEILA BLACK

American poet Sheila Black's "What You Mourn" is a poem about loving her body, and seeing the beauty in it when all others could see was her disability. Black has X-linked hypophosphatemia, a genetic disease that affects her height and causes her legs to bow.

"What You Mourn" is the first poem Black wrote about her disability. It references major milestones in her life—from the surgery she had to help straighten her legs as a teenager to her wedding day—as well as the changing monikers disabled people have been called by others, such as "crippled," "disabled," and "differently abled." Black says she is of a generation "where kids were operated on a lot" to try to "fix" their disabilities; "What You Mourn" makes it clear that she does not think she needs fixing or defining. While the world sees disability as something to be overcome, and her body as a prison, Black changes the narrative to portray her body as a beloved country—perhaps not perfect but home nonetheless.

Socially constructed

Black largely does not consider her work to be "crip poetry"—a more politicized genre associated with disability studies and activism. "What You Mourn" does, however, tackle common conceptions of disability as a tragic loss, fitting with crip poets' desire to show how perceptions of disability are socially constructed by the able-bodied. ∎

> [...] I loved it as you love your own country
> the familiar lay of the land, the unkempt trees,
> the smell of mowed grass [...]
> **"What You Mourn" (lines 27–29)**

See also: "Power" 286–287 ▪ "a survival plan of sorts" 308

HOW DOES A SHADOW SHINE?

SONATA MULATTICA (2009), RITA DOVE

Ludwig van Beethoven's *Violin Sonata No.9* was initially dedicated to George Polgreen Bridgetower, a Swabian–British violinist of African descent. More than 200 years later, his story was revived by Black American poet Rita Dove in her book-length work *Sonata Mulattica: Five Movements and a Short Play*.

The name of Dove's work comes from Beethoven's original title and his dedication to the "big wild mulatto composer" ("mulatto" being a contemporary term for someone who was mixed-race). *Sonata Mulattica* is a collection of short poems in different styles—some prose poems, some free verse—accompanied by diary entries, exploring the life of "Master B, little great man": Bridgetower's musical prowess, his meeting with Beethoven, and the tavern brawl that lost him his dedication.

Form and movements
Dove uses the fractured and nonlinear form of *Sonata Mulattica* to reflect Bridgetower's life and

I wanted to convey the sensation of how history had buried him.
Rita Dove
Interview in *Callaloo*, 2008

memory: "*those / broken sounds*," as she puts it. This narrative is in fragments because so much of Bridgetower's life is lost to history. While Dove used contemporary diary entries, she had to imagine many events herself.

Sonata Mulattica's form is influenced by Beethoven's violin sonata itself. Dove treats the five sections of the poem as musical movements, which continue to build upon a repeated theme with different variations. ∎

See also: "Middle Passage" 230–231 ▪ "a/coltrane/poem" 272–275 ▪ *for colored girls who have considered suicide/ when the rainbow is enuf* 284–285

WHO WE ARE AND CAN BE AS A SOCIETY*
"HAIR" (2014), ELIZABETH ACEVEDO
* Elizabeth Acevedo, 2018

IN CONTEXT

FOCUS
Performance poetry

OTHER KEY POETS
Walt Whitman, Allen Ginsberg, Maya Angelou, Adrienne Rich, Ntozake Shange, Amanda Lovelace

BEFORE
1986 Marc Smith organizes the first "poetry slam" in Chicago, Illinois.

1990 Three teams compete in the first National Poetry Slam in San Francisco, California.

AFTER
2017 American performance poet Sarah Kay is appointed the first spoken word artist in residence at San Francisco's Grace Cathedral.

2022 The US House of Representatives passes the CROWN Act (Creating a Respectful and Open World for Natural Hair).

Over the past century, performance poetry has become a popular platform for poets from minority backgrounds to express themselves. It has often provided a cathartic outlet for discussions on race, gender, LGBTQ+ rights, and colonialism. In 1973, Puerto Rican poet Miguel Algarín began organizing poetry readings in his living room for unheard minority communities, and he eventually opened the Nuyorican Poets Cafe in New York City as a diverse performance space.

The upsurge in performance poetry also came with the spread of slam poetry—where participants perform their poems to a live audience (often competitively)—in the late 1980s. Wishing to reconnect audiences with poetry, American poet Marc Smith's weekly poetry events encouraged aspiring poets to showcase their writing. One such poet was Elizabeth Acevedo, who uses her poetry to explore her identity as an Afro-Latina woman. Acevedo's performance of her poem "Hair" at a slam event in 2014 went

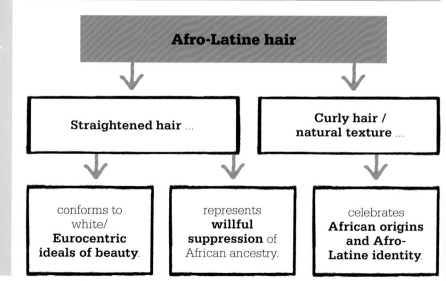

Elizabeth Acevedo

Born to Dominican parents in New York City in 1988, Elizabeth Acevedo was influenced by her parents' storytelling and her brothers' interest in music. Initially wanting to be a rapper, she first performed at age 15 at the Nuyorican Poets Cafe. She also took part in youth poetry slams, where she began to develop her unique performance style. Her interest in performance and poetry continued while she was at college.

In 2010, Acevedo graduated with a degree in performing arts from George Washington University in Washington, D.C., followed by a master's degree in creative writing in 2015. Acevedo's team won the 2014 National Poetry Slam. In addition to poetry, she has published several award-winning young adult novels-in-verse and in 2022 was named the Poetry Foundation's Young People's Poet Laureate.

Other key works

2016 *Beastgirl & Other Origin Myths*
2022 *Inheritance*

viral—leading to her becoming one of the best-known performance poets of the 21st century.

African identity

Written in free verse, "Hair" addresses some of the ways in which Western prejudices have been internalized in Afro-Latine (of Latin American and African descent) communities. The poem opens with Acevedo stating that she has been told to restyle her hair. The poet points out unflinchingly that fixing her hair means straightening it to conform to white beauty standards. She criticizes the way in which her Dominican community has willingly given up its own image and culture by adopting white styles, including straightening or flattening traditionally curly hair.

For Acevedo, her hair texture is a reminder of her African ancestry and the Dominican Republic's history of slavery. She compares subduing or tightly tying up natural curls to her enslaved African ancestors packed into the holds of slave ships, and also questions how her forbears would react to their descendants' attempts to eradicate their African identity. Acevedo accuses the Afro-Latine community of trying to forget their heritage, and uses the Dominican drink *morir soñando*—made with milk, orange juice, and sugar—to illustrate their attempts to whiten their history.

Racist attitudes

Acevedo goes on to denounce racist attitudes found within the Afro-Latine community. Based on her own experiences while in college, she recalls the Caribbean slurs used to describe those with darker skin and how people would discourage her from marrying a Black man, another member of an oppressed community.

In the face of such attitudes, Acevedo defiantly embraces her hair and history. In words unspoken to her critics, she describes the love she has for her partner and the beauty of their bodies entwined. Dreaming of her future children, she speaks of how she will raise them to love themselves and their hair. Reclaiming what was once stigmatized and discouraged, Acevedo resolutely ends "Hair" with the exhortation that its not necessary to fix something that has never been broken.

The performance element of the poem has allowed Acevedo to adapt "Hair" over time, using the poem to address generalized prejudices toward natural Afro hair in the US. In 2022, she published *Inheritance*, a revised, visual version of "Hair." ▪

Acevedo's parents were immigrants to the US from the Dominican Republic (flag on left), whose former plantation economy was based on the labor of enslaved Africans.

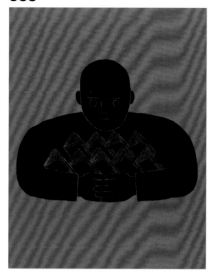

WRITE THE THING. THE WORLD NEEDS IT*
"a survival plan of sorts" (2017),
*Amanda Lovelace, 2023

IN CONTEXT

FOCUS
Instapoetry

OTHER KEY POETS
Adrienne Rich, Sheila Black, Elizabeth Acevedo

BEFORE
2013 New Zealand writer Lang Leav begins posting poetry on Tumblr; gaining a cult following, she becomes one of the first "Instapoets."

2014 "Typewriter Series," by American poet Tyler Knott Gregson—first posted on Instagram—is published as *Chasers of the Light* and becomes a bestseller.

AFTER
2018 British poet Rebecca Watts criticizes the populist approach of Instapoets in the poetry journal *PN Review*, sparking international debate.

2022 By the end of the year, more than 70 million Instagram posts are tagged as #poetry.

When American poet Amanda Lovelace self-published *the princess saves herself in this one* in 2016, they already had a strong fan base from the microblogging website Tumblr, where the book's poems were originally posted. One of the most popular poems in Lovelace's collection, "a survival plan of sorts" epitomizes "Instapoetry"—works written to be shared online. The poem presents the concept that words delivered digitally can be the ultimate modern weapon for women wanting a strong voice in a patriarchal world.

A controversial genre

"Instapoetry" is often characterized by empowering messages that deal with deeply personal or emotive themes with universal resonance. To this end, Lovelace frequently draws on the language of folk- and fairy-tales and their archetypes to explore modern issues and concerns such as womens' and LGBTQ+ rights, mental health, abuse, and trauma. Lovelace's poems, and works by others in this genre, such as Indian-born Canadian poet Rupi Kaur and Colombian–American poet R. M. Drake, share major stylistic similarities. These include the use of only lowercase letters; brevity; and simple, accessible language reflecting digital conventions.

Such features have led some critics to deride Instapoets for their supposed lack of substance. However, Lovelace has rejected the "Instapoet" label as reductive and divisive, stating that it seeks to separate her peers from "real" poets—the "dead white, straight, cisgender, males" of traditional literature. Lovelace identifies as queer and uses she/they pronouns. In this, Lovelace also represents the many Instapoets who come from—and describe the experiences of—marginalized communities. Providing a global platform for these underrepresented voices, the genre of Instapoetry plays an important role in bringing more diversity to modern poetry in both authors and their audiences. ∎

See also: "Diving Into the Wreck" 278–283 ▪ "What You Mourn" 304 ▪ "Hair" 306–307

LIFT UP OTHER PEOPLE*

"THE HILL WE CLIMB" (2021), AMANDA GORMAN

* Hillary Clinton

IN CONTEXT

FOCUS
Occasion poems

OTHER KEY POETS
Walt Whitman, Robert Frost, Maya Angelou

BEFORE
2009 "Praise Song for the Day" is American poet Elizabeth Alexander's inauguration poem for Barack Obama.

2013 At Obama's second inauguration, American poet Richard Blanco's "One Today" ends with a vision of hope and togetherness.

AFTER
2021 Gorman recites "Chorus of the Captains," written in honor of Covid-19 victims, before Super Bowl LV in Tampa, Florida.

2022 British poet Simon Armitage's elegy "Floral Tribute" for Queen Elizabeth II is a double acrostic—the first letters of 18 lines spell out "Elizabeth" twice.

J ohn Keats's "Ode to a Nightingale" was prompted by an occasion but is not occasional verse. To belong to this poetic category, a poem must mark a public occasion, often through performance, and/or have been specially commissioned for an occasion. Six US presidential inauguration ceremonies have featured a poet reading their work: John F. Kennedy's (1961), Bill Clinton's (1993 and 1997), Barack Obama's (2009 and 2013), and Joe Biden's (2021).

Amanda Gorman was 22 when she recited her poem "The Hill We Climb" for Biden. Among her inspirations were speeches by Kennedy; Civil Rights leader Martin Luther King, Jr.; President Abraham Lincoln; and UK Prime Minister Winston Churchill.

Engaging its audience with the use of an all-inclusive plural, "The Hill We Climb" mixes plain speech with wordplay, including double meanings and alliteration. The poem's blend of exhortation and affirmation is flecked with

[…] a message of hope, and unity, and healing […] that was the type of poem that the country and the world needed to hear.
Amanda Gorman
Interviewed on CNN, 2021

darker notes, especially a reference to the storming of the Capitol by supporters of former president Donald Trump in January 2021. In its final couplet, "The Hill We Climb" echoes an apocryphal motivational statement by Indian independence leader Mahatma Gandhi – the assertion that you have to be the change you want to see in the world. ∎

See also: "Song of Myself" 152–159 ▪ "The Road Not Taken" 182–187 ▪ "Still I Rise" 288–289

FURTHER READING

FURTHER READING

"THE HYMN TO INANNA"
(c. 2260 BCE), Enheduanna

Believed to have been written by
Enheduanna, a priestess of the
city-state of Ur during the reign of
her father, Sargon of Akkad, "The
Hymn to Inanna" addresses the
Sumerian goddess of love and
fertility. The poet praises the
goddess first, and then asks for her
help, specifically in taking revenge
on those who have ousted her and
driven her into exile. The poem
describes Inanna's wrath and
intervention, and finally thanks her
for answering the poet's prayers.
Although there is debate as to
whether the poem was written later
and attributed to her retrospectively,
Enheduanna is one of the earliest
known writers in history.

THEOGONY
(c. 700 BCE), Hesiod

Grounded in oral tradition and
credited to a contemporary of
Homer (see pp.24–31), the
Theogony is an instructional epic
that provides a prehistory of the
gods. The poem describes how
Chaos appeared out of nothing, and
gave birth to Gaia (Earth), Eros
(Desire), Tartarus (the Underworld),
Erebus (Darkness), and Nyx (Night).
The poem then moves on to recount
the "succession myth," whereby
Uranus, Gaia's son, is dismembered
by Cronos, his own son, who in
turn is overthrown by Zeus, who
becomes the king of the gods and
the permanent ruler of the cosmos.

Filled with heroes and monsters,
the Theogony also praises the
Muses (the goddesses of inspiration
and literature), who Hesiod claims
authorized him to tell this tale of
the gods.

OLYMPIAN 13
(464 BCE), Pindar

Celebrated as the greatest lyric
poet of ancient Greece, Pindar
wrote odes for the four Panhellenic
festivals, of which 45 survive. The
13th Olympian ode celebrates
the victories of Xenophon of Corinth,
who won both the foot race and the
pentathlon at the 79th Olympiad.
Pindar praises Xenophon and then
recounts the legend of Bellerophon,
a former prince of Corinth, who
(with divine assistance) pacified
the winged horse Pegasus. The poet
reminds his listeners that human
talents are divine gifts, and that
they should not be taken for granted.
To emphasize his point, Pindar
briefly alludes to Bellerophon's
fate: his audience would have been
aware that Bellerophon died when,
full of bravado, he attempted to fly
to the gods on Mount Olympus.

ARGONAUTICA
(c. 240 BCE), Apollonius of Rhodes

The Argonautica recounts the tale
of Jason and his fellow Argonauts,
who set sail to recover the Golden
Fleece (the wool of the winged ram
Chrysomallos) from a sacred grove
in Colchis on the coast of the Black
Sea. Arriving at Colchis, Jason

meets and falls in love with Medea,
a Colchian princess and sorceress,
who promises to help him if he
will marry her. After completing
a series of tasks set by the King of
Colchis, Jason succeeds in wresting
the fleece from its guardian dragon,
which Medea puts to sleep with
a spell. Following the style of a
Homeric epic (see pp.24–31), the
Argonautica became a model for
Virgil's Aeneid (see pp.34–39).

"I HATE AND I LOVE"
(c. 65 BCE), Catullus

The two-line poem or epigram,
"I Hate and I Love" (Catullus 85)
is one of the many poems written
by Gaius Valerius Catullus for his
lover, Lesbia. A declaration of his
conflicting feelings, it showcases the
poet's dramatic and highly personal
style. Writing in Latin at the time of
the late Roman Republic, Catullus
greatly influenced other writers,
including Virgil (see pp.34–39)
and Ovid (see pp.40–43).

THE CLEOPATRA ODE (1.37)
(c. 30 BCE), Horace

The foremost lyric poet during the
reign of the first Roman emperor,
Octavian (Caesar Augustus),
Quintus Horatius Flaccus (Horace)
wrote The Cleopatra Ode after
Octavian's victory at the Battle of
Actium (31 BCE). The poem recounts
how Octavian's fleet defeated the
combined forces of Cleopatra
(the queen of Egypt) and Roman
general Mark Antony. Although

Horace mentions neither of them by name, it is clear to whom he is referring when he rebukes the queen for being foolish enough to consider opposing Rome. However, in the final stanzas, Horace concedes that Cleopatra was brave—not least for her resolve to die by suicide.

"HOW SAD"
(c. 880 CE), Ono no Komachi

One of the greatest Japanese poets of her generation, Ono no Komachi specialized in a short verse form known as the "tanka" (sometimes referred to as the "waka"), which has a fixed number of syllables (5, 7, 5, 7, 7) over five lines. A forerunner of the haiku, which drops the final two lines (see p.111), the tanka typically expresses a single thought about an idea or event. Komachi's poem, which loses its structure in translation, expresses the poet's sadness at the transience of life.

"VÖLUSPÁ"
(c. 960)

"Völuspá", or "The Prophesy of the Völva" (seer), is the most famous poem of the Poetic Edda— a collection of Old Norse narrative poems of unknown authorship. It tells the story of the birth of the world, and its forthcoming death and rebirth, narrated by a seer to Odin, the god of war and wisdom. The seer prophesizes the end of the world—Ragnarök ("the doom of the gods")—a time when the sun will darken and lands will sink into the sea, after which the Earth will be reborn. Composed in Iceland toward the end of the first millennium, the poem appears to show the influence of Christian beliefs, and may even signify the waning of paganism as Christianity becomes the accepted religion.

THE SONG OF ROLAND
(c. 1100), Turold (attrib.)

Attributed to Turold, The Song of Roland (La Chanson de Roland) is one of the oldest surviving major works of French poetry. Composed around the time of the First Crusade (1096–1099), it recasts the Battle of Roncevaux Pass (778) and the death of Frankish leader Roland, killed fighting in Charlemagne's army, as a battle between Christians and Muslims. It is an example of a chanson de geste ("song of heroic deeds"), a French epic form that celebrated heroic historical figures.

LANVAL
(c. 1160), Marie de France

One of Marie de France's Breton lais (rhymed poems about love and chivalry), Lanval tells the tale of the eponymous knight of King Arthur's court. Lanval falls in love with a fairy who tells him that she will always appear for him, so long as he keeps her existence a secret. However, when the Queen accuses Lanval of disliking women because he spurns her advances, he feels compelled to defend his honor. Put on trial by King Arthur at the behest of his jealous wife, Lanval breaks his promise and reveals the identity of the fairy; the fairy appears (also breaking her promise) to verify his tale. At the end of the poem, the fairy carries Lanval away on her horse—saving him from the iniquities of the court.

PIERS PLOWMAN
(c. 1370s), William Langland

Written in Middle English and attributed to William Langland, of whom little is known, Piers Plowman describes a series of allegorical dream visions. It is narrated by a character named Will, who falls asleep in the English Midlands and encounters a host of allegorical characters. These include a plowman named Piers, who instructs Will on how to become a true Christian. The poem satirizes both secular society and the Church, which, it argues, are equally prone to being corrupted by greed. It is an

Verse drama

For much of history in Europe, stage plays were largely written in verse. The Greek tragedies of Aeschylus, Sophocles, and Euripides featured meter, as did long narrative poems, such as Homer's epics and those composed in Old English, which were probably performed. Shakespeare's plays, which became models for modern verse drama, are essentially poems that break into prose (see pp.88–93).

After Shakespeare, more "prosaic" forms of drama came into vogue, but verse drama remained popular, being the chosen form for plays such as Dryden's All for Love (1677), Goethe's Faust (1808 and 1832), and Henrik Ibsen's Peer Gynt (1876). Despite falling out of fashion in the 20th century, there is a growing interest in verse drama today.

example of alliterative verse, with Langland using repeated syllables instead of rhyme to create rhythm in the poem.

THE LOVER'S CONFESSION
(1390), John Gower

Written in Middle English, *The Lover's Confession* (*Confessio Amantis*) was composed for King Richard II (r. 1377–1399) and became one of the most circulated works of the 14th century. Divided into a prologue and eight books, the epic poem contains multiple narratives framed by the story of an aging man stricken with love. Wandering through a forest in May, he invokes Venus and Cupid who appear, and on hearing that he is dying from love, summon a chaplain, Genius, to hear his confession. The chaplain absolves the lover of his sins against love, and Venus cures his infatuation. Gower's poem would influence many later writers, including Shakespeare, who used the story of Apollonius from *The Lover's Confession* in his play *Pericles*.

"HIS LADY'S DEATH"
(c. 1560), Pierre de Ronsard

French poet Pierre de Ronsard addressed several poems, including "His Lady's Death," to a lady named Marie. In the previous poems he speaks to her directly, although it is never clear if his love is returned. In this final piece, he expresses his grief at the lady's death and confesses that, now she has gone, he is a lover of Death itself. His only consolation can be that her soul has gone to Heaven, where, in death, he may meet her one day.

"ON MY FIRST SON"
(1616), Ben Jonson

A short poem composed of six rhyming couplets, "On My First Son" is English playwright and poet Ben Jonson's lament for his son Benjamin, who died at the age of seven. Unlike a traditional elegy, which moves from intense sorrow to consolation, Jonson is unable to find solace, and ends the poem as heartbroken as he was at the start

of the piece. He even equates being a father with being a poet, and describes his son as his best piece of poetry—as if, with his son's death, his life as a poet is over.

"ABSALOM AND ACHITOPHEL"
(1681), John Dryden

Acclaimed as one of the greatest political satires in the English language, "Absalom and Achitophel" tells the Biblical tale of the rebellion against King David of Israel by his son Absalom and the royal advisor Achitophel. Written in heroic couplets, the poem recounts David's defense of his throne— echoing a very real crisis that was unfolding in England at the time. King Charles II (r. 1660–1685), who possibly asked Dryden to write the poem, had no legitimate heirs and was forced to defend himself against a rebellion mounted by supporters of his illegitimate son, the Duke of Monmouth.

"ON HER LOVING TWO EQUALLY"
(1682), Aphra Behn

Originally published under the title "How Strangely Does My Passion Grow," English playwright Aphra Behn's "On Her Loving Two Equally" is a short, three-stanza poem that expresses a woman's love for two men, and her anguish at having to choose between them. She wants Cupid to remove one of his arrows from her heart, but she cannot decide which: when she is with Alexis, she pines for Damon, and vice versa. The poem does not reach a resolution: it simply concludes that the woman needs both men.

Nonsense verse

For as long as there has been serious poetry, there have been traditions of nonsense verse in which writers have delighted in using made-up words and illogical phrases. Riddles are one of the oldest forms of poetry, as are nursery rhymes, although many of these may only appear bizarre because we have lost their original contexts. A still-recited British nursery rhyme, which asks: what has "Four dilly-dandies, Four stick standies, Two crookers, Two

lookers, And a wig-wag?" (the answer being a cow), may well date from Anglo-Saxon times.

In the modern period, when the phrase "nonsense verse" was first used, this type of poetry became an accepted genre. Its earliest exponents were Edward Lear (see opposite) and Lewis Carroll (see p.316), whose poems "The Owl and the Pussycat" and "Jabberwocky" respectively are classics of the form. More recent nonsense poets have included Dr. Seuss, Mervyn Peake, Spike Milligan, and Edward Gorey.

"TO THE NIGHTINGALE"
(1713), Anne Finch

English poet and courtier Anne Finch, Countess of Winchilsea, uses the image of the nightingale to express her wish to write poetry with total freedom—in particular without criticism from other, predominantly male, poets. Like many writers of the early 18th century, Finch was inspired by the Classical poets Horace, Ovid, and Virgil, who flourished during the reign of Caesar Augustus, the first Roman emperor. Along with her fellow "Augustans," Finch demonstrated that the individual, rather than nature or society, was a respectable subject for poetry.

"MIGNON'S SONG"
(1795), Johann Wolfgang von Goethe

Novelist, playwright, scientist, and poet Johann Wolfgang von Goethe is regarded as one of the greatest writers in the German language. His poetry inspired many composers, including Mozart and Beethoven. Music also features in much of his own work, with perhaps his most influential poem taking the form of a song. The piece "*Kennst du das Land*" ("Do You Know the Land"), often called "Mignon's Song," is performed by the 13-year-old female protagonist of his novel *Wilhelm Meister's Apprenticeship*. In the poem, Mignon, having been kidnapped in Italy by a troupe of acrobats and brought to Germany, fondly recalls the delights of her old home. Having been rescued from captivity by a young merchant, Wilhelm, she expresses her hope that she can travel there with him.

"A YOUTH ONCE LOVED A MAIDEN"
(1822), Heinrich Heine

A master of satire, German poet Heinrich Heine describes in a single stanza the blind nature of romantic love. The poem tells the story of how a boy loved a girl, who loved someone else, who in turn loved (and married) another. Furious and heartbroken, the girl marries the next man she meets, ultimately breaking the heart of the boy who loved her. One of the most popular poets in 19th-century Europe, Heine also produced many classics of the German *leid* tradition, in which poetry is set to music.

"CASABIANCA"
(1826), Felicia Hemans

Written in traditional ballad meter (alternating four-stress and three-stress lines, with an abab rhyme scheme), "Casabianca" tells the true story of a boy's death aboard the French ship *L'Orient* during the Battle of the Nile, fought between the French and British fleets in 1789. The boy, Casabianca, had been told to stay at his post by his father, the commander of the ship, who had been killed after giving the order. Rather than disobey, the boy remains at his post, even while the ammunition store catches fire and the ship is destroyed.

"I AM"
(1844), John Clare

Written during English poet John Clare's second stay at the Northampton General Lunatic Asylum, the three-stanza "I Am" depicts his struggle to find meaning in life and to be understood. It also conveys his great despair at having been abandoned by his family. In the last stanza, Clare finds solace in the knowledge that he will die, and expresses his longing to be in Heaven. The poem was transcribed for Clare by the asylum's house steward, W. F. Knight.

"REMEMBRANCE"
(1845), Emily Brontë

Penned by Emily Brontë, one of the British novel-writing sisters, "Remembrance" is an elegy addressed to someone who has died 15 years earlier. The poem was originally written in the voice of Rosina Alcona, a queen from the imaginary land of Gondal, which the Brontës invented and wrote about as children. However, the poet later removed all references to Gondal, leaving the published poem as a more universal lament for the death of a significant love and a meditation on intense grief.

"HOW PLEASANT TO KNOW MR. LEAR!"
(1846), Edward Lear

With the publication of his *Book of Nonsense*, English poet Edward Lear popularized "nonsense poetry" (see opposite), which revels in word-play and illogicality. Perhaps the most famous poem in the collection is "How Pleasant to know Mr. Lear," in which the poet describes himself as being physically grotesque, ill-tempered, prone to weeping, and a heavy drinker (although he never gets drunk). And yet, despite all of this, he seems to be pleasant to know.

"JABBERWOCKY"
(1871), Lewis Carroll

Appearing in complete form in his novel *Through the Looking-Glass and What Alice Found There*, "Jabberwocky" began as a single stanza (the final poem's first and last lines) that Carroll published in 1855. Titled "Stanza of Anglo-Saxon Poetry," the original work was a pastiche of Old English poetry, but Carroll extended it to form a seven-stanza poem about vanquishing a fictional monster, the Jabberwock. Featuring many made-up words, the poem is regarded as a classic of nonsense verse (see p.314).

A SHROPSHIRE LAD, XII
(1896), A. E. Housman

A collection of 63 poems set in a semi-fictionalized English pastoral location, A. E. Housman's *A Shropshire Lad* explores themes including war, the transience of youth and love, and mortality. The speaker in poem XII reflects these concerns, comparing the vibrancy and ephemeral nature of life with the silence and infinite nature of death. It is a reminder that death may be just around the corner, and this must be accepted as it cannot be escaped.

"THE DARKLING THRUSH"
(1900), Thomas Hardy

In four, short, ballad-meter stanzas, English novelist and poet Thomas Hardy paints a bleak vignette of a man standing at the edge of a forest at sunset in the depths of winter. Contemplating the frosty scene, he is surprised by a sound above him—an aged thrush in full song.

Puzzled by the bird's enthusiasm, the man concludes that it must be animated by some kind of hope of which he is unaware. Originally titled "By the Century's Deathbed," the poem is Hardy's reflection on the state of the world at the end of the 19th century, and the possibilities of an unknown future.

"ALGERNON"
(1907), Hilaire Belloc

One of Franco-British author Hilaire Belloc's *Cautionary Tales for Children: Designed for the Admonition of Children Between the Ages of Eight and Fourteen Years*, "Algernon" is a short, comic poem composed of rhyming couplets. Its full title—"Algernon, Who Played with a Loaded Gun, and, on Missing his Sister, was Reprimanded by his Father"—describes the poem in full, adding further absurdity to a tale that cautions children to stay away from firearms. Other poems in the collection include: "Matilda, Who Told Lies, and was Burned to Death" and "Jim, Who Ran Away from his Nurse, and was Eaten by a Lion."

"EL BESO"
(1909), Angelina Weld Grimké

El Beso ("The Kiss") describes a brief romantic encounter between the poet and her lover. Although it begins and ends in peace—the serenity of two people simply being together—it expresses the passion and ecstasy of love, as well as a profound sense of loss, as the poet surrenders to the moment. While this poem focuses on love, many of Grimké's other pieces tackle issues relating to race and civil rights. She became the first Black American

woman to have a play staged in public, and her work heralded the Harlem Renaissance.

"ITHAKA"
(1911), C. P. Cavafy

In "Ithaka," Greek poet C. P. Cavafy revisits the story of Odysseus's return home after the Trojan War. However, unlike in Homer's version of the tale (see pp.24–31), the narrator advises the hero not to think too much about his destination, which will always be there, but to focus on his travels instead. Simultaneously providing metaphorical advice on how to tackle the journey of life, he hopes that the voyage will be long and that Odysseus will learn from the people he meets, reaching home as an old man who has lived life to the fullest. Crucially, the narrator also advises that by tackling the journey (of life) with fortitude and optimism, Odysseus will avoid difficulties such as real (and metaphorical) monsters.

"SUSIE ASADO"
(1913), Gertrude Stein

Notoriously difficult to interpret, American writer Gertrude Stein's poem "Susie Asado" has been both dismissed and celebrated as nonsense poetry (see p.314), since it offers no clearly discernible plot or theme. However, it is also cherished as a work that leaves readers free to interpret it as they wish, and many see it as an upbeat feminist anthem. The power of the piece lies in the sound of its words rather than its literal meaning. Like many of Stein's works, its exuberant strangeness put it in the vanguard of Modernist poetry.

"THE SOLDIER"
(1914), Rupert Brooke

Written in the first year of World War I, Rupert Brooke's sonnet conveys a soldier's love for England, his homeland, at a time when he fears he will soon be killed. Shaped by England, he feels he owes his country his life, and in death, the essence of England will remain on the battlefield through his body and sacrifice. The patriotic message ends with the soldier hoping his memory will live on in an England finally at peace. Brooke died from septicemia a year after writing this poem, while stationed in Egypt. His body was buried in Greece.

"ALL IN GREEN WENT MY LOVE RIDING"
(1916), e e cummings

Composed in alternating three- and two-line stanzas, American poet e e cummings' "All in Green Went My Love Riding" describes a dream-vision in which a man pursues a woman he loves as she rides ahead of him, hunting a deer. However, when he finally gets a glimpse of her, he is struck dead, as though he is the prey she was hunting all along. According to one reading, he has been shot by Cupid's arrow, and so does not literally die. Another interpretation is that the woman has shot him dead to end his pursuit.

"ATTACK"
(1918), Siegfried Sassoon

"Attack" was written toward the end of World War I, at a time when the horrors of trench warfare, and the futility of much of the fighting, had become apparent to the public. Unlike Rupert Brooke (see left), Siegfried Sassoon expresses no love for England, but only the sheer terror of climbing out of a trench under a hail of artillery fire. A rare voice of protest against the continuation of the war, Sassoon survived the conflict and was decorated for his bravery.

"I SIT AND SEW"
(1918), Alice Dunbar-Nelson

"I Sit and Sew" describes a woman's anguish at having to sit and sew in the safety of her home while men are slaughtered on the battlefields of World War I. American poet Alice Dunbar-Nelson uses the title as a refrain throughout the poem, emphasizing the contrast between what the woman is doing and what she wants to do—to be on a battlefield, if only to help the wounded. She ends the poem with a desperate question, which goes unanswered: is sewing all that she is expected to do with her life?

"AMERICA"
(1921), Claude McKay

One of the most famous poets of the Harlem Renaissance, Claude McKay first published "America" in the socialist magazine *The Liberator*. In the poem, the speaker expresses genuine love for the US, while also acknowledging the extreme difficulties of living as a Black man in a white-dominated society. Full of racial pride, and without fear or malice, he looks to the future with optimism, reminding the reader that everything comes to an end—and that even the US, with all its pretensions to greatness, may fall.

Limericks

A five-line poem composed largely of anapests (see p.322) and with a rhyme scheme of aabba (see p.65), the limerick is one of the most popular forms of poetry. Limericks are usually humorous and can border on the absurd. One example, "A Young Lady of Lynn," by an anonymous poet, declares: "There was a young lady of Lynn / Who was so uncommonly thin / That when she essayed / To drink lemonade / She slipped through the straw and fell in."

Limericks were popularized in the 19th century by the English poet Edward Lear (see p.315). However, some scholars argue that the earliest known example was a composition by the medieval theologian St. Thomas Aquinas (1225–1274). Written in Latin, it is an entirely serious post-mass prayer of thanksgiving.

"MOTHERHOOD"
(1922), Georgia Douglas Johnson

First published in *The Crisis*, the official magazine of the National Association for the Advancement of Colored People, "Motherhood" expresses a Black woman's inner conflict about wanting a child, but not wanting to bring one into a cruel world where it will experience the evil of men. The child is poignantly depicted knocking on the mother's door; the mother explains why she must resist opening it. The poem contrasts with the view of the magazine's editor, American–Ghanaian sociologist W.E.B. du Bois, who argues in the preface to the same edition that children are the only hope for humanity. One of the first female Black American playwrights, Johnson was a leading figure of the Harlem Renaissance.

"WHAT LIPS MY LIPS HAVE KISSED, AND WHERE, AND WHY"
(1923), Edna St. Vincent Millay

In "What Lips My Lips Have Kissed, and Where, and Why," by American poet Edna St. Vincent Millay, the speaker meditates on the fact that although she has had many lovers, she can scarcely remember who they were. Regretting this loss of memories, she questions the purpose of love if it comes to nothing. In the final stanza, she compares herself to a tree in winter—silent and empty after a summer full of vitality and birdsong. Ironically, the poem is a sonnet (see p.91), which traditionally celebrates, rather than questions, romantic love. A prominent feminist during the 1920s and '30s, Millay also wrote under the pseudonym Nancy Boyd.

"THE WORLD AND I"
(1938), Laura Riding

In "The World and I," American poet Laura Riding meditates on the limits of language: how on the one hand, it is her only means of expression, but on the other, it fails to capture so much of what she wants to say. If a word cannot accurately portray the sun, she asks, how can she properly communicate her experience of it? She concludes, however, that language and experience are not total strangers and are best honored by acknowledging where the one fails to fully describe the other.

"DRINKING"
(1943), Gabriela Mistral

Lucila Godoy Alcayaga was a Chilean poet, educator, and diplomat who used the pseudonym Gabriela Mistral. In her poem "Drinking," she describes drinking water from a freezing stream in Argentina, and then from a calm pool in Mexico, before drinking milk from a coconut offered to her by a girl in Puerto Rico. Finally, she recalls drinking water given to her by her mother in her childhood home. In profound gratitude, she celebrates both the people and the lands that have sustained her. In 1945, Mistral became the first Spanish-American author to receive the Nobel Prize in Literature.

"LOS ENIGMAS"
(1950), Pablo Neruda

One of the 252 poems that comprise Pablo Neruda's *Canto General*—an epic history of the Americas from the Spanish-American perspective—"*Los Enigmas*" ("The Enigmas") is one of the poet's many reflections on nature. In the piece, he describes the ocean as a living entity and marvels at the creatures it contains. He also mourns the harm that humans inflict on nature, urging us to study the ocean and to celebrate whatever we learn—it alone can teach us about its mysteries, so we destroy it at our peril. A Chilean poet and diplomat, Neruda won the Nobel Prize in Literature in 1971.

"LIFE AT WAR"
(1966), Denise Levertov

In her poem "Life at War," Denise Levertov, who was born in the UK but became an American citizen, addresses the horrors of the Vietnam War (1955–1975). One of the most powerful anti-war poems ever written, it depicts in graphic detail the death and mutilation caused by armed conflicts, contrasting these with the extraordinary acts of kindness and creativity that human beings perform. Indeed, Levertov

Poetry in translation

Translating poems from one language into another is an art in itself. The translator must find a way of replicating the beauty, meaning, and rhythm of the poem—and this is not always possible. For example, a translation of a Japanese haiku (see p.111) may preserve the poem's meaning, but break its syllabic rules.

Despite these constraints, some remarkable translations have been produced. In English, many of the most celebrated have been translations of European classics, such as George Chapman's 17th-century translation of Homer's epics (see pp.24–31) and Dorothy L. Sayers' 20th-century translation of the works of Dante (see pp.58–61). More recent successes have been Ted Hughes' *Tales from Ovid* (1997), translated from the original Latin; Seamus Heaney's version of the Old English epic *Beowulf* (1999); and Simon Armitage's rendering of the alliterative Middle English masterpiece *Sir Gawain and the Green Knight* (2009).

suggests that the brutality of the Vietnam War permanently raises a question over the validity of our peacetime joys and achievements.

"ALDERSHOT CREMATORIUM"
(1971), John Betjeman

In two six-line stanzas, British poet John Betjeman describes the mundane sight of a crematorium, situated between a swimming pool and a cricket pitch, silently puffing smoke—all that remains of a life. Family and friends of the deceased depart, and, having no words to console each other, comment on the weather instead. The poem ends with Betjeman fearing that the mundane, material realities of the cremation suggest that death does not give entry to a higher spiritual plane. Although a committed Christian, Betjeman was terrified of dying and often used his poems as a means of wrestling with the paradoxes of faith.

"MUNICH, WINTER 1973 (FOR Y. S.)"
(1973), James Baldwin

Gay Black American poet James Baldwin often wrote love poetry using imagery that enabled him to express his feelings without revealing the gender or identity of his lover. In "Munich, Winter 1973 (For Y. S.)," the speaker describes lying in bed, waiting for someone to arrive to find him. Describing both the bed and himself as strange, the speaker implies that he and his lover are people living on the margins of society, and that they are probably meeting in secret. As well as anticipation,

the poem expresses the terror that all lovers can feel—that of letting go and embarking on a journey with an unknown destination, whatever the risks.

"WHEN I WAS GROWING UP"
(1973), Nellie Wong

"When I Was Growing Up" is a frank admission by an American poet that she had been ashamed of her Chinese heritage when she was a child, and had wanted to be white. Wong is openly impatient, telling her readers to stop asking how this could be, since all the great figures of American culture, both real and fictional, were exclusively white when she was young. With no positive validation of her identity, Wong confesses that she was happy to be considered exotic, and was grateful to go on a date with a white man. An active member of the feminist movement, Wong uses her poem to show that the fight for equality cannot just focus on women's rights but must recognize the struggles of different ethnicities.

"POEM ABOUT MY RIGHTS"
(1978), June Jordan

Using a stream-of-consciousness form, which frequently abandons punctuation, American poet June Jordan's poem is a furious diatribe against a legal system that refuses to accept the testimony of rape victims and assumes that a woman who claims to have been raped must have consented. The speaker reminds us that rape is an ancient crime, and that there have always been cultures that ignore or even condone it. The poem ends with

a threat—that the speaker is willing to kill to defend her body and her rights in such a system. Jordan wrote the poem after being attacked in her home in the US.

"THE WELDER"
(1983), Cherríe Moraga

Chicana poet Cherríe Moraga announces herself as a welder (who fuses things) rather than an alchemist (a magician) in this poem about forging new social identities. In order for "fusion" to occur, she suggests, we must acknowledge our biases and accept our personal differences. As a feminist and a lesbian woman of color, Moraga seems to be arguing that more cooperation is needed between marginalized groups in the fight for social justice. In the guise of the welder, she puts herself forward as someone who will proactively try to make this happen.

"the lost baby poem"
(1987), Lucille Clifton

In "the lost baby poem," American poet and two-time Pulitzer Prize finalist Lucille Clifton tackles the subject of abortion, addressing the nameless child of a terminated pregnancy. Using unconventional punctuation, she speaks sorrowfully of her impoverished state when she became pregnant, and how the child's life would not have been worth living. With painful frankness, she describes the unformed body of the baby passing through the sewers to reach the sea, and how unprepared she was for the sea of memory to turn its tide to haunt her. She ends by asking the sea to claim her, too, if she fails to look after the children she has had since then. In 2010, Clifton received a lifetime achievement medal from the Poetry Society of America.

"FACING IT"
(1988), Yusef Komunyakaa

"Facing It" describes an ex-soldier entering the walk-through Vietnam War Veterans Memorial ("The Wall") in Washington, D.C.—a gigantic structure of black granite inscribed with the names of more than 58,000 dead American soldiers. As he looks at the names, he sees his own reflection in the stone, as if trapped inside, perhaps one of the dead. Touching a name he recognizes, he remembers a booby trap detonating. As more memories return, the soldier describes himself as a window—an aperture between the still living and the dead. His unique perspective, and the contrast between those who stayed at home and those who have faced death in war, is captured in the poem's final image: a woman appears to be erasing names on the stone, but it is just a reflection—or perhaps a memory—of a woman brushing a boy's hair.

"THE ELEPHANT AND THE TRAGOPAN"
(1991), Vikram Seth

One of 10 fables in Indian writer Vikram Seth's collection *Beastly Tales From Here and There*, "The Elephant and the Tragopan" is a poem set in the imaginary world of Bingle, where animals have learned that humans are about to invade. The elephant, who understands humans best, educates the others about the nature of their enemy: humans exploit the environment,

show no kindness or gratitude toward animals, and are living contradictions—capable of being kind or merciless, sane or insane, whenever the mood takes them. The elephant's critique takes up most of the poem, and in the end, he convinces the animals that they should band together to face the approaching threat.

"THE WILD IRIS"
(1992), Louise Glück

In "The Wild Iris," American poet Louise Glück attempts to describe the processes of death and rebirth by recounting the experiences of a personified flower. The iris describes its terror at being buried alive, then how it survives, and reemerges transformed, having found a new voice. The poem does not specify whether the flower's account represents a metaphorical, spiritual, emotional, or physical rebirth, but Glück shows that the cycles of nature have much to teach us about life, acceptance, and growth.

"A NEW CHILD: ECL"
(1993), George Mackay Brown

Often cited as one of the most beautiful poems of the 20th century, "A New Child: ECL" was written by Scottish poet George Mackay Brown to celebrate the birth of a friend's daughter. It is a benediction given by an unknown speaker, telling the infant that one day she will embark on a journey (the rest of her life), but that she must be patient—building her vessel will take several summers. In the meantime, she must wait on the shore, enjoy being a child, and learn about the world around her.

A lifelong resident of the Orkney Islands, Brown found inspiration for his poem in the Icelandic *Orkneyinga Saga*.

"LIVING SPACE"
(1997), Imtiaz Dharker

An evocation of the slums of Mumbai, India, "Living Space" is a poem in which Pakistan-born British poet Imtiaz Dharker describes a ramshackle structure that has crooked edges and leans to one side but is somehow a family's home. In this lopsided mini-world, someone has hung a basket of eggs from one of the beams. The eggs, symbols of faith and life, simultaneously represent fragility and strength. This is the crux of the poem—on one hand a description of poverty, but on the other hand a celebration of endurance and ingenuity.

THE GRUFFALO
(1999), Julia Donaldson

Composed of rhyming couplets, *The Gruffalo* is a children's picture book written by Julia Donaldson. Inspired by a Chinese folk tale, it is the story of a mouse who walks through a forest and encounters three predators—a fox, an owl, and a snake. He persuades them not to eat him by claiming that he is friends with a Gruffalo—a huge, terrifying beast, which he believes he has just invented to scare them. However, he later encounters a real Gruffalo, who threatens to eat him. The mouse bargains for his life, saying he can prove that he is more terrifying than the Gruffalo. He takes the Gruffalo to meet the fox, the owl, and the snake, who all flee at their approach—apparently due to the mouse's fearsome reputation, or so the Gruffalo thinks.

"THE PASSING"
(2000), Don Paterson

In "The Passing," Scottish poet Don Paterson exhorts the reader to make the most of life, with the full awareness that death is only around the corner. Invoking the ancient Greek myth of the nymph Eurydice, whose life—and death—occasioned an outpouring of song, he determines that the passage from life to death should also be embraced with spirit. In the poem's final lines, Paterson counsels that part of this positive approach is accepting that we are insignificant in the wider scheme of things—when we die, nature will wipe us from the record.

"THINGS FALL APART"
(2005), Jackie Kay

Taking its title from the 1958 novel by Nigerian writer Chinua Achebe, "Things Fall Apart" expresses the disappointment of a woman on meeting her birth father, who had abandoned her as a child. Having tracked him down in Nigeria, she meets a man who has rejected his own African heritage in favor of Christianity and European culture. He is not the father she had imagined. In the end, alone in her hotel, she consoles herself that they must have something in common—if only the shape of their hands. Born in Scotland to a Scottish mother and Nigerian father, Jackie Kay was later adopted, and grew up in Glasgow. She has written extensively about post-colonialism and the nature of human identity.

"HOW TO TRIUMPH LIKE A GIRL"
(2015), Ada Limón

A feminist poem with a light touch, "How to Triumph Like a Girl" encourages women to look to female horses as exemplars of empowerment. The speaker praises the horses' speed, swagger, and success in races. She realizes that while outwardly horses and women do not resemble each other, inside they can embody the same traits—strength, determination, and the capacity for success. The author of numerous poetry collections, Limón became the US Poet Laureate in 2022.

"THE UNACCOMPANIED"
(2017), Simon Armitage

The threads that link our past, present, and future are the subject of British poet Simon Armitage's poem "The Unaccompanied." He describes a man walking home after dark, who hears a song from the opposite bank of a river. In the song, he recognizes the voices of his father, grandfather, and other forebears, as well as subjects ranging from the mythological to the modern. These are the threads that appear to support the man when, instead of stepping onto the bridge that spans the gorge to reach the far side, he sets out over the edge of the cliff. The suggestion is that our past builds a bridge to our future, and that even when we are alone we are never "unaccompanied."

Children's poetry

For most children, lullabies and nursery rhymes represent their first exposure to poetic language. These forms were traditionally seen as tools to soothe infants or to encourage them to speak. It is only in the modern period that poets began to write specifically for children.

The first examples of this type of poetry were religious and moral in nature, such as John Bunyan's *A Book for Boys and Girls* (1686). However, by the 19th century, poetry solely for entertainment, such as nonsense verse (see p.314), was increasingly popular. More recently, a number of poets, such as Americans Jack Prelutsky and Shel Silverstein, have written entirely for children, and picture books that use verse, such as those by Julia Donaldson (see opposite), are bringing poetry to new young audiences.

"WHAT IF"
(2020), Claudia Rankine

In "what if," the first poem in *Just Us: An American Conversation*—a collection of essays and poetry about racism—the speaker asks a series of questions about change, and whether it is possible. The sadness of the poem lies in the questions themselves—it implies that no matter what political steps are taken to eradicate racism, people of color will always suffer the subtle biases of white people. The poem acknowledges that progress has been made, but fears that the goal of true equality may never be reached.

GLOSSARY

In this glossary, terms defined within another entry are marked in **bold** type.

Accent The weight, or **stress**, given to a **syllable** when it is read or spoken.

Accentual-syllabic verse Poetry in which both **stressed** and unstressed syllables are counted. This forms the **feet** that define the **meter**.

Acrostic A poem in which the first letter of each line spells out a word or phrase. Acrostics were used in medieval poetry to highlight the name of a poet or patron.

Alexandrine A poetic line consisting of 12 **syllables** split into six **iambic feet**—one unstressed syllable followed by a **stressed** syllable (da-dah).

Allegory A poem that contains a veiled meaning or message—often moral—conveyed symbolically. For example, a knight fighting a dragon could be an allegory for the battle between good and evil.

Alliteration The repetition in a group of words of an initial **stressed** sound—usually the same first letter and most often a consonant. Alliterative **rhythms** are particularly important in **Old English poetry**.

Amphibrach A **foot** where one **accented syllable** is placed between two unaccented syllables (da-dah-da).

Anapest A **foot** consisting of two unaccented **syllables** followed by one **accented** syllable (da-da-dah).

Anaphora The repetition of a word or phrase, usually at the beginning of two or more lines.

Antithesis Placing together two terms or phrases that have opposite meanings, usually with a parallel structure to emphasize the contrast. For example, in John Milton's *Paradise Lost* (see pp.102–109), Satan says that it is "Better to reign in Hell, than serve in Heaven."

Aphorism A terse sentiment or statement of truth, usually relating to morality or philosophy.

Apostrophe A direct address to an absent person or entity—often a beloved or a muse. Shakespeare, for example, uses apostrophe in "Sonnet 18"—"Shall I compare thee to a summer's day?"

Assonance The repetition of vowel sounds, such as "beam" and "green," in words close to each other. Also known as "vowel rhyme."

Ballad A narrative verse form popular throughout Europe from the Middle Ages until the early 19th century. Ballads usually follow an abcb **rhyme scheme** and alternate between four-**stress** and three-stress lines. (See pp.172–173.)

Ballade A medieval French verse form with three eight-line **stanzas** and a four-line **envoi**, and a **rhyme scheme** of ababbcbc bcbc.

Blank verse Poetry that has **meter** but not **rhyme**. The meter is most often **iambic pentameter**, as, for example, in John Milton's *Paradise Lost* (see pp.102–109).

Cacophony Inharmonious, discordant sounds, particularly the repetition of consonants. The opposite of **euphony**.

Cadence The natural **rhythm** of speech; the rhythm **free verse**, which has no **meter**.

Caesura A break or pause within a line of poetry, usually in the middle.

Canto From the Italian word for "song," a section of a long poem—particularly an **epic**, such as Dante's *The Divine Comedy* (see pp.58–61).

Canzone Meaning "song" in Italian, a **lyric** poem that originated in late medieval Italy and France. The form—a precursor of the **sonnet**—usually consists of between one and seven **stanzas** of 8–10 lines, with each line 10–11 syllables long. The verse does not rhyme but repeats certain key words at the ends of lines.

Circumlocution The use of more words than necessary to convey a meaning. A poet might use this indirect way of writing to create a particular type of **meter**. Also known as "periphrasis."

Conceit An unusual or surprising extended **metaphor** or **simile**, often comparing deep feelings to something abstract. It is a favorite technique of **metaphysical** poets such as John Donne and George Herbert (see pp.94–99).

Concrete poetry A style where the meaning or subject of a poem is enhanced by the arrangement of its words on the page. "Easter Wings" by George Herbert (see pp.96–99) is an example. Also known as "visual poetry" or "shape poetry."

Consonance A similarity between the sounds of two words—or, more specifically, the repetition of consonant sounds, such as "fen" and "fine."

Couplet Two consecutive lines of poetry that usually **rhyme** and are mostly the same length.

Dactyl A **foot** consisting of one **accented syllable** followed by two unaccented syllables (dah-da-da).

Dactylic hexameter A type of **meter** where each line consists of six **dactyls**. This form was particularly common in ancient Greek and Roman **epics**.

Didactic verse Poetry that aims to give the reader a clear moral or practical message. Examples include John Milton's *Paradise Lost* (see pp.102–109) and "If—" by Rudyard Kipling (see p.180).

Dimeter A line of verse consisting of two **feet**.

Dirge A short **lyrical** poem of lamentation, usually composed for a funeral but shorter than an **elegy**.

Dissonance A deliberate disruption of harmonious sounds or **rhythms** in a line of verse.

Dramatic monologue A poem in which an imaginary speaker addresses one or more unknown characters, who remain silent. (See pp.144–145.)

Dream vision A poem that typically describes a person going to sleep and learning a fundamental truth in their dreams.

Echo verse Poetry in which the final one or two **syllables** of a line are repeated—like an echo—but have different meanings, such as "pane" and "pain."

Eclogue A short **pastoral** poem—usually a dialogue—idealizing rural life. The form originated in ancient Greece and was revived during the Italian Renaissance.

Ekphrasis From the Greek word for "description," an extended, portrayal of a work of visual art to amplify its meaning. An early example is in Homer's *The Iliad*, where the poet takes more than 100 lines to describe the shield of Achilles. (See pp.294–295.)

Elegiac stanza A **quatrain** written in **iambic pentameter**, with an abab **rhyme scheme**. Also known as a "heroic quatrain," it became the standard form for **elegy** in the mid-18th century.

Elegy Originally a **lyric** written in a particular meter on a range of subjects, which in English became a lament for the death of a person. (See pp.148–149.)

Elision The omission of an unstressed **syllable**—for example, using the word "o'er" instead of "over"—usually to make a word fit a poem's **meter**.

End-stopped Where a punctuation mark, such as a semicolon, dash, or period, creates a pause at the end of a line.

Enjambment The extension of a sentence or phrase from one line to the next with no punctuation—the opposite of **end-stopped**.

Envoi A short **stanza** that ends a poem, usually a **ballade** or **sestina**. (See pp.254–255.)

Epic A long narrative poetic form that details the adventures of historic or legendary heroes. Originating in oral traditions, epic poems are the world's oldest literary texts.

Epic simile A detailed, complex **simile** that unfolds over several lines. It is also known as a "Homeric simile," after Homer, the author of *The Iliad* and *The Odyssey* (see pp.24–31), who is believed to have originated the poetic device.

Epistle A philosophical or sentimental letter written in verse, usually addressed to someone close to the poet. The form was especially popular in the 18th century.

Epyllion A brief narrative poem resembling an **epic** in style, usually with a mythological or romantic theme. (See pp.86–87.)

Euphony The use of harmonious and pleasing word sounds, such as long vowels rather than consonants. The opposite of **cacophony**.

Eye rhyme Words that look similar on the page but do not **rhyme** when spoken, such as "move" and "love."

Figure of speech A word or an expression with an imaginative rather than simply literal meaning. Examples include **antithesis**, **metaphor**, and **simile**.

Foot The basic unit of **meter** in a line of **accentual-syllabic** verse. There are seven principal feet, each of which has a different **stress** pattern for its **syllables**: the **iamb** (da-dah), the **trochee** (dah-da), the **pyrrhic** (da-da), the **spondee** (dah-dah), the **anapest** (da-da-dah), the **dactyl** (dah-da-da), and the **amphibrach** (da-dah-da).

Free verse Poetry that has no consistent **rhyme** or **meter**. Instead, it follows the **rhythm** of natural speech. (See pp.152–159.)

Ghazal Pronounced "guzzle," an Arabic verse form of between five and 15 **couplets**, dealing with romantic love, loss, or longing. Each couplet ends on the same word or phrase, and is preceded by the couplet's rhyming word, which appears twice in the first couplet. The final couplet usually includes the poet's name. (See p.56.)

Gnomic verse Short poems full of proverbs, aphorisms, and other pieces of traditional wisdom.

Haiku A Japanese form of concise poetry that traditionally deals with aspects of the natural world. In English, a haiku has three lines of five, seven, and five **syllables** respectively. The form emerged in 17th-century Japan and became popular in Europe in the 20th century. (See pp.110–111.)

Iamb A **foot** consisting of one unaccented **syllable** followed by one **accented** syllable (da-dah).

Iambic pentameter A type of **meter** in which a line consists of five **iambs**. It is the most common meter in English poetry. (See p.103.)

Imagism An early 20th-century poetry movement that stressed the importance of precise, sharply drawn imagery using everyday language. Its principles were set out by Ezra Pound (see pp.232–235).

Internal rhyme Where words **rhyme** in the middle of a line rather than at the end—for example, "he fights the demons and rights the wrongs."

Juxtaposition Two words or phrases placed side by side for the reader to compare and contrast. *See also* **antithesis**.

Kenning Originating from Old Germanic, Norse, and Anglo-Saxon poetry, a **metaphorical** two-word compound phrase that replaces an ordinary noun. In *Beowulf*, for example, "battle-sweat" stands for blood. (See p.49.)

Lay An Old French form of **lyric** poem, usually about love and adventure, composed to be sung by minstrels. The term is also used to describe a type of songlike English narrative verse.

Light verse Playful poetry that may also make a serious point. The form includes the **limerick** and **nonsense verse**.

Limerick A pithy poem consisting of one five-line **stanza** with an aabba **rhyme scheme**. The subject matter is trivial and usually humorous. The form was popularized by British writer Edward Lear in the 19th century.

Litotes A form of ironic understatement that often incorporates a negative to create a positive, such as "not a bad idea." It appears often in **Old English poetry**—for example, the line "[the sword] was not useless to the warrior" from *Beowulf* (see pp.48–51) means that the sword was helpful.

Lyric A short, musical verse form, originating in ancient Greece to accompany the lyre—a harplike instrument. A lyrical poem is typically composed in the first person to reflect the emotions and thoughts of the speaker. The form includes the **dirge**, **elegy**, **ode**, and **sonnet**.

Metaphor A way of describing something imaginatively by comparing it with another thing that has similar characteristics, but without using the words "like" or "as" (see **simile**). For example, calling someone who stays up late a "night owl."

Metaphysical A term given to a group of 17th-century poets who wrote philosophical verse on subjects such as love, morality, and religion using **metaphors** and **similes** known as **conceits**.

Metonymy The replacement of one—often general or abstract—word with another related to it. For example, "the pen is mightier than the sword" suggests that "writing" achieves more than "violence."

Meter The pattern of **stressed** and unstressed **syllables** (see **foot**) in a line of poetry.

Mock-heroic The imitation of classical **heroic** verse style to satirize an unheroic subject.

Monometer A line of verse consisting of one **foot**.

Mosaic rhyme A type of **rhyme** in which a word of more than one **syllable** rhymes with two or more words of one syllable. For example, "know" and "it" could be pieced together to rhyme with "poet."

Negative capability The ability of a poet to reveal inner truths from a position of doubt and uncertainty, while free from the constraints of accepted facts and reason. The term was coined and defined by John Keats (see pp.138–141).

Nonsense verse A type of **light verse** that accentuates the absurd and the irrational. It often features invented words and deliberately ungrammatical sentences.

Octameter A line of verse that has eight **feet**.

Octave An eight-line poem or **stanza**, or the first eight lines of a **Petrarchan sonnet**.

Ode A formal **lyric** poem written as an address to—and often in praise of—a person, place, or thing. The form originated in ancient Greece, where it was performed accompanied by music. The ode became a feature of English **Romanticism**. (See pp.138–141.)

Old English poetry Anglo-Saxon poetry from early medieval England. It typically features four **stressed** and at least four unstressed **syllables** per line, with a firm **caesura** in the middle. The form makes heavy use of **alliteration** to tie together the two halves of a line and give the verse a chant-like **rhythm**. (See pp.48–51.)

Onomatopoeia The use of words that imitate the sound made by what they describe, such as "buzz," "bang," or "boom."

Ottava rima A **stanza**, originating in medieval Italy, that consists of eight 11-**syllable** lines and a **rhyme scheme** of abababcc. Lord Byron used a 10-syllable version of it in his poem *Don Juan* (see pp.136–137).

Oxymoron A descriptive device that combines contradictory words that seem to have opposite meanings, such as "deafening silence" or "living dead."

Paeon Originating in ancient Greek poetry, a **foot** that contains one **stressed** and three unstressed **syllables** in any order. It is called a "first," "second," "third," or "fourth" paeon depending on which of the syllables is stressed.

Pararhyme The partial **rhyme** of two words that have the same consonants but different vowels, such as "stirred" and "stared."

Pastoral Poetry that romanticizes the simplicity of the countryside and rural life, while exploring the harmonious connection between humans and nature. The pastoral dates back to ancient Greece and poets writing idealized visions of shepherds and their loves.

Pathetic fallacy A form of **personification** that applies human emotions to inanimate objects, particularly from nature—for example, William Wordsworth's "I wandered lonely as a cloud" (see pp.126–129). The term was coined by 19th-century British critic and writer John Ruskin to mock

the sentimentality of **Romantic** poets, such as Wordsworth and John Keats.

Pentameter A line of verse consisting of five **feet**.

Personification A device where a poet addresses something abstract or inanimate—"death" or a "rose," for example—as if it were human.

Petrarchan sonnet A **sonnet**, named after Petrarch (see pp.62–63), which divides 14 lines into two sections: an **octave** that rhymes abbaabba, and a **sestet** often rhyming either cdcdcd or cdecde, though its pattern varies.

Plangency The quality of being loud, deep, and resonant, and often also mournful. Usually used in relation to a sound.

Prose poem A piece of prose that does not break into the **rhythms** of poetry but relies heavily on poetic devices such as **metaphor**, **synecdoche**, and **metonymy**.

Prosody The study of **meter**, **rhythm**, and sound in poetry.

Psalm A sacred poem, usually taken from the biblical book *Psalms*, and primarily sung or spoken in Jewish and Christian services of worship.

Pyrrhic A **foot** consisting of two unaccented **syllables** (da-da).

Qualitative meter A type of **meter** in which **rhythm** is established by **syllables** that are **stressed** at regular intervals, such as **iambic pentameter**. It became the dominant metrical system in Europe after the Classical period.

Quantitative meter A type of **meter** where **rhythm** is dependent on the length of **syllables** rather than the number of **stresses**. It was the dominant system of ancient Greek and Italian poetry.

Quatrain A four-line **stanza**, or a four-line section of a 14-line **sonnet**.

Refrain A line or phrase that is repeated within a poem, often at the end of a **stanza**.

Rhyme The repetition of **syllables**, usually at the end of a line. Types of rhyme include **eye**, **internal**, **rich**, and **slant**.

Rhyme royal A **stanza** of seven 10-**syllable** lines, with a **rhyme scheme** of ababbcc. Popularized by Chaucer (see pp.64–71), it was named for its later use by King James I of Scotland.

Rhyme scheme The pattern of **rhymes** in a poem or **stanza**, either at the end or in the middle of lines. This pattern can be written out using letters of the alphabet, with rhyming words assigned the same letter, such as abcb.

Rhythm The pattern in spoken language created by **stresses** and the intervals between them.

Rich rhyme Words that have identical pronunciation but different spellings and meanings, such as "slay" and "sleigh." Particularly associated with French poetry, where it is known as *rime riche*.

Romance A long narrative poem, originating in France, based on stories of love, bravery, and chivalry. *Sir Gawain and the Green Knight* is an early English romance. (See p.57).

Romanticism A literary movement of the Romantic era, in the late 18th and early 19th centuries. Romantic poets looked to nature and the emotional world for inspiration and in search of the **sublime**. (See pp.126–141.)

Roundel An 11-line verse form invented by 19th-century British poet Algernon Charles Swinburne. It consists of three **stanzas**—a **tercet** sandwiched between two **quatrains**—with a **rhyme scheme** of abab bab abab. The start of the first line becomes a **refrain** that repeats in the 4th and 11th lines.

Sapphic stanza A **quatrain** with three 11-**syllable** lines, and a final five-syllable line, none of which **rhyme**. The stanza is named after the ancient Greek poet Sappho (see pp.32–33).

Satire Poetry that uses elements such as irony, sarcasm, and ridicule to expose or attack human failings or vices, often to reveal some deeper truth.

Scansion The analysis of a poem's **meter** to understand its pattern of **stresses** and **rhythm**. Scansion can also examine the wider structure of a poem, such as the **rhyme scheme** and the number and type of **stanzas**.

Sestet A six-line poem or **stanza**, or the final six lines in a 14-line **Petrarchan sonnet**.

Sestina A complex poem style composed of six **sestets** and a final three-line **envoi**. The lines usually do not **rhyme**, but the six end words of the first **stanza** are repeated in a different order in each subsequent stanza according to a strict set of rules. The envoi contains all six end words—three at the ends of its lines, three in the middle. (See pp.254–255.)

Sibilance The repetition of consonants—mainly "s" and "sh"—in a line of poetry to create a hushing, whispering, or hissing sound. For example, "silver sea shores" mimics the sound of waves.

Simile A comparison between two different things, which uses the words "like" or "as" to say that one thing is similar to the other.

Slam A competitive public event where poets perform **spoken word** poetry. Members of the audience score each performer, with the winner determined by total points awarded. (See pp.306–307.)

Slant rhyme A **rhyme** where the word sounds are similar but do not match. Usually, either the vowels or the final consonants of the stressed **syllables** are identical, such as "fate" and "save," or "port" and "chart."

Sonnet A 14-line poem that traditionally presents and comments on a single idea. The **Petrarchan sonnet** consists of an **octave** followed by a **sestet**, with a **volta** in between. In a Shakespearean sonnet, the volta comes after three **quatrains** and before a **couplet**. (See pp.62–63, 88–93, and 150–151.)

Spenserian stanza A nine-line **stanza**—eight lines in **iambic pentameter**, and the ninth line an **alexandrine**—with a **rhyme scheme** of ababbcbcc. It is named after English poet Edmund Spenser, who first used it in *The Fairie Queene* (see pp.82–85.)

Spoken word Poetry intended for public performance, which may also include drama and music. See also **slam**.

Spondee A **foot** consisting of two **accented syllables** (dah-dah).

Sprung rhythm A term coined by Gerard Manley Hopkins in the 19th century to describe his own **meter**, which mimics the patterns of natural speech. Each line contains a fixed number of **feet** between one and four **syllables** long, with **stress** on the first syllable. Lines can also have any number of extra unstressed syllables. (See pp.166–167.)

Stanza A group of lines separated out from the rest of a poem. Like a paragraph in prose, it can mark a change of mood or subject. There are seven main types of stanza, ranging from two to eight lines long: **couplet**, **tercet**, **quatrain**, quintain, **sestet**, septet, and octet.

Stepped line A line that unfolds in three descending, or "stepped," parts. Also known as "triadic line," it was invented by William Carlos Williams (see pp.216–217).

Stress The weight, or **accent**, given to a **syllable** when it is read or spoken. Combinations of stressed and unstressed syllables define the **feet** of **accentual-syllabic verse**.

Sublime A sense of transcending everyday experience, especially through the gateway of nature. The concept was part of **Romanticism**, embraced by poets such as William Blake and William Wordsworth.

Strophe A unit of grouped verses, or **stanzas**—sometimes of varying length—in a poem. In ancient Greek drama, the word meant "turning" and marked the first section of a spoken **ode**.

Syllabic verse A form of verse where the **meter** is defined by the number of **syllables** in a line rather than the number of **stresses**. (See pp.188–191.)

Syllable The smallest unit of sound, from which words are constructed. The natural patterns of **stressed** and unstressed syllables form the **rhythms** of language and poetry.

Synecdoche An expression that uses a small part of something to refer to the larger whole, or vice versa. For example, a poet may use a body part, such as a hand, heart, or eyes, to represent an entire person, as in "a hired hand."

Syntax The system for putting words together, including word placement and the rules for parts of speech and punctuation. A poet might manipulate syntax to emphasize particular words or to create unexpected effects.

Tanka Meaning "short poem" in Japanese, a 31-syllable verse form, traditionally written in a single line.

Tercet A three-line **stanza**, the lines of which can be **rhymed** or unrhymed.

Terza rima An Italian **stanza** form, meaning "third rhyme," popularized by Dante in *The Divine Comedy* (see pp.58–61). It consists of **tercets** that **rhyme** in an interweaving pattern—aba bcb cdc, and so on. It usually ends with a **couplet** that rhymes with the penultimate line of the final tercet.

Tetrameter A line of verse consisting of four **feet**.

Trimeter A line of verse consisting of three **feet**.

Triplet A type of three-line **stanza**, or **tercet**, where all three end words **rhyme**.

Trobairitz Female **troubadours**.

Trochaic See **Trochee**.

Trochee A **foot** consisting of one **accented** and one unaccented **syllable** (dah-da).

Trope Any kind of figurative language—such as **metaphor** or **metonymy**—used to enrich a poet's depiction of anything, including people, places, ideas, and experiences.

Troubadours Composers and performers of **lyric** poetry—using the Occitan language of southern France—in the 12th and 13th centuries. (See pp.54–55.)

Verse paragraph A **stanza** that constitutes a single set of ideas—the equivalent of a prose paragraph. Such stanzas can vary in length and may have an indented first line.

Villanelle A 19-line poem that originated in 16th-century France. It is composed of five **tercets** and a final **quatrain**, following an aba and abaa **rhyme scheme**. Lines 1 and 3 of the first **stanza** are repeated three times each: line 1 at lines 6, 12, and 18, and line 3 at lines 9, 15, and 19. (See pp.240–241.)

Volta A turn (change) in argument or thought partway through a poem, particularly a **sonnet**.

INDEX

ACKNOWLEDGMENTS

Dorling Kindersley would like to thank Ira Sharma, Shipra Jain, and Vanessa Hamilton for design assistance; Ankita Gupta, Chauney Dunford, and Abigail Mitchell for editorial assistance; Kathryn Hill for proofreading; and Helen Peters for indexing.

PICTURE CREDITS

The publisher would like to thank the following for their kind permission to reproduce their photographs:

(Key: a-above; b-below/bottom; c-center; f-far; l-left; r-right; t-top)

19 Alamy Stock Photo: IanDagnall Computing (cr). **21 Alamy Stock Photo:** The Picture Art Collection (tl). **23 Alamy Stock Photo:** Historic Collection (bl). **26 Alamy Stock Photo:** Classic Image (tl). **27 Alamy Stock Photo:** Heritage Image Partnership Ltd (br). **28 Alamy Stock Photo:** agefotostock / Historical Views (tr). **29 Alamy Stock Photo:** Eraza Collection (tr). **31 Alamy Stock Photo:** The Print Collector / Art Media / Heritage Images (tl). **33 Alamy Stock Photo:** Classic Image (tr). **SuperStock:** Mary Evans Picture Library (bl). **36 Alamy Stock Photo:** INTERFOTO / Personalities (bl). **37 Alamy Stock Photo:** Album (br). **38 Alamy Stock Photo:** Album (tr). **41 Alamy Stock Photo:** Classic Image (bl). **42 Alamy Stock Photo:** Artepics (tr); classicpaintings (br). **49 Alamy Stock Photo:** Arts & Authors (tr). **50 Alamy Stock Photo:** Chronicle (clb). **51 Bridgeman Images:** © British Library Board. All Rights Reserved (br). **53 Alamy Stock Photo:** Panther Media GmbH / Raymond Thill (cr). **55 Alamy Stock Photo:** GRANGER—Historical Picture Archive (tr); Prisma Archivo (bl). **56 Dreamstime.com:** Resul Muslu (cb). **59 Getty Images:** Hulton Archive / brandstaetter images / Imagno (tr). **60 Alamy Stock Photo:** Pictorial Press Ltd (b). **62 Bridgeman Images:** © Ashmolean Museum (bc). **63 Alamy Stock Photo:** Pictorial Press Ltd (tl). **66 Alamy Stock Photo:** Georgios Kollidas (bl). **67 Alamy Stock Photo:** Stewart Mckeown (tl). **68 Alamy Stock Photo:** The Picture Art Collection (t). **71 Alamy Stock Photo:** Granger, NYC (bl). **72 Alamy Stock Photo:** IanDagnall Computing (br). **73 Getty Images:** Hulton Archive / Culture Club (t). **81 Alamy Stock Photo:** FALKENSTEINFOTO (cr). **83 Alamy Stock Photo:** Heritage Images / The Print Collector (crb). **84 Alamy Stock Photo:** IanDagnall Computing (tr). **85 Alamy Stock Photo:** 19th era (tr); ART Collection (bl); eFesenko (tr). **90 Alamy Stock Photo:** Prisma Archivo (tr). **92 Alamy Stock Photo:** The Picture Art Collection (cl); The Picture Art Collection (br). **93 British Library:** (tr). **95 Alamy Stock Photo:** Chronicle (tl).

97 Alamy Stock Photo: Prisma Archivo (tr). **98 Alamy Stock Photo:** De Luan (cra). **104 Alamy Stock Photo:** Artepics (tr); The Print Collector / Heritage Images (bl). **107 Alamy Stock Photo:** Lebrecht Music & Arts (tr). **108 Alamy Stock Photo:** Amoret Tanner (tl). **109 Alamy Stock Photo:** Classic Image (br). **111 Alamy Stock Photo:** Chronicle (crb). **117 Getty Images:** Photos.com (bl). **119 Alamy Stock Photo:** Magite Historic (tr). **121 Alamy Stock Photo:** The Print Collector / Heritage Images (bl). **Shutterstock.com:** Everett Collection (tr). **123 Alamy Stock Photo:** Artokoloro (tl). **124 Alamy Stock Photo:** The Print Collector / Ann Ronan Picture Library / Heritage-Images (tl). **125 Alamy Stock Photo:** GRANGER—Historical Picture Archive (br); World History Archive (tc). **127 Alamy Stock Photo:** Gallery Of Art (tl); IanDagnall Computing (tr). **129 Alamy Stock Photo:** Ian Dagnall (bl). **130 Alamy Stock Photo:** © Fine Art Images / Heritage Images (bc). **131 Alamy Stock Photo:** CPA Media Pte Ltd / Pictures From History (tl). **133 Alamy Stock Photo:** © Fine Art Images / Heritage Images (tl). **Getty Images:** Universal History Archive / Universal Images Group (tr). **135 Alamy Stock Photo:** The Picture Art Collection (tl). **137 Alamy Stock Photo:** Masterpics (bl); Pictorial Press Ltd (tr). **139 Alamy Stock Photo:** Artepics (br). **140 Alamy Stock Photo:** IanDagnall Computing (tl). **141 Alamy Stock Photo:** GRANGER - Historical Picture Archive (bc). **143 Alamy Stock Photo:** Archive Collection (bl). **Getty Images:** Corbis Historical / Fine Art / VCG Wilson (tr). **144 Alamy Stock Photo:** ART Collection (tr). **145 Alamy Stock Photo:** Classic Image (tr). **146 Alamy Stock Photo:** AF Fotografie (bc). **147 Alamy Stock Photo:** INTERFOTO / Personalities (crb). **Getty Images:** Bettmann (tl). **148 Getty Images:** Ann Ronan Picture Library / Photo12 / Universal Images Group (cb). **149 Getty Images:** Hulton Archive / Print Collector / Ann Ronan Pictures (bl). **151 Getty Images:** Archive Photos / Stock Montage (tr). **154 Getty Images:** Archive Photos / Underwood Archives (bl). **156 Alamy Stock Photo:** North Wind Picture Archives (bl). **157 Alamy Stock Photo:** AF Fotografie (tr). **159 Alamy Stock Photo:** Pictorial Press Ltd (br). **161 Getty Images:** De Agostini Picture Library (cr). **163 Alamy Stock Photo:** Niday Picture Library (br); Universal Images Group North America LLC / PicturesNow (tl). **164 Alamy Stock Photo:** © Fine Art Images / Heritage Images (bl); Painters (tr). **165 Alamy Stock Photo:** GRANGER—Historical Picture Archive (bc). **167 Getty Images:** Universal History Archive (tr). **169 Alamy Stock Photo:** Atomic (tr). **171 Alamy Stock Photo:** Science History Images (tl). **172 Alamy Stock Photo:** Lordprice Collection (bc). **173 Getty Images:**

Napoleon Sarony / adoc-photos / Corbis (tr). **178 Alamy Stock Photo:** volkerpreusser (br). **179 Alamy Stock Photo:** photo-fox (tl). **180 Getty Images:** Universal Images Group / Pictures from History (bc). **184 Alamy Stock Photo:** Everett Collection Historical (bl). **185 Alamy Stock Photo:** Artefact (tl). **186 Shutterstock.com:** AP (clb). **187 Alamy Stock Photo:** GRANGER—Historical Picture Archive (bl). **190 Alamy Stock Photo:** Smith Archive (tl). **191 Getty Images:** Bettmann (tr). **193 Alamy Stock Photo:** Brian Harris for the CWGC (tc). **Getty Images:** Hulton Archive / Culture Club / Bridgeman (bl). **195 Alamy Stock Photo:** GRANGER - Historical Picture Archive (tr). **196 Getty Images:** Bettmann (bl). **197 Alamy Stock Photo:** AF Fotografie (bl). **201 Alamy Stock Photo:** Pictorial Press Ltd (bc); The Print Collector / Ann Ronan Picture Library / Heritage-Images (tr). **202 Getty Images:** Universal Images Group / Christophel Fine Art (tl). **203 Alamy Stock Photo:** Antiqua Print Gallery (bl); Everett Collection Historical (tr). **204 Alamy Stock Photo:** GRANGER—Historical Picture Archive (br). **206 Getty Images:** Hulton Archive / Fine Art Images / Heritage Images (cr). **210 Getty Images:** Library of Congress / Corbis / VCG (bl). **211 Collection of the Smithsonian National Museum of African American History and Culture:** Gift of Bobbie Ross in memory of Elizabeth Dillard (tl). **212 Alamy Stock Photo:** Everett Collection Inc (b). **213 Alamy Stock Photo:** Pictorial Press Ltd (br). **Library of Congress, Washington, D.C.:** LC-DIG-highsm-02802 / Highsmith, Carol M., 1946-, photographer (tl). **214 Alamy Stock Photo:** INTERFOTO / Personalities (bc). **215 Getty Images:** Universal History Archive (tr). **216 Alamy Stock Photo:** H.S. Photos (br). **217 Getty Images:** Corbis Historical / Pach Brothers / Oscar White (t). **219 Alamy Stock Photo:** incamerastock / ICP (tr). **221 Alamy Stock Photo:** GRANGER—Historical Picture Archive (tl). **222 Getty Images:** Picture Post / Hulton Archive / Kurt Hutton / Stringer (bl). **223 Getty Images:** Hulton Archive / John F. Stephenson / Stringer (bl). **228 Getty Images:** Hulton Archive / Fox Photos / Stringer (bc). **229 Alamy Stock Photo:** © Keystone Pictures USA / ZUMA Press, Inc. (tr). **231 Alamy Stock Photo:** Pictures Now (tr). **Getty Images:** Corbis Historical / Pach Brothers / Oscar White (tl). **233 Alamy Stock Photo:** Everett Collection Inc (br). **234 Alamy Stock Photo:** Peter Horree (bl). **235 Getty Images:** David Lees / Corbis / VCG (tl). **237 Alamy Stock Photo:** Everett Collection Inc (tr). **238 Alamy Stock Photo:** Shawshots (b). **240 Alamy Stock Photo:** National Museum of Wales / Heritage-Images (bc). **241 Alamy Stock Photo:** IanDagnall Computing (tr). **243 Alamy Stock Photo:**

Everett Collection Inc (tl). **244 Archives & Special Collections, Vassar College Library:** Ref.# 6.61 (br). **245 Alamy Stock Photo:** Everett Collection Historical (tr). **248 Getty Images:** Bettmann (bl). **249 Getty Images:** Corbis Premium Historical / Allen Ginsberg LLC (tr). **250 Alamy Stock Photo:** Everett Collection Inc (t). **253 Getty Images:** Premium Archive / MUUS Collection / Fred W. McDarrah (bl). **255 Alamy Stock Photo:** Everett Collection Historical (tr). **257 Alamy Stock Photo:** PA Images (tr). **259 Getty Images:** Picture Post / Hulton Archive / Leslie Davis / Stringer (tl). **261 Bridgeman Images:** © Mark Gerson Photography. All rights reserved 2023 (tr). **262 Shutterstock.com:** Nils Jorgensen (tl). **263 Shutterstock.com:** Philip Openshaw (bl). **265 Getty Images:** De Agostini Picture Library (cr). **267 Alamy Stock Photo:** CSU Archives / Everett Collection Historical (tl). **268 Alamy Stock Photo:** © Kino Lorber / Everett Collection Inc (bc). **269 Alamy Stock Photo:** Everett Collection Inc (tr). **273 Alamy Stock Photo:** WENN Rights Ltd (tl). **Getty Images:** Michael Ochs Archives / Stringer (br). **275 Alamy Stock Photo:** Ricky Fitchett / ZUMA Press (br). **277 Alamy Stock Photo:** Trinity Mirror / Mirrorpix (bl); ZUMA Press, Inc. (tr). **280 Getty Images:** Bettmann (bl). **281 Getty Images:** Archive Photos / Bev Grant (tr). **282 Getty Images:** Ullstein Bild / Reinhard Dirscherl (b). **284 Getty Images:** Bettmann (br). **285 Alamy Stock Photo:** CSU Archives / Everett Collection (tl). **287 Alamy Stock Photo:** CSU Archives / Everett Collection (tl). **289 Getty Images:** Michael Ochs Archives / Stringer (tr). **291 Alamy Stock Photo:** PA Images (tl); PA Images (br). **293 Alamy Stock Photo:** John Clarke (tl). **294 Alamy Stock Photo:** GL Archive (bc). **297 Claire Mcnamee:** (tl). **298 Getty Images:** Boston Globe / Erin Clark (br). **299 Getty Images:** J. Vespa / WireImage (tl). **301 Alamy Stock Photo:** Tristan Deschamps (tr). **302 Alamy Stock Photo:** Skimage (br). **Shutterstock.com:** Paula Alyle Scully / AP (tl). **307 Alamy Stock Photo:** Pako Mera (tl); Aleks Taurus (br)

All other images © Dorling Kindersley

TEXT CREDITS

pp.32–33 Sappho: excerpts from Poem #39 "He Is More Than A Hero" from *Sappho: A New Translation*, translated by Mary Barnard, copyright © The Regents of the University of California, 1958, 2019. Published by the University of California Press; **p.53 Saint Hildegard of Bingen:** excerpts from *Symphonia: A Critical Edition of the "Symphonia Armonie Celestium Revelationum"* (Symphony of the Harmony of Celestial Revelations), Second Edition, with Introduction, Translations, and Commentary by Barbara Newman. Copyright © Cornell University, 1988, 1998. Reprinted by permission of the publisher, Cornell University Press; **pp.54–55 Bernart de Ventadorn:** excerpts from "Now When I See the Lark Uplift"

translated by W. D. Snodgrass in *Selected Translations by W. D. Snodgrass,* copyright © W. D. Snodgrass, 1998. Reprinted with the permission of The Permissions Company, LLC on behalf of BOA Editions, Ltd., boaeditions.org; **pp.72–73 Christine de Pizan:** excerpts from "Letter of the God of Love" from *Poems of Cupid, God of Love*, translated by Thelma S. Fenster, edited by Mary Carpenter Erler, Brill, 1990. Reprinted with permission of the publisher via Copyright Clearance Center; **pp.142–143 Alexander Pushkin:** excerpts from Poem #39 in *Eugene Onegin*, translated by Stanley Mitchell, Penguin Classics, 2008. Translation copyright © Stanley Mitchell, 2008. Reprinted by permission of Penguin Books Ltd; **pp.162–165 Charles Baudelaire:** excerpts from *Les Fleurs du Mal*, translated by Richard Howard. Translation copyright © Richard Howard, 1982. Reprinted with the permission of The Permissions Company, LLC on behalf of David R. Godine, Publisher, Inc., www.godine.com; **pp.168–169 Emily Dickinson:** excerpts from "Because I Could Not Stop for Death" from *The Poems of Emily Dickinson*, edited by Thomas H. Johnson, Cambridge, Mass.: The Belknap Press of Harvard University Press, copyright © the President and Fellows of Harvard College, 1951, 1955. Copyright © renewed 1979, 1983 by the President and Fellows of Harvard College. Copyright © 1914, 1918, 1919, 1924, 1929, 1930, 1932, 1935, 1937, 1942, by Martha Dickinson Bianchi. Copyright © 1952, 1957, 1958, 1963, 1965, by Mary L. Hampson. Reprinted by permission. All rights reserved; **pp.182–187 Robert Frost:** excerpts from "The Road Not Taken" from *The Poetry of Robert Frost* edited by Edward Connery Lathem, Vintage, copyright © Henry Holt and Company, 1916, 1969. Copyright © Robert Frost, 1944. Reprinted by permission of Henry Holt and Company; and The Random House Group Limited. All rights reserved; **pp.198–205 T. S. Eliot:** excerpts from "The Wasteland" from *Collected Poems: 1909–1962*, Faber & Faber Ltd, 2020. Reprinted by permission of the publisher; **p.205 Ezra Pound:** excerpts from "Hugh Selwyn Mauberley, Part I" from *Personae*; and *Selected Poems 1908-1969*, Faber & Faber Ltd, copyright © Ezra Pound, 1926. Reprinted by permission of Faber & Faber Ltd; and New Directions Publishing Corp.; **p.206 Rainer Maria Rilke:** excerpts from *Duino Elegies / The First Elegy* translated by J. B. Leishman and Stephen Spender, Hogarth Press, 1968. Reprinted by permission of the Estate of Stephen Spender; excerpts from "Archaic Torso of Apollo" from *Ahead of All Parting: Selected Poetry and Prose of Rainer Maria Rilke*, translated by Stephen Mitchell, Modern Library, 1995; **p.207 Hilda Doolittle (H. D.):** excerpts from "Helen" from *Selected Poems*, edited by Louis L. Martz, Carcanet Press; and *Collected Poems, 1912-1944*, copyright © The Estate of Hilda Doolittle, 1982. Reprinted of Carcanet Press and New Directions Publishing Corp.; **pp.208–213 Langston Hughes:** excerpts from "I, Too;" "Mother to Son" and "The Weary Blues" from *The Collected Poems of Langston Hughes*, edited by Arnold Rampersad and David Roessel, Vintage,

1995. Reprinted by permission of David Higham Associates; and Penguin Random House LLC; **pp.214–215 Federico Garcia Lorca:** excerpts from "Ballad of the Moon, Moon" and "Ballad of the Spanish Civil Guard" from *Gypsy Ballads*, translated by Jane Duran & Gloria Garcia Lorca, Enitharmon Press, 2011. Reprinted by permission; **pp.216–217 William Carlos Williams:** excerpts from "The Sparrow" from *Collected Poems: Volume II, 1939-1962,* edited by Christopher MacGowan, copyright © William Carlos Williams, 1953. Reprinted by permission of Carcanet Press and New Directions Publishing Corp.; **pp.218–219 Wallace Stevens:** excerpts from "A Postcard from the Volcano"; "Anecdote of the Jar"; "Six Significant Landscapes"; and "Colloquy with a Polish Aunt" from *The Collected Poems of Wallace Stevens,* copyright © Wallace Stevens, 1936. Copyright © renewed 1964 by Holly Stevens. Reprinted by permission of Faber & Faber Ltd; and Alfred A. Knopf, an imprint of the Knopf Doubleday Publishing Group, a division of Penguin Random House LLC. All rights reserved; **pp.220–223 W. H. Auden:** excerpts from "September 1, 1939" from *Selected Poems of W. H. Auden*, edited by Edward Mendelson, copyright © W. H. Auden, 1940; renewed 1968. Reprinted by permission of Curtis Brown, Ltd; and Vintage Books, an imprint of the Knopf Doubleday Publishing Group, a division of Penguin Random House LLC. All rights reserved; **pp.220–223 Louis MacNeice:** excerpts from "For X" from *Collected Poems*, Faber & Faber Ltd. Reprinted by permission of David Higham Associates; **pp.228–229 Theodore Roethke:** excerpts from "My Papa's Waltz" and "The Waking" from *Collected Poems*. "My Papa's Waltz" copyright © Hearst Magazines, Inc., 1942; copyright © Beatrice Lushington, 1966, renewed 1994. "The Waking" copyright © Beatrice Lushington, 1966, renewed 1994. Reprinted by permission of Faber & Faber Ltd; and Doubleday, an imprint of the Knopf Doubleday Publishing Group, a division of Penguin Random House LLC. All rights reserved; **pp.228–229 John Ashbery:** excerpt from "Two Scenes" from *Collected Poems 1956-1987*, edited by Mark Ford, Library of America. Reprinted by permission of Carcanet Press; and Georges Borchardt, Inc; **p.229 Robert Frost:** excerpts from "Meeting and Passing" from *The Poetry of Robert Frost* edited by Edward Connery Lathem, Vintage, copyright © Henry Holt and Company, 1916, 1969. Copyright © Robert Frost, 1944. Reprinted by permission of Henry Holt and Company; and The Random House Group Limited. All rights reserved; **pp.230–231 Robert Hayden:** excerpts from "Middle Passage" from *Collected Poems of Robert Hayden* by Robert Hayden, edited by Frederick Glaysher, copyright © Robert Hayden, 1962, 1966. Liveright Publishing Corporation, 1985. Reprinted by permission of Liveright Publishing Corporation; **pp.232–235 Ezra Pound:** excerpts from "Canto LXXXI" from *The Cantos of Ezra Pound*, copyright © Ezra Pound, 1948. Reprinted by permission of Faber & Faber Ltd; and New Directions Publishing Corp; **p.235 Geoffrey Chaucer:** excerpts from *Selected Poems: Truth by Chaucer*, translated by

A. S. Kline, copyright © 2008, https://www. poetryintranslation.com/PITBR/English/ ChaucerPoems.php. Reprinted with kind permission of the translator; **pp.236–239 Gwendolyn Brooks:** excerpts from "The Anniad"; "the children of the poor"; and "The Womanhood, XV" from *The World of Gwendolyn Brooks*, Harper & Row, 1971. Reprinted by permission of Brooks Permissions; **pp.240–241 Dylan Thomas:** excerpts from "Do Not Go Gentle Into That Good Night" from *The Collected Poems of Dylan Thomas,* Weidenfeld and Nicholson; and *The Poems of Dylan Thomas*, New Directions, 2003, copyright © Dylan Thomas, 1952; The Dylan Thomas Trust. Reprinted by permission of David Higham Associates; and New Directions Publishing Corp.; **pp.240–241 William Empson:** excerpts from "Missing Dates" from *Landfill, Little Toller*, 1937, copyright © William Empson. Reprinted with permission of Curtis Brown Group Ltd, London on behalf of the Beneficiaries of the Estate of William Empson; excerpts from "Invitation to Juno" from *The Atlantic Book of British and American Poetry*, 1958, copyright © William Empson. Reprinted with permission of Curtis Brown Group Ltd, London on behalf of the Beneficiaries of the Estate of William Empson; **pp.242–245 Robert Lowell:** excerpts from "Skunk Hour" from *Collected Poems* by Robert Lowell, copyright © Harriet Lowell and Sheridan Lowell, 2003. Reprinted by permission of Farrar, Straus and Giroux. All Rights Reserved; **pp.246–253 Allen Ginsberg:** Excerpts from "Howl" from *Collected Poems 1947-1997*, copyright © The Allen Ginsberg Trust, 1956, 1961, 2006. Reprinted by permission of HarperCollins Publishers; and The Wylie Agency (UK) Limited; **pp.254–255 Elizabeth Bishop:** excerpts from "Sestina" and "One Art" from *Poems* by Elizabeth Bishop, Chatto & Windus, copyright © The Alice H. Methfessel Trust, 2011. Publisher's Note and compilation copyright © 2011 by Farrar, Straus and Giroux. Reprinted by permission of The Random House Group Limited; and Farrar, Straus and Giroux. All Rights Reserved; **pp.256–257 Philip Larkin:** excerpts from "An Arundel Tomb"; "Church Going"; "Talking in Bed"; and "The Whitsun Wedding" from *The Complete Poems of Philip Larkin* by Philip Larkin, edited by Archie Burnett, copyright © The Estate of Philip Larkin, 2012. Reprinted by permission of Faber & Faber Limited; and Farrar, Straus and Giroux. All Rights Reserved; **pp.258–259 Stevie Smith:** excerpts from "Not Waving but Drowning" from *Collected Poems & Drawings*, Faber & Faber Ltd, 2018; and *All The Poems*, copyright © Stevie Smith, 1937, 1938, 1942, 1950, 1957, 1962, 1966, 1971, 1972. Copyright © 2016 by the Estate of James MacGibbon. Copyright © 2015 by Will May. Reprinted by permission of Faber & Faber Limited; and New Directions Publishing Corp.; **pp.260–263 Ted Hughes:** excerpts from "Pike" from *Collected Poems* by Ted Hughes, Faber & Faber Ltd, 2003, copyright © The Estate of Ted Hughes, 2003. Reprinted by permission of Faber & Faber Limited; and Farrar, Straus and Giroux. All Rights Reserved; **p.265 Anna Akhmatova:** excerpts from "Poem Without a Hero: Chapter Three" from *The Complete Poems of Anna Akhmatova*, translated by Judith Hemschemeyer, edited and introduced by Roberta Reeder, Canongate Books Ltd, copyright © Judith Hemschemeyer, 1989, 1992, 1997. Reprinted with the permission of the Licensor Canongate Books Ltd through PLSclear; and The Permissions Company, LLC on behalf of Zephyr Press, zephyrpress.org; **pp.266–267 Sylvia Plath:** excerpts from "Daddy" from *The Collected Poems of Sylvia Plath*, edited by Ted Hughes, Faber & Faber Ltd, copyright © the Estate of Sylvia Plath, 1960, 1965, 1971, 1981. Editorial material copyright © 1981 by Ted Hughes. Reprinted by permission of Faber & Faber Limited; and HarperCollins Publishers; **pp.268–269 Amiri Baraka:** excerpts from "Black Art" from *S.O.S Poems 1961-2013,* copyright © The Estate of Amiri Baraka, 2014. Reprinted by permission of Grove/Atlantic, Inc. Any third-party use of this material, outside of this publication, is prohibited; **pp.270–271 Kamala Das:** excerpts from "The Looking Glass" from *Ten Twentieth-Century Indian Poets*, edited by R. Parthasarathy, Oxford University Press, 1976. Reprinted with the exclusive permission of The Estate of Kamala Das; **pp.272–275 Sonia Sanchez:** excerpts from "a/coltrane/poem" from *We a BaddDDD People* by Sonia Sanchez, Broadside Press, 1970. Reprinted by permission of the publisher; **pp.278–283 Adrienne Rich:** excerpts from "Diving Into the Wreck" from *Diving Into the Wreck: Poems:1971-1972* by Adrienne Rich, copyright © W. W. Norton & Company, Inc, 1973. Used by permission of W. W. Norton & Company, Inc.; excerpts from "Natural Resources" from *Collected Poems: 1950-2012* by Adrienne Rich, copyright © The Adrienne Rich Literary Trust, 2016, 2013. Copyright © 1978 by W. W. Norton & Company, Inc. Reprinted by permission of W. W. Norton & Company, Inc.; **pp.284–285 Ntozake Shange:** Excerpts from "for colored girls who have considered suicide/when the rainbow is enuf", from *for colored girls who have considered suicide when the rainbow is enuf*, Orion Publishing Group Ltd & Scribner, 1997, copyright © Ntozake Shange, 1975, 1976, 1977, 2010. Reprinted with the permission of the Licensor Orion through PLSclear; and Scribner, a division of Simon & Schuster, Inc. All rights reserved; **pp.286–287 Audre Lorde:** excerpts from "Power" from *The Collected Poems of Audre Lorde* by Audre Lorde, W. W. Norton & Company, Inc., copyright © Audre Lorde, 1978. Reprinted by permission of Abner Stein Agency; and W. W. Norton & Company, Inc.; **pp.288–289 Maya Angelou:** excerpts from "Still I Rise" and "On the Pulse of Morning" from *The Collected Poems of Maya Angelou*, Little Brown Books Ltd; *And Still I Rise: A Book of Poems* by Maya Angelou, copyright © Maya Angelou, 1978; and *On the Pulse of Morning* by Maya Angelou, copyright © Maya Angelou, 1993. Reprinted by permission of the Licensor Little Brown Book Group Limited through PLSclear; and Random House, an imprint and division of Penguin Random House LLC. All rights reserved; **pp.290–293 Seamus Heaney:** excerpts from "Casualty"; "Singing School"; and "Mossbawn: Sunlight" from *100 Poems*, Faber & Faber Ltd, 2018; and *Opened Ground: Selected Poems 1966-1996* by Seamus Heaney, copyright © Seamus Heaney, 1998. Reprinted by permission of Faber & Faber Limited; and Farrar, Straus and Giroux. All Rights Reserved; **pp.294–295 Carol Ann Duffy:** excerpts from "Standing Female Nude" and "Prayer" from *New Selected Poems* by Carol Ann Duffy, Picador, copyright © Carol Ann Duffy. Reprinted by permission of the author c/o Rogers, Coleridge & White Ltd., 20 Powis Mews, London W11 1JN; **pp.296–297 Michael Donaghy:** excerpts from "Machines" from *Dances Learned Last Night Poems 1975-1995*, Pan Macmillan, 2000. Reprinted by permission of the Licensor through PLSclear; **pp.296–297 Tony Harrison:** excerpts from "Marked with D" from *Selected Poems*, Penguin, 1984. Reprinted by permission of Faber & Faber Limited; **pp.300–303 Derek Walcott:** excerpts from "Omeros" from *Omeros* by Derek Walcott, Faber & Faber, 1990, copyright © Derek Walcott, 1990. Reprinted by permission of Faber & Faber Limited; and Farrar, Straus and Giroux. All Rights Reserved; **p.304 Sheila Black:** excerpts from "What You Mourn" first published in *Dancing with Cecil, Poems of Disability,* 2004. Reprinted by kind permission of the author; **p.305 Rita Dove:** excerpts from "Sonata Mulattica" from *Sonata Mulattica: Poems* by Rita Dove, W. W. Norton, 2010, copyright © Rita Dove, 2009. Reprinted by permission of W. W. Norton & Company, Inc.; **p.309 Simon Armitage:** excerpt from "Floral Tribute" from https://www.theguardian.com/uk-news/2022/sep/13/floral-tribute-poem-queen-elizabeth-simon-armitage-poet-laureate?CMP=Share_AndroidApp_Other. Reprinted by permission of Faber & Faber Limited.

In some instances we have been unable to trace the owners of copyright material, and we would appreciate any information that would enable us to do so.

QUOTE ATTRIBUTIONS

188 Marianne Moore
Frank Kermode, *London Review of Books*, 1998

276 Chinua Achebe
Chimamanda Ngozi Adichie, "To Instruct and Delight: A Case for Realist Literature," Commonwealth Lecture 2012 for The Commonwealth Foundation

298 Joy Harjo
An Art of Saying: Joy Harjo's Poetry and the Survival of Storytelling by Mary Leen, 1995, page 1

306 Elizabeth Acevedo
Interview with Emily Hub for *Literary Hub*, October 29, 2018

308 Amanda Lovelace
Interview for *Writing Routines*, 2023

309 Amanda Gorman
Interview with Hillary Clinton on *CNN*, March 8, 2021

DK BIG IDEAS SIMPLY EXPLAINED

For the curious